Foucault and the Iranian Revolution

Foucault and the Iranian Revolution

Gender and the Seductions of Islamism

Janet Afary and Kevin B. Anderson

The University of Chicago Press
Chicago and London

Janet Afary is associate professor in the departments of history and women's studies at Purdue University. She is the author of *The Iranian Constitutional Revolution, 1906–1911*, and president of the International Society for Iranian Studies (2004–2006). Kevin B. Anderson is associate professor of political science and sociology at Purdue University and the author of *Lenin, Hegel, and Western Marxism: A Critical Study*.

The University of Chicago Press, Chicago 60637
The University of Chicago Press, Ltd., London

Printed in the United States of America

14 13 12 11 10 09 08 07 06 05 2 3 4 5

ISBN: 0-226-00785-5 (cloth)
ISBN: 0-226-00786-3 (paper)

Library of Congress Cataloging-in-Publication Data

Afary, Janet.
Foucault and the Iranian Revolution : gender and the seductions of Islamism / Janet Afary and Kevin B. Anderson.
p. cm.
Includes bibliographical references and index.
ISBN 0-226-00785-5 (cloth : alk. paper) — ISBN 0-226-00786-3 (pbk. : alk. paper)
1. Foucault, Michel—Political and social views. 2. Iran—History—Revolution, 1979. I. Anderson, Kevin, 1948– II. Foucault, Michel. Selections. English. 2005. III. Title.
B2430.F724A63 2005
955.05'42—dc22

2004024383

♾The paper used in this publication meets the minimum requirements of the American National Standard for Information Sciences—Permanence of Paper for Printed Library Materials, ANSI Z39.48-1992.

The Western liberal Left needs to know that Islamic law can become a dead weight on societies hungering for change. The Left should not let itself be seduced by a cure that is perhaps worse than the disease.

—"Atoussa H.," Iranian feminist,
in response to Michel Foucault, November 1978

Contents

Acknowledgments

We decided to write this book a decade ago, during a visit to Paris, where we met some members of the Iranian community who were familiar with Michel Foucault's writings on the Iranian Revolution. We soon were engrossed in conversations about Foucault and, more generally, about Western intellectuals who had supported revolutionary movements in non-Western societies. Ever since then, we have been engaged in wide-ranging discussions with intellectuals and students from North America, Europe, Iran, and other parts of the Middle East over Michel Foucault, gender, and the Iranian Revolution. Our various interlocutors have given us literally hundreds of enthusiastic, albeit sometimes critical, responses. These have been so important and varied that it would be impossible to express our thanks adequately. Although we are of course solely responsible for any defects in this work, we would like to acknowledge those who have helped us along the way.

We are immensely grateful to the following people, who shared with us, through interviews or e-mail exchanges, their firsthand recollections of Foucault's encounters with the Iranian Revolution: Abolhassan Bani-Sadr (a former president of the Islamic Republic of Iran), Ehsan Naraghi, Ahmad Salamatian, and Hasan Shariatmadari (son of Ayatollah Kazem Shariatmadari). We also had exchanges with Fathi Triki on Foucault's 1966–68 sojourn in Tunisia. In addition, Nasser Pakdaman and Yann Richard shared their recollections of the debate over the Iranian Revolution in France.

We would like to thank the librarians of the Bibliothèque Publique d'Information Centre Pompidou, the Library of Congress, Northern Illinois University Library (especially Robert Ridinger), Northwestern University Library (especially the newspaper collection), and Purdue University Library (especially Larry Mykytiuk). We have a particularly important debt to the Regenstein Library of the University of Chicago, especially to Bruce Craig and Marlis Saleh of the Middle East Collection, and to Frank Conaway of the Social Science Division. In Los Angeles, we are grateful as well to Laleh Ghahreman and Bijan Khalili of Ketab Corporation bookstore, and to Mohammad Ali Sotoonzadeh Yazdi of Dekhoda Books, for exposing us to numerous Persian sources.

At the University of Chicago Press, we would like to express our thanks to our editor, John Tryneski, whose encouragement and judicious advice allowed for this book's publication in an improved and remarkably timely fashion. We also appreciate help from Rodney Powell and Ashley Cave on numerous issues, large and small. We thank as well our copyeditor, Nick Murray, and our production editor, Christine Schwab.

Among those who commented on earlier versions of this work, we are most indebted to those who read (very often longer) versions of the entire manuscript and who made unusually careful and helpful comments: Frieda Afary, Hélène Bellour, Mansour Bonakdarian, Samuel Kinser, Mark Lilla, Azar Nafisi, and two anonymous readers for the University of Chicago Press.

A much larger number of people offered important advice on earlier versions of specific chapters or parts of the book: Kamran Afary, Mona Afary, Said Amir Arjomand, Evelyn Blackwood, Albert Bowers, Berenice Carroll, Barbara Epstein, Ted Feldman, Jeff Goodwin, Mark Gottdiener, Inderpal Grewal, Sally Hastings, Mary Hegland, David Ingram, Manouchehr Kasheff, Nikki Keddie, Douglas Kellner, Jennifer Lehmann, Michael Löwy, Martin Matustik, Robert May, William McBride, Gail Melson, Robert Melson, Gordon Mork, Negar Mottahedeh, Orayb Najjar, Hal Orbach, Amir Pichdad, Arkhady Plotnitsky, Nick Rauh, Aparajita Sagar, Ruth Salvaggio, John Sanbonmatsu, Houman Sarshar, David Schweickart, Charlene Seigfried, Holly Shissler, Daniel Smith, David Norman Smith, Michael Smith, Maureen Sullivan, and Gordon Young. We would also like to express our gratitude for the responses to our presentations of parts of this work to annual meetings of the American Sociological Association, the International Society for Iranian Studies, the Middle East Studies Association, the Midwest Sociological Association, the Radical Philosophy Association, and the Socialist Scholars Conference, as well as to the Illuminations series at Purdue and a sociology colloquium at Northern Illinois University. In 2003, Janet Afary published an earlier version of parts of chapter 2 as an article, "Shi'ite Narratives of Karbala and Christian Rites of Penitence: Michel Foucault and the Culture of the Iranian Revolution, 1978–79," *Radical History Review* no. 86: 7–36. We are grateful for the helpful comments from issue editor Mansour Bonakdarian, Magnus T. Bernhardsson, and two anonymous reviewers for the journal.

Concerning the translations in the appendix, we would like especially to thank our primary translator, Karen de Bruin. We also benefited from a critique of the translations by anonymous reviewers for the University of Chicago Press.

Others assisted us with source material, useful suggestions, or important background at various points during our work on this book: Anvar Afary, Reza Afshari, Bahman Amin, Ahmad Ashraf, Sohrab Behdad, Donald Cress, Saeed Damadi, Nathalie Etoke, Rhonda Hammer, Hormoz Hekmat, Jacques d'Hondt, Peter Hudis, Houshang Keshovarz, Charles Kurzman, Ariane Lantz, Pierre Lantz, John Lie, Jim Miller, Hosein Mohri, Hasan Mortazavi, Homa Nategh, Hal Orbach, Danny Postel, John Rhoads, Maxime Rodinson, Yadollah Royai, Ahmad Sadri, Lawrence Scaff, and Patsy Schweickart. Regarding source materials, we would like to single out two individuals: Gita Hashemi generously shared with us her master's thesis, "Between Parallel Mirrors: Foucault, Atoussa, and Me, on Sexuality of History" (University of Toronto, 2000). Gholamreza Vantandoust sent us some important materials from Iran, especially the Persian translation of Foucault's writings on the revolution by Hussein M. Hamadani.

At Purdue University, numerous students responded, through insightful papers and other discussion, to parts of this work that we presented in graduate seminars. We also acknowledge valuable research assistance from the following graduate and undergraduate students: Albert Bowers, Keziah Fusco, Kaveh Hemmat, Petra Kleinlein, Li Fei, Shannon Linehan, Ashley Passmore, Neal Patel, Peishan Tan, and Tanya Tang.

We benefited from various forms of financial support during the course of researching this work, especially for support from the Research Incentive Grant program of Purdue University's School of Liberal Arts, without which the new translations for the appendix would not have been possible. In 1994, Afary's trip to Paris was supported by a Purdue University Research Foundation grant and Anderson's by a travel grant from Northern Illinois University. The American Philosophical Society underwrote Anderson's travel to Paris in 1996. Afary benefited from a one-semester research leave in the spring of 1999 through Purdue's Center for Humanistic Studies. The Soros Foundation funded Afary's travel to Paris in 2003.

Additionally, we would like to thank the following members of the support staff at Purdue University for various forms of assistance, including photocopying and scanning: Michelle Conwell, Barbara Corbin, Linda Doyle, Karen Ferry, Jennie Jones, Nancy Mugford, and Margaret Quirk.

Finally, we would like to express our thanks to our parents and other family members for their numerous forms of help and support, and to our daughter Lena, for all the joy she has brought to our lives.

We would like to acknowledge the following individuals and institutions for permission to publish the texts in the appendix:

To Baqir Parham and Agah Publications, for permission to publish our translation from the Persian of his dialogue with Michel Foucault.

To Éditions Gallimard, for permission to publish our translations of Foucault's journalistic writings on Iran, which originally appeared in Foucault, volume 3 of *Dits et écrits, 1976–1979*, © 1994, Éditions Gallimard, Paris.

To Garnet Publishing, for permission to reprint the translation by Roger Hardy and Thomas Lines of Maxime Rodinson's "Islam Resurgent?" *Gazelle Review*, no. 6 (1979); and to Éditions Fayard for the translation rights of the French original, as it appears in Maxime Rodinson, *L'Islam, politique et croyance*, © 1993, Librairie Arthème Fayard.

To Éditions Fayard, for permission to publish our translations of Rodinson's "Khomeini and the 'Primacy of the Spiritual'" and "Critique of Foucault on Iran," from Maxime Rodinson, *L'Islam, politique et croyance*, © 1993, Librairie Arthème Fayard.

To Maryam Matin-Daftari, for permission to publish our English translation of the Iranian women's statement of March 10, 1979.

To Margaret Simons, the editor of the English edition of Simone de Beauvoir's collected writings, for permission to publish Marybeth Timmerman's translation of de Beauvoir's statement on Iranian women.

To Claudie and Jacques Broyelle, for permission to publish our translation of their article "What Are the Philosophers Dreaming About?"

To Taylor and Francis for permission to reprint Alan Sheridan's translation of "Spirit of a Spiritless World," an interview with Foucault by Claire Brière and Pierre Blanchet, which appeared in Michel Foucault, *Politics, Philosophy, Culture: Interviews and Other Writings, 1977–1984*, edited by Lawrence D. Kritzman, © 1988, reproduced by permission of Routledge/Taylor & Francis Books, Inc.; and to Éditions du Seuil for the translation rights of the French original, as it appears in Claire Brière and Pierre Blanchet, *Iran: la révolution au nom de Dieu*, © 1979, Éditions du Seuil.

Introduction

> The author is an ideological product, since we represent him as the opposite of his historically real function.
>
> Foucault, "What Is an Author?"

In 1978–79, in the course of a massive urban revolution with several million participants, the Iranian people toppled the regime of Muhammad Reza Shah Pahlavi (r. 1941–79), which had pursued an authoritarian program of economic and cultural modernization. By late 1978, the militant Islamist faction led by Ayatollah Ruhollah Khomeini had come to dominate the antiregime uprising, in which secular nationalists, liberals, and leftists also participated.[1] The Islamists cast the struggle against the shah as a reenactment of the Battle of Karbala (680 CE), which Shi'ite Muslims mark annually in the month of Muharram by commemorating the martyrdom of Imam Hussein (grandson of Muhammad). Hussein died at the hands of his enemy Yazid in the desert of Karbala (present-day Iraq), in a battle that sealed Yazid's succession to the caliphate. In 1978, Khomeini personified the innocent Hussein, the shah stood for his nemesis Yazid, and those protestors killed by the shah's brutal repression were seen as martyrs in the tradition of Hussein's seventh-century followers.

Increasingly, in the name of national unity, the secular, nationalist, and leftist demands of many of the anti-shah demonstrators were articulated in religious terms and through the rituals that commemorated the death of Hussein. The Islamists controlled the slogans and the organization of the protests, which meant that many secular women who joined the protests were pressured into donning the veil (*chador*) as an expression of solidarity with traditional Muslims. Muharram fell in December in 1978, at the height of the uprising, and its celebration brought a million people to the streets. By February 1979, the shah had fled, and Khomeini returned from exile to take power. The next month, he sponsored a national referendum that declared Iran an Islamic republic. Soon after, as Khomeini began to assume nearly absolute power, a reign of terror ensued.

Progressive and leftist intellectuals around the world were initially divided in their assessments of the Iranian Revolution. While they supported the overthrow of the shah, they were usually less enthusiastic about the notion of an Islamic republic. A major exception to this ambivalence was Michel Foucault. He visited Iran twice in 1978, and wrote and spoke enthusiastically and uncritically on the revolution.

Throughout his life, Foucault's concept of authenticity meant looking at situations where people lived dangerously and flirted with death, the site where creativity originated. In the tradition of Friedrich Nietzsche and Georges Bataille, Foucault had embraced the artist who pushed the limits of rationality, and he wrote with great passion in defense of irrationalities that broke new boundaries. In 1978, Foucault found such transgressive powers in the revolutionary figure of Ayatollah Khomeini and the millions who risked death as they followed him in the course of the revolution. He knew that such "limit" experiences could lead to new forms of creativity, and he passionately lent his support. This was Foucault's only firsthand experience of revolution, and it led to his most extensive set of writings on a non-Western society.

Foucault first visited Iran in September 1978 and then met with Khomeini at his exile residence outside Paris in October. Foucault traveled to Iran for a second visit in November, when the revolutionary movement against the shah was reaching its zenith. During these two trips, Foucault was commissioned as a special correspondent of the leading Italian newspaper *Corriere della sera*, and his articles appeared on the front page of that paper. Foucault's interest in the Iranian Revolution was much more than a journalistic curiosity. His earlier work had shown a consistent though subtle affinity for the Orient and the more traditional social norms of the East, as well as a preoccupation with messianic Eastern thought. Foucault believed that the demise of colonialism by the 1960s had brought Western thought to a turning point and to a crisis. During a 1978 encounter at a Zen temple in Japan, Foucault remarked that this was "the end of the era of Western philosophy. Thus if philosophy of the future exists, it must be born outside of Europe or equally born in consequence of meetings and impacts between Europe and non-Europe" (1999, 113).

Later that year, Foucault went to Iran "to be there at the birth of ideas." He wrote that the new "Muslim" style of politics could signal the beginning of a new form of "political spirituality," not just for the Middle East, but also for Europe, which had adopted a secular politics ever since the French Revolution. As he wrote in *Corriere della sera* in November 1978:

> There are more ideas on earth than intellectuals imagine. And these ideas are more active, stronger, more resistant, more passionate than "politicians" think. We have to be there at the birth of ideas, the bursting outward of their force: not in books expressing them, but in events manifesting this force, in struggles carried on around ideas, for or against them. Ideas do not rule the world. But it is because the world has ideas (and because it constantly produces them) that it is not passively ruled by those who are its leaders or those who would like to teach it, once and for all, what it must think. This is the direction we want these "journalistic reports" to take. An analysis of thought will be linked to an analysis of what is happening. Intellectuals will work together with journalists at the point where ideas and events intersect. (cited in Eribon 1991, 282)

In addition to *Corriere della sera,* Foucault wrote on Iran in French newspapers and journals, such as the daily *Le Monde* and the widely circulated leftist weekly *Le Nouvel Observateur*. Iranian student activists translated at least one of his essays into Persian and posted it on the walls of Tehran University in the fall of 1978. In spring 1979, the Iranian Writers Association published an interview with Foucault from the previous September on the concept of revolution and the role of the intellectual. All of Foucault's published writings and interviews on Iran appear in English in their entirety for the first time in the appendix to this volume, alongside those of some of his critics.

Foucault staked out a series of distinctive political and theoretical positions on the Iranian Revolution. In part because only three of his fifteen articles and interviews on Iran have appeared in English, they have generated little discussion in the English-speaking world. But this itself is curious. Why, given the accessibility in English of even his interviews and other minor writings, have these texts not previously been made available to the English-speaking public, especially given the wide interest in Foucault by scholars of non-European societies? Many scholars of Foucault view these writings as aberrant or the product of a political mistake. We suggest that Foucault's writings on Iran were in fact closely related to his general theoretical writings on the discourses of power and the hazards of modernity. We also argue that Foucault's experience in Iran left a lasting impact on his subsequent oeuvre and that one cannot understand the sudden turn in Foucault's writings in the 1980s without recognizing the significance of the Iranian episode and his more general preoccupation with the Orient.

Long before most other commentators, Foucault understood that Iran was witnessing a singular kind of revolution. Early on, he predicted that this revolution would not follow the model of other modern revolutions. He wrote that it was organized around a sharply different concept, which he called "political spirituality." Foucault recognized the enormous power of the new discourse of militant Islam, not just for Iran, but for the world. He showed that the new Islamist movement aimed at a fundamental cultural, social, and political break with the modern Western order, as well as with the Soviet Union and China:

> As an "Islamic" movement, it can set the entire region afire, overturn the most unstable regimes, and disturb the most solid. Islam—which is not simply a religion, but an entire way of life, an adherence to a history and a civilization—has a good chance to become a gigantic powder keg, at the level of hundreds of millions of men. . . . Indeed, it is also important to recognize that the demand for the "legitimate rights of the Palestinian people" hardly stirred the Arab peoples. What would it be if this cause encompassed the dynamism of an Islamic movement, something much stronger than those with a Marxist, Leninist, or Maoist character? ("A Powder Keg Called Islam," app., 241)[2]

He also noted presciently that such a discourse would alter the "global strategic equilibrium" (ibid.).

Foucault's experience in Iran contributed to a turning point in his thought. In the late 1970s, he was moving from a preoccupation with technologies of domination to a new interest in what he termed the technologies of the self, as the foundation for a new form of spirituality and resistance to power.[3] The Iranian Revolution had a lasting impact on his late writing in several ways. In his Iran writings, Foucault emphasized the deployment of certain instruments of modernity as means of resistance. He called attention to the innovative uses that Islamists made of overseas radio broadcasts and cassettes. This blending of more traditional religious discourses with modern means of communication had helped to galvanize the revolutionary movement and ultimately paralyzed the modern and authoritarian Pahlavi regime.

Foucault was also fascinated by the appropriation of Shi'ite myths of martyrdom and rituals of penitence by large parts of the revolutionary movement and their willingness to face death in their single-minded goal of overthrowing the Pahlavi regime. Later, in his discussion of an "aesthetics of existence"—practices that could be refashioned for our time and serve as the foundation for a new form of spirituality—Foucault often referred to Greco-Roman texts and early Christian practices. However, many of these practices also had a strong resemblance to what he saw in Iran. Additionally, many scholars have wondered about Foucault's sudden turn to the ancient Greco-Roman world in volumes 2 and 3 of *History of Sexuality*, and his interest in uncovering male homosexual practices in this era. We would suggest an "Oriental" appropriation here as well. Foucault's description of a male "ethics of love" in the Greco-Roman world resembles some existing male homosexual practices of the Middle East and North Africa. Foucault's foray into the Greco-Roman world might, therefore, have been related to his longstanding fascination with *ars erotica* and the erotic arts of the East in particular, since he sometimes combined the discussion of sexual practices of the contemporary East with those of the classical Greco-Roman society.

The Iranian experience also raises some questions about Foucault's overall approach to modernity. First, scholars often assume that Foucault's suspicion of utopianism, his hostility to grand narratives and universals, and his stress on difference and singularity rather than totality would make him less likely than his predecessors on the Left to romanticize an authoritarian politics that promised radically to refashion from above the lives and thought of a people, for its ostensible benefit. However, his Iran writings showed that Foucault was not immune to the type of illusions that so many Western leftists had held with regard to the Soviet Union and, later, China. Foucault did not anticipate the birth of yet another modern state where old religious technologies of domination could be refashioned and institutionalized; this was a state that propounded a traditionalist ideology, but equipped itself with modern technologies of organization, surveillance, warfare, and propaganda.

Second, Foucault's highly problematic relationship to feminism becomes more than an intellectual lacuna in the case of Iran. On a few occasions, Foucault reproduced statements he had heard from religious figures on gender relations in a possible future Islamic republic, but he never questioned the "separate but equal" message of the Islamists. Foucault also dismissed feminist premonitions that the revolution was headed in a dangerous direction, and he seemed to regard such warnings as little more than Orientalist attacks on Islam, thereby depriving himself of a more balanced perspective toward the events in Iran. At a more general level, Foucault remained insensitive toward the diverse ways in which power affected women, as against men. He ignored the fact that those most traumatized by the premodern disciplinary practices were often women and children, who were oppressed in the name of tradition, obligation, or honor. In chapter 1, we root his indifference to

Iranian women in the problematic stances toward gender in his better-known writings, while in chapters 3 and 4, we discuss Foucault's response to attacks by Iranian and French feminists on his Iran writings themselves.

Third, an examination of Foucault's writings provides more support for the frequently articulated criticism that his one-sided critique of modernity needs to be seriously reconsidered, especially from the vantage point of many non-Western societies. Indeed, there are some indications that Foucault himself was moving in such a direction. In his 1984 essay "What Is Enlightenment?" he put forth a position on the Enlightenment that was more nuanced than before, also moving from a two-pronged philosophy concerned with knowledge and power to a three-pronged one that included ethics. However, the limits of his ethics of moderation with regard to gender and sexuality need to be explored, and this is the subject of the last chapter of this book.

As against Foucault, some French leftists were very critical of the Iranian Revolution early on. Beginning in December 1978 with a series of articles that appeared on the front page of *Le Monde*, the noted Middle East scholar and leftist commentator Maxime Rodinson, known for his classic biography of Muhammad, published some hard-hitting critiques of Islamism in Iran as "a type of archaic fascism" ("Islam Resurgent?" app., 233). As Rodinson later revealed, he was specifically targeting Foucault in these articles, which drew on Max Weber's notion of charisma, Marx's concepts of class and ideology, and a range of scholarship on Iran and Islam. In March 1979, Foucault's writings on Iran came under increasing attack in the wake of the new regime's executions of homosexual men and especially the large demonstrations by Iranian women on the streets of Tehran against Khomeini's directives for compulsory veiling. In addition, France's best-known feminist, the existentialist philosopher Simone de Beauvoir, protested the Khomeini regime's suppression of women's rights and sent a message of solidarity to Iranian women ("Speech by Simone de Beauvoir," app., 246–47). Foucault refused to respond to the new attacks, issuing only a mild criticism of human rights in Iran that refrained from any mention of women's rights or gay rights, and he soon lapsed into silence on Iran.

In France, the controversy over Foucault's writings on Iran is well known and continues to undercut his reputation. For example, during the debate over the September 11, 2001, terrorist attacks on New York and Washington, a prominent French commentator referred polemically and without apparent need for any further explanation to "Michel Foucault, advocate of Khomeinism in Iran and therefore in theory of its exactions" in a front-page op-ed article in *Le Monde* (Minc 2001).[4] Even French commentators more sympathetic to Foucault have acknowledged the extremely problematic nature of his stance on Iran. Biographer Didier Eribon, himself an editor at *Le Nouvel Observateur* and a friend of Foucault, wrote, "The criticism and sarcasm that greeted Foucault's 'mistake' concerning Iran added further to his despondency after what he saw as the qualified critical reception" of volume 1 of *The History of Sexuality*. Eribon added: "For a long time thereafter Foucault rarely commented on politics or journalism" (1991, 291). Eribon has furnished us with what is to date the most detailed and balanced discussion of Foucault and Iran. Another biographer, Jeannette Colombel, who was also a friend of Foucault, refers to "his error" on Iran and concludes that the controversy "wounded him" (1994, 216).

In the English-speaking world, there have been fewer criticisms of Foucault over his involvement with Iran. One exception to this is the critical biography by the political philosopher James Miller, who characterized Foucault's Iran episode as one of "folly" (1993, 309). Miller was the only biographer to suggest that Foucault's fascination with death played a part in his enthusiasm for the Iranian Islamists, who emphasized mass martyrdom. In a discussion of Miller's book, the social philosopher Mark Lilla picked up this theme, writing that during the Iran episode, Foucault had "again heard the siren call of a 'limit experience' in politics" (2001, 154). The political theorist Mitchell Cohen has suggested that Foucault's writings on Iran were "a symptom of something troubling in the kind of left-wing thinking that mixes postmodernism, simplistic thirdworldism, and illiberal inclination" (2002, 18).[5] David Macey, the author of the most comprehensive biography of Foucault to date, was more equivocal. Macey regarded the French attacks on Foucault over Iran as exaggerated and mean-spirited, but he nonetheless acknowledged that Foucault was so "impressed" by what he saw in Iran in 1978 that he misread "the probable future developments he was witnessing" (1993, 410).

Elsewhere in the English-speaking world, where Foucault's writings on Iran have been only selectively translated, and the contemporary French responses to him not translated at all, Foucault's Iran writings have been treated more kindly. His last two articles on Iran, where he rather belatedly made a few criticisms of the Islamic regime in the face of the attacks on him by other French intellectuals, have been the most widely circulated among the ones that have appeared in English. James Bernauer, a Jesuit scholar sympathetic to Foucault, translated one of these over two decades ago (Foucault 1981). This article and another somewhat critical one, both something of an exception among Foucault's writings on Iran, are the only examples of his work on Iran that appear in a comprehensive, English-language selection of his shorter writings (Foucault 2000a). In a review of that volume, the literary critic Edward Said, hardly unsympathetic to Foucault, sought to distance himself from the two Iran writings included there by suggesting that they "seem very dated" (2000b, 16–17).

Another factor that has minimized the discussion of Foucault's writings on Iran in the English-speaking world has been the tendency of scholars sympathetic to him to group the Iran writings together with a number of other ones on political issues during the same period. Macey did so in his 1991 biography. Soon after, James Bernauer and Michael Mahon wrote that the Iranian Revolution and Poland's Solidarnosc were "two events in the political realm" on which Foucault commented during his last years (1994, 144). In his introduction to Foucault's shorter writings on power, James Faubion extended this list to include Foucault's 1979 intervention on behalf of Vietnamese boat people (see Foucault 2000a, xxxvi).

While in no way minimizing the political significance of these interventions over Poland and the Vietnamese boat people, each of which had an impact on French politics, we maintain that they had a character very different from Foucault's writings on Iran. Quantitatively, he simply wrote far more on Iran than on Poland, let alone the Vietnamese boat people. Qualitatively, there were also major differences between his writings on Iran and these other interventions. On the Vietnamese boat people, an issue that came to the fore in the spring of 1979, Foucault joined with other intellectual luminaries such as Jean-Paul Sartre and Raymond Aron to demand asylum for people fleeing a repressive Stalinist dictatorship. Concerning Poland, he worked during 1981 and 1982 alongside the well-known sociologist Pierre Bourdieu and the famous actress Simone Signoret, among others, to support Solidarnosc, driven underground in December 1981. Thus, he did not carve out much of a distinctive position on these issues, and he may in fact have used these interventions to regain his standing in the Parisian intellectual world after the embarrassment of the Iran episode in 1978–79. In addition, on Poland and Vietnam, Foucault's positions were part of a broad shift within the French intellectual Left, after decades of leaning toward Russian and then Chinese versions of communism. On Iran, however, Foucault stood virtually alone.

Instead of merging his Iran episode with these other, less controversial, political interventions, we therefore emphasize its *singularity*, to use a favorite term of Foucault's. We believe that, except for his more intensive and long-term organizing activities in the prisoner support movement during the early 1970s, his writings on Iran represent the most significant and passionate political commitment of his life. It was an episode that ended in failure, as he himself seemed to recognize in his silence on Iran after May 1979. We also believe that, like his writings and activism concerning modern forms of punishment, the Iran writings express characteristic aspects of Foucault's worldview.

We have been unable to locate any discussions by Foucault about the Nicaraguan Revolution of 1979, one that featured a form of political spirituality, liberation theology, that was more open and humanistic than Iranian Islamism. Latin American liberation theology did not develop a cult of martyrdom and death, nor was it an authoritarian movement. The example of liberation theology is also important for another reason. There have been numerous forms of political spirituality in the past century. Some, like liberation theology, Gandhianism, or much of the U.S. Civil Rights Movement, favored a politics of democracy, tolerance, humanism, and to a degree, women's rights.[6] The same could be said of the progressive Muslim thinkers who have joined Iran's Reform Movement since 1997. Others, like Iranian Islamism in 1978–79, were authoritarian movements that targeted religious and ethnic minorities as well as women. In our present exploration of Foucault's relationship to Iranian Islamism, we limit our critique of political spirituality to such authoritarian forms. In the Islamic world today, they can be compared to Western Christian fundamentalism, to extremist currents within Zionism, or to authoritarian Hindu revivalism in contemporary India.

A few of Foucault's supporters in the English-speaking world have attempted to exercise damage control in their discussions of the Iran episode.[7] However, English-language scholars sympathetic to Foucault from the field of religious studies have approached his Iran writings with somewhat greater care. Jeremy Carrette, who has produced two volumes on Foucault and religion, distanced himself from Foucault's uncritical embrace of the Iranian ayatollahs and wrote, "There were clearly huge miscalculations of Iran and Islam in Foucault's journalistic work, but the force of his interest in the power of religious subjectivity in the shaping of human life is clear" (Carrette 2000, 140; see also Carrette 1999). The Amsterdam-based philosopher Michiel Leezenberg held that "Foucault correctly saw the decisive importance of political Islam in the protests" of 1978, but this insight was "paired, however, with a number of seriously flawed or oversimplified remarks on shi'ism" (1998, 79). The notion that Foucault made some "miscalculations" on Iran usually refers to the fact that the regime of the ayatollahs quickly became a brutal theocracy, something Foucault did not anticipate. A deeper questioning of Foucault's generalized enthusiasm for Islamist "spiritual politics" and his vehement rejection of other alternatives to the shah's regime, whether liberal, nationalist, or social democratic, is not to be found here. Another issue with regard to Foucault's own project is whether his interest in the Iranian Revolution was tied to a search for alternate forms of non-Western modernity that could rejoin spirituality and politics.

The more common attempts to bracket out Foucault's writings on Iran as "miscalculations," sometimes with the implication that they are not really Foucauldian, remind one of what Foucault himself had criticized in his well-known 1969 essay, "What Is an Author?" When we include certain works in an author's career and exclude others that were written in "a different style," or were "inferior" (Foucault 1969, 111), we create a stylistic unity and a theoretical coherence. We do so by privileging certain writings as authentic and excluding others that do not fit our view of what the author ought to be: "The author is therefore the ideological figure by which one marks the manner in which we fear the proliferation of meaning" (Foucault 1969, 110). For these reasons as well as those mentioned earlier, we invite the reader to join us in exploring Foucault's writings on the Iranian Revolution. We write these lines in 2004, the twentieth anniversary of Michel Foucault's death and the twenty-fifth anniversary of the Iranian Revolution.

PART I

Foucault's Discourse: On Pinnacles and Pitfalls

Chapter 1

The Paradoxical World of Foucault

The Modern and the Traditional Social Orders

Why did Foucault decide to travel twice to Iran and write on the Iranian Revolution in 1978–79 when he showed no similar interest in the Nicaraguan Revolution, and only slightly greater concern for the Solidarnosc movement in Poland? Why, in his writings on the Iranian Revolution, did he give his exclusive support to its Islamist wing? Certain modalities in Foucault's oeuvre seemed to resonate with the revolutionary movement that was unfolding in Iran. There was a perplexing affinity between this post-structuralist philosopher, this European critic of modernity, and the antimodernist Islamist radicals on the streets of Iran.[1] Both were searching for a new form of political spirituality as a counterdiscourse to a thoroughly materialistic world; both clung to idealized notions of premodern social orders; both were disdainful of modern liberal judicial systems; and both admired individuals who risked death in attempts to reach a more authentic existence. Foucault's affinity with the Iranian Islamists, often construed as his "error" over Iran, may also reveal some of the larger ramifications of his Nietzschean-Heideggerian discourse.

This chapter begins with an exploration of Foucault's original contributions on power, discourse, and the body. We look at his attraction to Oriental forms of ascetic speculation and suggest that his comments on the latter, although sporadic, nonetheless form an important subtext to his oeuvre. We then turn to Foucault's genealogical method, which, he claimed, broke with a suprahistorical method of historiography. We argue, however, that Foucault's methodology can itself be seen as a suprahistorical grand narrative. The difference between the Foucauldian grand narrative and the liberal or Marxian ones is that Foucault's narrative privileges not modernity but the traditional social orders. In particular, we look at Foucault's writings on Christian monastic literature, including lectures that he gave before his travels to Iran and as he prepared to write volumes 2 and 3 of *The History of Sexuality*. In the tradition of Martin Heidegger, Foucault was interested in a secular, hermeneutic reading of Christianity, especially of those rituals and techniques that could be reinvented for a new spirituality, a modern form of penitence. Foucault also appropriated another Heideggerian concept, "freedom-toward-death," as a liminal space for artistic and political creativity. The last section of this chapter turns again to Iran in 1978 when Ayatollah Khomeini, leader of the Iranian Revolution, helped convince millions to risk their lives in the struggle against the shah. For Foucault, he seemed to become the personification of Nietzsche's "will to power."

Foucault's Original Contribution: Power, Discourse, and the Body

What makes Foucault such an irresistible thinker, even to many of his critics, are his original formulations on power and what he calls the discourses of modernity. Modern power is not only repressive, negative, and restrictive, he argued; it is also positive, productive, and creative. "Power produces realities" and establishes "rituals of truth," he wrote in *Discipline and Punish*. Power games manifest themselves not only in relations between the state and its subjects, or between members of various social classes. Modern power is far more pervasive. It seeps through the web of all social, political, and economic relations down to the "very depth of society" (Foucault 1977a, 27). A whole generation of feminist and postcolonial theorists has stressed that forms of knowledge are not independent of power. Foucault articulated this notion in a crisp theoretical formulation: "There is no power relation without the correlative constitution of a field of knowledge, nor any knowledge that does not presuppose and constitute at the same time power relations" (27).

As is well known, in his historical studies on the mental institution, the military, the school, the hospital, and the prison, Foucault argued that modern "technologies of power" create docile, utilitarian bodies. The instruments of modern power are simple: a "hierarchical method of observation" is established at the military, the school, or the prison "making it possible for a single gaze to see everything constantly" (Foucault 1977a, 173). A "normalizing judgment," a set of rules that require continuous observance, is then put in place. Students, soldiers, mental patients, and prisoners internalize these rules. All are now subject to a small penal mechanism. It "compares, differentiates, hierarchizes, homogenizes, excludes. In short, it *normalizes*" (183;

original emphasis). Finally there is the "examination," the highly ritualized process that rewards the conformists and penalizes the nonconformists. Thus, modern power operates ostensibly by gathering a body of knowledge about individuals (students, mental patients, soldiers, prisoners) through which they are constantly monitored. The system becomes more successful once the new "disciplinary power" is enforced not only by the teacher, the sergeant, or the warden, but also by the individual subject, who has internalized it.

The purpose of modern power is both to attain "maximum intensity" and to do so at a minimal cost, in both economic and political terms. The aim is to aggregate large numbers of individuals in an institution, yet employ such discreet and invisible methods of control as to arouse "little resistance." In short, the purpose of the new technology of power is to "increase the docility and utility of all the elements of the system" (Foucault 1977a, 218). In most of his writings before 1976, Foucault suggested that there could be no successful challenge to the unitary, disciplinary power of modernity. Later, however, his matrix of power was not completely devoid of resistance either, as is seen in *The History of Sexuality*, first published in 1976. Since power operates at the micro levels of society, points of resistance, which "are present everywhere in the power network" (Foucault 1978a, 95), would also be local, manifesting themselves in everyday practices. Multiple sites of resistance could break norms and prevent the creation of hegemonic and homogenized societies. He referred as well to "a plurality of resistances": "Resistances do not derive from a few heterogeneous principles; but neither are they a lure or a promise that is of necessity betrayed. They are the odd term in relations of power; they are inscribed in the latter as an *irreducible opposite*" (96; emphasis added). Two years later, Foucault's writings on Iran focused on the Islamist movement, which, as we will see, he was to characterize as an "irreducible" form of resistance to Western hegemony.

One of Foucault's more provocative challenges to liberalism, and at least to orthodox Marxism, was his rejection of the emancipatory claims of the Enlightenment. He argued that the dominant classes of Western societies gradually abandoned traditional and more violent forms of power, not because the elites had become more "civilized" and caring but because they had devised a more subtle "technology of subjection" by the eighteenth century, one that was more effective and productive than brute punishment. In Foucault's view, "the 'Enlightenment,' which discovered the liberties, also invented the disciplines" (1977a, 222). The more egalitarian juridical framework of the French Revolution masked the more insidious controlling mechanisms that operated in the factory, the military, the school, and the prison:

> The development and generalization of disciplinary mechanisms constituted the other, dark side of these processes. The general juridical form that guaranteed a system of rights that were egalitarian in principle was supported by these tiny, everyday, physical mechanisms, by all those systems of micro-power that are essentially non-egalitarian and asymmetrical that we call the disciplines. And although, in a formal way, the representative régime makes it possible, directly or indirectly, with or without relays, for the will of all to form the fundamental authority of sovereignty, the disciplines provide, at the base, a guarantee of the submission of forces and bodies. The real, corporal disciplines constituted the foundation of the formal, juridical liberties. (222)[2]

Foucault's highly critical stance toward modernity and the Enlightenment has been debated for decades. His most prominent intellectual adversary, Jürgen Habermas, also criticized the instrumental rationality of the Enlightenment and its technological domination. But Habermas was not willing to reject the achievements of the Enlightenment and modernity. Instead, he argued that Foucault's genealogical method of writing history was constructed on major gaps and omissions. Why was it that when Foucault spoke of the reforms of the Enlightenment era in the eighteenth and early nineteenth centuries, he singled out issues such as the problems of the Kantian theory of morality, the development of a penal justice system, and the formulation of a utilitarian philosophy, yet failed to discuss in any substantial way the establishment of constitutional forms of government that transferred state power "ideologically from the sovereignty of the prince to the sovereignty of the people" (Habermas 1995, 289)?

Furthermore, why was it that Foucault saw so little importance in those modern laws in the last two centuries that have significantly expanded civil liberties for many previously disenfranchised members of society, both women and minorities? Why did he see such civil codes merely as sources of deception: "We should not be deceived by all the Constitutions framed throughout the world since the French Revolution, the Codes written and revised, a whole continual and clamorous legislative activity: these were the forms that made an essentially normalizing power acceptable" (Foucault 1978a, 144). Habermas conceded that the legal mechanisms that secure freedoms for citizens in the modern welfare state are the same ones that "endanger the freedom of their presumptive beneficiaries." But he argued that instead of critically addressing these problems, and building upon the "emancipatory impulses" of the Enlightenment, Foucault so "levels down the complexity of modernization" that such differences simply disappear from his fragmentary archaeological studies (Habermas 1995, 290).

A Heideggerian Orientalist Subtext?

Perhaps more than any other philosophical position, Martin Heidegger's criticism of technology and modernity influenced Foucault's work. Heidegger had tried to distance himself from both the metaphysical and the rational, scientific, and technological traditions of the West. In charting a new ontological and antihistoricist perspective, he employed many Roman Catholic theological concepts for his ostensibly secular inquiry into the "fall" of modern man (Heidegger 1962). He characterized modernity by subjectivity, a move away from the theocratic and traditional values that had defined ethics and politics for centuries. In the absence of traditions that had given meaning, structure, and certainty to the world, the modern subject relied on human perception, on feeling and on rationality. Mastery over nature through science and labor became the goal of life. Modern historical inquiries produced a notion of progress based on the acquisition of technology and the control over nature. To Heidegger, however, this never-ending drive for mastery over objects (and by definition over other subjects) had catastrophic consequences. The pursuit of humanity in the modern world produced an utter "inhumanity." Subjectivity and modernity culminated in a "totalitarian world technology," whether in its American, Soviet, or Nazi versions, even though Heidegger was not unsympathetic to the latter (Steiner 1987, 28; see also Gillespie 1984, 127–28). Only through recognizing human limitations, through facing the reality of their own eventual death, could human beings free themselves from the dogma of science and technology and live authentic lives.

Heidegger's call of conscience and questioning of Western modernity have been likened to Oriental forms of meditation, including Japanese traditions of ascetic speculation (Steiner 1987, 33; Gillespie 1984, 174). This too has been linked to Foucault. Several commentators, especially Ua Schaub, have pointed to Foucault's preoccupation with various forms of mysticism (Christian and Jewish), as well as magic, hermeticism, and gnosticism (Schaub 1989, 306). Others have wondered if a preoccupation with Eastern thought, including Buddhism, lies beneath Foucault's criticism of Western technologies of power and Western morality. Schaub suggests that Foucault's constant questioning of limits and his explorations of transgressivity were influenced by an Eastern "counter-discourse that appropriates Oriental lore in opposition to Western strategies of control," an East that remained supposedly incomprehensible to the modern, rational European world (308). Indeed, similar to a passionate Romantic, Foucault may have exoticized and admired the East from afar, while remaining a Westerner in his own life (Brinton 1967, 206).

In the original preface to *Madness and Civilization* (1961), however, Foucault criticized notions of the East as the absolute "other" of the expansionist rational West:

> In the universality of the Western ratio, there is this divide that is the East; the East thought of as the origin, dreamt of as the dizzy point that is the place of birth, of nostalgia and promises of return, the East which offers itself to the colonizing reason of the West but is indefinitely inaccessible, for it remains always as a boundary, the night of beginning in which the West was formed but where it drew a dividing line, the East is for the West everything which the West is not, yet it is here that it has to seek whatever might be its originating truth. It is necessary to do a history of this great divide. (Foucault 1961, iv)

Nonetheless, Foucault's own work suffers from a similar type of dualism.

In an unusual turn, however, Foucault's "Orient" seems to include the Greco-Roman world as well as the modern Eastern one, since the contrast he draws is primarily between tradition and modernity rather than East and West as such. A somewhat related taxonomy appears in Nietzsche's *Genealogy of Morals*, where he includes in his category of "noble races"—and in his description of necessary manifestations of violence—a number of quite diverse premodern societies: "One cannot fail to see at the bottom of all these noble races the beast of prey, the splendid *blond beast* prowling about avidly in search of spoil and victory; this hidden core needs to erupt from time to time, the animal has to get out again and go back to the wilderness: the Roman, Arabian, Germanic, Japanese nobility, the Homeric heroes, the Scandinavian Vikings all shared this need" (1967, 40–41).

In Foucault, a dualism emerges in which the premodern social order (assumed also to operate in many Middle Eastern, African, and Asian societies of today) is privileged over the modern Western one. This notion is problematic, not only because Foucault assumes a pristine, idyllic East, as against a "rational" West, but also because Foucault's subjectless historiography and idealized East reproduces androcentric patterns of discourse. In a 1982 interview, for example, Foucault combined an admiration for the Orient with a certain nostalgia for the aristocratic, ostensibly paternalistic system of taking care of one's subordinates, which modernity had replaced with a callous form of individualism. Such hierarchical traditions regulated relations between adults and youths, men and women, and upper and lower classes in premodern societies, something of which Foucault seems blissfully unaware in the following encomium to silence:

> Silence may be a much more interesting way of having a relationship with people. . . . I think silence is one of those things that has unfortunately been dropped from our culture. We don't have a culture of silence; we don't have a culture of suicide either. The Japanese do, I think. Young Romans or young Greeks were taught to keep silent in very different ways according to the people with whom they were interacting. Silence was then a specific form of experiencing a relationship with others. This is something that I believe is really worthwhile cultivating. I'm in favor of developing silence as a cultural ethos. (cited in Carrette 1999, 40)[3]

Here again, there are echoes of Heidegger, who wrote in *Being and Time* that the discourse through which the self is finally brought back from the loud idle talk of others and conscience is achieved is one of silence. "Remaining silent has been characterized as an essential possibility of discourse. . . . The discourse of conscience never comes to utterance" (Heidegger 1962, 246). As we shall see throughout the course of this study, to the extent that there is an Orientalist subtext in Foucault's work, it is not a geographical and spatial one, but a philosophical and temporal one, a discourse that moves across the East/West divide and relies heavily on both Nietzsche and Heidegger. Foucault's "East" implicitly privileges intuition and silence (read the silence of mostly youth, women, and the lower classes in premodern social orders) as the preferred modes of discourse and opens up the possibility that pre-rational forms of thought could be mistaken for supra-rational ones.[4]

For Foucault, silence was especially valued in the Eastern discourse on sex (i.e., what feminists working on the East are just beginning to challenge). In *The History of Sexuality* he wrote that there were two great procedures for producing the truth of sex. The West produced a *scientia sexualis*, procedures for telling the truth of sex that were geared to a form of knowledge as power, while the East produced something quite different. Note, however, how Rome is here grouped together with Asian and Middle Eastern cultures:

> China, Japan, India, Rome, the Arabo-Moslem societies . . . endowed themselves with an *ars erotica*. In the erotic art, truth is drawn from pleasure itself. . . . There is formed a knowledge that must remain secret, not because of an element of infamy that might attach to its object, but because of the need to hold it in the greatest reserve, since, according to tradition, it would lose its effectiveness and its virtue by being divulged. Consequently, the relationship to the master who holds the secrets is of paramount importance; only he,

> working alone, can transmit this art in an esoteric manner. (Foucault 1978a, 57–58)

From this, one might conclude that, for Foucault, those who questioned this romanticization of *ars erotica,* or wished to unveil such silences, simply reproduced modern Western attitudes toward sexuality. If Orientalism means stereotyping the East and its way of life (either by glorifying it or vilifying it), if it means romanticizing the exotic sexuality of the East (heterosexual or homosexual), then Foucault was probably an Orientalist. This is the case even though his intellectual and political sympathies seemed to be on the side of the East, because of its more pre-technological lifestyle and its victimization by Western imperialism.

A second consequence of this binary worldview appears in Foucault's analysis of modern European sexualities, also in *The History of Sexuality.* In exploring the origins of the new technologies of sexuality in the eighteenth and nineteenth centuries, Foucault briefly mentioned the impact of colonialism on scientific claims and analyzed racism as it was expressed in the West. As Ann Stoler has argued, the modern European discourse of sexuality was constructed, at least in part, on the basis of certain social practices that were a result of Western imperialism. Indeed, many other aspects of European economics, politics, and culture were formed through this relationship as well. Stoler writes that bourgeois identities in both the colonies and the imperial metropolis were "emphatically coded by race" and reflected a host of anxieties that originated from the porous margins between the European elite and their colonial subjects, with poor whites and mixed-blood children defining that arbitrary boundary. The new concepts of sexuality were meant to draw the line amid these constantly shifting social taxonomies (Stoler 1995, 100).[5]

Foucault, however, argued that in the new Western technologies, the discourse of sex was not aimed at enslaving and exploiting the other (working-class or colonized), but at affirming the bourgeois self. Though he came tantalizingly close to a recognition that the bourgeois body had to be "isolated" from these "others," Foucault did not identify the racialized nature of what amounted to a fear of *métissage*:

> The primary concern was not repression of the sex of the classes to be exploited, but rather the body, vigor, longevity, progeniture, and descent of the classes that "ruled." . . . It has to be seen as the self-affirmation of one class rather than the enslavement of another. . . . [The bourgeoisie] provided itself with a body to be cared for, protected, cultivated, and preserved from the

> many dangers and contacts, to be isolated from others so that it would retain its differential value. (Foucault 1978a, 123)

As Stoler points out, Foucault's use of the passive voice in this sentence covered up the fact that this pampering and cultivation of the bourgeois body required a whole host of maids, servants, butlers, and wet-nurses, who performed these functions in the colonies. These new technologies of the body relied on "an intimate set of exploitative sexual and service relations between European men and native women, between European women and native men, shaped by the sexual politics of class and race" (Stoler 1995, 111).

But why did Foucault avoid a more in-depth discussion of colonial culture, when a number of contemporary French intellectuals were engaged precisely in such a project? Foucault's fascination with the more traditional social norms of the East and the binary distinction he maintained between modern and premodern social orders might have prevented him from exploring the colonial roots of the European technologies of sexuality. A closer exploration of imperialism would have required a discussion of the gradual transformation of the East by modernity and Western modalities, as well as interracial sexual relations between Western intellectuals, colonialists, or tourists and the indigenous population. All of this could have led him to seriously rethink his project. Thus, a more porous, fluid, and hybrid interchange between the East and the West is missing from Foucault's discourse, though it can be found in the writings of several of his contemporaries, including Frantz Fanon and Albert Memmi, whose psychoanalytic observations on sex across the racial divide relied on Freud and Lacan, as well as Hegel, Marx, and Sartre (see Fanon 1967; Memmi 1965).

Foucault's Grand Narrative

As Foucault wrote in 1971, in "Nietzsche, Genealogy, History," the social world showed an endless repetition of the process of domination, which played itself out in "rituals that imposed rights and obligations" (Foucault 1971, 85). The search for truth in history was not possible. The desire for knowledge, the ultimate task of history, was useless and even destructive, since "it may be that mankind will eventually perish from this passion for knowledge" (96). Therefore, the main point in doing history was to discover discontinuities. In this new way of writing history, which he alternately called "genealogy" or "effective history," Foucault suggested that the genealogist does not pretend that he can go back in time only to "restore an unbroken continuity." His work did not resemble "the evolution of a species," nor was he interested in mapping "the destiny of a people." Rather, his or her concern was with accidents and "minute deviations," with "errors" that gave birth to the modern axes of power and knowledge (81). Thus, in the tradition of Nietzsche, Foucault called for a different type of history and a break with what he termed "supra-historical" historiography.

But a closer look at Foucault's genealogical writings suggests that he often replaced the earlier grand narratives of modernity with his own metanarrative, a binary construct wherein traditional social orders were privileged over modern ones. Foucault replaced the liberal, Marxist, and psychoanalytic historical narratives with a discourse on power, knowledge, and pleasure (and sometimes resistance), the central axis of which was a binary contrast or construct between modern and premodern European societies. In each of his more empirical genealogical explorations, Foucault attempted to show the process whereby premodern physical forms of restraint and punishment were replaced by more psychological and discursive modern ones. These new forms of constraint gave the appearance of being more humane, but were in fact more pervasive and powerful because they categorized, labeled, diagnosed, and monitored according to a regimen.

In *Madness and Civilization* (1961), Foucault argued that in Western Europe at the time of the Renaissance, madness was a mundane fact of life and was even endowed with a certain respect. He cited Shakespeare and Cervantes to show that the insane led "an easy, wandering existence" in the open countryside or aboard a "ship of fools" (Foucault 1965, 8). Madness assumed a liminal position in these societies. Sometimes, it became a window to wisdom and knowledge, giving one a glimpse of another world. Only when he became mad did Shakespeare's King Lear recognize the true nature of his unkind daughters and the folly with which he had treated his younger daughter, Cordelia. Lady Macbeth revealed the truth of her crime when she collapsed into insanity. At other times, madness was a tragic destiny deserving of our sympathy, as was the case with Ophelia in *Hamlet*. In the premodern world, madness almost always opened a window to the imagination, and the very "invention of the arts" owed much to the "deranged imagination" of poets, painters, and musicians (29).

Beginning with the seventeenth century, the insane were incarcerated, tortured, and tormented. During and after the French Revolution, Foucault argued, the physical torment lessened but was replaced with a psychological one. As James Miller notes, for Foucault, the seemingly humane application of scientific knowledge turned out in fact to be a "subtle and insidious new form of social control" (1993, 14). In France and England, the mad were freed from chains and brought into asylums. Foucault had almost no words of support for the two great reformers of the period, the Quaker William Tuke (1732–1822) in England and the French revolutionary Phillippe Pinel (1745–1826). The two reformers had simply subjected the insane to the intense gaze of the "other." Gradually, through regimented work, observation, surveillance, and the alternation of reward and punishment, they had instilled a system of self-observation and self-discipline. The purpose of this new treatment was not to understand the mentally ill better or even to relieve them of their traumas. It was to control their behavior and conduct in order to make them adhere to society's codes of normality and proper morality. Here again, Foucault followed Nietzsche in his negative assessment of the French Revolution. Where Nietzsche argued that the French Revolution represented the triumph of the slave morality, of "leveling" and of "wanting to set up a supreme rights of the majority" (Nietzsche 1967, 54), Foucault critiqued the normative power of the French Revolution and its new institutions.[6]

Foucault made a similar argument in 1963, in *The Birth of the Clinic,* where he wrote that a new medical "gaze" emerged in the eighteenth century, breaking with the earlier, traditional form of medicine, which had relied on classifying illness and curing a particular category of illness. Instead, medicine began focusing on the symptoms of the individual. This transformation took place as a result of the new sociopolitical climate of the French Revolution. Once the patient is treated as an individual, a new conception of life and death also emerges: "Disease breaks away from the metaphysic of evil, to which it had been related for centuries" (Foucault 1994a, 196). This new empirical science of medicine immediately defines human beings by their limits. The magic of modern medicine is that it endlessly repudiates death: "health replaces salvation" and scientists become philosophers. Medicine "is fully engaged in the philosophical status of man." Contemporary thought was still in this empirical straitjacket: "We are only just beginning to disentangle a few of the threads which are still so unknown to us that we immediately assume them to be either marvelously new or absolutely archaic" (199).

In *The Order of Things,* first published in 1966, Foucault developed similar perspectives, this time focusing on the evolution of language and its relation to scientific inquiry in the seventeenth century. Until the modern period, human beings had assumed that there was a relationship of "sympathy and similitudes" between the objects of nature and their purpose. For example, he noted, the walnut's shape was similar to the human head and, therefore, walnuts were regarded as a cure for various forms of head ailments. The Renaissance and the introduction of the printing press elevated language to the same sacred position. Knowledge about an object involved a combination of rational and magical discourses.[7] Each text had infinite interpretations, and each interpretation was the object of a further discursive reading. Then, in the seventeenth century, there was a great break—a mutation in thought. Foucault wrote nostalgically about what was lost in this period, when, with the introduction of the empirical sciences, the "profound kinship of language with the world" ended, and one "began to ask how a sign could be linked to what it signified?" (1973, 42–43). Language became arbitrary, representing something else. Then Hobbes, Berkeley, Hume, and Condillac led the way toward the creation of a new scientific domain, with man at its center. New theories in the fields of grammar, natural history, and economics soon "toppled the whole of Western thought," and undermined the intrinsic relationship that had existed between nature and its objects, and between words and things (239).[8] Only in the realm of literature, in the writings of Friedrich Hölderlin, Stéphane Mallarmé, and others such as Antonin Artaud, did language maintain an "autonomous existence" outside the empirical world (44). Foucault famously ended *The Order of Things* by proclaiming the death of the modern humanist subject: "Since man was constituted at a time when language was doomed to dispersion, will he not be dispersed when language regains its unity? . . . One can surely wager that man would be erased, like a face drawn in sand at the edge of the sea" (386–87).

Foucault made a similar argument in *Discipline and Punish,* first published in 1975. The book began with the description of a grotesque 1757 execution in Paris by torture, which Foucault then contrasted to the methodical timetables of modern Western prisons. At first glance, the reader might assume that Foucault was condemning the horrible bodily torment of the pre-1789 system of justice, but this was not the case. Here again, he seemed to echo Nietzsche, who had famously declared, "when mankind was not yet ashamed of its cruelty, life on earth was more cheerful than it is now" (1967, 67). Foucault constructed a historical narrative in which he argued the following: Our modern world has replaced public torture with a less visible penal system that pretends to be more humane and less cruel, but is in fact quite the opposite. Modern society has invented new disciplinary practices that are more subtle, but also more insidious. These methods of controlling the body and the mind are not limited to the prisons, but permeate our entire society, in the military, schools, factories, and other workplaces. Moreover, the disciplinary practices of modern society are internalized by citizens, who police themselves. To Foucault, these modern disciplinary practices in fact allow less freedom than the earlier physical punishments of the insane or the criminal. This is because in the premodern era individuals at least had the freedom to consider themselves wronged and inhumanely treated. The modern age takes that defense away with its medicalization of deviance and its transformation of punishment from an open and public act to one that is hidden from view.

In volume 1 of *The History of Sexuality*, Foucault pushed the time-line forward, but the basic argument remained quite similar. Premodern European society, like many other traditional ones, was engaged in a "deployment of alliances." For example, marriage was based on status, kinship ties, and other non-individualist linkages between partners. Among the dominant classes, marriage was mainly a vehicle for transferring the family name and property. The eighteenth century superimposed on the old pattern a new apparatus, which Foucault called "the deployment of sexuality." The monogamous, heterosexual marriage, expected to be based on love and affection, became the new norm. It was imposed first upon the bourgeoisie and then gradually on the working classes.

Foucault held that these patterns, developed in the eighteenth and nineteenth centuries, had far-reaching ramifications for modern Western societies because they penetrated and controlled the body and constructed new definitions of sexuality in an increasingly detailed way. These included four techniques of sexualization, which corresponded to four types of abnormalities: (1) within medicine, the "hysterization of women's bodies" as thoroughly saturated with sexuality (Foucault 1978a, 104); (2) the prohibition of masturbation by children; (3) the regulation of fertility and the construction of pseudoscientific statements about blood, heredity, and colonized peoples; (4) the psychiatrization of the societal response to perverse pleasure. As a result, the family's role was "to anchor sexuality and provide it with permanent support," thus becoming an "obligatory locus of affect, feeling, and love" (108).

Foucault showed perceptively how the new "family" could not bear the straitjacket imposed on it and was gradually opened to the scrutiny of medical doctors, priests and ministers, and psychiatrists. Suddenly, a whole range of "abnormalities" was discovered. The new field of psychology took it upon itself to remold individuals to fit back into "normal" life patterns. Here, he examined the workings of disciplinary power as "bio-power." The new medical, psychiatric, penal, and pedagogical discourses monitored, classified, channeled, molded, and "treated" individual behavior. They established new normative distinctions: legal/illegal, healthy/sick, and normal/abnormal. Hence, what seemed to be liberating—more talk about sex, more openness in sexual relations, and the removal of traditional restraints on sexual practices—was in fact not so liberating, since the new discourses were involved in constructing new forms of "deviance." In sum, Foucault's new perspective was aimed at countering the prevailing theories of the time (including some forms of feminism), which equated the post-Enlightenment period with the emergence of greater democracy and greater freedoms, at least for the middle classes.

Thus, in each of his major writings Foucault privileged premodern social relations over modern ones. In *Madness and Civilization,* he argued that the Renaissance regarded madness as a fact of life and even endowed it with a certain amount of wisdom and creativity. In *Discipline and Punish,* he held that the seemingly more brutal disciplinary practices prevalent until the mid-eighteenth century exerted less control over mind and body than modern forms of punishment. And in *The History of Sexuality,* he claimed that premodern marriages of the elite, which were based on political and economic alliances, allowed for greater sexual freedom, including same-sex relations, and were hence more desirable when compared to the monogamous, heterosexual marriages of modern bourgeois society and their normalizing power. Foucault's one-sided critique of modernity and his minimizing of the harsh and confining disciplinary practices of the premodern world—including those that shackled women's sexuality—may explain his problematic relationship to the issue of women's rights, a subject to which we now turn.[9]

Foucault and Feminism: A Nonreciprocal Affair?

There is very little in Foucault's writings on women or women's rights. At the same time, Foucault's theoretical writings have had an immense influence on a generation of feminist academics, even though his attitude toward feminism was ambiguous and sometimes even dismissive. As many of the contributors to Diamond and Quinby's 1988 volume have argued, feminism and Foucault converge on several points concerning theories of power. Both identify the body as a site of power, a location upon which domination is established and docility is accomplished. Both point to the minute operations of power in all spheres of life (family, economics, science, law, literature, etc.), rather than focusing on the power of the state or capital alone. Both speak of the crucial role of discourse in constructing hegemonic power and in exploring potential challenges that might emerge from marginalized discourses.[10] As a result, a number of feminists have found Foucault's theoretical insights in works such as *Discipline and Punish* and volume 1 of *The History of Sexuality* extremely important to their own work (Bartky 1990; Bordo 1988; Deveaux 1994; Sawicki 1988; Hekman 1990; Butler 1990). Other feminists have found Foucault's concept of the technologies of the self, which appeared in his later works in the 1980s, to be useful, since Foucault moved from an exclusive focus on the domineering forms of power, or technologies of domination, to a more diffuse concept of power. This latter concept focused on the production of power through certain social and cultural practices. These technologies were aimed at creating one's life as one would a work of art. This new concept of power recognized that individuals exercised a certain level of autonomy and agency in their daily lives. People chose certain practices from the available repertoire of social and cultural traditions in order to change them, "to make their life into an oeuvre that carries certain aesthetic values and meets certain stylistic criteria" (Foucault 1985, 10–11). The interstices between "technologies of domination" and "technologies of the self" formed a multifaceted point of equilibrium, where technologies that imposed coercion on the body coexisted with self-imposed technologies.[11] Lois McNay writes that Foucault's notion of technologies of the self is a useful concept for a feminist politics of difference, where women are no longer seen as "powerless and innocent victims of patriarchal social structures" (1992, 67). Not just in the West, but also in the Middle East, women themselves have been involved in the subjugation of other women, using privileges of class, race, ethnicity, and seniority associated with the patriarchal order. They have also used different practices of the self to refashion their lives in new ways, not always according to feminist sensibilities (Kandiyoti 1991; Afary 2001).

But historians and philosophers have also criticized Foucault's work for its factual inaccuracies on gender in modern Europe and for its disregard of feminist concerns, especially on issues such as pedophilia, rape, and monogamous marriage.[12] The British feminist philosopher Kate Soper argues that despite Foucault's minimal engagement with feminist writings, even when compared to Lacan and Derrida, his clinical detachment veils a "somewhat less than objective male-centeredness of outlook." This "covert androcentricity" shows him to be indifferent or insensitive to feminist concerns (Soper 1993, 29). Soper points out that sexuality and the body are mediated culturally, but gender and sex are not entirely cultural constructs. There are prediscursive realities that should be recognized. Foucault ignores the specific forms in which power is exercised in any "sexually hierarchical society" (39). As Sandra Bartky (1990) has also suggested, Foucault glosses over the differences between disciplinary procedures as they operate on the bodies of women as compared to those of men. Foucault is attractive because of his "iconoclastic rupture with the two 'grand narratives' of Marxism and psychoanalysis" on which feminists have relied. Foucault's paradigm freed feminists from both the determinism of economics and of childhood experience, but his concept of power was not sufficiently theorized. There is a clash between "the existentialist impulse of his argument and his otherwise relentless deconstruction of the autonomous Enlightenment subject" (Soper 1993, 36). In this individualistic conception of the self, it is desirable to be free of all duties and obligations in the pursuit of pleasure. It is a sort of "sexual monad" that is "accountable only to the dictates of our personal tastes" and is entirely abstracted from questions of impersonal need. Soper concludes that Foucault advocates an "individualistic and narcissistic conception of liberation" in *The History of Sexuality*. This is not necessarily parallel to the feminist conception of emancipation; rather, it is another version of the "familiar, isolated individual of liberal theory" (36).

Foucault's discussion of the repressive hypothesis in *The History of Sexuality* merits special attention, especially with regard to his individualistic notion of freedom and his unwillingness to explore the dynamics of power in a sexually hierarchical society.[13] Foucault writes that in 1867, a simple-minded male farmhand in the village of Lapcourt was reported to the mayor for "a few caresses from a little girl, just as he had done before and seen done, by the village urchins round about him . . . who would play the familiar game called 'curdled milk.'" The girl's parents complained to the mayor. The gendarmes were informed, and the man was examined by a medical doctor, brought before a judge, and indicted, although he was later acquitted. What is most disturbing about this story, however, is not so much the incident, which happened over a century ago, but Foucault's commentary on it in 1976: "What is the significant thing about this story? The pettiness of it all; the fact that this everyday occurrence in the life of village sexuality, these inconsequential bucolic pleasures, could become, from a certain time, the object not only of a collective intolerance but of a judicial action, a medical intervention, a careful clinical examination, and an entire theoretical elaboration" (Foucault 1978a, 31). We know that the fight against sexual abuse and molestation has been at the core of the feminist movement. Was Foucault trying to undermine contemporary feminist discourse by calling protests against child molestation an example of "collective intolerance"?[14] Or was his hostility to modern state power, and especially its regulation of sexuality, so one-sided that he could oppose state intervention even of this sort? Nor is this an isolated example of Foucault's position on these issues. During the campaign to criminalize sexual acts between adults and children below the age of fifteen in France, Foucault had opposed the campaign, arguing that sexuality was not the business of the law (Alcoff 1996).

A close reading of the subsequent two volumes of *The History of Sexuality*, both first published in 1984 and subtitled *The Uses of Pleasure* and *The Care of the Self*, will similarly show that Foucault's brief ruminations on child molestation cited above were no aberration. One can argue that when the subject under discussion is sex, and those who initiate sex are adult men, while the discursive bodies upon which sex is practiced belong to children or adolescents (boys or girls), Foucault suddenly abandons his brilliant insight on the body as a location where docility is achieved through minute operations of power.[15]

Nancy Fraser enters this debate by pointing to multiple ambiguities in Foucault's concept of power. Foucault stressed that power permeates everything, that "power-free cultures, social practices, and knowledges are in principle impossible." He also claimed that his own description of modern power was "normatively neutral." However, Foucault's descriptions of the modern power/knowledge axis are filled with phrases such as "domination" and "subjugation" (Fraser 1989, 29). Even when one agrees that all cultural practices involve power relations, Fraser sees some serious problems in Foucault's conceptualization of power: "It doesn't follow that all forms of power are normatively equivalent, or that any social practices are as good as any others. Indeed, it is essential to Foucault's own project that he is able to distinguish better from worse sets of practices and forms of constraint. But this requires greater normative resources than he possesses" (32). Fraser compares Foucault unfavorably to both Max Weber and Habermas. In contrast to Weber, Foucault did not make systematic distinctions among various forms of power such as "authority, force, violence, domination and legitimation." However, in the tradition of Nietzsche and the earlier Frankfurt School theorists Theodor Adorno and Max Horkheimer, Foucault critiqued Western rationality. This led him to a dead end, for two reasons, Fraser concludes. First, he proposed no criteria for distinguishing forms of power that dominate and subjugate from those that express emancipatory impulses. Second, he endorsed "a one-sided, wholesale rejection of modernity," without suggesting anything to put in its place (33). This position was not so far removed from the late Adorno's "negative dialectics."

The tension between feminism and Foucault can also be located in his work on sexuality studies. Foucault turned to a genealogy of (male) homosexual relations in the Greco-Roman world in his last two published books. But he was not an enthusiastic supporter of the gay and lesbian liberation movement in France and Western Europe in the 1970s. He did not share the new enthusiasm for "gay pride." He feared that the new emphasis on a gay lifestyle would sustain the binary division between heterosexual (normal) and homosexual (pathological) in the modern world. In his view, upholding a gay identity meant acknowledging one's pathology, for "to betray the law of normality means continuing to recognize its existence" (cited in Nye 1996, 234). One had to break altogether with notions of a specific homosexual pleasure and adopt a "polymorphism" that refused any limits on one's objects of sexual desire. Only in this way could the old "regimes of desire" be deposed (Nye 1996, 235).[16]

Messianic Confessions

How far can we extend the dualism in Foucault's oeuvre? Can we also suggest an emerging theological subtext to his discourse? In the late 1970s Foucault was exploring a new "political spirituality," most notably in his Iran writings. He engrossed himself in the Christian monastic literature and in Eastern religious text. This material was apparently intended for a projected fourth volume of *The History of Sexuality*, which remains unpublished, since Foucault had requested no "posthumous publications" (cited in Carrette 1999, 46).

Jeremy Carrette, editor of *Religion and Culture: Michel Foucault* (1999), and the Jesuit philosopher James Bernauer, who wrote the introduction to that book, both suggest that Foucault was indeed mapping out a new spirituality. Bernauer characterized this as "a Christian style of liberty, which combined a care of the self with a sacrifice and mortification of that self" (Bernauer, in Carrette 1999, xiv). This new spirituality did not shun the world; it was a "spiritual existence" that exposed subjects to the mysteries of themselves and others (xv).[17] Foucault rejected the notion that the premodern Christian world was a time of sexual austerity. "Never did sexuality enjoy a more immediately natural understanding and never did it know a greater 'felicity of expression' than in the Christian world of fallen bodies and of sin" (Foucault 1963, 57). Foucault's interest in the Iranian Revolution was clearly related to his wider fascination with the concept of "political spirituality." He wished to explore this new idea, not only by returning to the practices and rituals of the early church, but also by searching for it in non-Christian societies (Carrette 1999, 43). By 1979, Foucault was developing a new hermeneutics of Christianity, a reading of Christian rituals and techniques that involved a new concept of spirituality, one that he hoped would accommodate late twentieth-century attitudes toward sexuality (Hadot 1992).

In April 1978, only months before he visited Iran, Foucault presented the broad outlines of his future work in a lecture at Tokyo University. He reiterated his familiar contrast between the East, here again including the Greco-Roman world as part of the East, and the West. He soon reached, without reservation, the following conclusion: The discourse on sexuality had very quickly developed into a scientific discourse in the West, whereas, in the East, it was shaped around methods that intensified pleasure, hence constituting "sexuality as an art." The East had erotic arts, and the West had sexual science.

These were "two completely different discourses, belonging to two equally different kinds of society" (Foucault 1978b, 119).

In this formulation about "two completely different discourses," Foucault was surely in the realm of Orientalism. This notion of two separate discourses was of course inaccurate with regard to the Middle East. To take one example, the writings of scientists and philosophers such as Avicenna (980–1037 CE) on anatomy were taught at European medical institutions until the seventeenth century. Thus, Foucault was imposing a type of homogeneity on Eastern thought that seemed at variance with his frequently expressed rejection of metanarratives. By 1978, he further divided the history of Western sexuality into three periods, Greco-Roman, Christian, and bourgeois:

> The First moment: Greek and Roman antiquity, where sexuality was free, expressed itself without difficulties, and developed effectively, was devoted, in any case, to a discourse in the form of an erotic art. Then Christianity intervened, Christianity which, for the first time in the history of the West, would pose a great prohibition on sexuality, which said "no" to pleasure and by the same token to sex. This "no," this prohibition, led to a silence on sexuality, a silence on sexuality essentially founded on these moral prohibitions. But the bourgeoisie, starting in the sixteenth century, finding themselves in an hegemonic situation, a situation of economic dominance and cultural hegemony, somehow recaptured for themselves, in order to reapply—*more severely and with more rigorous means*—this Christian asceticism, this Christian refusal of sexuality, and in consequence prolonged it until the nineteenth century, where, finally, in the very last years, we began to lift the veil with Freud. (Foucault 1978b, 120; emphasis added)

Here, Foucault surely recognized the limitations that Christianity had imposed on sexuality. As we shall see below, he also pointed out that Roman culture had already instituted many of the prohibitions we attribute to Christianity and that the modern bourgeoisie had applied these prohibitions with a meticulous rigor that had not been intended in the Christian era: "Polygamy, pleasure outside of marriage, valorizations of pleasure, [sexual] indifference toward children, had already essentially disappeared from the Roman world before Christianity" (121). Only a small, rich elite refused to adhere to these prohibitions. By increasing the responsibility of both Roman and bourgeois ethical concepts for the modern prohibitions on sexuality, was Foucault trying to reduce the burden on the Church for instituting these prohibitions and hoping to present a more favorable view of medieval Christianity?

Earlier, in the first volume of *The History of Sexuality*, Foucault had stressed the continuity between Christian methods of confession and modern techniques of psychoanalysis and pedagogy. He had argued that the confessional techniques of Christianity, including the need to reveal all transgressive and evil thoughts to a priest, gradually lost its ritualistic dimension. It also lost its exclusivity, spreading through other relationships, whether those of "children and parents, students and educators, patients and psychiatrists, [or] delinquents and experts." Thus, by the nineteenth century there was "too much rather than not enough discourse" on sexuality (Foucault 1978a, 65). Only two years later, in 1978, Foucault seemed to have moved away from this earlier focus on the continuity between the Christian confessional or penitential methods and the modern technique of confession. Now he was more interested in the differences between monastic and modern disciplinary techniques.

The pastor required obedience from his flock, and the believers were required to confess all truth to the pastor. But Foucault now stressed that, in contrast to the modern psychiatrist, the priest did not label people abnormal.[18] The assumption that all human beings could be fooled by the devil meant that repentance could be achieved through true confession. Christianity, it now turned out, had constructed a "moderate morality" between asceticism and civil society: "The Christian flesh was never conceived as an absolute evil which had to be got rid of, but as a perpetual source, within subjectivity, within individuals, of temptation which risked leading the individual beyond the limits posed by the common morality: marriage, monogamy, the sexuality of reproduction, and the limitation and disqualification of pleasure" (Foucault 1978b, 126).

Foucault also made a distinction between the verbal methods of confession and the physical methods of penitence. He tried to formulate new "technologies of the self" that drew on and refashioned the old Christian rituals. Given his new reading of Christianity, Foucault's interest in the religious dimension of the Iranian Revolution was surely more than a journalistic curiosity. As we shall see in chapter 2, he was moved both by the political message of the revolution and by its use of rituals of penitence, which were in some respects similar to the Christian practices he had started to explore.

Freedom-Toward-Death: A Liminal Space for Creativity

Foucault belongs to a group of Western thinkers, from Schopenhauer to the existentialists, for whom the reality of death has not only to be acknowledged but also embraced by the living. Nietzsche's "overman" (*Übermensch*) remained "joyfully and proudly" aware of death as the proper finale to his life's performance. For Freud and Heidegger, genuine living grew out of an awareness of death. Only in this realization, and in the sense of urgency it produced among us, could we achieve an authentic existence (Olson 1967, 306–9).

Foucault's debt to Freud was pervasive, though at times unacknowledged, since Foucault's project was essentially aimed at turning Freud on his head.[19] In his *Civilization and Its Discontents*, written in 1930, Freud had argued that in addition to humanity's psychic drives for food and sex, there was also a drive toward death. Civilization dealt with these aggressive and destructive drives through the process of sublimation, channeling them into work and the creation of culture. Meanwhile, the superego controlled the ego and limited the insatiable demands of the id, as Freud wrote in a famous military metaphor: "Civilization obtains mastery over the individual's dangerous desire for aggression by weakening and disarming it, by setting up an agency within him to watch over it, like a garrison in a conquered city" (Freud 1989, 84).

In his libertarian celebration of the death drive, Foucault claimed that the project of civilization had to be reversed. His celebration of near-death experiences was built on Freud's assumption that the suppression of our death drive results in the crushing of our imaginative, instinctual impulse. Freud had argued that humanity pays a very heavy price for civilization, that our "permanent internal unhappiness" stems from this renunciation and the ever-present sense of guilt that plagues us (Freud 1989, 89). Foucault wanted to do no less than reverse this course.[20]

Foucault's challenge to Freud's death drive built on Heidegger's most central category, being-toward-death. Here, we are thrown into this world; we have no personal choice in the matter. The world exists before us and will be there after us. Nor do we know toward what end we have entered this world. We live inauthentically because we live according to the dictates of others and their "idle chatter." We are not to be blamed for this inauthentic living. This "fallenness" is a necessary part of existence. As George Steiner points out, for Heidegger "social reform or revolution will not eliminate inauthenticity, nor will therapy or psychological amendments of personality," whether in the traditions of Marx or Freud (1987, 108). But there was the possibility of a dialectical transcendence, a way out of this absolutely necessary state of "fallenness" leading to a more authentic grasp of the world. By coming to terms with death, through "care" and "solicitude," we might experience a "calling," a certain "resurrection." Ultimately we might reach a stage at which we accept the possibility of our own death, a stage of "freedom-toward-death" that is released from the illusions of others (Heidegger 1962, ¶ 264, 266).

Foucault seemed to have lived Heidegger's "freedom-toward-death"—

and not only intellectually. Biographer James Miller (1993) has suggested that Foucault's statements on the subject of dying and his fascination with pain and death formed a central aspect of his thought. Mark Lilla has written that the influence of surrealist and other avant-garde intellectuals such as Georges Bataille, Antonin Artaud, and Maurice Blanchot on Foucault's generation is often missed by readers outside France: "In them, Foucault saw the possibility of exploring personally what lay even further outside the bounds of ordinary bourgeois practice, to seek what he called 'limit experience' in eroticism, madness, drugs, sadomasochism, even suicide" (Lilla 2001, 143–44). Indeed, many examples in Foucault's life pointed in this direction: his youthful attempts at suicide; his personal involvement with sado-masochism in California and elsewhere; his painful brush with death in an automobile accident, which he later described as one of the most "intense pleasure(s)" of his life (Miller 1993, 306). It seems that in these liminal spaces that exist between life and death, in these near-death experiences, Foucault recognized the possibility for extraordinary artistic and sensual creativity, including in his own personal life.

Foucault remained similarly fascinated by the subjects of death, suicide, and martyrdom in his genealogical writings and spoke with passion of the link between madness and death. Madness, as the final stage before death, offers the individual freedom from the fear of death. In Foucault's terminology, madness was the closest stage to Golgotha, the Jerusalem hill named as the place where Jesus was crucified. Foucault wrote that Jesus was not only surrounded by madmen, he chose also to pass for one: "Madness thus became the ultimate form, the final degree of God in man's image, before the fulfillment and deliverance of the Cross" (Foucault 1965, 80). Similarly, Foucault praised artistic, musical, and literary works that grappled with the concept of death. In "What Is an Author?" Foucault spoke of the continuous relationship of writing to death. In the Greek epic, the hero who spoke was willing to die young, trading life for immortality. Concerning the Arabian *Thousand and One Nights*, in which storytelling became a way of avoiding death, he wrote, "Scheherazade's narrative is an effort, renewed each night, to keep death outside the circle of life" (Foucault 1969, 102).

Foucault embraced the author or artist who pushed the borders of rationality and explored near-death experiences. In distancing himself from both the possibility of attaining absolute knowledge, and the Hegelian dialectic of mutual recognition, Foucault instead celebrated the French author Marquis de Sade. He admired Sade because through him "man rediscovers a truth he had forgotten," that deadly desire and immoral passions are indeed quite natural and hence rational. Echoing Sade, he wrote, "What desire can be contrary to nature since it was given to man by nature itself?" (Foucault 1965, 282; Sade 1992).

Foucault's discussion of the Spanish painter Francisco de Goya followed the same logic. Goya has been celebrated for his two series of etchings known as the *Caprichos* (1799) and *The Disasters of War* (1810–20). Most critics see the *Caprichos* as the embodiment of the best ideals of the Enlightenment. The satirical caricatures of monks, witches, and goblins suggest that humanity can be improved through science, that reason can eradicate superstition and religious dogma. *The Disasters of War*, a commentary on the Peninsular War between Spain and Napoleonic France, is in turn regarded as a magnificent criticism of violence and brutality in war, and of the limits of both modernity and the Enlightenment. Finally in some of his last etchings, Goya turned to the subject of cannibalism (Licht 1979).[21] Foucault's interest lay in the representations of madness and insanity in these works as a liminal experience. In Goya's work "madness has become man's possibility of abolishing both man and the world" (Foucault 1965, 281). Through Sade and Goya "the Western world received the possibility of transcending its reason in violence and of recovering tragic experiences beyond the promises of dialectic" (285).

The "Will to Power" on the Streets of Tehran

Foucault's long-standing preoccupation with the near-death experience as a locus for human creativity would find a kindred spirit in the daily unfolding of the Iranian Revolution. In Persia (Iran), the dualistic principles of the ancient Zoroastrian religion were first formulated nearly three thousand years ago, around the fight between the forces of good (Ahura Mazda) and the forces of evil (Ahriman). In Iranian Shi'ite Islam, aspects of the old Persian religion would find a new articulation. As we shall see in chapter 2, Shi'ite theologians saw a reenactment of this fight between good and evil in a war that took place in 680 CE between two men, the saintly Hussein (grandson of the prophet Muhammad) and the supposedly evil Yazid, his rival. The battle ended in the massacre of Hussein and his supporters and the martyrdom of Hussein, which is commemorated annually in the month of Muharram by Shi'ites the world over.

In 1978, Ayatollah Ruhollah Khomeini, an ascetic Muslim cleric known for his uncompromising opposition to Muhammad Reza Shah Pahlavi (r. 1941–79), emerged as the leader of the revolutionary movement. He cast himself in the role of Hussein and portrayed the shah in the mantle of Yazid. He also reenacted the old epic, which was now combined with powerful anti-imperialist rhetoric.[22] The Islamist tendency and even many Iranian leftists of the time shared something of Foucault's peculiar "Orientalism," in the sense that they also privileged an idealized, premodern past—the period of early Islam—over modernity. Many of them were also searching for a new form of political spirituality in the late twentieth century. The Islamists and many others who joined the Iranian Revolution seemed to believe that by adopting an attitude of "freedom-toward-death," by recognizing and submitting to the finitude and limitation of their own insignificant human existence, and by aspiring to a cause greater than themselves, they could bring about the collective authentic existence of the Iranian community. Foucault was a witness to this reenactment of a grand old epic, where the Nietzschean "will to power" seemed to gain ascendancy over the "will to exist" under oppression.

As a keen admirer of Nietzsche, Foucault might have been more cautious about supporting a revolution led by a religious ascetic. In his "What Is the Meaning of Ascetic Ideals?" Nietzsche had given plenty of warnings about priestly asceticism, which he regarded as "the best instrument for wielding power [and] also the 'supreme' license for power" (Nietzsche 1967, 97). The "chief trick of the ascetic priest" was to exploit the believer's sense of guilt. Life was a "wrong road," and it was the believer's obligation to put it right by scrupulously following his advice. For the ascetic priest, life itself was a contradiction, since he wished "to become master not over something *in* life but *over* life itself, over its most profound, powerful, and basic conditions." The priest turned his back to all the beautiful and joyful manifestations of physical existence and embraced all that negated living. He celebrated death, "self-mortification, self-flagellation, self-sacrifice" (118). The ascetic was not motivated by moral scruples, nor did he choose this lifestyle because he was repulsed by pleasure. His ability to control himself, his powerful will, gained the admiration and respect of others. Mastery over self led eventually to mastery over others. In retrospect, the essence of Khomeini's ascetic ideal could not have been better described. But perhaps Foucault was also impressed with Khomeini because he went beyond the role of the ascetic priest. Khomeini knew how to exploit the religious sentiment of guilt, the public *ressentiment,* in more than one way. He did so with regard to both personal expressions of repentance through self-flagellation (a basic ritual of Shi'ite Islam) and outward political acts of revolutionary self-sacrifice. The millions of believers who joined Khomeini on the streets (many of whom were leftist secular students) seemed to exemplify the Heideggerian freedom-toward-death, as they aimed at a more authentic collective life.

In some ways, Khomeini was the personification of Nietzsche's "will to power," a ruthless historical figure with saintly self-mastery. He was a man who dared to think the unthinkable and convinced millions of others to risk their lives. To be sure, in unleashing the passion of death and the desire to go beyond life, Khomeini was hardly advocating a Nietzschean release of passions, one that would challenge the dominant Judeo-Christian-Islamic ethics in order to embrace the pleasures of life. But Khomeini was able to become the charismatic leader of millions who joyfully cast "the dice for death," and to set in motion on the streets of Iran a movement wherein "life sacrifices itself for power" (Nietzsche 1976, 228).

Chapter 2

Processions, Passion Plays, and Rites of Penance

Foucault, Shi'ism, and Early Christian Rituals

The motifs of pain and suffering from injustice, as well as rituals that glorify martyrdom, have been at the core of Iranian Shi'ism since the sixteenth century.[1] But these rituals of penitence found a new political meaning in the course of the Iranian Revolution, when Ayatollah Khomeini reappropriated them for his movement to establish an Islamist government. In fall 1978, thousands of people joined the anti-shah demonstrations on the streets of Tehran wearing white shrouds as a sign of their willingness to face death. Demonstrators carried pictures of martyred political prisoners and chanted slogans calling for their deaths to be avenged. Even secular and leftist political organizations of this period drew their legitimacy from the number of martyrs they had given to the revolutionary cause. Many newspapers of the revolutionary period, especially those of the Islamic-leftist Mujahedeen Khalq and the Marxist-Leninist Fedayeen-i Khalq, were filled with pictures of young martyrs who had lost their lives in the prisons of the shah.[2]

Foucault's writings on "practices of the self" in early Christian communities provide us with a very useful way of understanding the phenomenon of the Iranian Revolution, specifically the Islamists' utilization of Shi'ite narratives and ritual practices.

Foucault was fascinated by the dramatic mass demonstrations he witnessed in Iran, especially by the Islamists' appropriation of Shi'ite rituals to create what he called a "political spirituality." In the rhythmic chants of the protesters, the self-flagellation of the demonstrators, and the exuberance of the death-defying crowds—the men dressed in black shirts, the women in black veils—Foucault may have been reminded of rituals of early Christianity. Indeed, his later writings on Christian rites resonated strongly with some practices of Shi'ite Islam. Foucault and the Islamist movement in Iran seemed to share three passions: (1) an opposition to the imperialist and colonialist policies of the West; (2) a rejection of certain cultural and social aspects of modernity that had transformed gender roles and social hierarchies in both the East and the West; and (3) a fascination with the discourse of death as a path toward authenticity and salvation, a discourse that included rites of penitence and aimed at refashioning the self. Foucault recognized the Iranian public's fascination with the seemingly archaic rituals of Shi'ite Islam. He was moved by the active participation of the clerics in the anti-shah movement and was intrigued by the use of religious processions and rituals for ostensibly political concerns. Every time government troops shot and killed protestors on the streets, the response was larger demonstrations. As was customary in Iran, new processions were organized on the fortieth day after the killings, commemorating the dead. Foucault grasped the crowds' enormous fascination with death and the trust in the militant religious leadership this implied. He understood that the religious gatherings, processions, and theatrical performances of Shi'ism, like their counterparts in Christianity, were politically charged ceremonies that forged new forms of communal solidarity. What Foucault saw on the streets of Tehran may therefore have been a realization of some of his fantasies and desires.

Despite his familiarity with the fascist Right in Europe, Foucault never related the Islamists' selective reading of "modernity," nor their equating of "modernity" with a loss of spirituality, to similar political invocations by the Right in Europe four decades earlier. There are many examples of such political manipulations in Europe, and a comparison of these with the Iranian experience could have demystified any notion that the Islamist movement and its propaganda techniques were a distinctively "Oriental" phenomenon. Perhaps Foucault's reading of Islam was "Orientalist" because he failed to point out that Shi'ite narratives, like other invented traditions and identities around which imagined national or religious communities are formed, lend themselves to multiple readings (Anderson 1983). Instead, Foucault made an abstraction of Islam and Shi'ism, never exploring the fact that a group of opposition clerics and intellectuals had adopted a particular reading of Shi'ism in the course of the revolution. Nor did he pay attention to the fact that Khomeini's "anti-modernist" stance involved innovations, as well as inventions of tradition. What Foucault witnessed in Iran was the result of a carefully staged and crafted version of Shi'ism that had been first developed in the 1960s and 1970s as a response to the authoritarian modernization of Muhammad Reza Shah's government. This was a militant and political reading of Shi'ism and its annual Muharram celebrations, a reading that for some Islamist intellectuals, such as Ali Shariati, was also influenced by Western philosophic discourses (Boroujerdi 1996). It was a synthesis of orthodox Marxism, existentialism, Heideggerianism, and a militant form of traditional Shi'ite Islam. In this hybrid discourse, the rituals of prayer and fasting, and even care for fellow Muslims, orphans, and widows, were neglected. "Authentic Islam" was defined as the willingness to face martyrdom in order to attain an ostensibly better world for others.

In this chapter we explore a single aspect of Foucault's writing on Iran: his preoccupation with Shi'ite rituals of martyrdom in the form of the centuries-old festival of Muharram. We will delineate three issues: (1) the place of Muharram in Iranian culture, (2) the political use of Muharram by the Islamists in 1978, and (3) Foucault's writings on Muharram and on Christian rites of penitence. We begin with the central narrative of Shi'ite Islam, the story of Karbala,[3] which is remembered and reenacted every year in the month of Muharram.

The Karbala Paradigm

As opposed to the majority Sunni branch of Islam, Shi'ites claim that after the death of Muhammad (632 CE), leadership of the Muslim *umma* (community of believers) should have been vested in the family of Muhammad and his descendants, beginning with Muhammad's cousin and son-in-law Ali Ibn Abu Talib (d. 661). Instead, after Muhammad's death, Abu Bakr, his father-in-law, became the first caliph (ruler) of the Muslim community. Abu Bakr's short rule (632–634) was followed by that of Umar (r. 634–644) and Uthman (r. 644–656). Umar and Uthman were both assassinated, and Ali's opponents accused him of having had a hand in the assassination of Uthman. The tribal council eventually elected Ali as the fourth caliph (r. 656–661). After five years as caliph, Ali was also assassinated, and the leadership of the community was transferred to the influential warrior Mu'awiyah (r. 661–680), a member of the prominent Umayyad family and the governor of Syria.

During his twenty-year reign, Mu'awiyah built an empire, fought the Byzantines, and developed a large and disciplined army. The enmity between the clan of Muhammad and the Umayyads ran deep. Mu'awiyah had opposed the Prophet until nearly everyone else in Mecca had converted to the new faith. He had then reversed himself and joined Muhammad as his secretary. Mu'awiyah had also been a staunch enemy of Ali and blamed him for the assassination of Uthman. Mu'awiyah wanted to keep the leadership in his family. He concluded a pact with Ali's first son Hassan (d. 670), who withdrew from politics.

But after Mu'awiyah's death, Ali's second son, Hussein, chose to pursue his claim and challenged Mu'awiyah's son Yazid, who was poised to become the sixth caliph. Hussein counted on the support of the residents of the city of Kufah (today in southern Iraq), where his father Ali had ruled as caliph and where the Arab armies that had been sent east to conquer Iran were headquartered (Richard 1995, 28). According to legend, Hussein, along with seventy-two male supporters and their families, moved in the direction of Kufah. The more politically influential Yazid won over the Kufan leadership and forced Hussein and his entourage to camp outside the city in the desert of Karbala. Led by 'Umar Ibn Sa'ad, Yazid's army now encircled the camp, cutting off its access to the waters of the nearby Euphrates River. The siege lasted ten days. On the tenth of Muharram (October 10, 680 CE), commemorated by the Shi'ites as the mournful Ashura day, the army of Yazid massacred Hussein and his followers. The women and children were sold into captivity. Yazid then assumed power as the caliph, ruling from Damascus from about 680 to 683.

Supporters of Hussein, known as Shi'ite Ali (Party of Ali), refused to recognize the Umayyads as legitimate caliphs. In the centuries that followed, Karbala became a site of pilgrimage for Shi'ites around the world and eventually also a center of theological learning. Shi'ite doctrines include all the principal beliefs of Islam, such as the oneness of God, recognition of Muhammad as messenger of God, resurrection of the dead on Judgment Day, and belief in God's justice. But Shi'ites also claim that the direct descendents of Muhammad are designated by God as the true leaders of the community (Momen 1985, 176–77). In Twelver Shi'ism, the official religion of Iran, the term *imam* is reserved for Ali, his two sons, Hassan and Hussein, and the subsequent nine descendents of the clan of Ali, who became leaders of this Shi'ite community. The Very Pure Fourteen—the Prophet Muhammad, his daughter Fatima, and the twelve imams who succeeded him—are also considered infallible (Richard 1995, 6).

Twelver Shi'ites claim that enemies and rival groups assassinated the first eleven imams and that the twelfth imam went into occultation in 874 CE. He will reappear at the end of the world as the Mahdi (i.e., the messiah/the promised one), declare God's judgment, and reinstate justice.[4] A large number of holidays in the Shi'ite calendar are devoted to the commemoration of the martyred imams, whose stories are told in countless sermons. While not all Shi'ites follow the Twelver line of the succession of imams, in Iran, Lebanon, southern Iraq, Bahrain, Kuwait, Pakistan, and parts of Afghanistan and India, the anniversary of the martyrdom of Hussein remains the most important ceremonial event of the year among the various Shi'ite denominations.

Twelver Shi'ism did not become Iran's official religion until the Safavid dynasty (1501–1722), when Sunni-Shi'ite divides helped to fuel political and military conflicts between the Sunni Ottomans and the Shi'ite Safavids. The founder of the Safavid dynasty, Shah Isma'il (1501–24), claimed to be a descendent of the seventh Shi'ite imam, as well as a representative of the Hidden Imam, at a time when few prominent Iranians were adherents of Shi'ism. His successor, Shah Tahmasb (1524–76), did much to encourage an orthodox interpretation of Twelver Shi'ism. Clerics known as *mujtahids* gained the right to interpret the Quran and the *shariat* (Islamic law), while Shi'ite centers of learning in present-day Iraq gained the right to appoint leaders of communal prayers in every town and village. They openly cursed the first three Muslim caliphs and persecuted Sunnis. These actions led in turn to the persecution of Shi'ites in Mecca and Medina by Sunni Muslims. The Safavids conquered the Shi'ite shrines of Najaf and Karbala (Iraq), a political victory with immense symbolic value, and expanded the Shi'ite shrines in Qom and Mashhad inside Iran.

Many of the bloodier rituals of Muharram (wounds to the forehead with knives and swords, or scorching of the body) were gradually introduced in the sixteenth and early seventeenth centuries. Under Shah Abbas I (r. 1588–1629), Muharram rituals became elaborate civil and religious festivals that also borrowed some traditions from older Persian Now Rouz (New Year) ceremonies that had originated in pre-Islamic Iran. Shah Abbas encouraged "gladiatorial displays," a form of factional strife between rival gangs as part of the festivities. In this way, sociopolitical discontent among corporate entities such as artisans, guild members, and ethnic groups was channeled into these controlled public spectacles. The annexation of Najaf and Karbala, as well as the rebuilding of the shrines of Qom and Mashhad, created new public spaces. These were used for horse racing, polo, military parades, animal fights, and public executions, as well as religious rituals (Calmard 1996, 164). By the time of Shah Suleiman I (r. 1666–94), spectacular features of Muharram ceremonies reached the point where the "festivals tended to shift from pure devotional assemblies to public entertainment in which displays of social influence were part of the show" (Calmard 1996, 158).

In 1687, Muhammad Baqir Majlisi, a leading theologian and author of numerous works in Persian and Arabic, became the power behind the throne of the puritanical Sultan Hussein Shah (r. 1694–1722). Majlisi suppressed all Sufi and philosophical tendencies within Shi'ite Islam and sanctioned the relentless persecution of Sunnis. He propagated a dogmatic and legalistic reading of Twelver Shi'ism, and stressed the role of the imams as "mediators and intercessors for man with god" (Momen 1985, 117). This new interpretation aimed to transfer the public's devotion from the Sufi mystics to the twelve Shi'ite imams. A 1695 edict prohibited all activities not approved by the *shariat*. Wine from the royal court cellars was destroyed, and coffeehouses shut down. Music, dance, gambling, backgammon, chess, opium, and herbs that induced hallucinations became illegal. The shah also banned many previously acceptable social practices for women. Henceforth, for example, women could not go on the streets unless they had a valid and legitimate reason: "They should not stroll in gardens and go on pleasure promenades with anyone other than their husbands. They should not loiter in public gatherings (*ma'rika*). They were to move out of their private harem only with the permission of their husbands or their male legal guardians" (Babayan 1996, 117–18).

Majlisi was the first major theologian to translate into Persian a wide-ranging series of books and manuals on Shi'ite theology, history, and rituals, rather than leaving them in Arabic, the language of the Quran. He also encouraged travel to the shrines and sites of pilgrimage, such as Karbala, an activity that the expansion of the Safavid Empire had made possible. Both of these measures spread Shi'ism and its rituals farther throughout the whole region (Taremi 1996, 98; Browne 1956, 4:404). Today, members of the various Shi'ite denominations number about one hundred million and make up some 10 percent of the world's Muslim population.

A Genealogy of Muharram Rituals

The twin concepts of *jihad* (in its broad definition, ranging from striving for personal religious improvement to holy war in defending and expanding the faith) and *shahadat* (martyrdom) appear in the Quran (sura 5, verse 35; sura 25, verse 52). There is also a large body of literature on the conditions and circumstances under which jihad (in its narrow definition of holy war) is required and martyrdom is encouraged (Abedi and Legenhausen 1986). But in Shi'ism, because of the central narrative of Muharram, the themes of martyrdom and unjust usurpation of power by earthly rulers are even more pronounced than in Sunni Islam.

Devout Iranian Shi'ites commemorate and reenact the events of Karbala and the martyrdom of Hussein and Ali in three ways. First, there is a dramatic narration of the life and the suffering of the saints, the *rowzeh khvani*. This is a social gathering of relatives, neighbors, and guild members at one's garden or house. A mullah (in the men's hall) or a female mullah baji (in the women's hall) recites the tragedy of Hussein or mourns the events of Karbala, using passages from a sixteenth-century book, known as *The Garden of the Martyrs*.[5] The audience laments and grieves in memory of Ali and Hussein. Meanwhile, the host serves tea and coffee, and sometimes there are a few rounds of water pipes. Eventually, the guests are entertained with a lavish feast.

Second, Iranian Shi'ites commemorate the events of Karbala through a public *sinehzani*, a predominantly male ritual of self-flagellation and mourning.[6] This is a funeral procession where participants, dressed in black, march through the streets and bazaars during the ten days of Muharram. At the head of the parade is a coffin or shrouded effigy representing the martyred Imam Hussein. The men chant eulogies and beat their chests and backs rhythmically, often with chains, sticks, or swords. These processions also include festive elements, which helps explain the enormous popularity and staying power of these rites.[7]

Third is the Ta'ziyeh performance, which is similar to Christian passion plays and was influenced by them. It is a theatrical representation of the Karbala events. Ta'ziyeh is one of the oldest forms of theater in the region, and ordinary citizens eagerly anticipate the annual performances. This highly melodramatic performance, which is a fusion of the first two traditions mentioned above with European theatrical ones, is staged by local groups throughout the country before large audiences. The performances single out the suffering of Hussein's entourage, especially that of the women and the children, on Ashura day. The narrator and the actors describe in great detail the thirst of the besieged community in the heat of the desert of Karbala and the deviousness of Yazid, who chose Friday at noon, the time of Muslim communal prayer, to slaughter his rivals. The audience weeps bitterly during the last scenes of the play and is reminded of the treachery and guilt of the Kufan community, which did not side with its savior Hussein, thereby allowing the tyrant Yazid to commit his dastardly deed. These rituals of Muharram, much more than a single belief or dogma, define Shi'ite communities (Halm 1997, 41; Mahjub 1979, 142; Momen 1985, 240; Fischer 1980).

Most scholars believe that Muharram rituals have pre-Islamic origins. The anthropologist William Beeman argues that they are similar to those marking the death of Dionysus in ancient Greece, or Osiris in ancient Egypt, which symbolize cosmic renewal and rebirth. Muharram is also traced to ancient Mesopotamian rituals, which helped give birth to similar traditions in Manicheanism, Judaism, or Christianity (Beeman 1979). Ritual lamentation, wailing, and self-flagellation are practiced in all of these religions as a means of purifying the body and the whole community (Halm 1997, 41–85). The historian Ehsan Yarshater supports the theory of a pre-Islamic Iranian origin for these rituals, especially in the mythic story of Siyavosh, son of Key Kavus. This story is recounted in the Persian epic *Shahnameh* (Book of kings), the 1010 CE masterpiece that is a compilation of many earlier epic tales and is the foundation for Iranian national literature. Like Hussein, Siyavosh had seventy-two companions. The King of Turan murdered him, along with his entourage. In parts of Iran, the celebration of Ashura is still called Suvashun, after Siyavosh (Yarshater 1979; Curtis 1993, 74–75; Abedi and Legenhausen 1986, 228). Mahmoud Ayoub writes that Ashura might originally have been a day of celebration, one that commemorated the "day that God forgave Adam" or the day that "God accepted David's repentance," since there are references to traditions that regard it as a "day of joy and festivity." Ayoub also suggests a possible Jewish origin for the holiday in Yom Kippur (Ayoub 1988, 258–59).[8]

In Iran, the reenactment of the events of Karbala as a theatrical performance has been traced to the sixteenth century. By the middle of the eighteenth century, the mourning rituals had developed into a new form of theatrical performance. In the nineteenth century, numerous guilds of players and performers were organized with the support of the royal court and the elite (Chelkowski 1991, 214). European diplomats and scholars who observed the performances were often overwhelmed. The French diplomat Joseph-Arthur de Gobineau traveled to Iran twice between the years 1855 and 1863. The author of the notorious *Essai sur l'inégalite des races humaines* (1854), he found the Ta'ziyeh a highly creative theatrical performance, one that was superior to both the Roman and the modern European theatre. Gobineau was particularly moved because the Ta'ziyeh reached a mass audience, whereas the contemporary European theater only attracted a small elite group (Manafzadeh 1991, 317). The late nineteenth-century British diplomat Sir Lewis Pelly was equally charmed by the public reception of the Ta'ziyeh: "If the success of the drama is to be measured by the effects which it produces upon the people for whom it is composed, or upon the audiences before whom it is represented, no play has ever surpassed the tragedy known in the Mussulman world as that of Hasan and Hussein" (1970, iii). In the late nineteenth century, Naser al-Din Shah (r. 1848–96) built a large theater, known as a *takyeh,* for Ta'ziyeh performances. There were perhaps thirty other *takyehs* in Tehran and each accommodated close to three thousand people. Thus, very large crowds, even by current standards, attended the annual Ta'ziyeh performances (Khaki 1991, 256).

Reza Shah Pahlavi (r. 1925–41), who sought to secularize and modernize the nation, banned many rituals of Muharram, including the processions marked by self-flagellation and self-mutilation. But the public never really abandoned the ceremonies, including Ta'ziyeh performances. In 1941, when Britain and Russia forced the shah to abdicate, these rituals were revived, though in less elaborate forms. The publication of Bahram Bayza'i's *Theater in Iran* (1965) drew the academic and artistic communities of Iran to Ta'ziyeh passion plays. In 1976, at the Shiraz festival of the arts, which was sponsored by the royal court, Ta'ziyeh was developed into an elite theatrical experience and embraced by Iran's literary and artistic communities, even as the government continued to discourage local performances (Ghafary 1991).

Muharram and the Practices of the Self

The events of Muharram and the accompanying rituals in the month of Safar, as well as the mourning processions of the month of Ramadan on the anniversary of Ali's martyrdom, occupy about two months of the year. In this period, the subliminal messages of Muharram are chiseled into the hearts and minds of participants, helping to shape their worldview. Much of the appeal of Ta'ziyeh lies in the physical, spiritual, and emotional links forged between the actors and the audience, as well as among the members of the audience. Hussein Esma'ili describes the ways in which all the senses are invoked and engaged, both in the mourning processions and in the performances at the *takyeh* playhouses. The scent of rose water, wildrue (to avert the evil eye), and incense blends with the smoke of tobacco from water pipes and sweat from the huddled crowds. Food is an important part of the festivities, and sharing food is part of the ritual. The aroma of juicy kebabs prepared on hot charcoal mixes with the sweet smell of saffron rice pudding, sour-cherry syrups, and cardamom tea that is served constantly. The sounds of various musical instruments—drums, tambourines, trumpets, horns, and flutes—fill the air, along with the chants and singing of the performers (Esma'ili 1991). The Ta'ziyeh is based on material that is literary in origin and embellished by colloquialisms. The heroes sing, while the villains speak, and the entire script of the Ta'ziyeh is rhymed (Elwell-Sutton 1979).

The festivities also engage the eyes. The crystal decorations, bright lights, ornate costumes, and props mesmerize the young and old. The protagonists are dressed in green and black, the colors of Islam; the antagonists are dressed in red, the color of blood and passion. The angels of God wear wings on their backs; the devils hold spiked clubs. The imams carry prayer beads and wave copies of the Quran, while Yazid and his cohorts hold symbolic glasses of wine (forbidden by Islam) in their hands, suggesting their evil intentions. The performance is especially exciting to children. Some actors gallop around the platform on fast horses, others might dress up as animals (often a lion). There is also a lot of clowning, and many Ta'ziyehs include grotesque comedy and epic tales with little connection to the story of Karbala.

The Ta'ziyeh continuously transgresses the temporal and spatial boundaries of real and imagined worlds.[9] This dramatic device, known as *goriz* (diversion) allows the actors to perform a play within a play. Hussein can travel to India to aid a local king just before his death. And the ghosts of the earlier Biblical prophets appear and give him the "good news" that he will soon become a martyr. Peter Chelkowski, the foremost scholar of Ta'ziyeh, writes that neither time nor place is real and definite. What happened in the year 61 of the Muslim era (680 CE) on the battlefield of Karbala becomes a reality today: "Ta'ziyeh breaks the boundaries of time and space." The past and the present meet, and the "audience is both here and in the desert of Karbala" (Chelkowski 1991, 220). According to the well-known dramaturge Peter Brook,

> I saw in a remote Iranian village one of the strongest things I have seen in theater: A group of four hundred villagers, the entire population of the place, sitting under a tree and passing from roars of laughter to outright sobbing—although they all knew perfectly well the end of the story—as they saw [Hussein] in danger of being killed, and then fooling his enemies, and then being martyred. And when he was martyred, the theater became a truth—there was no difference between past and present. An event that was told as remembered happening in history 1,300 years ago, actually became a reality in that moment. (cited in Chelkowski and Dabashi 1999, 80)

Yann Richard turns our gaze to the crowd and the mourning processions on the streets. He writes of the young unshaven men, dressed in black, many wearing white shrouds in order to show their willingness to die. Some smear dirt on their foreheads, indicating their eagerness to be buried for Hussein. They beat their chests rhythmically, sometimes with a small chain, cut their scalps in moments of frenzy, and seem oblivious to any sense of pain. At the head of the procession, which moves slowly through the winding streets, is a large, heavy, decorated metal emblem. From time to time, the young men who carry the heavy symbol stop and perform daring acrobatic stunts with it. They mount it on their foreheads, bounce it on their navels, and attempt to impress the young women (and men) in the crowd, who watch them with great excitement and admiration (Richard 1995, 97–99).

Muharram rituals routinely transgress gender boundaries. Muharram has been an occasion for unrelated individuals of the opposite sex to meet in public (Calmard 1996, 170).[10] In the weeks preceding the Muharram processions, many young men attend traditional bodybuilding clubs. Young women sometimes send marriage proposals to handsome leaders of the procession.[11] In a society where the accusation of femininity is a great affront to men, male actors in Ta'ziyeh performances, including many amateurs, willingly dress as women and perform the female roles (Chelkowski 1991).[12] An unacknowledged and unspoken, but clearly palpable, sexual energy is released on the streets. Richard reports:

> All my informants confirm that Ashura is a day for fondling, furtive caresses, and flirtations. All at once the sexual nature of this festival of death hits me. The pole of the majestic emblem supported on the belly and raised skywards to be exhibited to the women's [and men's] view; the macho display of virility to attract compassion and admiration; the sweetness of the syrups, the tenderness of stolen glances, of love for Hoseyn and his companions; the bewitching rhythm of the processions, usually in four-time-three flagellations and one pause, or three lightly swung flagellations and one step forward is more like a dance than a funeral march; and the whip and the little chains that the men twirl around to lash their shoulders suddenly resemble the multicolored scarves that the tribal women wave over their heads while dancing lightly in their finest dresses at weddings. (Richard 1995, 99–100)[13]

The Shi'ite rituals of mourning also play a crucial psychological role. In a culture where saving face and hiding one's failures are important social customs, communal grieving and lamentation provide important psychological relief. Participation in a *rowzeh khvani* gathering is an acceptable form of expressing one's grief. A recent account of one such gathering, held on the anniversary of the martyrdom of Ali (nineteenth day of the month of Ramadan), shows how this routine social gathering can renew religious identity and act as a catharsis:

> At one well-appointed apartment in Tehran, about 60 women, clothed head to toe in black, sat on the floor, facing toward Mecca. A dirge singer . . . keened into a microphone. She told the women to place small copies of the [Quran] on their heads and ask Ali for their wishes. They closed their eyes and raised their hands in the air as if summoning him. Then the singer began pressing the buttons. She moaned the story of Zainab, Ali's daughter, watching him die: "The daughter is looking at her father who is dying, whose eyes are becoming dim, he is dying, this is Zainab, who is watching her father die, who is cleaning father's bloody head, she is saying baba baba, father father, talk to me, open

> your eyes and talk to me." One woman, then two, then dozens began to weep, as if it were their own father's death was being described. "Cry everyone, cry," the singer crooned. "If you do not have enough tears, your sins will not be forgiven." The women cried as if their after-lives depended on it. Boxes of Kleenex circulated through the room. The praying settled into a rhythm, and the women began beating their chests in time to it. It was 1:30 A.M., and there were several hours more of praying and weeping before the women could attack a waiting table laden with food. (Waldman 2001, A5)

These rituals of penance thus address the believers' spiritual needs in a very concrete way. By appealing to Hussein and his family, one can hope for a swift resolution of one's problems. As Mary Hegland has similarly argued, the figure of Imam Hussein has served as "an intercessor between God and human beings."[14] Hussein's martyrdom earns him a special place in the heavenly panoply. He is gifted with the saintly power of forgiving sins and fulfilling believers' wishes, no matter how mundane.

Foucault on the Discourse of Death and Christian Rituals of Confession

In the fall of 1978, during the early stages of the Iranian Revolution, a variety of nationalist and leftist students joined the Islamists in mass antiregime demonstrations. Soon, however, the Islamist wing dominated. The struggle against the shah was cast as a reenactment of the historic battle between Hussein and Yazid, and the ostensibly secular, nationalist, and leftist demands of many of the demonstrators were articulated in religious garb and through Muharram rituals. In the name of national unity, Islamists took control of all the revolutionary slogans and demanded that the more secular women don the veil as an expression of solidarity with the more traditional ones.

Foucault compared the political reenactments of Shi'ite rituals by the Islamists during the 1978–79 Iranian Revolution to European Christian rites of penitence:

> On December 2, the Muharram celebrations will begin. The death of Imam Hussein will be celebrated. It is the great ritual of penitence. (Not long ago, one could still see marchers flagellating themselves.) But the feeling of sinfulness that could remind us of Christianity is indissolubly linked to the exaltation of martyrdom for a just cause. It is a time when the crowds are ready to advance toward death in the intoxication of sacrifice. During these days, the Shi'ite people become enamored with extremes. ("The Revolt in Iran Spreads on Cassette Tapes," app., 216)

Foucault, who personally observed the anti-shah demonstrations, was nearly mesmerized by the new attitude of the unarmed masses on the streets toward death. For him, Iranian Shi'ites had a different "regime of truth," an entirely different attitude toward life and death. This set them apart from the logic of the modern West.

Foucault was interested in both the festive manifestations of the rituals of mourning and their healing power. During a visit to the shrine of an imam, he wrote,

> All around the mausoleum, there is stamping and jostling. The European is probably wrong to seek to discern what part is village fair and what part devotion. The present monarch has tried indeed to harness some of this current. Very close to here, he erected the tomb of his own father. The father Reza Shah also laid out a large avenue and designed concrete platforms where there had been only vegetable gardens. He threw parties and received foreign delegations, all for nought, for in the rivalry between the dead, the [great-grand-]son of the imam wins, every Friday, over the father of the king. ("Tehran: Faith against the Shah," app., 199)

Foucault was likewise intrigued by the relationship between the discourse of martyrdom and the new form of political spirituality to which the Islamists aspired. He held that the Western world had abandoned this form of spirituality ever since the French Revolution. In the Paradise of Zahra Cemetery, the largest cemetery near Tehran, political debates routinely followed mourning rituals.

To Foucault, it seemed that Shi'ism had a different approach to death. It was not seen as the end but simply one more stage in the drama of life. In an imaginary conversation with an Iranian sociologist, he summarized this worldview: "What preoccupies you, you Westerners, is *death*. You ask her to detach you from life and she teaches you how to give up. As for us, we care about the *dead*, because they attach us to life. We hold out our hands to them in order for them to link us to the permanent obligation of justice. They speak to us of right and of the struggle that is necessary for right to triumph" ("Tehran," app., 201).

Foucault feared that future historians would reduce the Iranian Revolution to a merely social movement, with the religious elite joining the masses to address social, economic, and political grievances. This would miss the point, he warned. The driving force of the Iranian Revolution was religious and cultural, he maintained. This could be seen in the public nostalgia for the rituals and the discourses of Shi'ism, traditions that many Iranians had abandoned in a forced assimilation to modernity. This was a correct assessment, at least in part, but Foucault also made the highly questionable assertion that the Islamist discourse deployed in the course of the Iranian Revolution was not an ideology, that it did not "mask contradictions." Nor was it a constructed "sacred union" of "divergent political interests." Moving from a discourse of cultural imperialism to a more universal discursive paradigm of the tyranny of modernity, Foucault argued that the Shi'ite discourse was something more intrinsic and unmediated, "the vocabulary, the ceremonial, the timeless drama into which one could fit the historical drama of a people that pitted its very existence against that of its sovereign" ("Iran: The Spirit of a World without Spirit," app., 252).

In the next few years, after his return from Iran, and likely under the influence of his sojourns there, Foucault returned to these themes. Several scattered statements in Foucault's writings, lectures, and interviews in the early 1980s show his interest in early Christian ritual practices of the self, practices that believers adopted to mold their own thought in order to gain a "certain state of perfection, of happiness, of purity, of supernatural power" (Foucault 1980, 162).

Speaking in the fall of 1980, Foucault pointed out that in early Christianity there were two types of confessions, two practices of punishing the self. Only the first of these moved him. This was the practice of *exomologesis*, a public manifestation of penitence, which involved fasting, wearing tattered clothes, baring the chest, heaping ashes on one's head, and scarring the body. The penitents had to "prove their suffering and show their shame, make visible their humility, and exhibit their modesty." One told the truth, not by verbally confessing to a sin, but by fasting, self-mutilation, and various other ways of manifesting public grief. There was no verbal enunciation in this particular ritual and no analysis of the sin by a higher authority. Confession did not involve a graphic telling of what one had done or a focusing on the details of one's bodily, familial, or religious transgressions. Like a cleansing bath, this method of confession rubbed out the sin from one's skin and "reinstated the previous purity." The sinner had committed a type of spiritual suicide. Therefore, his repentance was "the theatrical representation of the sinner, willing his own death as a sinner." It was a most dramatic self-renunciation: "Exomologesis obeyed a law of dramatic emphasis and of maximum theatricality." The sinner expressed a sense of "martyrdom to which all would be witness(ed) and through this act (was) reinstated" (Foucault 1980, 172–73).

In the week before Easter, certain days were set aside for this public and collective ritual. The sinners gathered and acted out their grief and shame. Foucault quotes an account by St. Jerome (331–420 CE) describing the rituals suffered by Fabiola, a Roman noblewoman who had remarried before the death of her first husband and was to repent for this sin: "During the days that preceded Easter, Fabiola was to be found among the ranks of the penitents. The bishop, the priests, and the people wept with her. Her hair disheveled, her face pale, her hands dirty, her head covered in ashes, she chastened her naked breast and the face with which she had seduced her second husband. She revealed to all her wound, and Rome, in tears, contemplated the scars on her emaciated body" (Foucault 1980, 172). The Church Fathers justified this method of repentance by using medical language. Patients had to show their wounds to the physician if they wished to be healed. More important, however, the Church used the model of martyrdom as justification. The martyrs preferred to face death rather than abandon their faith: "The sinner abandons the faith in order to keep the life of here below; he will be reinstated only if in his turn he exposes himself voluntarily to a sort of martyrdom to which all will be witness and which is penance, or penance as exomologesis" (173). It is interesting that Foucault here chooses to cite Jerome, surely one of the harshest of the Church Fathers, whose theology included the stringent ferreting out and persecution of heretics, as well as an aversion to women and to sexuality of any kind, even within marriage.

The second type of Christian confession, the one that Foucault disliked, was what he termed "an analytical and continuous verbalization of the thought" to the priest (Foucault 1980, 179). A monk was required to control all of his thoughts, not just his actions and his deeds, so that his heart, his soul, and his eyes were pure to receive God. He accomplished this by confessing everything to a spiritual father. He confessed not only his sinful deeds but also his thoughts, dreams, and aspirations. This second form of confession, developed in the monastic orders, was called *exagoreusis*. Foucault believed that this second practice was a model for our modern forms of disciplinary social control, where teachers and psychiatrists replaced the abbot.

In both rituals, one had to sacrifice oneself to learn the truth about oneself. Foucault pointed to the complex Christian theology of the self, the notion that "no truth about the self [was possible] without the sacrifice of the self" (Foucault 1980, 180). This renunciation of the self was either in the flesh (which Foucault seems to have preferred and was perhaps tied to his interest in sadomasochism as a form of discovery of the self through pain), or in words, which Foucault criticized alongside modern disciplinary techniques.

The criticism that Foucault leveled at modern Western culture was that it had attempted to establish a hermeneutics of the self, but not one that was based on the early Christian (or, we could add, Muslim) principles of *sacrifice of the self*. The modern hermeneutics of the self was based on a theoretical and practical *emergence of the self*. Medical and psychiatric practices, political and philosophical theory, all went in this direction. Subjectivity was the root of a positive self. There was an attempt to substitute "the positive figure of man for the sacrifice which for Christianity was the condition for the opening of the self as a field of indefinite interpretation." Foucault believed this might have been a wrong course of action: "Do we need, really, this hermeneutics of self?" (Foucault 1980, 181). He held that the modern practices of the self should instead be changed. Foucault suggested a reenvisioning of the practice of exomologesis, of bodily repentance, not in its exact medieval form, but through public and private (nonverbal) rituals of self-mastery, a starting point from which one could refashion Western culture.[15]

Foucault's reading of Christian rites of penance can help explain the endurance of, and affinity for, similar rituals of penance in Shi'ite Islam. In Muharram, self-adulation, self-mutilation, and the "baring of the flesh and the body" are not individual, lonely acts of repentance. Rather, they take place as part of a collective, dramatic public festival. The community joins this drama of repentance and representation of death. Penitence, which is also a form of self-purification and a renunciation of guilt, is combined with a variety of ceremonies that engage the body in the physical, emotional, and spiritual sense, leading to an enormously gratifying experience. The annual penance of Muharram is a time for the individual sinner to place under everyone's eyes the body and the flesh that has committed the sin, not just the historical sin of betraying Hussein, but also one's own individual sin, without the need for an individual, verbal confession. In crying for Hussein, one also gains absolution from the Almighty for one's own personal guilt.

Participants in religious social gatherings, street processions, or Ta'ziyeh performances are routinely encouraged to remember (but not articulate) their individual grief and sin.[16] They are told to compare their own tragedies and losses in life to the suffering experienced by Hussein and his family, and to conclude that the Kufan tragedy was a much greater one. The play is also meant to comfort the audience by reminding it that untimely death happens to even the best of us, and therefore one should be prepared to accept the will of God. At the end of a Ta'ziyeh performance, members of the audience confirm and renew their profound expressions of grief and guilt over the events they have witnessed. The annual performance thus creates a sense of community as the participants "ritually renew their commitment to a religion and ideological order of which they are already an integral part" (Beeman 1979, 30). The individual is therefore involved in an act of public confession. Rather than a verbalization of personal sins and shortcomings, it is a public manifestation of penitence. The participants experience a sense of salvation and hope, as they believe that the Almighty might now redeem them as a result of their appeals to the clan of Hussein.

Troubling Appropriations of Shi'ite and Christian Passion Plays

What many contemporary discussions of Muharram fail to mention is that the message of Karbala is not just about adoration and veneration of the good. The medieval passion plays of Europe contrast the purity, decency, and love of Jesus with the fiendish, mischievous actions of the Jews, who were blamed for his death. Likewise in the Iranian Shi'ite passion plays, the saintly qualities of the Shi'ite leaders are contrasted to the unethical and vile conduct of the early Sunni leaders, who supposedly snatched the mantle of leadership unjustly, taking it away from Hussein and showing no mercy toward his family, including the infants.

The rituals of Muharram condemn the founders of the Umayyad dynasty, and by implication their followers, that is, the majority Sunni Muslims. Straw effigies of the enemies of the clan of Muhammad, including that of the second caliph, Umar, who is highly respected in the Sunni world, are spat upon and set on fire. In parts of Iran, certain days are designated as "the killing of Umar" days, when people celebrate the assassination of the second Muslim caliph, Umar, whom Shi'ites also see as a usurper. Often the play includes a Christian character (the Foreign Ambassador), who witnesses the martyrdom of Hussein and is so moved that he converts to Islam. The implication is clear: non-Muslims will convert to Islam if they are exposed to the truth of Karbala. The audience is also told that all the celestial beings (including the devil) and every dead or living person (including all the former biblical prophets) offered to save Hussein before his predestined death. These ceremonies and processions remind non-Shi'ite and non-Muslim Iranians of their marginal and precarious status. The frenzied Muharram processions sometimes lead to violence. Often, when two rival factions (*dasteh*), which are performing the *sinehzani* (self-flagellation rituals), come face to face in a narrow alley, neither gives the other the right-of-way. As a result, there are at times violent outbursts, resulting in injuries or even deaths, and terrifying non-Shi'ite communities (Mazzoui 1979, 232).

Muharram is also about total obedience to higher religious authorities. This is not a script where the father sacrifices himself for the son, or where the son asserts his authority over the father. Rather, as in the story of Abraham and his son, it is the child who is asked to give his life willingly for the glory of the father and, unlike the story of Abraham, a child is always martyred in the play. The authority of the patriarch is continuously reasserted. Women are recognized for two attributes: They are givers of martyrs (as sisters, wives, and mothers of the men who die) and the eventual victims in the play. The wives of Hussein never speak, but Zainab, the sister of Hussein, is glorified because she accepts the eventual destiny of her brother, helps prepare him for his last battle, and eventually lives to tell the story. The ethics and politics of Muharram, like the black shirts and the white shrouds of the mourners, are unambiguous. Hussein and the entire clan of Muhammad are good, decent, ethical, and pure, while the enemy is wicked, impure, unethical, and immoral. Only a sinner or an unbeliever would ask if the clan of Hussein was justified in its claim to the eternal leadership of the entire Muslim community by virtue of its birthright.

In his accounts of both Christian and Muslim rituals, Foucault's omissions are surprising and troubling. He belonged to a generation that was well aware of the uses that fascist movements had made of Christian rituals of martyrdom and passion plays. Why was there no reference to any of this in his 1978–79 writings on Iran, or even in his work on the hermeneutics of religion in the 1980s, which was written much later and far away from the frenzy of the revolutionary moment? These omissions were all the more surprising, given the political agenda of Khomeinism, with its intolerance toward minority religions and ethnicities, its hostility toward "atheistic" leftists and secularists, and its dismissal of women's rights.

For Christians raised on the story of the crucifixion of Jesus and related passion plays, the story of the martyrdom of Imam Hussein sounds remarkably familiar.[17] If we compare Ta'ziyeh performances with the longest-surviving passion play in Europe, the one that has been held in the village of Oberammergau (Bavarian Alps) since 1634, we find numerous similarities. The Oberammergau passion play centers on Jesus and his supporters, while the Ta'ziyeh centers on Hussein and his clan. Jesus is betrayed by those who are initially loyal to him, while Hussein is betrayed by the once-loyal Kufans. The Christian play is devoted to the "passion" of Jesus, meaning his suffering and gruesome death, just as the Ta'ziyeh is devoted to the tragic suffering and death of Hussein and his family. A significant part of both stories deals with the grieving, as well as the courage, of women, whether of Mary who mourns the loss of her son, or of Zainab, who lives to tell the story of her brother's martyrdom (Pinault 1998; Humayuni 1979). Both plays include flashbacks to Old Testament stories, such as the expulsion of Adam and Eve from the Garden of Eden, Abraham's near-sacrifice of his son, and Moses leading the Hebrews across the Red Sea. As Gordon Mork points out, Jesus is not portrayed as a "powerful avenger." Rather, he is seen as a "suffering servant" of God, who allowed him to be sacrificed "to atone for the sins of all the world" (Mork 1996, 154–55). Similarly, Michael Fischer suggests that Hussein "had to witness for Islam and thereby shock people back to the true path, to serve as an example throughout the ages that sometimes death can create a lasting testament that people will remember" (1980, 72).

The similarities between Christian and Shi'ite Muslim passion plays extend to their appropriation for political aims as well. Roman Catholics have played an important role in a number of nationalist and democratic movements around the world, including the oppositional culture of Poland's Solidarnosc movement, the hunger strikes of Irish Republican Army prisoners in Northern Ireland, and, of course, liberation theology in the Caribbean and Latin America. But Christian rituals, like those of Islam, lend themselves to multiple readings, including ones that demonize the "other." The attempt to mold, shape, and manipulate passion plays has not been limited to twentieth-century Iran. European fascism was not, as it is sometimes assumed to be, entirely anti-Christian or anti-clerical. Hungarian, Slovak, and Croatian fascist movements drew on Christian symbols and rituals as well as on Christian millenarian beliefs. The Iron Guard and the Legion of Archangel Michael in Romania had some similarities to militant Shi'ite movements of late twentieth-century Iran. Romanian fascist organizations employed the priests and the churches in their appeals to the masses and drew their inspiration from religious icons. They were also characterized by "extraordinary cults of suffering, sacrifice, and martyrdom" and regarded their ultimate goal as the "resurrection in Christ" (Arjomand 1988, 208–9).

Even the Nazis, who glorified pre-Christian Germanic traditions and were somewhat anti-religious, realized that in the absence of a unifying cultural heritage, religious rituals could be reappropriated for their purposes. Adolf Hitler was acutely aware of the political message of the Oberammergau passion play and encouraged his party to use the play for disseminating anti-Semitism. He attended these performances twice, in 1930 and in 1934, and declared the play "a German national treasure." He further argued that the play had to be kept alive because of its highly negative portrayal of Jews: "One of the most important tasks will be to save future generations from a similar political fate and to maintain forever watchful in them knowledge of the menace of Jewry. For this reason alone it is vital that the Passion Play be continued at Oberammergau" (Hitler 1953, 457). In 1939, the Nazi Propaganda Ministry, which backed the performance, declared the event "important for the Reich," while a leading member of the party announced that "the Passion Play is the most anti-Semitic play of which we are aware" (cited in Mork 1996, 157).

Reinventing Traditions: Martyrdom and Authenticity

The preceding comparison between fascism and Iranian Islamism is not arbitrary. Much has been written about some European intellectuals of the late nineteenth and early twentieth centuries who, in their rejection of individualism, rationalism, and democracy, turned to a new Christian identity, one that borrowed some elements from socialism and nationalism, and eventually contributed to the birth of European fascism (Sternhell 1996; Birnbaum 1996). A similar process took place in Iran. In the 1960s and 1970s, a generation of leftist Iranian intellectuals with religious leanings gradually carved out a new militant discourse of Islam, one that also borrowed from the West. It was a strange synthesis of Soviet and Chinese Marxism, the existentialism of Sartre, Kierkegaard, and Heidegger, and a militant form of traditional Shi'ite Islam. This new discourse arose under a government that tolerated no political opposition or even dissent. The new discourse also expressed solidarity with several more traditional religious figures, especially Ayatollah Khomeini, who opposed the government of Muhammad Reza Shah and his agenda of reform.

In 1963, the shah held a national referendum for a new program of political and social reform called the "White Revolution," in obvious contrast to the "Red" Russian and Chinese Revolutions. The proposal included land reform, the establishment of a national literacy corps, and women's suffrage. Almost all of the major clerics, as well as the more secular National Front, called for a boycott of the referendum, for various reasons. Khomeini went further than others in attacking the shah, claiming that the White Revolution undermined Islam. The shah ordered an assault on the Fayziyeh Theological Seminary, Khomeini's headquarters, killing several students and arresting others. He labeled Khomeini and his supporters "black reactionaries" and cut government funding for the ranking clerics. He also ordered the army to draft the young theology students ('Aqeli 1993, 2:153–54).

On June 3, 1963, the day of Ashura during Muharram, when thousands of believers poured into the holy city of Qom to hear religious sermons, Khomeini escalated his verbal attacks, making one of the most incendiary statements that had ever been pronounced against the shah. He compared the shah to Yazid, the enemy of Hussein and the most hated figure in the Shi'ite tradition: "It is now the afternoon of Ashura. Sometimes when I recall the events of Ashura, a question occurs to me: If the Umayyads, and the regime of Yazid, son of Mu'awiyah, wished to make war against Hussein, why did they commit such savage and inhumane crimes against the defenseless women and innocent children?" (Khomeini 1963, 177). He answered the question himself. The Umayyad clan wished to uproot the entire family of the prophet, to uproot Islam itself. Khomeini then extended this polemic to the shah and went so far as to accuse his soldiers of destroying the Quran. "If the tyrannical regime of Iran simply wished to . . . oppose the ulama, what business did it have tearing the Quran to shreds . . . what business did it have with the *madrassa* [religious schools] or with its students?" As with the Umayyads, the shah was "fundamentally opposed to Islam itself and the existence of the religious class" (177).

Khomeini's June 1963 speech marked the beginning of a new discourse in Iranian politics in another respect as well. Iranians were used to the longstanding power struggle between the state and the *ulama* (clerical establishment), as well as to leftist and nationalist attacks on Western governments for their imperialist interventions. The new element in Khomeini's discourse, which helped galvanize a mass opposition movement, was a masterful weaving of Shi'ite mythology into these denunciations of Western imperialism. In addition, he linked his attack on Israel, which was also becoming a staple of leftist and nationalist discourse, to denunciations of Iran's minorities and feminists. At a time when Arab nationalist leaders like Egypt's Gamal Abdel Nasser stood fast in their uncompromising rejection of the Jewish state, the Iranian government's official neutrality and unofficial alliance with Israel were a source of national and religious humiliation to many Iranian Muslims. Khomeini recognized the regime's ideological weakness here and masterfully appropriated it for his own purposes.[18] He rekindled dormant religious biases that progressive intellectuals had tried to erase for decades. Khomeini said that the shah was carrying out the wishes of the Jewish state, a government that planned to uproot Islam and seize the economy, with the help of Iran's minorities. He thus linked together opposition to the West, to Israel, and to the shah, and to Iran's non-Muslim minorities, especially Baha'is and Jews, who had gained new rights under the Pahlavi regime: "Henceforth, Jews, Christians, and the enemies of Islam and the Muslims were to decide on the affairs, the honor, and the person of the Muslims." He then asked rhetorically if the shah was in fact a "Jew" (Khomeini 1963, 175). Khomeini was quickly arrested as a result of this speech, but his arrest unleashed protests throughout the country. The U.S.-trained army launched brutal attacks on demonstrators in Qom, Tehran, Shiraz, Mashhad, Isfahan, Kashan, and other cities that turned bloody, giving the movement martyrs.[19] The shah sent Khomeini into exile in Najaf, Iraq, where he developed plans for a new Islamist state in Iran.

Without the support of some of the leftist intellectuals within Iran, however, Khomeini's blueprint for an Islamist revolution might have remained in the drafting stage. Jalal Al-Ahmad (1923–69), author of the now-classic 1963 book *Plagued by the West,* was one of these, the first leftist to contribute to the new discourse of militant Islam. By the early 1960s, Al-Ahmad saw Islam as the only remaining barrier to Western capitalism and rampant consumerism. *Plagued by the West* blended a Nietzschean critique of modern technology with a Marxian one of alienated labor, also attacking the cultural hegemony of the West.[20] The text was peppered with references to Albert Camus, Eugene Ionesco, Jean-Paul Sartre, and Franz Kafka, who had written on the contradictory impulses of modernity in philosophical treatises, novels, and plays. To Al-Ahmad, the plagues and demons in the works of these authors referred to a modern technocratic capitalism that had run amuck. It was a world that had abandoned all faith and all ideas, except for science and materialism. This scientific worldview had ushered in the atomic age, beginning with the destruction of Hiroshima and Nagasaki: "I understand all of these fictional destinies to be omens, foreboding the Hour of Judgment, warning that the machine demon if not harnessed and put back into the bottle, will place a hydrogen bomb at the end of the road for mankind" (Al-Ahmad 1982, 111).

Al-Ahmad believed that modern technology could only be tamed through a return to the twin concepts of martyrdom and jihad, the latter in its strictly combative meaning. For nearly two centuries, he wrote, a variety of nationalist camps in Iran, Egypt, and the Ottoman Empire had used Islam as a weapon to resist Western colonialism in the Middle East. But the Muslim world had been weakened by the Shi'ite-Sunni divide and especially by the institutionalization of Shi'ism in Iran under the Safavids. Shi'ism had lost its vitality and exuberance once the discourses of jihad and martyrdom had been abandoned. From "the day we gave up the possibility of martyrdom, and limited ourselves to paying homage to the martyrs, we were reduced to the role of the doormen of cemeteries" (Al-Ahmad 1982, 68).

Ali Shariati (d. 1977), one of the most influential Muslim thinkers of his generation, was another leftist intellectual who contributed to this new line of thinking. A lay Muslim theologian who was the son of a cleric, he became involved in the international movement for Algerian Independence while studying in France (Keddie 1981, 294). Shariati, who had a Ph.D. in Persian philology from the Sorbonne, galvanized the youth, helping to pave the way for Khomeini's hegemony over the revolutionary movement in 1978–79. Shariati's reinterpretation of jihad and martyrdom was influenced by his philosophical studies in France, though he also claimed to present an "authentic Islam."

In considering Al-Ahmad and Shariati here, we should not forget that a far larger number of Iranian students and intellectuals of the 1960s were fascinated by Western schools of thought, such as Marxism and existentialism, and were not interested in Islamic politics. But men like Al-Ahmad and Shariati modernized the old religious narratives by connecting them to some of the themes of leftist thought, thus making them more palatable to students and intellectuals. Soon after his return to Iran in 1964, Shariati gained a reputation as a powerful lecturer. When Husseiniyeh Ershad, a somewhat modern theological seminary, opened in Tehran in 1969, Shariati lectured there and soon found a mass following. His lectures were recorded and distributed, and his controversial ideas were discussed widely, despite the jealousy and resentment of the traditional Shi'ite clergy. All along, the regime had allowed some limited space for oppositional discourse within the religious community, while cracking down much harder on the secular Left. This was part of the overall Cold War mindset, which saw "international Communism" as the main threat to the established power. Although Shariati was allowed to lecture for a few years, he left the country in 1977 after a series of confrontations with the regime. He died shortly afterward from a heart attack in London at the age of only forty-four. Rumors implicating the regime in his death soon elevated his stature to that of a *shahid* (martyr). More than anyone else except Khomeini, Shariati, through his writings and speeches, would become the ideological inspiration of the 1978–79 revolution (Dabashi 1993, 102–46).

Shariati introduced an existentialist reading of the Karbala narrative that was also informed by Heidegger's work. He elevated the concept of martyrdom above all else and called it the defining moment of Shi'ism (Shariati 1970, 154). He called for a revolutionary concept of Islam, one that could challenge the monarchy and bring a new generation of Muslim thinkers like him to power. In his search for what he considered to be an "authentic" interpretation of Islam, Shariati castigated the external influences on Islam, which had been many in over a thousand years of rich intellectual ferment and cross-fertilization. In particular, he wished to drive out Greek philosophy, Indian and Iranian mysticism, as well as Christian and Jewish theology. He also rejected the more tolerant interpretations of Islam found in Persian poetry (e.g., Omar Khayyam), in Muslim philosophy (e.g., Farabi [al-Farabi], 870–950; Avicenna, 980–1037), or even in Sufi mysticism (174). Finally and most controversially for Iran's leftist youth, he rejected Marxism as a "Western fallacy," singling out Marx's humanism for particular attack (Shariati 1980).

Shariati's new "authentic Islam" centered on a reinterpretation of the story of Karbala. He wrote that Hussein's martyrdom had taken place because

Shi'ite Muslims remained passive and ignorant of political and ideological issues. If Iranians could recapture the original revolutionary meaning of Shi'ite Islam and the concept of the "ideal" Muslim man and woman, they could overcome another Yazid (the shah) and bring about a society based on true Muslim values. Shariati called his revolutionary interpretation of Shi'ism the "Shi'ism of Ali," distinguishing this "Alavid Shi'ism" from the more conservative "Safavid Shi'ism," the institutionalized Shi'ism in Iran dating back to the Safavid dynasty. For Shariati, this "Alavid Shi'ism" was the "true" Islam, one that did not build divisions "between intellectuals and the people" (cited in Dabashi 1993, 111–12; see also Shariati 1986).

Shariati delivered one of his most moving lectures in 1970, on the eve of Ashura, at a time when several of his students, who were members of the People's Mujahedeen, had been killed by the shah's police. Shariati did not dwell on themes commonly invoked in the sermons of the clerics, such as the murder and enslavement of the women and children from Hussein's clan after the battle of Karbala, the cruelty of Yazid, the treachery of Hussein's allies, or the promise of paradise for the saintly clan of Muhammad and the true believers. Instead, he emphasized almost exclusively Hussein's willingness to embrace martyrdom. Conventional theologians had downplayed the significance of this type of jihad in Islam. There were eight gates to heaven, and jihad was only one of them—one that could be avoided. They told their followers:

> You are not obligated to enter only through the door of jihad. Jihad is simply one of the keys, which opens the doors to paradise. Prayer, other forms of worship, and incantation are safer keys and you can use them without harm, loss, danger, or risk! There are a lot of charitable affairs that will take you to the same point, such as feeding the needy, looking after poor families, visiting the holy places, praying, asceticism, piety, making vows, dedication, helping your neighbor, incantation, prayer ceremonies, lamentation, and intercession. You will reach the same goal as the person who chooses jihad, so why cause yourself suffering and pain by choosing the much more difficult action of jihad? (Shariati 1970, 183)

Shariati ridiculed such notions, as well as some of the practices of Muharram. Paradise could not be bought so cheaply through prayer, fasting, and rituals! Only through a continuous reenactment of the tragedy of Karbala could one live the life of a genuine Muslim. This reenactment could not be achieved by attending Ta'ziyeh performances or Muharram processions, nor was it an intellectual or "mental jihad." It could only be achieved through embracing personal martyrdom in the present day (173).

For Shariati, the key point in the story of Karbala was Hussein's existential choice. Hussein could not fight and win over the more powerful Yazid, nor could he remain silent. Therefore, he chose a third option, death, which opened the possibility of an authentic Shi'ite Islam for others. Martyrdom, as defined by Shariati, was a mystical experience, full of erotic charge, and beyond "science and logic." The story of Hussein's martyrdom was "so exciting that it pulls the spirit toward the fire. It paralyzes logic. It weakens speech. It even makes thinking difficult." Martyrdom was the combination of "a refined love and a deep, complex wisdom" (Shariati 1970, 154). The martyr was a "model" and an "example" for other human beings; the efficacy and the resonance of martyrdom were "broader, deeper, more continuous than that of jihad, even one that is victorious" (194, 207). Martyrdom was a privilege because one invited death at a time of one's own choosing. It was "a choice, whereby the warrior sacrifices himself on the threshold of the temple and the altar of love and is victorious" (193). Despite the claim that he was presenting an "authentic Islam," Shariati's reading was heavily indebted to Western thought, including some of the most virulent forms of Christian anti-Semitism. For example, he referred to "money-worshipping Jews" and to "deceitful Christ-killing rabbis" (208). Many leading clerics and even some secular Muslim intellectuals of this period shared such sentiments.

But there was also a stronger philosophical and hermeneutical appropriation of aspects of Western thought in Shariati's work. In *Being and Time,* Heidegger had reinterpreted the crucifixion and resurrection of Jesus to arrive at a new philosophical meaning. When faced with the possibility of one's own death, one adopted an attitude of freedom-toward-death and thereby experienced authentic living, he had written. Shariati was influenced by this and similar hermeneutical readings of Christianity. But his notion of authenticity was aimed at the community rather than the individual. When Shi'ites faced a formidable enemy of Islam, one who could not be defeated, they had two options: (1) to remain silent and allow the oppression to continue, or (2) to choose death and at least create the possibility of authentic (Muslim) living for others. In a morbid appeal to the youth, both young men and women, Shariati argued that this type of death was as beautiful as a "necklace" around the neck of a young and beautiful girl, that such martyrdom was "an adornment for mankind" (Shariati 1970, 177).

Shariati also parted company with Christian theologians, who had argued that Jesus "sacrificed himself for humanity" (Shariati 1970, 209). A similar reading of the story of Karbala could have suggested that Yazid's forces had also acted according to the will of God and hence deserved some mercy. But Shariati's vitriolic discourse lacked mercy or forgiveness. The mission of Ashura was "revolt and jihad for the devastation of the regime of Yazid" (209). He wrote that Hussein knew that death at the hands of his enemies would mark them for life. They became "transgressors," who had murdered the grandson of Muhammad. Hussein realized that he could achieve more by facing martyrdom at the hands of his enemies (and tainting their reputation) than by living. This was not a type of death through which God forgave the sins of humanity; it was one that pointed toward revenge, a death that marked the enemy as a horrible sinner: "It is in this way that the dying of a human being guarantees the life of a nation" (213).

According to Shariati, martyrdom was thus "the only reason for existence" and a "goal in itself." It was "an invitation to all generations, in all ages, if you cannot kill your oppressor, then die." Martyrdom was so noble in Islam that the corpse required no ritual bath. The martyr was also under no obligation "to give an account of himself on the day of Judgment" (Shariati 1970, 214). Martyrdom was a pass straight to heaven.[21] Such thinking was soon to become influential among leftists. In January 1974, when Khosrow Golsorkhi, a poet and journalist, was tried and condemned by a military tribunal for an attempt on the shah's life, he used the occasion to declare that the objectives of Marxism and Islam were one and the same. He called the Shi'ite saint Ali "the world's first socialist" and argued further as follows:

> The life of Imam Hussein is similar to ours, as we stand trial in this court, willing to sacrifice our lives for the deprived people of our nation. He was in the minority, while Yazid had ruled in the royal court, had an army, a government, and power. [Hussein] stood fast and was martyred. Although Yazid occupied a brief moment of history, what remained for all time was the path of Hussein, not the government of Yazid. The masses have continued and will continue the perseverance of Hussein, not the government of Yazid. . . . In this way, in a Marxist society, genuine Islam can be justified as a superstructure, and we approve of such an Islam, the Islam of Hussein and the Islam of Imam Ali. (cited in Nabavi 2001, 263)

Reenacting the Karbala Paradigm: The Revolution

After Shariati's death in 1977, Khomeini, long respected for his opposition to the shah and his austere lifestyle in exile, quickly assumed the mantle of leadership within the Islamist opposition.[22] The shah had long been criticized by the international community for his extensive violations of human rights, including the arrest and torture of political opponents. In 1977, after the election of Jimmy Carter to the U.S. presidency, the shah also came under criticism by the United States. In the 1970s, a vibrant but clandestine nationalist and leftist movement was active alongside the Islamist one, including members of the National Front, the Tudeh Party, the Fedayeen and the People's Mujahedeen guerrilla organizations, and a variety of nationalist and leftist student groups (including pro-Soviet and pro-China ones), which were involved in the Confederation of Iranian Students abroad. Gradually, the Islamists, who took their cue from Khomeini, came to dominate the anti-shah movement. Shariati's radical students, including many followers of the Mujahedeen, flocked to Khomeini's side and bestowed on him the title of "imam." This designation insinuated a stature similar to that of the Twelfth Imam, who by tradition was to return from occultation to announce the Day of Judgment. As the opposition movement against the shah gained momentum inside Iran, the exiled Khomeini called upon his close confidants inside Iran to organize a form of street demonstration that borrowed many elements from the Muharram processions.

What happened in Iran in 1978 was therefore the result of a twofold set of appropriations: the revival of the old and sometimes forbidden rituals of Muharram and, simultaneously, a new interpretation of Shi'ite traditions, one that emphasized martyrdom. In his reinterpretation of Shi'ite rituals, Khomeini removed the borders between the audience and the actors, turning the entire country into a stage for his casting. He imbued the old passion plays with a passionate hatred of the shah, of Israel, the United States, and the West, of Iran's non-Muslims, especially Baha'is and Jews (the latter tracing their heritage in Iran back to 500 BCE), and of women's rights advocates. Drawing on some long-held prejudices of Shi'ite theology concerning gender and the rights of non-Muslims, and in language that was reminiscent of fascist propaganda of the 1930s, Khomeini and a group of theologians embarked on a militant and belligerent interpretation of the Karbala incident, one with overtly political dimensions. The emphasis was no longer on the innocence of Hussein. It was on Hussein's willingness to make the supreme sacrifice of giving his life for the sake of justice. Muslims were expected to follow the example of Hussein and give their lives for the cause of justice as defined by Khomeini, who had accused the shah of acting like a modern Yazid and of supporting the Jews and the Baha'is. He thereby sanctioned a religious insurrection against the regime.

On January 9, 1978, soldiers broke into the house of Ayatollah Kazem Shariatmadari in Qom, where a group of protesting theology students had taken sanctuary. Shariatmadari was a moderate and pro-constitutionalist cleric, who was not an outspoken critic of the monarchy. The soldiers fired upon the students, killing one and injuring several others. The Islamist leadership now had a martyr. In keeping with Shi'ite traditions, forty days later a commemoration for the martyred student was held in a mosque in Tabriz, Shariatmadari's home base. When the police again broke into the mosque, killing many more people, the cycle of mourning processions and commemorations, modeled after Muharram, was initiated.

Khomeini kept reminding the public of the glories of martyrdom, of what Hussein had done for Islam, and of the need to give one's life for the sake of the Iranian Revolution. The February 18 memorial procession led to a bloody demonstration in which a hundred more demonstrators were killed. Forty days later demonstrations in memory of the martyrs of February resulted in more riots and strikes throughout the country. The March-April memorial events in turn led to riots in thirty-four cities. On May 9, two theology students were killed. This event triggered new demonstrations in Qom and other major cities. On September 8, government forces shot at protesters who had gathered at Jaleh Square in Tehran, killing at least two hundred and fifty and wounding another thousand (Ashraf and Banuazizi 1985).

This event, known as the "Black Friday Massacre," further radicalized the movement and ended the possibility that the moderate camp of reformers might assume the leadership of the movement (Milani 1998, 250). Khomeini encouraged women and children to march at the head of processions.

> Our brave women embrace their children and face the machine-guns and tanks of the executioners of this regime. . . . Sisters and Brothers, be resolute, do not show weakness and lack of courage. You are following the path of the Almighty and his prophets. Your blood is poured on the same road as that of the [martyred] prophets, imams, and their followers. You join them. This is not an occasion to mourn but to rejoice. (Khomeini 1999, 3:510–12)

Over and over, he resurrected the imagery of Karbala:

> My dears, do not fear giving martyrs, giving life and property for God, Islam, and the Muslim nation. This is the custom of our great prophet and his clan. Our blood is no more precious than the blood of the martyrs of Karbala . . . You, who have stood up for Islam and devoted your life and property [to it], are now in the ranks of the martyrs of Karbala, for you follow this doctrine. (4:155)

But Khomeini also combined this type of militant Shi'ite discourse with an anti-imperialist one that distanced itself from both the Russian and the Chinese regimes, striking an independent nationalist chord.

In September 19, 1978, just after the Black Friday massacre in Tehran, Khomeini declared,

> Today, the so-called Red revolutionary China, the U.S., which stands for international oppression, the Soviet Union, which is the source of lies and deceit, Britain, this old rogue of colonialism, have all risen to defend the shah and demolish a nation that wishes to stand on its own feet rather than rely on the East or the West. Under such circumstances, the shameless shah labels the defenseless Iranian people a mixture of Red communists and Black reactionaries. However, I am sure that the victory of our nation is certain. (Khomeini 1999, 3:476–77)

It was at this point that Foucault first visited Iran.

PART II

Foucault's Writings on the Iranian Revolution and After

Chapter 3

The Visits to Iran and the Controversies with "Atoussa H." and Maxime Rodinson

On September 16, 1978, Foucault arrived in Iran for a ten-day visit, at a time when the uprising was beginning to make headway. In addition to the wave of anger inside the country, the September 8 massacre in Tehran had also sparked a fifteen-thousand-strong anti-shah demonstration in Paris ("Quinze mille" 1978). Before 1978, Foucault had occasionally signed statements against the Pahlavi regime. He was also acquainted with some of the French and Iranian anti-shah activists in Paris, including National Front leader Ahmad Salamatian. The latter reported that his contacts with Foucault went back as far as 1973 and that he had visited Foucault's home several times over the years. Foucault had been extremely modest during their encounters and took the time to listen carefully to what his Iranian interlocutors had to say (personal communication from Ahmad Salamatian, December 12, 2002). Also in 1978, the editors of *Corriere della sera* had asked Foucault to write regularly for their publication, Italy's most respected daily newspaper. Foucault called together a group of younger intellectuals to work with him, among them his lover Thierry Voeltzel, André Glucksmann, and Alain Finkielkraut. This group accepted his proposal to write reports on world events as a collective. Besides Foucault's articles on Iran, the only other result of this initiative was a November 1978 article by Finkielkraut on Carter's America, for which Foucault wrote an introduction. Biographer David Macey has suggested that *Corriere della sera*'s owner, Rizzoli Publications, was also contemplating "subsequent republication in book form" of these reports, something that never materialized either. Be that as it may, the newspaper's editors treated Foucault's articles as a major event. In a front-page statement accompanying his first dispatch from Iran, *Corriere della sera*'s editors intoned enthusiastically that Foucault's article would begin "a series of reports . . . which will represent something new in European journalism and which will be entitled 'Michel Foucault Investigates'" (cited in Macey 1993, 406).

In preparation for his trip to Iran, Foucault met with Thierry Mignon, a human rights lawyer active on Iranian issues, and his wife, Sylvie Mignon. In addition, Salamatian furnished Foucault with books, pamphlets, and, most important, contacts inside Iran. Foucault also met twice with Abolhassan Bani-Sadr, the European-educated Iranian exile who was to become the first president of the Islamic Republic. (In 1981, he had to flee for his life back to Paris.) Years later, Bani-Sadr reported that Foucault's interest in Iran in 1978 had turned on two issues. First, he had asked about the conditions under which a large spontaneous movement could form and be in the process of making a revolution, all of this outside the traditional political parties. Second, recounted Bani-Sadr, he had expressed interest at a more general level in the ways in which a discourse of subjection to power was being replaced by one of resistance. Bani-Sadr went on to suggest that the encounter with Iran was a crucial turning point in Foucault's thinking and that as a result of the Iranian events, he was to become more interested in notions of human agency and resistance (personal communication, December 11, 2002).

On October 6, three weeks after Foucault arrived in Iran, Khomeini received authorization to move from his exile in Iraq to the Paris suburb of Neauphle-le-Château, where he became the subject of intense international media attention. By mid-October, the two most important internal opposition groups, the Freedom Movement (headed by Khomeini's supporter Mehdi Bazargan) and the secular National Front (led by Karim Sanjabi) had announced their support for Khomeini's leadership of the movement against the shah. In September, the political situation inside Iran was still somewhat fluid, however, and not all observers recognized the depth and seriousness of the opposition. For example, the U.S. Defense Intelligence Agency concluded that month that the shah would remain in power for another decade. Within weeks, however, sustained strikes in the communications, water, railroad, manufacturing, and especially the oil sectors would change that prognosis. During September and October, the shah's appointed government, led by Prime Minister Ja'far Sharif-Imami, was desperately trying to maintain the regime by releasing political prisoners. Among those released were two key supporters of Khomeini, Ayatollah Hussein Ali Montazari and Ayatollah Mahmud Taleqani. By late October, angry civil servants were pulling pictures of the shah and his wife down from the walls of government offices. Former Prime Minister Ali Amini tried to work out a compromise by encouraging the shah to resign and leave the country. On November 6, the government of Sharif-Imami resigned. In a nationally televised speech, the shah reluctantly gave a measure of recognition to the revolutionary movement. He appointed General Gholamreza Azhari head of a new military government, but warned him that he did not want another bloodbath in the streets of Tehran. Playing for time, the government now arrested a few prominent officials and also promised to change all laws that were "contrary to Islam" (cited in Menashri 1980, 491). On November 8, National Front leader Sanjabi visited Khomeini in Paris, where he declared the monarchy "illegitimate" and gave conditional approval to the idea of an "Islamic government." Khomeini was now becoming the uncontested leader of the opposition to the shah, which weakened the position of more senior and more moderate clerics like Ayatollah Shariatmadari.

During October and November, Khomeini's supporters in France were coaching him on how to soften the harshness of his Islamist discourse. He did so a bit, also calling for independence, freedom, and democracy in Iran. Among those who coached Khomeini in Paris was Bani-Sadr. For his part, the shah warned ominously of the danger of a Communist takeover, a possibility that remained of serious concern to the United States. On November 26, only a few days before the month of Muharram began, government troops shot a group of protesters who had sought sanctuary at the Shrine of Imam Reza in Mashhad. Khomeini and three other Grand Ayatollahs, Ayatollah Golpaygani, Ayatollah Marashi Najafi, and Ayatollah Shariatmadari, declared a day of national mourning. By late 1978, Khomeini began to put forward more forcefully his demand for "an Islamic government." On the streets of Tehran and other major cities, support for Khomeini intensified. A novel strategy employed by protesters was to mount rooftops in the evening and chant "Allah o Akbar" (God is great). The loud vibrating noise was a tremendous blow to the morale of the soldiers, weakening their support for the shah.

In December, the Pahlavi regime began to crack. On December 2, the month-long Muharram celebrations began, and, as we saw in chapter 2, the clerics deftly turned it into a massive mobilization against the shah. The religious mobilization reached its peak on December 10–11, when mass demonstrations involving hundreds of thousands commemorated Ashura on the streets of Tehran and other cities. During these days, strikes spearheaded by oil workers also brought the entire economy to a halt. On December 13, in his first public admission of defeat, the shah offered the prime ministership to the regime's most prominent secular opponent, Karim Sanjabi of the National Front. Sanjabi publicly spurned the offer. After several others also declined, on December 28, Shapour Bakhtiar accepted the position. Bakhtiar was immediately expelled from the National Front and denounced by the entire opposition.

A Brief Note on Gender and Politics in Iran, 1906–1978

To Iranians and those familiar with the country's history, the revolutionary uprising of 1978–79 was part of a series of turbulent events stretching back to 1906, in which the themes of democracy versus autocracy, nationalism versus imperialism, socialism versus capitalism, secularism versus clericalism, and women's emancipation versus tradition had played themselves out at several key junctures. In this brief sketch, we will highlight the politics of gender, a topic on which Foucault was largely ignorant, but an important one for the analysis of the events of 1978–79.[1]

Iranian democrats, whether liberal or socialist, usually saw the 1906–11 Constitutional Revolution as a founding moment, a time when the nation came to the forefront of the Muslim world in its quest for democracy, equality, and national sovereignty. Inspired by the Russian Revolution of 1905, in which Iranian migrant workers and merchants in Baku (then in the Russian Empire but today in the Republic of Azerbaijan) had participated, Iranian constitutionalists won the right to form a *majlis* (parliament). They set up a constitutional monarchy along European lines that limited royal and clerical authority, and established equal rights for all (male) citizens regardless of religion or ethnicity. The revolution also had a more radical social democratic dimension, and while women certainly did not win equality, important gains occurred, especially in women's education.[2]

A new democratic public sphere included newspapers where leading male and female intellectuals argued for women's rights and an end to polygamy, veiling and seclusion of women, and easy male divorce. The conservative wing of the Shi'ite clergy opposed the revolution, targeting especially its gender reforms. The most prominent member of the clerical opposition, the royalist Sheikh Fazlullah Nuri, was tried and executed by a revolutionary court in 1908, making him a martyr in the eyes of later Islamists, including Khomeini. The revolutionary period came to an end in 1911, when Britain and Russia intervened militarily and helped to reestablish royal power. Even at its high point, however, the Constitutional Revolution had acceded in 1907 to a supplementary law that allowed for a council of Shi'ite clerics to veto any law they found "offensive" to Islam.

By the mid-1920s, Iran was traveling down a different road, that of authoritarian modernization from above. In 1925, Reza Khan, a mid-level military officer who had suppressed a communist uprising, assumed the title of Reza Shah with the backing of the British, the leading clerics, and the remnants of the 1906–11 parliament. Modeling himself on Mustafa Kemal (Ataturk), but without the latter's anti-imperialist credentials, Reza Shah created a modern military and state bureaucracy. In addition to thoroughly crushing the Left, he reduced the powers of the clerical establishment, and muzzled the parliament.[3] Reza Shah also encouraged a stronger sense of national identity, one that glorified the pre-Islamic past. He promulgated a more secular legal code, but left most gender and family issues under the religious courts. Educated women were granted a few new rights. Most dramatically, in 1936 he issued a formal decree ordering women to unveil, violently crushing sporadic resistance from conservative religious forces.

In 1941, the Allies deposed Reza Shah because of his government's pro-Axis sympathies, placing his son, who was twenty-two, on the throne as Muhammad Reza Shah. The years 1941 to 1953 saw the reemergence of democratic and leftist forces. During this decade, the pro-Soviet Tudeh Party also came onto the scene as a major force. The more open political climate allowed the *ulama* to reappear on the political scene as well. As a junior cleric, Khomeini published *Kashf al-Asrar* (The unveiling of secrets) in 1943, a book that advocated a return to clerical supervision of the entire legal code, the return of the veil, as well as "Quranic" physical punishment. At the same time, in an innovation for clerical politics, Khomeini wished to take over rather than dismantle the state apparatus built by Reza Shah.[4]

From 1951 to 1953, the left-of-center Prime Minister Muhammad Mossadeq headed a nationalist and social democratic coalition, the National Front, whose leadership included some nationalist clerics. Mossadeq's government was overthrown in 1953 during a confrontation with the United States and Britain. These two powers, outraged by Mossadeq's immensely popular nationalization of the vast holdings of the Anglo-Iranian Oil Company, conspired with the military and parts of the clergy. The CIA orchestrated a coup that overthrew Mossadeq and restored the shah to absolute power.[5] As feminist historians Parvin Paidar (1995) and Maryam Matin-Daftari (2001) have shown, an often ignored but crucial issue in the breakup of Mossadeq's coalition prior to the coup was the burgeoning movement for women's suffrage, which by 1952 had won voting rights for women in local elections.

After 1953, the previous policy of authoritarian modernization from above was attempted anew. On the one hand, the SAVAK, a U.S.-trained political police, ruthlessly crushed all opposition, while on the other, many urban, middle-class women obtained new rights. By the 1960s, thousands of women had gained university degrees and taken up professional, civil service, and corporate positions. At a cultural level, the media were filled with images of women in short skirts and other "provocative" clothing. This led not only the clerics, but also many first-generation university students to believe that "Western corruption" had infiltrated the Shi'ite Muslim culture.[6] As we saw in the previous chapter, the Shi'ite clergy, now led by Khomeini, organized protests against the shah's 1963 White Revolution. A major factor here was the *ulama*'s opposition to women's suffrage, which was nonetheless enacted. In the decade after 1963, the country experienced strong economic growth as well as burgeoning class polarization. In 1966, the regime established the Women's Organization of Iran (WOI). Within the context of the authoritarian state, the WOI fought for gender reforms, most importantly for the 1967 Family Protection Law. Female-initiated divorce now became possible and, with the law's 1975 amendments, so did a wife's limited right to child custody.

It was during the 1970s that Ali Shariati, and later Khomeini, began to win a mass following among urban, educated youth for the new, anti-imperialist form of Islamist politics discussed in the last chapter.[7] Crushed by the shah, who refused any type of democratic opening, the remnants of the National Front and the Tudeh either compromised with the regime or gravitated in the direction of the new Islamist opposition, which was allowed at least some refuge in the mosques and seminaries. A third but numerically much smaller element, the youthful leftists of the Mujahedeen and Fedayeen guerrilla movements, both (and especially the latter) influenced by Maoism, also played a role. Increasingly, the leftist discourses began to emphasize that the shah had been installed and was propped up by the United States. This led to the predominance of an anti-imperialist politics that saw the regime not as an indigenous growth, but as a creation of Western imperialism. In this period, secular nationalists and leftists argued that the shah's gender reforms had nothing to do with true equality and were instead an example of Western imperialist influence.[8]

A Conversation in Iran on Intellectuals and Revolution

Soon after his arrival in Iran, Foucault, accompanied by Voeltzel, traveled to several cities and met with various sectors involved in the revolutionary movement, including Ayatollah Shariatmadari. In a dialogue during his stay in Iran with the writer Baqir Parham, Foucault explained his fascination with the Islamist movement and his reasons for coming to Iran. He held that Europe and the West had witnessed two "painful" social upheavals in the past two centuries, movements in which philosophers and intellectuals had been implicated. The first were the liberal revolutions of the eighteenth and nineteenth centuries, which were influenced by French, English, and German philosophers. Locke, Rousseau, Kant, and later Hegel elaborated principles of good government. However, out of their hopes and aspirations for a balanced and just world came the monstrosity of industrial capitalism. Outbidding even the Marxists in his attack on capitalism, Foucault called it "the harshest, most savage, most selfish, most dishonest, oppressive society one could possibly imagine" ("Dialogue between Michel Foucault and Baqir Parham," app., 185).

The second upheaval, which Foucault called "tragic," was that of the socialist and communist movements of the twentieth century. Here again, out of the dreams of Marx and other socialists of the nineteenth century, out of their desire for a more rational society, had emerged a second monstrosity, totalitarian communism. Intellectuals were not directly responsible for either one of these painful events, but their writings had contributed to the process. Foucault held that even perfectly justifiable movements against colonialism or U.S. imperialism in Third World countries, as in Vietnam or especially Cambodia, "a struggle that was just and right at its foundation," had brought about highly authoritarian societies in which "freedom, a classless society, a non-alienated society," were completely absent ("Dialogue," app., 185).

Foucault told Parham that he was in Iran because he believed all philosophical and political principles had to be rethought. Every principle that had contributed to oppression had to be reexamined. He stated that in 1978 humanity was at "point zero" insofar as political thought was concerned and that Iran now offered a new hope ("Dialogue," app., 185). No "Western intellectual with [any] integrity" could afford to be indifferent to what was going on Iran, a nation that had reached "dead ends" on a number of social and political fronts and was doing precisely this type of rethinking (ibid., 185–86). The Iranian revolutionaries wished to create a society that was the absolute "other" in relation to the modern Western world. They wished to take "nothing from Western philosophy, from its juridical and revolutionary foundations. In other words, they try to present an alternative based on Islamic teachings" (ibid., 186). Foucault said that he was in Iran to observe and to learn. Having already immersed himself in the history of Western Christianity, he hoped to take back to Europe something from the revolutionary movement of Iran.

When Parham asked him about the role of religion in modern social and political thought, Foucault presented one of his clearest explanations of this issue. He suggested that revolutionary religious movements—whether the kind he was witnessing on the streets of Tehran in 1978, or those that

Europe had experienced as part of the English Revolution of the seventeenth century—could provide a new point of departure in thought and in actuality. Foucault reported that a number of people in Iran had told him that Marx's 1843 statement that religion was "the opium of the people" was either wrong or inapplicable to the case of this predominantly Shi'ite society. Khomeini was making similar statements during this period, as seen in his October 30 denunciation of Marxism aimed at Iranian students abroad: "They say Islam is opium! That religion as a whole is opium! . . . [When in fact] the prophet of Islam, and other Muslims, fought the wealthy. Now [the leftist opposition] has injected the thought [in people's minds] that it is the rich who introduced religion! All these machinations are so they could separate you from one another and from the Quran" (Khomeini 1999, 4:240).

Foucault indicated that there was something special about Shi'ism, here recalling some of the statements of the Islamist theoretician Ali Shariati. Foucault suggested that Shi'ism had played a key role in "inciting and fomenting political awareness" in Iran, as well as an "oppositional role" ("Dialogue," app., 186). Christianity had played a similar oppositional role at certain periods in European history, especially in religious and political movements of the early modern period. Religious movements had sometimes fought against feudal lords, against the state, and alongside the revolutionary peasantry. Here, Foucault singled out the Anabaptist movement and its role in the German peasant uprisings of the sixteenth century. He declared that the Anabaptists "rejected the power of the state, government bureaucracy, social and religious hierarchies, everything" (ibid., 186–87). They also supported the right to individual conscience, as well as the independence of small religious groups from the powerful centralized church. That was why these religious movements, as well as the history of religion and its connection to politics, had to be studied anew, to provide an alternative foundation for a new type of revolutionary social movement. Foucault concluded that Marx's statement on religion as the opium of the people was correct for a particular period in history, the rise of capitalism in Europe, when the state and the churches had colluded to induce workers to "accept their fate." However, in his view Marx's statement could not be regarded "as a general statement on all eras of Christianity, or on all religions" (ibid., 187).

Foucault's First Report from Iran: The Clerics and the Local Councils

Foucault's first report from Iran, "The Army—When the Earth Quakes," was published on September 28, 1978, in *Corriere della sera,* a few days after his return to France. (All of his reports in *Corriere* were datelined Tehran, even though they were actually written in Paris upon his return.) He was moved deeply by the grassroots local organizations that were established by the Shi'ite clergy for the relief of victims of an earthquake that had shaken the town of Tabas just before his arrival in Iran. He recounted an incident in 1968 after an earthquake at Ferdows in which twenty-six thousand people perished. Under the leadership of a Shi'ite cleric, the local community bypassed the relief team that had been sent by the royalist government:

> On one side, there was the town of administration, the Ministry of Housing, and the notables. But a little further away, the artisans and the farmers rebuilt their own town, in opposition to all these official plans. Under the direction of a cleric, they collected the funds, built and dug with their own hands, laid out canals and wells, and constructed a mosque. On the first day they planted a green flag. The new village is called Islamiyeh. Facing the government and against it, Islam: already ten years old. ("The Army—When the Earth Quakes," app., 189–90)

Foucault related this history to the present earthquake in Tabas. In 1978 as well, he reported, the mullahs succeeded in passing the word that the people should channel their relief contributions through them and not through the government. He viewed this as a highly important challenge to the modernist Pahlavi regime, which had in fact grossly mishandled the earthquake relief in Tabas. A British reporter noted at the time that the army stockpiled relief supplies, but refused inexplicably to distribute them. Meanwhile, the clerics had quickly organized effective relief programs, including field kitchens. People "in the streets all said how much the clergy were achieving, and how little the Government." However, this reporter also noted something missing entirely from Foucault's account, the presence of a "third faction," neither the army nor the clergy: "A third faction consisted of radical students from Mashhad University, led by the medical faculty. They were busy inoculating against typhus, carrying out first aid, and checking water supplies, but were quick to criticize the clergy's efforts as 'propaganda,' while being even more scathing about the official aid effort" (Cooper 1978, 38).

Grassroots associations have had a long and complex history in twentieth-century Iran, beginning with the Constitutional Revolution of 1906–11. On the one hand, when a new democratic space was created, whether in 1906–11 or 1941–53, many grassroots councils (*anjomans*) had put forward progressive, democratic, class-based, secular, or even feminist demands. On the other hand, ever since the Constitutional Revolution, orthodox Shi'ite clerics opposed to the democratic movement had also instituted their own grassroots councils, often called Islamiyehs. During the Constitutional Revolution, the Islamiyehs were highly conservative cultural institutions that provided the clerics with groups of vigilantes for confrontations with the Constitutionalists, who were supported by a large body of progressive mullahs.[9] The Islamiyehs opposed the demands of the more liberal and left-wing grassroots associations, and openly campaigned against Iran's non-Muslim minorities and secular democrats. In 1908, for example, the Islamiyeh council in Tabriz, Azerbaijan, had been the headquarters of forces opposed to the Constitutional Revolution. In 1953, Ayatollah Abulqasem Kashani had relied on similar grassroots Islamic societies in his struggle against the nationalist Mossadeq regime, overthrown that year by the CIA. Since his exile in 1963, Khomeini had encouraged the formation of thousands of Islamiyic Coalition Councils, which now existed throughout the country. These grassroots associations raised money for the needy, but they also propagated an authoritarian and intolerant interpretation of Islam. Unfortunately, Foucault seemed unaware of this checkered history.

The Shah and the "Dead Weight of Modernity"

Foucault's second article on Iran, published on October 1, shows a more obvious connection to larger themes in his work, especially his critique of modernity. Foucault's proposed title for this second piece, "The Dead Weight of Modernity," changed by the newspaper editors to a more modernist "The Shah Is a Hundred Years Behind the Times," suggested a substantial continuity between his overall critique of modernity and his writings on Iran. This was the article that Iranian students would translate into Persian and paste on the walls of Tehran University.

In this article, Foucault stressed the dependent nature of Iran's modernization and the limited success of Reza Shah in constructing a coherent policy of nationalism and secularism:

> [Reza Shah] had three objectives borrowed from Mustafa Kemal: nationalism, secularism, and modernization. The Pahlavis were never able to reach the first two objectives. As to nationalism, they neither could nor knew how to loosen the constraints of geopolitics and oil wealth. The father placed himself under English domination in order to stave off the Russian threat.

> The son substituted American political, economic, and military control for the English presence and for Soviet penetration. For secularism, things were equally difficult. ("The Shah Is a Hundred Years Behind the Times," app., 196)

While correct in his assessment that the modernization project of Reza Shah was far less successful than that of Ataturk in Turkey, Foucault seemed to deny the fact that Reza Shah had been able to generate a degree of support for his agenda inside Iran.

More significantly, Foucault's objection was not to the limited nature of this modernization, but to the very principle of modernization itself. He argued that as far as the Iranian people were concerned, "This modernization is now utterly rejected, not only because of the setbacks that have been experienced, but also because of its very principle. With the present agony of the regime, we witness the last moments of an episode that started almost sixty years ago, the attempt to modernize the Islamic countries in a European fashion" ("The Shah," app., 196–97). Foucault's reference above to "sixty years ago" was very important, for it was in May 1919, almost exactly sixty years earlier, that Ataturk had first begun to dominate Turkish politics. Thus, Foucault was dismissing an entire era in the Muslim world as a mere "episode" that was now ended. Besides the reforms in Turkey and Iran, this era had included radical educational and social reforms in the predominantly Muslim societies of Soviet-ruled Central Asia and reforms elsewhere in the Middle East from Egypt to Afghanistan. Where all this left secular-minded readers in the Muslim world was unclear.

Foucault also mocked "ambitious" Iranian technocrats, who "have not understood that in Iran today it is modernization that is a dead weight" ("The Shah," app., 197). The glue that kept together the Pahlavi regime, this strange contraption of despotism and modernization, was "corruption." It made everyone from the landed elite to the bazaar merchants discontented:

> It is true that all the great efforts undertaken by the regime since 1963 are now rejected, by all social classes. It is not only the big property owners who are discontented with the agrarian reform, but also the small peasants, who fall into debt as soon as they are granted a parcel of land, and are then forced to emigrate to the city. The artisans and the small manufacturers are discontented, because the creation of an internal market benefited mainly foreign products. The bazaar merchants are discontented because the current forms of urbanization suffocate them. The wealthy classes, who counted on a

> certain level of national industrial development and who can now only imitate the governing caste by placing their capital in California banks or in Parisian real estate, are also discontented. (Ibid., 196)

Before he left France, everyone had told him that "Iran is going through a crisis of modernization" in which members of its "traditional society" did not want to follow this pathway but instead to "seek shelter among a retrograde clergy" (ibid., 194).

As against this, Foucault concluded, implicitly situating himself in a postmodern position, modernization itself had become an "archaism":

> I then felt that I had understood that recent events did not signify a shrinking back in the face of modernization by extremely retrograde elements, but the rejection, by a whole culture and a whole people, of a *modernization* that is itself an *archaism*. The shah's misfortune is to have espoused this archaism. His crime is to have maintained, through a corrupt and despotic system, that fragment of the past in a present that no longer wants it. Yes, modernization as a political project and as a principle of social transformation is a thing of the past in Iran. ("The Shah," app., 195–96)

Thus, the shah's plan for secularization and modernization, handed down by his father Reza Shah, a brutal dictator known for "his famous gaze," was itself retrograde and archaic ("The Shah," app., 197). Here the allusion to his *Discipline and Punish* was quite clear: The Pahlavi shahs were the guardians of a modernizing disciplinary state that subjected all of the people of Iran to the intense gaze of their overlords, most recently through the SAVAK.

Some French intellectuals were more critical of the Islamist movement, however. One example is a September 30 opinion piece in *Le Monde* entitled "The Future Is Fundamentalist," by the novelist and poet Gabriel Matzneff, who had lived for many years in Tunisia and other Arab lands.[10]

Like Foucault, he acknowledged that Islamism was rapidly gaining headway, "from the sands of Libya to the cities of Iran." Unlike Foucault, however, Matzneff sounded a discordant note when he referred to "the severe beauties of the Quran," and pointed out that "the Quran and the Book of Leviticus have a family resemblance" (Matzneff 1978). Chapter 20 of the Book of Leviticus, it should be recalled, mandated the death penalty for adultery and homosexuality, as well as stoning to death for witchcraft. Although the negative tone of Matzneff's commentary was rather the exception (see Rezvani 1978; Bromberger and Digard 1978), few French commentators at this time were as uncritical of the Islamist movement as was Foucault. Several others (Jospin 1978; Gueyras 1978) gave far greater and more favorable attention to the secular opposition than he was doing in his reports in *Corriere della sera*.

"Faith against the Shah"

On September 20, during this first visit to Iran, Foucault traveled to Qom to meet Ayatollah Shariatmadari, at that time the most prominent member of the Islamist opposition operating openly inside the country. While he had allied himself with Khomeini by now, Shariatmadari was less supportive of the idea of an Islamic republic. For example, as a traditionalist, he refused to exclude the possibility of a constitutional monarchy. To be sure, he wanted some restrictions in the name of Islam, such as an end to coeducation and the sale of alcohol, but he also suggested that after the shah's departure, the clerics should retire from politics.[11] In late 1979, he began to express reservations about the nature of the new Islamist regime, after which he was sidelined and placed under house arrest.

According to one witness, his son Hasan Shariatmadari, members of the Committee for the Defense of Freedom and Human Rights were there on September 20 and were staging a sit-in at the Ayatollah's residence. Foucault arrived in the middle of all this and saw the police violently break up the sit-in (personal communication from Hasan Shariatmadari, December 12, 2002). Foucault himself may have been beaten up by the police (personal communication from Ahmad Salamatian, December 12, 2002). During Foucault's conversation with Shariatmadari, Mehdi Bazargan, the founder of the Committee for the Defense of Freedom and Human Rights and the future Prime Minister of the Islamic Republic, who like Shariatmadari was later pushed aside as too moderate, served as interpreter. In retrospect, Hasan Shariatmadari complained that Foucault had brushed aside the reservations his father had expressed during that conversation about the notion of an Islamic republic.

In "Tehran: Faith against the Shah," an October 8 article in *Corriere della sera* based largely on this meeting, Foucault noted that Iran's modernization policies had driven peasants into the cities. There, he noted perceptively, they often found only unemployment, eventually seeking refuge in the mosques:

> "At this point, what else do they have left?" is a frequent question. "They have been cut off from their traditional existence. To be sure, their life was narrow and precarious. However, by tearing them away from their farms

> and their workshops, by promising them a salary that can only be found in earth-moving or construction (and this only sporadically), one exposes them to permanent unemployment. Displaced in this manner, what refuge do they have except the one they can find in the mosque and the religious community?" ("Tehran: Faith against the Shah," app., 199)

Foucault continued to look at the dilemma of the displaced peasants and their gravitation toward the Islamist movement: "Where can protection be sought, how can *what one is* be found, if not in this Islam, which for centuries has regulated everyday life, family ties, and social relations with such care?" (ibid., 200; emphasis added). Here Foucault had fused the search for an authentic personal identity—finding "what one is"—with a return to traditional Islam.

Now he began to summarize the comments of an Iranian sociologist on Islam:[12] "Have not its rigor and its immobility constituted its good fortune? A sociologist told me of its 'value as a refuge.'" Foucault, inspired as he was by the mobilizing power of Shi'ite Islam, was critical of the Iranian sociologist's expression about Islam's "immobility": "It seems to me, however, that this man, who knew his country well, erred (out of discretion, perhaps, in front of the European that I am) by an excessive Westernness" ("Tehran," app., 200). At this point, something rather striking emerged in Foucault's writings on Iran. On the one hand, when confronted with an Iranian voice that was less religious, more leftist, or otherwise "Western," Foucault appeared to suggest that such thinking was inauthentically Iranian. On the other hand, he seemed to view as authentic those Iranians (including former leftists and secularists) who had come to support Khomeini uncritically. Foucault saw only this latter group as the true and indigenous Iranian voice. "I know more than one student, 'left-wing' according to our categories, who had written in big letters, 'Islamic Government,' on the placard on which he had written his demands and that he was holding up with outstretched arms" (ibid.).

Considering the angry sermons of the Shi'ite clergy, he compared them to those of the fifteenth-century Italian religious leader Girolamo Savonarola and of early Protestant revolutionaries:

> In the mosques during the day, the mullahs spoke furiously against the shah, the Americans, and the West and its materialism. They called for people to fight against the entire regime in the name of the Quran and of Islam. When the mosques became too small for the crowd, loudspeakers were put in the streets. These voices, as terrible as must have been that of Savonarola in Florence, the voices of the Anabaptists in Münster, or those

> of the Presbyterians at the time of Cromwell, resounded through the whole village, the whole neighborhood. ("Tehran," app., 200–201)

Foucault also took note of the rituals of martyrdom that were used to commemorate Muslim youth killed in the struggle against the regime: "White, red, and green lanterns were lit up after nightfall on big tree branches standing in front of hundreds of houses. It was the 'wedding bed' of the boys just killed" (ibid., 200). The colors were those of Iran's national flag, with green for Islam, while the "wedding chamber" for young men who died without marrying was a funerary custom common in Muslim communities.

Religion, Foucault argued, was the defining principle of the Iranian people, and their very mode of resistance:

> Do you know the phrase that makes the Iranians sneer the most, the one that seems to them the stupidest, the shallowest? "Religion is the opium of the people." Up to the time of the current dynasty, the mullahs preached with a gun at their side in the mosques. Around 90 percent of Iranians are Shi'ites. They await the return of the Twelfth Imam, who will create the reign of the true order of Islam on earth. While this creed does not announce each day that the great event will occur tomorrow, neither does it accept indefinitely all the misery of the world. When I met Ayatollah Shariatmadari (he is undoubtedly the highest spiritual authority in Iran today), one of the first sentences he uttered to me was: *"We are waiting for the Mahdi, but each day we fight for a good government."* Shi'ism, in the face of the established powers, arms the faithful with an unremitting restlessness. It breathes into them an ardor, wherein the political and the religious lie side by side. ("Tehran," app., 201; emphasis added)

However, he chose to ignore Shariatmadari's very carefully formulated phrase above, calling for "good government" now, while awaiting the eventual appearance of the Mahdi or savior, which was somewhat at variance with Khomeini's call for the immediate establishment of an Islamic government.

Foucault also seemed to see the clerics' sermons in 1978 as the unmediated expression of the popular will of the masses: "These men of religion are like so many photographic plates on which the anger and aspirations of the community are marked" ("Tehran," app., 202). In addition, Foucault extolled "the wisdom, and the exemplary sacrifices of the imams," who had been "persecuted by the corrupt government of the caliphs, these arrogant aristocrats who had forgotten the old egalitarian system of justice" (ibid.,

201). Not only was Foucault infatuated with the revolutionary rhetoric of militant Shi'ism, but he also parroted Shi'ite prejudices against Sunni Muslims. Among them was the claim that the Shi'ite imams (twelve descendents of the Prophet Muhammad, beginning with Ali) were all egalitarian religious leaders, whereas the early Sunni caliphs were all corrupt.

After much other praise for the Shi'ite imams and clerics, Foucault seemed finally to qualify his argument slightly, in an apparent attempt to avoid sounding naïve to his readers: "Let us not embellish things. The Shi'ite clergy is not a revolutionary force" ("Tehran," app., 202). He acknowledged that it was part of the establishment and noted that one of its number, Ayatollah Abulqasem Kashani, had opposed Mossadeq in 1953. He seemed to view this incident as an aberration, however, for he now repeated the explanation that the Islamists had evidently given him, that this violated the spirit of the rank-and-file clerics, who were "most often on the side of the rebels" (ibid., 202).

Shi'ism, he continued, was the very language of mass discontent and revolt, not only in 1978, but also throughout Iranian history:

> It is much more than a simple vocabulary through which aspirations, unable to find other words, must pass. It is today what it was several times in the past, the form that the political struggle takes as soon as it mobilizes the common people. It transforms thousands of forms of discontent, hatred, misery, and despairs into a *force*. It transforms them into a force because it is a form of expression, a mode of social relations, a supple and widely accepted elemental organization, a way of being together, a way of speaking and listening, something that allows one to be listened to by others, and to yearn for something with them at the same time as they yearn for it. ("Tehran," app., 202–3)

Unfortunately, he seemed unaware of the fact that Shi'ism was first imposed on the majority of the population as late as the Safavid dynasty of the sixteenth century. He also ignored the fact that, despite occasional clashes over influence and authority, religious institutions ostensibly remained committed to government rulers. Their challenges to the state had often been over social and political reforms that threatened to undermine existing class, religious, or gender hierarchies

Instead, Foucault continued in the same vein, suggesting that the mullahs were a deeply rooted, even "irreducible" force of opposition to established power, and not only in 1978: "Persia has had a surprising destiny. At the dawn of history, it invented the state and government. It conferred its models of state and government on Islam, and its administrators staffed the Arab Empire. But from this same Islam, it derived a religion that, throughout the centuries, never ceased to give an *irreducible* strength to everything from the depths of a people that can oppose state power" ("Tehran," app., 203; emphasis added). Here all qualifiers were removed, and the Shi'ite clergy stood alone as a popularly rooted force that had fought tyranny over the centuries. Additionally, in using the term *irreducible* to refer to Shi'ite Islam, Foucault seemed to make a philosophical point. As we will see below, he would employ the term *irreducible* at several crucial junctures in his writings on Iran, using it, for example, as an adjective referring to Khomeini. Two basic meanings were probably intended here: (1) Something that is irreducible cannot be reduced (essentialized) to something more basic, or split into constituent elements; thus, Islamism was not a mere ideology behind which lurked "real" economic or social contradictions, as a "reductionist" Marxist might suggest. (2) Something that is irreducible cannot easily be co-opted, subdued, or conquered, in the sense of a fortress that cannot be reduced by its enemies. And as we saw in chapter 1, the notion of irreducibility had already become a crucial aspect of Foucault's theory of resistance, articulated two years earlier in the *History of Sexuality*.

Foucault's Meeting with Ayatollah Khomeini and "Political Spirituality"

Almost immediately after Khomeini's arrival in France on October 6, Foucault went to see Bani-Sadr, hoping to be granted an interview with the Ayatollah. According to his biographer, Didier Eribon, "Foucault asked Bani-Sadr to explain to the ayatollah that it would be better to avoid denouncing the shah too violently because he would risk immediate expulsion" (1991, 285–86). Khomeini did in fact soften his language on this and other issues, as mentioned above. Some days later, Foucault was granted a meeting with Khomeini at his residence outside Paris:

> During a visit to Neauphles with Ahmad Salamatian and Thierry Mignon, Foucault witnessed a minor incident. A mullah from Khomeini's entourage wanted to prevent a German journalist from entering the yard because she was not veiled. Salamatian protested: "Is that the image you want to give of your movement?" The ayatollah's son and son-in-law intervened, reproaching the mullah for having been too zealous. The German journalist was allowed to enter. During their return trip in the car, Foucault said how impressed he had been, while in Iran, to see that wearing the veil was a political gesture; women who were not in the habit of wearing it insisted on putting it on to participate in demonstrations. (Eribon 1991, 286)

This brief visit seemed only to intensify Foucault's enthusiasm for Khomeini and the Islamist wing of the movement.

However, despite his attempts to project a more tolerant and moderate image of himself in his interviews at Neauphle-le-Château, even at this juncture Khomeini occasionally revealed the depth of his hostility toward the National Front, the Left, Iran's non-Muslim minorities (including Zoroastrians), and anyone whom he perceived as standing in the way of an Islamic government. In an October 8 address to Iranian students as the new school term opened, Khomeini denounced teachers who did not support his vision of revolution:

> If you see that your professors, your teachers, or leaders of the nation, are being diverted from their national and religious obligations, at the head of which obligation[s] is the uprooting of this decrepit regime, you must vehemently protest and *suggest to them the way of the nation, which is the way of God*. If they do not accept [argument], then avoid them and clearly explain their deviant ways to the innocent people. [Say] that [the teachers] are traitors to religion, to the nation, and to the country, that they want the shah and his owners, the international thieves, to continue their plundering and to keep the nation poor and backward. (Khomeini 1999, 3:486; emphasis added)

In an October 12 interview with the BBC, Khomeini hinted at the authoritarian pathway he had in mind for Iran, when he declared that he had no intention of restoring the 1906–7 Constitution. He termed it "an old and reactionary thing," adding, "Islamic law is the most progressive law" (3:514–15).

On October 26, again speaking in Persian, Khomeini castigated the regime for granting civil liberties to Zoroastrians, declaring that the shah's rule had

> resulted in the development of fire-worshipping [Zoroastrianism] and the strengthening of fire-worshippers and in the deepening of the foundations of injustice, especially in Iran. . . . Likewise, the Zoroastrians of the United States . . . thanked him. They wrote that "No other [leader] has supported and glorified our religion as you have." Now, all that will be over. Thank God our nation awakened, although somewhat late, and did not allow him to continue with such actions. (Khomeini 1999, 4:161–62)

Here, Khomeini was continuing his earlier attacks on Jews, Baha'is, and other non-Muslim Iranians.[13]

During this period, when the nationwide strikes began, Foucault decided to publish his views on Iran in French for the first time. Entitled "What Are the Iranians Dreaming About?" his article appeared on October 16 in the widely circulated leftist weekly, *Le Nouvel Observateur,* whose main editor, Jean Daniel, had been a friend of Foucault since the 1960s.[14] *Le Nouvel Observateur* dubbed Foucault its "special correspondent" in Iran. Alongside a photo of a contemplative Khomeini, presumably outside his new residence in France, the editors summarized Foucault's main point provocatively, underneath the title: "Perhaps the shah's rebellious subjects are in the process of searching for the thing that we have forgotten for so long in Europe: a political spirituality."

In the article, Foucault recounted a remark by an Iranian oppositionist: "They will never let go of us of their own will. No more than they did in Vietnam." Underlining Iran's strategic importance to Washington, Foucault added,

> I wanted to respond that they are even less ready to let go of you than Vietnam because of oil, because of the Middle East. . . .
>
> Will the Americans push the shah toward a new trial of strength, a second "Black Friday"? The recommencement of classes at the university, the recent strikes, the disturbances that are beginning once again, and next month's religious festivals, could create such an opportunity. The man with the iron hand is Moghadam, the current leader of the SAVAK. This is the back-up plan, which for the moment is neither the most desirable nor the most likely. ("What Are the Iranians Dreaming About?" app., 203)

Opposed to this system of power, Foucault wrote, was "an immense movement from below" that had faced down the shah's tanks. Its slogans included not only "Death to the Shah," but also "Islam, Islam, Khomeini, We Will Follow You" ("Iranians Dreaming," app., 204). Foucault described the current struggle in nearly mythic terms: "The situation in Iran can be understood as a great joust under traditional emblems, those of the king and the saint, the armed ruler and the destitute exile, the despot faced with the man who stands up bare-handed and is acclaimed by a people" (ibid.). Here there was the evocation of a cultural motif that captured the theatricality of the conflict, but remained outside history.

Foucault wrote that between the shah and the masses looking to Khomeini stood a group of compromisers, who wanted to confine the movement within modernist categories. To Foucault, here echoing the Islamist position, these included the secular Left, as well as forces close to the regime: "Whether advisers to the shah, American experts, regime technocrats, or groups from the political opposition (be they the National Front or more 'socialist-oriented' men), during these last weeks everyone has agreed with more or less good grace to attempt an 'accelerated internal liberalization,' or to let it occur" ("Iranians Dreaming," app., 203).

The "politicians" of the opposition, he wrote, thought that if the dictatorship were abolished, they would take control, and Khomeini would then recede into the background. These politicians thought Khomeini had no program, that he had come to temporary prominence because all political parties had been abolished since 1963. In attacking such assessments, Foucault was indeed reading the balance of forces much more correctly than most secular oppositionists and their Western supporters.

Foucault noted that he had been speaking not with "professional politicians" but with "religious leaders, students, intellectuals interested in the problems of Islam, and also with former guerrilla fighters who had abandoned the armed struggle in 1976 and had decided to work in a totally different fashion, inside the traditional society." He had found that these people were speaking not of "revolution," but most often of "an Islamic government" ("Iranians Dreaming," app., 205). Some specific features of Shi'ite Islam accounted for this massive support for Islamic politics, he concluded:

> Indeed, Shi'ite Islam exhibits a number of characteristics that are likely to give the desire for an "Islamic government" a particular coloration. Concerning its organization, there is an absence of hierarchy in the clergy, a certain independence of the religious leaders from one another, but a dependence (even a financial one) on those who listen to them, and an importance given to purely spiritual authority. The role, both echoing and guiding, that the clergy must play in order to sustain its influence—this is what the organization is all about. As for Shi'ite doctrine, there is the principle that truth was not completed and sealed by the last prophet. After Muhammad, another cycle of revelation begins, the unfinished cycle of the imams, who, through their words, their example, as well as their martyrdom, carry a light, always the same and always changing. It is this light that is capable of illuminating the law from the inside. The latter is made not only to be conserved, but also to release over time the spiritual meaning that it holds. Although invisible before his promised return, the Twelfth Imam is neither radically nor fatally absent. It is the people themselves who make him come back, insofar as the truth to which they awaken further enlightens them. (Ibid.)

Presumably, Foucault was drawing a contrast to the Catholic Church, which appointed its clerics from above, whereas leadership in Shi'ite Islam was based on education, training, financial base of support, and influence. In addition, Foucault suggested that all of this would lead to a more open society, noting that when he met Shariatmadari, the ayatollah "was surrounded by several members of the Committee on Human Rights in Iran" (ibid., 206).

Summarizing what a "religious leader" had told him about an "Islamic government," Foucault reported enthusiastically,

> One thing must be clear. By "Islamic government," nobody in Iran means a political regime in which the clerics would have a role of supervision or control. To me, the phrase "Islamic government" seemed to point to two orders of things.
>
> "A utopia," some told me without any pejorative implication. "An ideal," most of them said to me. At any rate, it is something very old and also very far into the future, a notion of coming back to what Islam was at the time of the Prophet, but also of advancing toward a luminous and distant point where it would be possible to renew fidelity rather than maintain obedience. In pursuit of this ideal, the distrust of legalism seemed to me to be essential, along with a faith in the creativity of Islam.

Foucault continued in this effusive manner:

> A religious authority explained to me that it would require long work by civil and religious experts, scholars, and believers, in order to shed light on all the problems to which the Quran never claimed to give a precise response. But one can find some general directions here: Islam values work; no one can be deprived of the fruits of his labor; what must belong to all (water, the subsoil)[15] shall not be appropriated by anyone. With respect to liberties, they will be respected to the extent that their exercise will not harm others; minorities will be protected and free to live as they please on the condition that they do not injure the majority; between men and women there will not be inequality with respect to rights, but difference, since there is a natural difference. With respect to politics, decisions should be made by the majority, the leaders should be responsible to the people, and each person, as it is laid out in the Quran, should be able to stand up and hold accountable he who governs. ("Iranians Dreaming," app., 206)

Foucault's critics would cite several of the above formulations.

In his own defense, in later debates Foucault would stress that he had also mentioned in this article that some of the above pronouncements were "not too reassuring." It is important, however, to specify the nature of his doubts, to wit: "The definitions of an Islamic government . . . seemed to me to have a familiar but, I must say, not too reassuring clarity. 'These are basic formulas for democracy, whether bourgeois or revolutionary,' I said. 'Since the eighteenth century now, we have not ceased to repeat them, and you know where they have led'" ("Iranians Dreaming," app., 206). Thus, Foucault's problem with the Islamist vision he had evoked above was not centered on women's rights or on the danger of a clerical authoritarianism. Instead, the danger he saw lurking underneath the Iranian upheaval was that of a liberal democracy. Apparently, his doubts flowed from his two decades of theoretical work exposing the confining and oppressive features of modern forms of political and social power that had grown up alongside liberal democracy.

Foucault also alluded to the Islamist movement as "a form of 'political will'" and to its spiritualization of politics: "I do not feel comfortable speaking of Islamic government as an 'idea' or even as an 'ideal.' Rather, it impressed me as a form of 'political will.' It impressed me in its effort to politicize structures that are inseparably social and religious in response to current problems. It also impressed me in its attempt to open a spiritual dimension in politics" ("Iranians Dreaming," app., 208). It was this element, "a spiritual dimension in politics," that was at the center of Foucault's interest in the Iranian Revolution. Also crucial here was another notion, that of the "political will" of the Iranian people, which he would soon describe as perfectly unified. He concluded the article by referring to the crucial place of "political spirituality" in Iran and the loss of such spirituality in early modern Europe. This was something, he wrote, "whose possibility we have forgotten ever since the Renaissance and the great crises of Christianity." Poised for the sharp responses he knew such views would receive in the highly charged world of Parisian intellectual debate, he said he could "already hear the French laughing" at such a formulation. But, he retorted, "I know that they are wrong" (ibid., 209). This evocation of "political spirituality" was surely intended to provoke controversy in France, a country whose political and intellectual culture was the most determinedly secular of any Western country.[16] What's more, Foucault had not limited his remarks to Iran, which would have been controversial enough to French readers, but also suggested that France itself had important lessons to learn from Iranian political spirituality.

The lack anywhere in the article of a sustained critique or even a questioning of Khomeinism was most striking. Even in this early period, when the repressive and obscurantist character of Khomeinism had not come out into the open, and during which many other leftist and liberal commentators were also expressing enthusiasm about the impending revolution in Iran, Foucault's writings stood out among those of his contemporaries for their uncritical enthusiasm for the Islamist movement of Iran.

The Debate with "Atoussa H.," an Iranian Woman of the Left

Foucault's suggestion that his *Le Nouvel Observateur* article would stir up controversy turned out to be correct, perhaps more so than even he had anticipated. One of his closest friends, the Gallimard editor Claude Mauriac, later recalled a private conversation in which he had expressed reservations to Foucault about his support for a "political spirituality." Mauriac recounted their conversation in his memoirs, in an entry for November 23, 1978:

> MAURIAC: I read your paper in *Nouvel Observateur*, but not without surprise, I must say. I speak of the last sentence [citing it]. FOUCAULT: And you laughed? You are among those that I could already hear laughing? MAURIAC: No . . . I only said to myself that as to spirituality and politics, we have seen what that gave us. FOUCAULT: And politics *without* spirituality, my dear Claude? (Mauriac 1986, 322–23)

This conversation indicates that even one of his closest friends had doubts about Foucault's stance on Iran. It also shows the degree to which Foucault's writings on Iran were part of a larger critique of modern secular culture, a critique that was grounded in a notion of political spirituality.

During these weeks, the Tehran University sociologist Ehsan Naraghi, whom Foucault had visited in September, wrote an opinion piece for *Le Monde*. Published on November 3, Naraghi's article expressed the then extremely popular wish for a return to the 1906–7 Constitution, which, he pointed out, "gave religious leaders the assurance of laws not in contradiction with Islam." At the same time, he hinted that he had some reservations concerning the proposal for an Islamic republic, adding that the constitution also "allowed political groups as well as all Iranians to take part in national life." While he did not say so openly, this suggested equal rights for non-Muslim minorities and secular groups. Arguing that "the Iranian people" had been "an example of tolerance for the Muslim world," Naraghi cautioned the religious leaders against "the error of attempting to destroy a Constitution that was founded on the separation of powers" (Naraghi 1978).

On November 6, *Le Nouvel Observateur* published excerpts of a letter from "Atoussa H.," a leftist Iranian woman living in exile in Paris, who took strong exception to Foucault's uncritical stance toward the Islamists. She declared: "I am profoundly upset by the untroubled attitude of French leftists toward the possibility of an 'Islamic government' that might replace the bloody tyranny of the shah." Foucault seemed "moved by the 'Muslim spirituality' that would advantageously replace, according to him, the ferocious capitalist dictatorship that is tottering today." Why, she continued, apparently referring to the 1953 overthrow of Mossadeq, must the Iranian people, "after twenty-five years of silence and oppression" be forced to choose between "the SAVAK and religious fanaticism"? Atoussa H. then brought in a well-known verse from the Quran on women, which reads, "Your wives are for you a field; come then to your field as you wish." This, she wrote, showed "clearly" that "the man is the lord, the wife the slave; she can be used at his whim; she can say nothing." Unveiled women were already being insulted on the streets, and Khomeini supporters had made clear that "in the regime that they wish for, women should behave or else be punished." With respect to Foucault's statements that ethnic and religious minorities would have their rights "on the condition that they do not injure the majority," Atoussa H. asked pointedly, "At what point do the minorities begin to 'injure the majority'?" ("An Iranian Woman Writes," app., 209).

Returning to the problematic notion of an Islamic government, Atoussa H. pointed to the brutal forms of justice in Saudi Arabia: "Hands and heads fall, for thieves and lovers." She concluded,

> It seems that for the Western Left, which lacks humanism, Islam is desirable . . . for other people. Many Iranians are, like me, distressed and desperate about the thought of an "Islamic" government. We know what it is. Everywhere outside Iran, Islam serves as a cover for feudal or pseudo-revolutionary oppression. Often also, as in Tunisia, in Pakistan, in Indonesia, and at home, Islam—alas!—is the only means of expression for a muzzled people. The Western liberal Left needs to know that Islamic law can become a dead weight on societies hungering for change. The Left should not let itself be seduced by a cure that is perhaps worse than the disease. ("Iranian Woman," app., 209–10)

This critique was extremely hard-hitting because it came from an Iranian who strongly opposed the regime from the Left, and who was very familiar with the key issues, especially those of gender, that Foucault had avoided in his writings on Iran.

Foucault, in a short rejoinder published the following week in *Le Nouvel Observateur*, made two arguments against Atoussa H. First, he said, she "did not read the article she criticizes," because he never claimed that Islamic spirituality was superior to the shah's dictatorship. Foucault mentioned that he had pointed to "several elements" in the Iranian upheaval that "did not seem to me to be very reassuring" ("Foucault's Response to Atoussa H.," app., 210). But he did not take the opportunity to detail what those elements were. In particular, he ignored the issues she had raised about women's rights.

His second argument was more substantive, however. What was "intolerable" about Atoussa H.'s letter, he wrote, was how it "merges together" all forms of Islam into one and then proceeded to "scorn" Islam as "fanatical." It was certainly prescient on Foucault's part to note as he did that "Islam as a political force is an essential one for our time and the coming years." But this very discerning prediction was seriously undercut by his utter refusal to share her critique of the implications of an Islamist politics, even with regard to Saudi Arabia. Instead, he concluded his rejoinder by lecturing Atoussa H.: "In order to approach [Islam] with a minimum of intelligence, the first condition is not to begin by bringing in hatred" ("Response to Atoussa H.," app., 210). While we are aware of no other public attacks in France on Foucault's Iran writings at this time, we should also note that, none of his supporters came publicly to his defense, as they had on several previous occasions when he had been attacked. In March and April 1979, once the Khomeini regime's atrocities against women and homosexuals got underway, this exchange would come back to haunt him.

Foucault's dismissive attitude toward Atoussa H. has made even some of his strongest supporters cringe. One of them later wrote of "this remarkably forceful rejection of a comment by an intelligent and concerned woman" (Stauth 1991, 266). The mystery about Atoussa H.'s identity has also led to some creative readings of their exchange by contemporary Iranian feminists. One of them, the visual artist Gita Hashemi, has focused on how *Le Nouvel Observateur* had shortened Atoussa H.'s letter,[17] also evoking Foucault's curt reply:

> There is the editor: Sitting at his desk, chopping chunks of Atoussa's letter, probably thinking them unimportant, perhaps irrelevant, definitely requiring too much space. Subjective, he (for it is quite likely that the editor is a man) must be thinking. Perhaps she has made stronger accusations, but I'll never know because the letter was not published in full. And here, in this room, I cannot help but ponder the power that vested the writer and the editor with the authority to cut her voice, to silence it, to decide what part of what she said could be heard and countered and what not. But this was the kind of theater

> that was the Revolution. Men talking. Behind closed doors, in print, on the airwaves. (Hashemi 2000, 30)

Her overall theme was the silencing of women, not only in Iran, but also across the world: "In what language haven't we been called stupid for daring to say what we think? . . . In all languages they veiled us: Body and Thought. Public and Private" (25).

November 1978: "The First Great Insurrection against the Global Systems"

During these same days, on November 5, *Corriere della sera* published another of Foucault's articles on Iran, "A Revolt with Bare Hands." Here he began by contrasting the Iranian Revolution to earlier ones in China, Cuba, and Vietnam, calling the Iranian movement "a tidal wave without a military leadership, without a vanguard,[18] without a party" (app., 211). He appealed to his readers' awareness that vanguardist movements had so often led to single-party dictatorships after a revolution's victory. But to disabuse those who might therefore link Iran in 1978 to the more spontaneous and diffuse student-worker revolt in France in 1968, Foucault quickly added that the Iranian Revolution was very different from what happened in France in 1968. This was "because the men and women who protest with banners and flowers in Iran have an immediate political goal: They blame the shah and his regime, and in recent days they are indeed in the process of overthrowing them" (ibid.).

Foucault argued that the success of the anti-shah movement lay in its ability to maintain a very broad coalition of highly diverse interests, including students, newly released political prisoners, oil workers, merchants of the bazaar, and even the new industrial sectors in a "clear, obstinate, almost unanimous will" behind a single clerical leadership:

> The revolt spread without splits or internal conflicts. The reopening of the universities could have put into the forefront the students, who are more westernized and more Marxist than the mullahs from the countryside. The liberation of over a thousand political prisoners could have created a conflict between old and new oppositionists. Finally, and most importantly, the strike by the oil workers could have, on the one hand, worried the bourgeoisie of the bazaar, and on the other hand, started a cycle of strictly job-oriented demands. The modern industrialized sector could have separated itself from the "traditional" sector (by immediately accepting pay raises—the government

> was counting on this). But none of this happened. ("Revolt with Bare Hands," app., 211)

Foucault again attacked the old secular opposition parties like the National Front and more generally "renewal of political life, including the political parties" (ibid., 212). Clearly, he was worried that a corrupt compromise might keep the regime in power.

However, it was more than that. What seemed to be at issue was the outright rejection of politics in any form. Foucault's position here mirrors that of the Islamist and the far leftist opposition, the latter including groups like the Mujahedeen and the Fedayeen, who wished to avoid a "compromise" solution at all costs. He especially applauded the way that all concrete political questions were being postponed so that the "political maneuvering" of parties could not take over the movement ("Revolt with Bare Hands," app., 212). Since the clerics were supposedly a direct expression of the "collective will," presumably Islamist politics alone served to assure a fully just and democratic outcome. He castigated the liberal democratic political process and its "politics." Many before Foucault had described mass revolutionary movements as expressions of an undifferentiated collective will, but it is rather surprising to find such language in the writings of a philosopher so identified with the concepts of difference and singularity. Evidently, in conceptualizing Iranian society and culture as a site of radical difference and singularity vis-à-vis Western Europe, Foucault had allowed this sense of dichotomy to overwhelm any effort to discern difference and singularity—whether of class, gender, ethnicity, or sexual orientation—within Iranian society itself.

Again and again, Foucault applauded the ways in which Khomeini and the Islamist leadership inside Iran had kept the movement outside "politics" and pushed aside the demands of the secular parties in order to center everything on the single issue dear to the clerics, an "Islamic republic":

> Ayatollah Khomeini and the clerics who follow him want to force the shah's departure solely through the strength of the people's movement that they have organized, unconnected to the political parties. The clerics have forged, or in any case sustained, a collective will that has been strong enough to hold at bay even the most police-ridden monarchy in the world. . . . Khomeini has just this very morning proposed a different type of referendum. It would be held after the shah is forced out solely by the pressure of the ongoing movement, and it would center on the establishment of an "Islamic government." The political parties would then find themselves in a very embarrassing position. These parties would either have to reject one of the essential themes of the

> people's movement. (The politicians would then be opposed to the religious leaders and would certainly not win.) Or they would have to bind their own hands in advance by accepting a form of government under which the political parties would have precious little room for maneuver. ("Revolt with Bare Hands," app., 212–13)

The last alternative mentioned above is of course what happened in the early days of the Islamic Republic, in spring 1979, after the March 30–31 referendum on an Islamic republic was ratified. Soon, all political parties in Iran had to prove their "Islamic" credentials to be authorized, a situation that still exists today. In early November of 1978, as Foucault was writing this article, he noted the hegemonizing aims of Khomeini's movement, but seemed not to see any danger in them. Moreover, he actually applauded the hegemony of the Islamists as a break with the politics of modernity, whether liberal or socialist.

Corriere della sera published another of his articles, "The Challenge to the Opposition," two days later, on November 7. In this article, Foucault once again employed the term *irreducible,* now concerning Khomeini himself: "The shah finds himself up against the religious leaders, the mullahs, and the *irreducible ayatollah*" (app., 215; emphasis added). On November 5, later dubbed "Black Sunday," uprisings broke out in Tehran and other cities. Crowds attacked and set fire to police stations and government buildings. In a dramatic gesture of defiance, they collected pictures of the shah from these offices and burned them on the streets in big bonfires. As mentioned earlier, on November 6, Prime Minister Sharif-Imami abruptly resigned and was replaced by General Azhari, but this did not stem the tide of revolt.[19]

November 1978: Foucault's Second Trip to Iran

Before his second trip to Iran on behalf of *Corriere della sera* from November 9 to November 15, Foucault had another lengthy meeting with Bani-Sadr, who recalled, "He wanted to understand how this revolution was able to be produced, developing with no reference to any foreign power, and stirring up an entire nation, despite the distance between towns and the difficulties of communication. He wanted to reflect on the notion of power" (cited in Eribon 1991, 286).

In his next article, "The Revolt in Iran Spreads on Cassette Tapes," published in *Corriere della sera* on November 19, Foucault reported on the deepening revolt and especially the role of new media in the revolution. He wrote glowingly of Khomeini, referring to him again as an "old saint" (app., 217).

During this second visit to Iran, Foucault met with two groups of workers who were involved in what were by then ongoing nationwide strikes against the regime. These were, on the one hand, the relatively well-off and westernized airline pilots and flight attendants, and on the other, blue-collar workers who were laboring in the far harsher environment of the Abadan Oil Refinery. Again, he found what he had previously termed a "collective will," now going so far as to refer to a universal "love" for Khomeini:

> The point of connection is found outside of the country, outside of the political organizations, outside of all possible negotiations. This is in Khomeini, in his inflexible refusal to compromise and in *the love that everyone individually feels for him*. It was impressive to hear a Boeing pilot say in the name of his workmates: "You have in France the most precious thing that Iran has possessed for the last century. It is up to you to protect it." The tone was commanding. It was even more impressive to hear the strikers of Abadan say: "We are not particularly religious." "Whom do you trust then? A political party?" I asked. "No, no one." "A man?" I asked. "No, no one, except Khomeini, and he alone." ("Revolt in Iran Spreads," app., 218; emphasis added)[20]

Foucault mentioned the Marxist groups involved in the Abadan strike, but only in passing. He also noted, without comment, the strikers' "continual call for the foreigners to leave" Iran, here mentioning not only "American technicians" and "French air hostesses," but also "Afghan laborers." Foucault might have asked what the latter group had to do with Western hegemony.[21]

He ended this article with the use of cassette tapes by the Islamists to spread their message. He termed these cassettes "the tool *par excellence* of counter-information," before launching into a reverie with lyrical overtones:

> But one can find, outside the doors of most provincial mosques, tapes of the most renowned orators at a very low price. One encounters children walking down the most crowded streets with tape recorders in their hands. They play these recorded voices from Qom, Mashhad, and Isfahan so loudly that they drown out the sound of cars; passersby do not need to stop to be able to hear them. From town to town, the strikes start, die out, and start again, like flickering fires on the eve of the nights of Muharram. ("Revolt in Iran Spreads," app., 219–20)

Foucault's last article in his fall 1978 series for *Corriere della sera*, "The Mythical Leader of the Iranian Revolt," appeared on November 26. Not so much a reporting on events as a theoretical analysis of the significance of the revolution, this article underlined what Foucault saw as its deeply radical character and pointed to how the revolutionaries believed that the departure of the shah and the establishment of an Islamist regime would solve their social, economic, and political problems.

Foucault made five astute observations about the nature of the revolutionary movement in Iran: (1) that the Iranian Revolution was not a cultural movement aimed at a "liberation of desires" in the tradition of the 1960s movement in the West; (2) that the vast antiregime coalition held together because its objective was defined so narrowly; (3) that Khomeini was a consummate political leader, since his amorphous, down-to-earth, and at the same time purposely obfuscatory discourse allowed different groups to assume that their respective objectives would be realized once the shah was overthrown; (4) that this seemingly antimodern revolution relied on modern means of communication (tape recorders, overseas radio broadcasts, newspapers) to disseminate its ideas; (5) that a blending of tradition and modernity, of modern means of communication with centuries-old rituals of penitence, made it possible to paralyze the modern authoritarian police state of the Pahlavis, with hundreds of thousands of demonstrators in the streets, as well as a general strike.

Foucault concluded that the Iranian Revolution was beyond politics, an expression of a totally unified society that rooted itself in thousand-year-old cultural traditions:

> This movement has no counterpart and no expression in the political order.
>
> The paradox, however, is that it constitutes a *perfectly unified collective will.* It is surprising to see this immense country, with a population distributed around two large desert plateaus, a country able to afford the latest technical innovations alongside *forms of life unchanged for the last thousand years,* a country that is languishing under censorship and the absence of public freedoms, and yet demonstrating an extraordinary unity in spite of all this. . . . Somewhat like the European students in the 1960s, the Iranians want it all, but this "all" is not one of a "liberation of desires." This political will is one of breaking away from all that marks their country and their daily lives with the presence of global hegemonies. ("Mythical Leader," app., 222; emphasis added)

Foucault assured his readers that there was no danger in this because "there will not be a Khomeini party; there will not be a Khomeini government" (ibid.).

This of course turned out to be a serious error of political judgment, albeit one shared by many others on the Left, both inside and outside Iran. However, one could argue that there was an equally important theoretical problem in the above passage, not unconnected to Foucault's overall philosophical stance. In referring to "forms of life unchanged for the last thousand years," Foucault seemed to fall into what Sartre had once called "the rejection of history."[22] There were also some unfortunate overtones here of the Orientalist discourse of an unchanging "East."

Foucault recognized the global potential of the Islamist movement and the possibility that it would become an example for many other predominantly Muslim countries of the Middle East, North Africa, and South Asia. The Iranian Revolution was "perhaps the first great insurrection against global systems, the form of revolt that is the most modern and the most insane" ("Mythical Leader," app., 222). He deemed the Iranian Revolution "insane," because it transgressed the Western borders of rationality. Perhaps, as Foucault had expressed the hope in *Madness and Civilization*, such a transgression, not only in the realm of discourse, but also in reality, could break down the binary logic of modernity. Finally, a question arises concerning his characterization of the Islamist movement as "the form of revolt that is the most modern." Was he attempting to redefine and reappropriate the concept of modernity by suggesting that there could be alternative forms of modernity—not the Western (or communist) ones that had become "archaic," but new Eastern ones that were rejoining spirituality and politics?

Maxime Rodinson's Critique of Foucault: Khomeinism as a "Type of Archaic Fascism"

While many prominent French intellectuals had become caught up in the enthusiasm of the Iranian upheaval in late 1978, none, to our knowledge, followed Foucault in siding with the Islamists against the secular Marxist or nationalist Left. Others with more background in Middle East history were less sanguine altogether, notably the leading French specialist on Islam, Maxime Rodinson. A historian who had worked since the 1950s in the Marxian tradition, Rodinson was the author of the classic biography *Muhammad* (1980) and of *Islam and Capitalism* (1973). He had strong leftist credentials and was also one of the most prominent French supporters of the Palestinian cause.[23]

Rodinson's prescient three-part article entitled "The Awakening of Islamic Fundamentalism [*Intégrisme*]?" appeared on the front page of *Le Monde* beginning on December 6, 1978, and was later published in English as "Islam Resurgent?"[24] As he indicated some years later, in this article he "wanted to respond to Foucault," especially to his evocation of a "political spirituality." However, Rodinson chose not to name Foucault, writing later that he had carried out his critique "more or less implicitly" ("Critique of Foucault on Iran," app., 271).[25] For those in France who had followed Foucault's writings on Iran, however, Rodinson's references in this December 1978 article were clear enough. This was especially the case when he referred polemically to "those who come fresh to the problem in an idealistic frame of mind" and to "Europeans convinced of the vices of Europe and hoping to find elsewhere (why not in Islam?) the means of assuring a more or less radiant future" ("Islam Resurgent?" app., 233 and 236). Despite Rodinson's obvious differences with Foucault here, they agreed on one point at least: Iran's revolutionary movement had a quite different character from that of previous leftist or nationalist revolutions.

It was a mark of Rodinson's stature as France's leading expert on the Islamic world that these articles received more space than any other opinion piece that *Le Monde* published on Iran during the months before and after the revolution.[26] His series poured cold water on the hopes of many on the Left for an emancipatory outcome in Iran. He began by mentioning the new Islamist military regime in Pakistan, also pointing to the "spectacular excesses" with which Quranic law had been recently applied in Saudi Arabia and Libya ("Islam Resurgent?" app., 223). Over the last few centuries, various expressions of fundamentalism had continually emerged in the Islamic world, he wrote. As against modern Western Europe, he added, "religious law remains the supreme authority in the eyes of the masses" (ibid., 224). In the West, numerous schisms and other intellectual currents had challenged the hegemony of the Catholic Church from the early modern period onward. However, he wrote, such an evolution, present for a while in the Islamic world as well, was "brought to a halt within Islam in the eleventh century by the vigorous Sunni reaction," here referring to the attacks on the writings of the neo-Aristotelians Farabi (al-Farabi) and Avicenna and the ascendancy of orthodoxy (ibid., 225).

As a result, a strict moralism that blamed societal problems on a lack of piety among the leaders had not receded. Instead, attacked by the Christian world during the Crusades, then by the Mongols and the Turks, and most recently by Western imperialism in the last two centuries, Islam, he wrote, had come to see itself as embattled. It viewed outside threats in a manner that "can only be compared either with Catholic paranoia in the nineteenth century in the face of increasing decline of religion (supposedly inspired by the Judeo-Protestant-Masonic conspiracy, led by Satan), or with the analogous fears and obsessions felt by the communist world" ("Islam Resurgent?"

app., 226). He noted that a small part of the educated classes in the Islamic world had become, under Western influence, more skeptical in recent years, quickly adding:

> But the conversion of these people to such Westernizing trends has reinforced the attachment to Islam, in its most rigidly traditional form, among the more numerous masses. The poor, driven to the limit of famine or wretched subsistence, direct their anger and recrimination against the privileges of the rich and powerful—their ties with foreigners, their loose morality, and their scorn of Muslim injunctions, the most obvious signs of which are the consumption of alcohol, familiarity between the sexes, and gambling. (Ibid.)

This included attacks on "the places of worship of 'heretics' or non-Muslims" (ibid.). Here, there was an acknowledgment of the deep oppression and anger of the masses, but, in strong contrast to Foucault, there was also an analysis of the retrogressive features of Islamism.

Since the nineteenth century, continued Rodinson, much of the Muslim elite had been attracted to new ideologies such as nationalism or socialism. However, the masses often reinterpreted these ideologies in religious terms: "It happened that foreign domination was the work of infidels and that the exploiters were infidels or else one's fellow countrypeople in the pay of infidels" ("Islam Resurgent?" app., 227). However, there also had been instances when significant parts of the population had been touched by modernizing ideas. As Rodinson also argued: "In areas of the Arab East where there were religious minorities, the national and social struggles were often fought in common by Muslims, Christians, and (until quite recently) Jews" (ibid.). However, these secular nationalist tendencies had lost ground in recent years.

Additionally, Rodinson reviewed the checkered results of secular Arab nationalist movements in the post—World War II period. In 1978, the rulers of predominantly Muslim countries were often attracted to Western lifestyles and technology. However, the more religious majority was incensed by what it considered to be the Westerners' "impious morality, their debauchery and drunkenness," and "their bad example regarding the equality of the sexes, if not indeed female domination" ("Islam Resurgent?" app., 229). Because of this, nationalism in the Muslim world had become more and more Islamicized. Islam's persistent traditionalism had also strengthened the notion of male domination: "As with Latin Catholicism in the past, for example, religious tradition can be exploited in order to dominate the sex which the males unquestioningly consider to be weak and subordinate" (ibid., 230). Rodinson harbored no illusions about an Islamist government and saw it as leading straight to despotism. Islamism had similarities not to progressive nationalism but to fascism: "*The dominant trend is unquestionably a type of archaic fascism*. By this I mean a wish to establish an authoritarian and totalitarian state whose political police would brutally enforce the moral and social order" (ibid., 233; emphasis added).

Citing the well-known historian of Iran Nikki Keddie,[27] Rodinson contrasted Sunni Islam, long dominated by the state, with Iranian Shi'ism. Already in the 1906 Constitutional Revolution, clerics had sided for a period with secular revolutionaries against the state. The opposition to the shah, as well as similar movements for democracy in other Muslim lands had again become interested in an alliance with the clerics. Rodinson termed this "a provisional alliance against one form of despotism which usually numbered among its members people dreaming of another form of despotism" ("Islam Resurgent?" app., 235). He pointed to specific ways in which the ideology of an Islamic state carried with it many reactionary features:

> the minimum Muslim fundamentalism, according to the Quran, requires the cutting off of a thief's hand and the halving of a woman's inheritance. In returning to tradition, as the men of religion require, anyone caught drinking wine must be whipped, and an adulterer either whipped or stoned. . . . Nothing is easier or more dangerous than this time-honored custom of dubbing your adversary an "enemy of God." (Ibid., 235–36)

He concluded by addressing the notion of an Islamic Left. The problem with such a notion was that the same ideology that opposed America or the West also exerted "pressure to maintain an archaic moral order" (ibid., 238). Bringing to bear the perspectives of historical materialism, he wrote: "It is astonishing, after centuries of common experience, that it is still necessary to recall one of the best-attested laws of history. Good moral intentions, whether or not endorsed by the deity, are a weak basis for determining the practical policies of states" (ibid., 237).

These articles by Rodinson were published not in specialist journals but on the front page of *Le Monde* and were thus available to the broad French public. They, and the doubts expressed by others about the events in Iran, would have a strong effect on the future response within France to Foucault's writings on Iran. However, most French commentators continued to be far more sanguine about the revolution. On December 30, the same day that Bakhtiar accepted the prime ministership, the historian Jacques Julliard published an opinion piece on religion and politics in *Le Nouvel Observateur*, of which he was also an editor. Perhaps he was responding to Rodinson. The title, "Walking on Both Legs," alluded to the familiar image of Western culture as standing on two legs, the Greco-Roman rationalist tradition and the Christian one (Julliard 1978). Julliard's main point was to question Enlightenment and Marxist notions of religion as an inherently reactionary force. Pointing to Pope John Paul II's impact on the movement for democracy in Poland, to Alexander Solzhenitsyn's Christian-based critique of the Soviet Union, to Latin American liberation theology, and especially to the recent events in Iran, Julliard wrote that an "extraordinary situation" had arisen, one where "religious freedom has again become one of the touchstones of human freedom and dignity." He called the Polish version of these developments "a major scandal" for "arrogant Marxist thought, the worthy and legitimate heir of the Enlightenment." Without mentioning Foucault's controversial October *Nouvel Observateur* article that had concluded with a call for "spiritual politics," Julliard nonetheless came close to Foucault's position. He did so when he wrote, using the two legs analogy: "To me, the primacy of the spiritual, and the importance and independence of the political, would seem to constitute a two-fold and inseparable rule for any social organization sincerely interested in escaping the slide toward totality." In calling for the "independence of the political," however, Julliard was expressing a note of caution that had been lacking in Foucault's deliberately provocative earlier article.

Ashura, the tenth day of Muharram, fell on December 11, 1978. By this time, the Islamists had proceeded to transform the traditional processions of Muharram into a formidable political weapon. At the invitation of Ayatollah Taleqani, over a million people participated in the demonstrations throughout Iran. Participants became actors in a massive reenactment of the Ta'ziyeh: "Instead of inflicting wounds on their bodies in the traditional way, they stood ready to expose themselves to bayonets and bullets. Those in the vanguard, who were totally ready for martyrdom, would wear symbolic burial shrouds to show their willingness to sacrifice their lives" (Chelkowski and Dabashi 1999, 83).

On January 4, 1979, at the Guadeloupe economic summit, leaders of the Western powers and Japan asked the shah to leave Iran. A day later, as the army was beginning to fracture, the United States sent General Robert E. Huyser, who knew much of the officer corps personally, on a special mission to Iran. The purpose was twofold: (1) prevention of a pro-shah coup, since the United States regarded the shah's situation as hopeless and thought Huyser's efforts might smooth U.S. relations with the new regime; and (2) safeguarding sensitive U.S. military equipment. As millions celebrated in the streets, the shah left the country on January 16, and the large army he had created "melted like snow" (Milani 1998, 251). From exile, Khomeini immediately established a secret Revolutionary Council that acted as a shadow government. U.S. Attorney General Ramsey Clark now met with Khomeini in Paris and recognized the obvious by announcing that there could be no resolution to the Iranian crisis without the participation of Khomeini in a new government ('Aqeli 1993, 2:397).

As the level of mass participation in Iran reached its zenith during the first weeks of January 1979, many French intellectuals became more enthusiastic about the Iranian Revolution. These included Matzneff, who, as we saw earlier, had initially expressed more skepticism. In a January 13 opinion piece in *Le Monde* entitled "L'autel contre le trône" (The altar against the throne), Matzneff contrasted the political irrelevance of European religious leaders to the way in which the Shi'ite clergy of Iran had been able to galvanize a mass movement. Referring to the prominent scholar of Islam Louis Massignon's notion that Shi'ism was marked by "the desire for justice on earth and the thirst for eternal life," he concluded that if this was so, "we should all, I hope, consider ourselves a little bit Shi'ite" (Matzneff 1979). Similar sentiments were voiced by the scholar of religion Jacques Madaule (1979).

Nonetheless, amid the enthusiasm some discordant voices could still be heard on the Left, both inside and outside Iran. The noted philosopher Mahmoud Enayat (1979) warned of an incipient dictatorship. On January 19, the Fedayeen, which had grown considerably in recent months, issued an open letter to Khomeini referring to numerous physical attacks on secular, anti-shah groups by Islamists. The Fedayeen warned that "if the purpose of appealing to Islam . . . is the repressing of every opposing thought, form, and opinion . . . we are certain every liberationist patriot will condemn it, and we believe the people will also rise to expose it because they see it as a ploy of imperialism and reaction" ("People's Fedayi" 1979, 31). While this letter was published in Persian, Agence France Press also reported on January 21 that ten thousand secular leftists had marched in Tehran, chanting that they "had not emerged from the dictatorship of the shah to fall into an Islamic dictatorship" ("Marxist Demonstration" 1979, 32).

In France, the prominent historian Emmanuel Le Roy Ladurie now entered the debate, pointing to troubling parallels between the Iran's Islamists and some harshly intolerant movements in Western history. Le Roy Ladurie had been strongly influenced by structuralism, although he was closer to the Annales School. Like Foucault, he was a professor at the prestigious Collège de France. In an opinion piece in *Le Nouvel Observateur* of January 22, he wrote, "The Iranian paradox is the alliance of forces that could be considered broadly 'reactionary' on the one hand, and as 'progressive,' on the other"

(Le Roy Ladurie 1979). Referring to Khomeini and the clerics as advocates of "a chauvinist Islamism," Le Roy Ladurie argued that the Shi'ite clerics of 1979 shared many characteristics with French Catholic fanatics of the late sixteenth century. Organized into a Catholic League, they had reacted violently against the continuing threat of Protestantism, even after the horrific St. Bartholomew Day massacre of thousands of Protestants in 1572. By 1588, the League had succeeded in mobilizing large sectors of the urban population. In this and in their "democratic demands," the Iranian Islamists resembled the League. "The organization of the masses, the dictatorship of secret revolutionary committees, the participation of the common people, but also the middle classes—bazaar merchants in particular—accentuate the resemblance," he added. He concluded by referring to "the figure of Khomeini, this lethargic and dangerous equivalent of our hysterical preachers of the 1580s." Such strong warnings were the exception during the heady weeks of January 1979, however.

Surveying Foucault's writings in the months up to Khomeini's triumphal return on February 1, and comparing them to those of other French intellectuals at the time, we find that he had carved out a nearly unique and very problematic position for himself. Foucault realized that the movement against the shah included many diverse elements, but found Khomeini's ability to maintain the anti-shah focus remarkable. He also saw the possibility that the Islamist movement, through its use of modern means of communication, might develop a global reach. Finally, he celebrated the Islamist movement as a rejection of a European form of modernity. He hoped that what he called its "insane" transgressive discourse would fracture the boundaries of a "rational" modernity. If this could happen, Foucault argued, the Iranian Revolution might become the harbinger of similar movements in both the East and the West. In this sense, he had no serious qualms about the way in which the Islamists had come to dominate the revolutionary movement, displacing the Marxist and nationalist Left. In the next chapter, we examine the public controversy that broke out in March and April 1979 over Foucault's uncritical embrace of the Iranian Islamists.

Chapter 4

Debating the Outcome of the Revolution, Especially on Women's Rights

Foucault and Rodinson Respond to Khomeini's Assumption of Power

Khomeini, who was now addressed by the honorific title, "Imam,"[1] returned to Iran on February 1, 1979, an event celebrated on the streets of Tehran by about three million people. He went directly to the Paradise of Zahra Cemetery, where he outlawed the monarchy, the *majlis*, and the senate. He labeled the visual media—television, radio, and cinema—"centers of moral corruption." Addressing the army, he called on the soldiers to choose "Islam" and national independence. Iran was freeing itself from a foreign yoke, he said (Khomeini 1999, 6:15). As Khomeini moved to seize power from the shah's last prime minister, Shapour Bakhtiar, the French press began to express greater wariness about Iran. On February 3, *Le Monde* editorialized, "The concern and sometimes the exasperation of the secular forces and the Left are beginning to express themselves in the face of the emergence of an Islamic Republic that, despite its noble declarations, could well prove to be intolerant and oppressive" ("Le tout ou rien" 1979). *Le Monde* also carried a report on the widespread, organized persecution of Baha'is.

On February 6, Khomeini formed a provisional government headed by the moderate Islamist Mehdi Bazargan. This gave the clerical regime in formation a relatively benign face, prompting many to predict that Khomeini, already 77, would now retreat to a contemplative life, allowing a broad coalition government involving secular as well as religious parties to rule. On February 8, a million people, including hundreds of soldiers, filled the streets of Tehran in a demonstration calling for Bakhtiar to resign immediately in favor of the government Khomeini had appointed. As the military started to crack, Air Force technicians began to back Khomeini openly, while the Immortals, an elite military unit, continued to resist. Barricades now went up in the streets, and on February 11, the final remnants of resistance by the old regime collapsed, as Bakhtiar resigned and went into hiding.

It was at this point, on February 13, that Foucault's last article for *Corriere della sera*, "A Powder Keg Called Islam," appeared. He wrote that until now, it had been hard to label the events in Iran a revolution in the traditional sense of the word. With the barricades in the streets, "a known figure finally appears," he suggested ("Powder Keg," app., 239). Mocking French Marxist discourse, he continued:

> Today, we feel as though we are in a more familiar world. There were the barricades; weapons had been seized from the arsenals; and a council assembled hastily left the ministers just enough time to resign before stones began shattering the windows and before the doors burst open under the pressure of the crowd. History just placed on the bottom of the page the red seal that authenticates a revolution. Religion's role was to open the curtain; the mullahs will now disperse, taking off in a great flight of black and white robes. The decor is changing. The first act is going to begin: that of the struggle of the classes, of the armed vanguards, and of the party that organizes the masses, and so forth. (Ibid.)

Foucault's dismissal of predictions that the secular nationalist or Marxist Left would now take center stage would certainly prove to be accurate.

Even more important, he noted, a new type of revolutionary movement had emerged, one that would have an impact far beyond Iran's borders:

> Maybe its historic significance will be found, not in its conformity to a recognized "revolutionary" model, but instead in its potential to overturn the existing political situation in the Middle East and thus the global strategic equilibrium. Its singularity, which has up to now constituted its force, consequently threatens give it the power to expand. *Thus, it is true that as an "Islamic" movement, it can set the entire region afire, overturn the most unstable regimes, and disturb the most solid ones. Islam—which is not simply a religion, but an entire way of life, an adherence to a history and a civilization—has a good chance to become a gigantic powder keg, at the level of hundreds of millions of men.* Since yesterday, any Muslim state can be revolutionized from the inside, based on its time-honored traditions. ("Powder Keg," app., 241; emphasis added)

Here again, Foucault showed an extraordinarily keen insight into Islamism's global reach. During the coming years Islamist movements would stage uprisings and/or gain wide followings in a number of key countries in the Muslim world. Additionally, Foucault argued that its global impact would surpass that of Marxism, which was not as deeply rooted in society, extolling "the dynamism of an Islamic movement, something much stronger than the effect of giving it a Marxist, Leninist, or Maoist character" (ibid., 241). But, as in his previous writings on Iran, there was no note of criticism, or even hesitation. Instead, the tone was almost laudatory.

By mid-February, Iran had reached the center stage of world politics. This prompted a torrent of commentaries by French intellectuals in the next couple of months.[2] The debate reached a crescendo in March and April, in the wake of the feminist protests in Iran and abroad against Khomeini's order that women re-veil. While Foucault remained silent about Iran during these feminist protests, his earlier writings on Iran were now attacked by feminist, leftist, and liberal intellectuals.

With Khomeini now beginning to consolidate his rule, Rodinson followed up his earlier critique of Foucault on Iran with an article in the February 19 issue of *Le Nouvel Observateur* entitled "Khomeini and the 'Primacy of the Spiritual.'" Although Rodinson stated that he was responding to Jacques Julliard's article, discussed in the previous chapter, which had ended with a notion similar to that of Foucault, "the primacy of the spiritual," his real but still unacknowledged target was Foucault.[3] As in his December *Le Monde* series, Rodinson warned of the dangers of Islamist rule. Using Marx's concept of ideology and Weber's notion of the mobilizing power of religious charisma, he also pointed to the "credulity" of Western intellectuals concerning the Iranian Revolution:

> There is neither improbability nor scandal in revolutionary mobilizations that take place in the name of religion. They can succeed better than others. However, it is necessary to be vigilant toward their victories. It is also necessary to maintain a critical attitude toward both the propaganda of the intellectuals within these movements and the credulity of those outside them. A revolutionary tendency can easily continue to be put forward under the banner of Islam. But what superior facilities religion has for those who want to smother society with conservative and reactionary options! Religions are not dangerous because they preach belief in God, but rather because the only remedy they have at their disposal concerning the inherent evils of society is moral exhortation. The more they seem to have such remedies at their

> disposal, the more they make sacred the social *status quo* that more often than not suits their clerics. In power, they succumb more often than not to the temptation of imposing, in the name of moral reform, an order of the same name. ("Khomeini and the 'Primacy of the Spiritual,'" app., 244)

Referring to religious revolutionaries in early modern Europe, Rodinson suggested that Khomeini "could be a Savonarola" or perhaps, if he could develop "some politically practical ideas, a Calvin or a Cromwell." However, Rodinson concluded, there was also the danger that he might "reveal himself to be a Dupanloup tending toward a Torquemada" (ibid., 245), here referring to the nineteenth-century French liberal Bishop Félix Dupanloup and the infamous Spanish Inquisitor of the fifteenth century. These last points also constituted a specific rejoinder to Foucault's October 8 article for *Corriere della sera,* where he had written that the angry "voices" of the Iranian clerics were "as terrible as must have been that of Savonarola in Florence, the voices of the Anabaptists in Münster, or those of the Presbyterians at the time of Cromwell" ("Tehran: Faith against the Shah," app., 201). Many French intellectuals continued to express sympathy for the new regime, even occasionally on feminist grounds. In a March 1 opinion piece in *Le Monde* entitled "The Veil Is Not Only a Mark of Oppression," two feminist anthropologists argued that the veil allowed "women to affirm their role as activists, equal to that of men" (Desmet-Grégoire and Nadjmabadi 1979).[4]

By late February, real power in Iran lay in the hands of the Revolutionary Council, the small and secretive group of clerics around Khomeini. On the surface, the Bazargan government seemed relatively pluralistic, with no clerics and four members of the National Front, including Karim Sanjabi as Foreign Minister. However, Khomeini's council frequently countermanded its orders and changed its policies by fiat. The new regime also started to round up former officials of the shah's regime, some of whom it executed after summary trials. Additionally, it established a rigid control over the broadcast media and started to institute public whippings for alcohol consumption. Bazargan now began to issue frequent verbal attacks on "Marxists," whom he threatened to crush if they attempted to destabilize the country, warnings aimed mainly at the Fedayeen, the Mujahedeen, and other far left groups, which had begun to criticize the new government. The latter naïvely concentrated their initial criticisms on the "liberal-bourgeois" makeup of the Bazargan government, rather than on the hard-line clerics around Khomeini. Another potential source of opposition, the pro-Soviet Tudeh Party, immediately announced its unconditional support for Khomeini.

Already, *Le Monde* reported on February 17, the Tehran University campus had become "one of the rare places, perhaps the only one, where women come alongside men and hold discussions with them as equals" (Balta 1979a). On February 25, Ali Shaygan, a prominent National Front leader who had been a close friend of Mossadeq, returned to Iran after years of exile in France and the United States. Shaygan, who had also played a key role in coordinating the anti-shah activities of the Confederation of Iranian Students in the United States, was expected by many to become Iran's first president. He expressed approval for some Islamist projects, such as the prohibition of alcohol. But after his first meeting with Khomeini, Shaygan voiced strong reservations about the direction of the revolution: "Iran cannot return to the first century of Islam and must instead come up with a new government that meets international standards" (Shaygan 1979).

On March 1, the left-leaning Association of Iranian Writers warned publicly that the "democratic character of the revolution must be preserved." The association complained that the provisional government had refused to recognize the elected councils of workers and civil servants that had been instrumental in the general strikes during the revolution. Censorship had returned, and limits on freedom of expression were being reinstituted. Vigilantes intimidated newspapers and targeted public demonstrations and lectures with threats of violence. They "cleansed" library books, "abrogated the rights of women, who had played an important role in the revolution, and in the name of religious sentiments, eliminated discussion of Iran's [non-Islamic] national festivals and rituals [such as Now Rouz] from textbooks" (Kanun-i Nevisandegan-i Iran 1979).

On March 6, the secular leftist and nationalist parties were able to prove their strength at a mass rally commemorating the anniversary of the Mossadeq's death. As reported in *Le Monde*, the crowd that day, comprising hundreds of thousands, was dominated by supporters of the Left. It included many women, few of whom wore the chador. Slightly distancing himself from Khomeini, Ayatollah Taleqani gave a major address calling for tolerance and unity among the forces that had supported the revolution. Mossadeq's grandson Hedayat Matin-Daftari gave the most dramatic speech, calling for the founding of a new political group, the National Democratic Front. Evoking principles from the 1906 Constitutional Revolution, he demanded a real debate rather than the plebiscite that had been announced for March 30–31 on a single question, whether Iran should become an Islamic republic. Matin-Daftari also advocated an end to censorship and to discrimination against women, as well as cultural and political autonomy for Iran's minorities (Balta 1979b).

For his part, Khomeini moved quickly to restrict women's rights. On February 27 he issued a letter abrogating the Family Protection Law, which had been a milestone for women's rights (see chap. 3). On March 3, the new regime prohibited women from serving in the judiciary. The day after, Khomeini announced that initiating divorce was to become an exclusively male prerogative. On March 9 came a ban on women in sports, including the Olympic team. On March 8, he ordered women to wear the chador, touching off a national and international controversy.

The March 1979 Controversy over Women's Rights in Iran

At the March 8 International Women's Day demonstration, the repressive character of Iran's new Islamist regime suddenly became quite apparent to many of its international supporters. On that day, Iranian women activists and their male supporters demonstrated in Tehran and Qom against an order for women to re-veil themselves in the traditional chador worn by highly religious women. The demonstrations continued for five days. At their height, they attracted tens of thousands in Tehran, men as well as women. Some leftist men formed a cordon around the women, fighting off armed attackers from a newly formed group, the Hezbollah or "Party of God." The demonstrators chanted "No to the Chador," "Down with the Dictatorship," and even the occasional "Down with Khomeini." One banner read, "We made the Revolution for Freedom, But Got Unfreedom," while others proclaimed "In the Dawn of Freedom, We Have No Freedom." For their part, the Hezbollah chanted "You will cover yourselves or be beaten," but their response was mainly nonverbal: stones, knives, and even bullets.

An important figure in the international feminist movement witnessed and participated in these events. Kate Millett, the author of *Sexual Politics* (1970), had arrived from New York a few days before March 8. (French feminists also came to Iran at this time.) As part of the Committee on Artistic and Intellectual Freedom in Iran (CAIFI) in the years before the Revolution, Millett had given numerous presentations at campuses across the United States on human rights abuses under the U.S.-backed regime of the shah. Now she came to Iran at the invitation of CAIFI and feminists in Tehran. She later published a sprawling, impressionistic, yet ultimately very moving memoir, *Going to Iran* (Millett 1982). Millett's entire three-hundred-page memoir is devoted to this single week, when women's issues came to the fore.[5] Millett's reports were something of a counterpoint to those of Foucault. Both had shown a passionate affinity for the Iranian people, and both had devoted a significant part of their lives as public intellectuals to the anti-shah cause. Where Foucault had stressed the totally unified character of the revolutionary movement, Millett focused on the multiplicity of forces involved. Millett's Iran was more varied than Foucault's. It was secular and religious, female and male, gay and straight, non-Islamic and Islamic. Where Foucault saw an undifferentiated totality united behind Khomeini, Millett saw deep contradictions within the movement that had overthrown the shah. Where Foucault had supported the anti-shah movement only to become silent when these contradictions emerged, Millett, who had been even more active than Foucault in the anti-shah movement, plunged into those contradictions, seeking to deepen them in a way that meant supporting the rights of women, of gay men, of workers, of religious and ethnic minorities.

In the days leading up to March 8, women activists attempting to organize a celebration of International Women's Day had been attacked in the press. The Iranian newspaper *Women's Re-Awakening* responded forcefully to clerical allegations that feminism was a Western conspiracy:

> The words "woman" and "international" resurrect nightmares of blasphemy in their tiny brains and they naturally conclude that "this is an international conspiracy by corrupt and promiscuous women." But such thoughts are far from our conscious and freedom-loving women. Our militant and suffering women have borne the weight of such slanders and bullying from their homes to their farms, factories, offices and schools. Today, when the greatest source of bullying and dictatorship in the past fifty years of our country has been overthrown by the determined and brave struggle of these women and their menfolk, they will not tolerate any more exploitation and coercion. (cited in Azari 1983, 194)

The Komiteh, a shadowy political and police force that was controlled by Khomeini and other mullahs close to him, had also harassed and occasionally detained women activists. Despite these difficulties, feminists had continued with their plans for a March 8 demonstration. Millett mentioned summary trials and executions of real or perceived regime opponents, as well as floggings for drinking alcohol. But as a lesbian activist, she was particularly shocked by the anti-gay killings already taking place: "As for the homosexuals, they were shot right in the road, judgment took seconds" (Millett 1982, 109).

On the morning of March 8, when Khomeini gave his infamous order compelling women to wear the chador, hundreds of feminists had already begun to gather in the courtyard of Tehran University for their International Women's Day demonstration. They reacted with bitter derision to this news. Despite severe verbal pressure from hostile men on the campus, some five thousand women marched out of the university onto the streets, where Islamist counterdemonstrators physically harassed them. Two days later, on Saturday, March 10, many thousands marched for women's rights, after which fifteen thousand women held a sit-in at the Ministry of Justice. The statement the women presented to the government called for "freedom" for all, "regardless of gender, color, race, language, and opinion." Their eight demands included free choice concerning dress, freedom of expression, and the removal of "all inequalities between men and women in national law" ("Statement by Iranian Women Protestors," app., 245, 246). By this time, the government had announced that the new dress code was a recommendation, not a requirement, and that the Family Protection Law would be restored, but both of these concessions turned out to be only temporary. The most popular slogan of the day was: "In the Dawn of Freedom, We Have No Freedom" (Millett 1982, 139).

Claudine Moullard of the French women's movement, also present by invitation of the Iranian feminists, spoke at a press conference on March 11, stating that she was "from the women's liberation group in France called Politique and Psychoanalysis," and the journal *Des femmes en mouvement*. She added, "The struggle of women is international: since the first day. When Iranian women break their chains, women of the whole world can advance" (Millett 1982, 160–62).

By March 12, the women's demonstrations had spread to numerous cities around the country. After a long public debate at Tehran University, with the Fedayeen bowing out from helping to protect the marchers, and other leftist groups urging the women to call off the march, thousands stepped out into the streets again, still shielded to an extent by numerous male leftists, who continued to form a chain of protection against the Islamist vigilantes. March 12 was the last big feminist demonstration. Soon after, the women's movement called off its public demonstrations, in large part because of pressures from leftist groups such as the Fedayeen, the most influential group on the campus of Tehran University. The Fedayeen argued that the paramount issue now was the need to avoid a new civil war within the revolutionary camp, in the face of possible foreign intervention or royalist plots (Gueyras 1979b).

The French media covered the women's demonstrations in great detail, and *Le Monde* reported that an "Islamic tribunal" had carried out the execution of two "corrupt" men found guilty of "homosexual perversions"

(Gueyras 1979a). Feminists connected to the journals *Des femmes en mouvement* and *Histoires d'elles* now held large public debates over Iran, with both French and Iranian women taking the floor. The Trotskyist Revolutionary Communist League (LCR), the largest group to the left of the Communist Party, called for "solidarity" with the Iranian women, who, as reported on March 14 in the leftist paper *Libération*, "were fighting for the right to control their own lives and against an Islamic normalization that threatens the freedoms of all workers, of minorities, and of homosexuals." On Friday, March 16, as recounted enthusiastically by *Libération*, a thousand turned out for a demonstration in Paris in support of the Iranian feminists. Slogans included "We will give in neither to the shah nor the ayatollah" and "The veil will fall, from Tehran to Casablanca." Among the participants were Iranian and French feminists, as well as gay and lesbian activists (Delacour 1979a). In Iran that same day, about a hundred thousand demonstrators, many of them women clad in black chadors, rallied in Tehran to defend Khomeini and to denounce the women's demonstrations of the previous week. Much larger than the feminist demonstration of March 10, this one enjoyed the full support of the regime, including free transportation, and did not have to contend with violent harassment on the streets.[6]

In Paris, Simone de Beauvoir called a press conference on March 19 to announce that an international delegation composed of feminist activists and intellectuals was heading to Iran to gather information. While she had to cancel her own plans to travel to Iran for health reasons, de Beauvoir made a public statement of solidarity:

> We have created the International Committee for Women's Rights (CIDF) in response to calls from a large number of Iranian women. Their situation and their revolt have greatly moved us. . . . The first task we have taken up is a very, very burning one for today. It is the task of acquiring information concerning the struggle of the Iranian women, communicating that information, and supporting their struggle. We have received an appeal from a very large number of these women. We have also seen their struggles, their fights, and their actions. We have appreciated the depth of the utter humiliation into which others wanted to make them fall, and we have therefore resolved to fight on their behalf. . . . It is very possible that the mission will fail, inasmuch as they might turn it away the moment it arrives. Nevertheless the die will have been cast, and it is important to have a demonstration—on the part of a very large number of Western women, French women, Italian women, and others—of solidarity with the struggle of Iranian women. ("Speech by Simone de Beauvoir," app., 246–47)

In fact, all signs suggested that the delegation would not make much progress, for that very day, Millett arrived in Paris, having been expelled by the new regime for "provocations against the Islamic Revolution" (Delacour 1979b).

At her own press conference at Orly airport, Millett expressed how deeply moved she had been by the demonstrations in Tehran: "The Iranian women are marvelous human beings" and "armed with great courage." Millett also testified to the increasingly repressive atmosphere in Iran (Delacour 1979b; see also Kempton 1979). The prominent feminist Gisèle Halimi, the editor of the popular feminist magazine *Choisir*, sometimes compared to the American feminist magazine *Ms.*, published an article in *Le Monde* on March 21 in response to the expulsion of Millett. Halimi asked, "How did so many revolutions, movements of resistance to oppression, and independence movements in colonized lands occur amid exploitation of and scorn for women? These women who were, at the least, the equals of their male comrades in withstanding torture, in courage, in death?" Halimi also pointed to the rise of a new feminist internationalism in the wake of the demonstrations in Iran: "For feminists today, the first concrete signs of an international solidarity have appeared" (Halimi 1979). The April issue of the more leftist feminist monthly *Histoires d'elles* also carried a strong defense of the Iranian feminists, entitled, "In Iran, the Chador Goes On, in Paris It Burns," in which the Franco-Algerian writer Leila Sebbar called the Iranian women's demonstrations an unprecedented event in the history of revolutionary movements. This was because women had stepped forward as an independent force that brooked no control from the male leadership: "Up to now, revolutions (Algerian, Chinese, Vietnamese) have brought women to heel, put them in their place, or shifted them into a mixed-gender egalitarianism in conformity with socialist or nationalist political necessity. For the first time, women, Iranian women, are in a situation of insubordination toward a revolutionary order, the Islamic Revolution" (Sebbar 1979).[7]

Other internationally prominent feminists also spoke out on Iran. From Detroit, the Marxist feminist Raya Dunayevskaya issued a strong statement of support for the Iranian women on March 25. She protested Khomeini's expulsion of Millett: "The expulsion of Kate Millett is but a symbol of how he intends to roll the clock backward in his attempt to exorcise all these specters." She also referred to his efforts "to stop those fighting for self-determination with guns in hand, the Kurds" (Dunayevskaya 1979, 3).[8] Dunayevskaya first singled out the self-organization and determination of the Iranian feminists. Like Millett, she stressed the solidarity of male leftists: "That certainly was an advance over the beginnings of the Portuguese Revolution in 1975 where the Left males attacked women's demonstrations with impunity. 1979 in Iran showed, at one and the same time, that male revolutionaries would not permit attacks on women revolutionaries, and women were striking out on their own as a way of deepening the content of revolution" (1979, 2–3). Additionally, Dunayevskaya lauded the openness to international links on the part of the Iranian feminists. She placed the current upheaval in the context of the Constitutional Revolution, citing Morgan Shuster's 1912 eyewitness account of what she called the "historic role" of women at that juncture as well: "The Persian women since 1907 had become almost at a bound the most progressive, not to say radical, in the world. That this statement upsets the ideas of centuries makes no difference. It is the fact. . . . In their struggles for liberty and its modern expressions, they broke through some of the most sacred customs which for centuries past had bound their sex in the land of Iran" (cited in Dunayevskaya 1979, 8–9). Finally, she poured scorn on those leftists, both inside and outside Iran, who placed anti-imperialism in the forefront in such a way as to excuse the internal oppression of an ascendant mullocracy that was hemming in the rights of women, workers, and national minorities.

In France and elsewhere, however, not all leftist intellectuals supported these feminist criticisms of the revolution. Marc Kravetz wrote in *Libération* that, according to his sources among Iranian women, "the situation of Iranian women is more complex than the views expressed at meetings in Paris." He also downplayed reports of executions of homosexuals, writing that they were not "for homosexuality as such," but for "homosexual pimping and sexual violence against minors," as if the claims of Khomeini's secret tribunals were to be taken at face value (Kravetz 1979). Not surprisingly, Kravetz's article soon received a sharp rebuke from a gay male activist, Lola Steel, who had participated in the March 16 demonstration in Paris: "As a homosexual, I participated in the demonstration in support of Iranian women because I had heard talk of 'shooting' of homosexuals." Steel then mocked Kravetz's assertions that these were merely executions of pedophiles. He pointed out that homosexuality existed in all societies, including Islamic ones, albeit in different forms (Steel 1979).

Criticism of international efforts to support the Iranian feminists came from other quarters as well. In mid-March, Edward Said had attended a meeting convened by Sartre and de Beauvoir on the Arab-Israeli conflict. At the meeting, de Beauvoir seems to have expressed her strong opposition to the re-veiling of Iranian women. In a rather condescending account published two decades later, Said described her attitude toward the Iranian feminists:

> Beauvoir was already there in her famous turban, lecturing anyone who would listen about her forthcoming trip to Tehran with Kate Millett, where they

> were planning to demonstrate against the chador; the whole idea struck me as patronizing and silly and although I was eager to hear what Beauvoir had to say, I also realized that she was quite vain and quite beyond arguing at that moment. . . . Beauvoir had been a serious disappointment, flouncing out of the room in a cloud of opinionated babble about Islam and the veiling of women. (Said 2000a)

During these same days, Rodinson published a report on the growing persecution of Baha'is: "Baha'is have been killed, their houses burned, their tombs profaned, their children kidnapped, and their parents required to convert to Islam for their return." This had been orchestrated by the regime, he concluded, since most Baha'i places of worship had already been closed down by the police (Rodinson 1979). There were many more reports in the French press on demands for autonomy by Iranian Kurds, against whom the new regime sent helicopter gunships, before negotiating an uneasy truce.

The mainly French delegation of eighteen women that had gone to Iran on March 19 returned after two weeks. During and after their trip, a few of the delegates tried to put a positive face on their visit, adopting a stance very different from Millett's. Writing in the March 24 issue of *Le Matin de Paris*, a leftist daily paper, the feminist theorist Catherine Clément reported that many Iranian women felt ambivalent about the March 8 demonstration, because they also supported Khomeini. Clément quoted one woman demonstrator who claimed that right-wing elements had swelled the feminist march on the last day. This demonstrator also attacked Millett: "Where were these American women who came to Iran today when the SAVAK was torturing four thousand Iranian women?" (cited in Clément 1979b; see also Clément 1979a; Brière and Macciocchi 1979). She was evidently unaware of Millett's years of anti-shah activism in New York, something Clément did not inform her readers about either. Such opinions were something of an exception among members of the international feminist delegation to Iran, however. Most of the reports by the women delegates painted a very bleak portrait of women's rights in Iran (see for example Kaup 1979; Macciocchi 1979).

For her part, Millett continued to stress the courage and intelligence of the Iranian feminists, implying that the struggle was not over yet: "These are the most polished feminists I have ever seen. God, are they good at what they do. They fought the shah at the risk of their lives, and they're fighting on. When we marched, men volunteers—friends, brothers, husbands, lovers—made a circle around us to protect us. They understood that women's rights were democratic rights. Those marches were the whole spirit of the insurrection" (cited in Kempton 1979).[9]

"I Am 'Summoned to Acknowledge My Errors'": Foucault on the Defensive over Iran

It was at this point that Foucault began to be attacked by name over his writings on Iran. On March 24, a highly polemical article against Foucault appeared in *Le Matin*, a leftist daily paper that had, with the exception of Clément's articles, been very critical of Khomeini. Written by the veteran leftist journalists Claudie and Jacques Broyelle, the attack on Foucault was entitled "What Are the Philosophers Dreaming About?" The title was an obvious allusion to Foucault's October 1978 article in *Le Nouvel Observateur*, "What Are the Iranians Dreaming About?" This was the only one of his Iran articles to have appeared in French, and it had already generated a sharp exchange with an Iranian woman, "Atoussa H.," at the time it had appeared (see chap. 3). The subtitle was provocative: "Was Michel Foucault Mistaken about the Iranian Revolution?" Although they became much more conservative in later years, in 1978 the Broyelles had strong feminist and leftist credentials. In 1977, they had published a scathing account of women in China that had helped to move the Parisian Left away from its earlier Maoist sympathies (Broyelle, Broyelle, and Tschirhart 1980).

The Broyelles began by ridiculing Foucault's enthusiastic praise of the Islamist movement:

> Returning from Iran a few months ago, Michel Foucault stated that he was "impressed" by the "attempt to open a spiritual dimension in politics" that he discerned in the project of an Islamic government.
>
> Today there are little girls all in black, veiled from head to toe; women stabbed precisely because they do not want to wear the veil; summary executions for homosexuality; the creation of a "Ministry of Guidance According to the Precepts of the Quran"; thieves and adulterous women flogged. Iran has had a narrow escape. When one thinks that after decades of ferocious dictatorship under the shah and the SAVAK, this country almost fell into the trap of a "Spanish-type" solution, of a democratic parliament, this news is proof enough of that country's good fortune. ("What Are the Philosophers Dreaming About?" app., 247–48)

The last two sentences referred to the 1977 transition in Spain from fascist dictatorship to a constitutional monarchy in which leftist political parties had secured a majority in the parliament, as did leftist-led trade unions in the economic sphere. Here, the connection to Foucault's Iran article lay in the fact that he had attacked proposals for a similar democratic transition in Iran.

Some of the Broyelles' argument also touched upon Foucault's critique of the modern liberal system of justice in works like his *Discipline and Punish.* They implied that his critique of modernity failed to indicate the progress that had been achieved since the democratic revolutions of the eighteenth century and thus minimized the oppressiveness of premodern forms of justice. Alluding to Foucault's overall theoretical position, as well as the new regime in Iran, the Broyelles referred ironically to "this spirituality that disciplines and punishes" ("Philosophers Dreaming," app., 248). They derided his previous statements about "absence of hierarchy in the clergy" and about the Islamists' notion of law based upon what Foucault had termed a spiritual "light that is capable of illuminating . . . [the] law" and a necessary "distrust of legalism" (ibid.).

Next, the Broyelles noted that a great many leftist intellectuals had excused the crimes of Stalin or Mao and that the anti-Semitic writings of rightists like Léon Daudet had anticipated the Holocaust: "No, the philosopher is not responsible for the blood that flows today in Iran. . . . He is no more responsible than Léon Daudet for the Holocaust, or than the Western communist intellectuals for the socialist gulags" ("Philosophers Dreaming," app., 248). However, they continued, the privileged Western intellectual whose ideas had sometimes excused fascism or totalitarian communism did have a responsibility: to seek and then avow the truth. It was at this point that the Broyelles called upon Foucault to admit that his thinking on Iran had been "in error":

> When one is an intellectual, when one works both on and with "ideas," when one has the freedom—without having to fight at the risk of one's life in order to obtain it—not to be a sycophantic writer, then one also has some obligations. The first one is to take responsibility for the ideas that one has defended when they are finally realized. The philosophers of "people's justice" should say today, "Long live the Islamic government!" and it would be clear that they are going to the final extreme of their radicalism. Or they should say, "No, I did not want that, I was mistaken. Here is what was wrong in my reasoning; here is where my thinking is in error." They should reflect. After all, that is their job. (Ibid., 249)

Next to this article, *Le Matin* ran an announcement that a response by Foucault would appear in the next issue.

Foucault's response, published two days later, on March 26, was in fact a nonresponse. He would not respond, he wrote, "because throughout 'my life' I have never taken part in polemics. I have no intention of beginning now." He wrote further, "I am 'summoned to acknowledge my errors.'" Hinting that it was the Broyelles who were engaging in thought control by the manner in which they had called him to account, Foucault continued: "This expression and the practice it designates remind me of something and of many things, against which I have fought. I will not lend myself, even 'through the press,' to a maneuver whose form and content I detest. 'You are going to confess, or you will shout long live the assassins.'" He added that he would be willing "to debate here and now the question of Iran, as soon as *Le Matin* will give me the opportunity" ("Foucault's Response to Claudie and Jacques Broyelle," app., 249–50). In an accompanying note, *Le Matin*'s editors indicated that "we expect to publish an article by Michel Foucault after the March 30 referendum in Iran." That referendum was the one that established an Islamic republic.

Foucault's attempt to turn the tables on his critics, to imply that they were conducting an inquisition of some sort, seemed to backfire. *Le Matin* ran a second highly critical piece on Foucault in the form of a long letter to the editor three days later, on March 31. Entitled "Foucault, Iran, and Responsibility," its author was Paul Martin, a teacher from Marseilles who expressed an affinity with the anti-authoritarian leftist philosopher Cornelius Castoriadis. Martin accused Foucault in his response to the Broyelles of "hiding behind a haughty silence when harsh reality has disproved what one has said." Concerning Foucault's rejoinder, Martin added:

> It is insinuated that asking someone to explain himself, to indicate where he has been in error (and how he has contributed to error since his discourse was public), is to be "Stalinist," totalitarian. (It is quite definitely this that was meant when Foucault recollected "something and many things.") In effect, what the whole text by Michel Foucault implicitly calls for is the right of the professional intellectual to say anything at all and never have to be haunted by his errors. If obstinate, non-amnesiac and therefore disrespectful people demand explanations, our intellectual wraps himself in his offended dignity and cries inquisition. Here the intention is to dodge the truth and one's responsibility. (Martin 1979)

No subsequent articles by Foucault on Iran appeared in *Le Matin*. Perhaps he thought it better to cut his losses. In addition, Foucault faced a much broader challenge in the critical reviews of a book on Iran that contained a lengthy interview with him that now appeared in several newspapers and journals.

The Fallout over Foucault's Interview in *Iran: The Revolution in the Name of God*

One of Foucault's lengthiest treatments of the events in Iran was in an interview with Claire Brière and Pierre Blanchet that formed the appendix to their book *Iran: The Revolution in the Name of God*. Published at the end of March 1979, this book was based on reporting by these two journalists in *Libération*. They had been in Iran as well as around Khomeini during his brief Paris exile in 1978, and Brière had returned to Iran on the same plane as the ayatollah in February 1979. The interview, which appears to have been conducted at the end of 1978, was entitled "Iran: The Spirit of a Spiritless World." Unfortunately for Foucault's reputation, this rather enthusiastic discussion of Iran's Islamist movement was published in the immediate aftermath of the March women's demonstrations and amid the growing reports of atrocities against gay men, Baha'is, and Kurds. The book was widely read because of its timeliness, and, months later, *Iran: The Revolution in the Name of God* was still the most prominently displayed title on the Iranian Revolution in Paris bookstores.[10]

The editors of a subsequent French reprint of Foucault's interview seemed at great pains to indicate that he was not to be blamed. They implied that it was the journalists Brière and Blanchet, rather than Foucault, who had been too enthusiastic about the Islamist movement in Iran (Foucault 1994b, 743, editor's note). A close reading of the interview suggests the opposite: that the two journalists were themselves rebuffed at several points when they nudged Foucault to take a more nuanced and critical stance toward the Islamist movement in Iran. In the interview, Foucault began his analysis of Iran by complaining that "the Iran affair and the way in which it has taken place have not aroused the same kind of untroubled sympathy as Portugal, for example, or Nicaragua." He also found fault with the actions of a newspaper editor (unnamed, but possibly the editor of *Libération*), who had added the word "fanatic" to a reporter's phrase about "Islamic revolt" in publishing a dispatch from Iran ("Iran: The Spirit of a World without Spirit," app., 250). Blanchet then criticized parts of the French Left, "whether of the [Socialist Party] or . . . the more marginal left around the newspaper *Libération*," which had tended to distance itself from the Iranian Revolution. These groups expressed "irritation" over two points: (1) "religion is the veil, is an archaism, a regression at least as far as women are concerned"; (2) "the second, which cannot be denied, because one feels it: if ever the clerics come to power and apply their program, shouldn't we fear a new dictatorship?" (ibid., 250–51).

It was unclear why only the second of these dangers was undeniable, but at least Blanchet had raised for discussion a feminist criticism of the Islamist movement. Instead of acknowledging either of these dangers, however, Foucault took the conversation back to where it had started: his complaint that the Western Left had not been very enthusiastic about what was happening in Iran:

> It might be said that, behind these two irritations, there is another, or perhaps an astonishment, a sort of unease when confronted by a phenomenon that is, for our political mentality, very curious. It is a phenomenon that may be called revolutionary in the very broad sense of the term, since it concerns the uprising of a whole nation against a power that oppresses it. Now, we recognize a revolution when we can observe two dynamics: one is that of the contradictions in that society, that of the class struggle or of social confrontations. Then there is a political dynamic, that is to say, the presence of a vanguard, class, party, or political ideology, in short, a spearhead that carries the whole nation with it. Now it seems to me that, in what is happening in Iran, one can recognize neither of those two dynamics that are for us distinctive signs and marks of a revolutionary phenomenon. What, for us, is a revolutionary movement in which one cannot situate the internal contradictions of a society, and in which one cannot point out a vanguard either? ("Iran," app., 251)

Foucault continued to stress the uniqueness of the events in Iran, as well as their profundity. Once again he had attacked the weaknesses of the secular Left, but he had refused to discuss problems in the Islamist movement itself.

Foucault now moved on to characterize the place of religion in the Iranian Revolution:

> It is true that Iranian society is shot through with contradictions that cannot in any way be denied, but it is certain that the revolutionary event that has been taking place for a year now, and which is at the same time an inner experience, a sort of constantly recommenced liturgy, a community experience, and so on, all that is certainly articulated onto the class struggle: but that doesn't find expression in an immediate, transparent way. So what role has religion, then, with the formidable grip that it has on people, the position that it has always held in relation to political power, its content, which makes it a religion of combat and sacrifice, and so on? Not that of an ideology, which would help to mask contradictions or form a sort of sacred union between a great many divergent interests. It really has been the vocabulary, the ceremonial, the

> timeless drama into which one could fit the historical drama of a people that pitted its very existence against that of its sovereign. ("Iran," app., 252)

This was a fitting criticism of the vulgar Marxist notion of religion as a permanently conservative ideology that masked something deeper, such as class conflict. Instead, Foucault saw religion as a discourse that could take on different political meanings at different times. But what was curious was how Foucault characterized Iranian Shi'ism as a "timeless," unified, historico-cultural discourse system, one that completely overrode those "contradictions" with which, he acknowledged in passing, "Iranian society" was "shot through."

Blanchet countered that while in the fall of 1978 the mass movement had seemed unified, by early 1979 this was beginning to change: "Obviously, afterwards, things will settle down and different strata, different classes, will become visible" ("Iran," app., 252). Foucault disagreed. He again extolled the "absolutely collective will" he had witnessed among the Iranian masses. He compared the Iranian Revolution to previous anticolonial struggles and referred to the United States and other Western backers of the shah. There was more. The Iranian Revolution expressed something greater and deeper than nationalism: "But national feeling has, in my opinion, been only one of the components of a still more radical rejection: the rejection by a people not only of foreigners, but of everything that had constituted over the years, the centuries, its political destiny" (ibid., 253). Here, what Foucault perceived to be the deeply antimodernist themes of the Iranian Revolution drew his attention.

Blanchet again warned of uncritical euphoria with respect to the events in Iran, referring to his and Brière's experience in China during the Cultural Revolution. In particular, Blanchet expressed skepticism about Foucault's notion of an "absolutely collective will":

> There was the same type of collective will. . . . Afterwards, we came to realize that we'd been taken in to some extent; the Chinese, too. It's true that, to an extent, we took ourselves in. And that's why, sometimes, we hesitate to allow ourselves to be carried away by Iran. In any case, there is something similar in the charisma of Mao Zedong and of Khomeini; there is something similar in the way the young Islamic militants speak of Khomeini and the way the Red Guards spoke of Mao. ("Iran," app., 253)

Once again, Foucault refused the implications of a more questioning, critical stance. Disagreeing directly with Blanchet, he insisted on the uniqueness of the events in Iran vis-à-vis those in China:

> All the same, the Cultural Revolution was certainly presented as a struggle between certain elements of the population and certain others, certain elements in the party and certain others, or between the population and the party, etc. Now what struck me in Iran is that there is no struggle between different elements. What gives it such beauty, and at the same time such gravity, is that there is only one confrontation: between the entire people and the state power threatening them with its weapons and police. One didn't have to go to extremes; one found them there at once, on the one side, the entire will of the people, on the other the machine guns. (Ibid., 253–54)

Here, Foucault's denial of any social or political differentiation among the Iranian "people" was absolutely breathtaking. He continued in this vein, again and again parrying Blanchet's urgings that he discuss differences, contradictions, or dangers within Iran's revolutionary process. For example, Foucault declared that with regard to the Iranian Islamists, "religion for them was like the promise and guarantee of finding something that would radically change their subjectivity" (ibid., 255). Then he suggested that Marx's famous sentence on religion had been misconstrued: "People always quote Marx and the opium of the people. The sentence that immediately preceded that statement which is never quoted says that religion is the spirit of a world without spirit." Foucault argued that by 1978, the better-known part of Marx's statement had become inappropriate: "Let us say, therefore, that Islam, in the year 1978, was not the opium of the people precisely because it was the spirit of a world without spirit" (ibid.). Thus, where dogmatic Marxists had quoted only the latter part of Marx's statement, "religion is the opium of the people," Foucault now wanted to interpret the statement in a different way, emphasizing its first part, that "religion is the spirit of a world without spirit."

Finally, about nine-tenths of the way through the interview, after more prodding by both Blanchet and Brière, Foucault acknowledged very briefly a single contradiction within the Iranian Revolution, that of xenophobic nationalism and anti-Semitism. We can quote these statements in full, since they are so brief:

> There were demonstrations, verbal at least, of virulent anti-Semitism. There were demonstrations of xenophobia, and not only against the Americans, but also against foreign workers who had come to work in Iran. . . .
>
> What has given the Iranian movement its intensity has been a double register. On the one hand, a collective will that has been very strongly expressed politically and, on the other hand, the desire for a radical change in ordinary

> life. But this double affirmation can only be based on traditions, institutions that carry a charge of *chauvinism, nationalism, exclusiveness,* that have a very powerful attraction for individuals. ("Iran," app., 259 and 260; emphasis added)

Here, for the first time in his discussions of Iran, Foucault had acknowledged that the religious and nationalist myths through which the Islamists had mobilized the masses were full of "chauvinism, nationalism, exclusiveness." At the same time, however, and what continued to override the possibility of a critical perspective, was the fact that he was so enamored by the ability of the Islamists to galvanize tens of millions of people through such traditions that he ignored the dangers. Strikingly, in the entire interview, Foucault never addressed the dangers facing Iranian women, even after Brière recounted, albeit with a big apologia for the Islamists, an incident in which she had been physically threatened for trying to join a group of male journalists during a 1978 demonstration.

In the conclusion of the interview, Foucault argued forcefully that the events in Iran could not be grasped through traditional, especially Marxist, categories. He then stressed the alterity of the Iranian people. Since they were not Westerners, the Iranians "don't have the same regime of truth as ours, which, it has to be said, is very special, even if it has become almost universal" ("Iran," app., 259). He ended the interview on a similar note of absolute difference:

> Many here and some in Iran are waiting for and hoping for the moment when secularism will at last come back to the fore and reveal the good, old type of revolution we have always known. I wonder how far they will be taken along this strange, unique road, in which they seek, against the stubbornness of their destiny, against everything they have been for centuries, "something quite different." (Ibid., 260)

In addition to the prediction that secular and leftist forces would not displace the Islamists, there was also a certain exoticizing of Iranian culture as an oppositionless collectivity defined by its absolute difference from modern Western societies. Given the opposition to clerical rule that had emerged from feminists, minorities such as the Kurds, and leftists, such a view was a grossly inadequate theorization of Iran's concrete social and political situation in March 1979. Had this interview appeared in January 1979 or earlier, at a time when the Islamists had not begun to implement their idea of an Islamic government, it might have aroused less attention. But it was Foucault's misfortune that it appeared in March 1979, after the women's demonstrations and the first executions of homosexuals.

On March 29, soon after *Iran: The Revolution in the Name of God* appeared, a review in *Le Monde* raised further questions about Foucault's position on Iran. The reviewer, Paul-Jean Franceschini, praised the book as a whole for having summed up the Islamist movement in Iran as well as the grievances of Iranians against Western imperialism and Western stereotypes of their culture. However, Franceschini concluded,

> To the caricature of the West, the Iranian Revolution responded with a blaze of fundamentalism that was itself just as much a caricature, one that became from then onwards quite powerful. Human rights cannot be split apart. The bloody encounter of a country with its past, its identity, its religion, does not justify the excesses that Mr. Bazargan is trying to bring to a close. In this regard, the attempt by Michel Foucault to read these events, which concludes the book, appears questionable. (Franceschini 1979)

This review set the tone for most of the others that were to follow.[11]

A week later, on April 7, Catherine Clément published a review of *Iran: The Revolution in the Name of God* in *Le Matin* that defended Foucault's views on Iran. Clément saw Foucault's interview as a most prescient analysis of the situation on the eve of the fall of the shah: "This dialogue with Michel Foucault . . . has already spilled a lot of ink because, the three of them, including Brière and Blanchet, tried to discern what has escaped our intellectual expectations in this story. After this book—but only after it—and that is now, come the questions regarding freedom and social contradictions" (Clément 1979c). Clément's review stressed that for millions of Iranian revolutionary women, the chador was "the symbol of a veiled Iranianism that was opposed to Westernization."

Clément also argued that the notion of universal human rights could not be applied to Iran, linking the events there to China's Cultural Revolution:

> No disillusionment, no schema, including that of "Human Rights" within our tradition, can be applied *directly* to this country, which makes its revolution from its own culture. . . . Cultural revolution—we know the enthusiasm and the reversals of that. Nonetheless, it makes one think. And to think about it truly, in silence and *without ethnocentrism, Iran: The Revolution in the Name of God* is undoubtedly the best point of departure. (Clément 1979c)

Evidently, Clément was still caught up in the enthusiasm that had greeted the Iranian Revolution in many quarters of the Left, as well as some lingering nostalgia for Mao's Cultural Revolution. Additionally, her article cast the human rights perspective in terms of avoiding "ethnocentrism." This seems to have been the only public attempt to defend Foucault's Iran writings during this period.

A week after Clément's defense of Foucault, another strong critique appeared in a review of *Iran: The Revolution in the Name of God*. Jean Lacouture, the veteran journalist and biographer, gave the book a mixed, albeit somewhat positive review in the April 14 issue of *Le Nouvel Observateur*. Lacouture's criticism again focused on Foucault's interview, arguing that the book "poses important issues with a rather abrupt simplicity that becomes most apparent in the concluding conversation between the two authors and Michel Foucault." The biggest problem with the book and with Foucault's contribution, Lacouture added, was the way in which "the unanimous character of the movement" was emphasized in a one-sided fashion. Something similar to this so-called "unanimity" for Islam was also observed, he concluded, erroneously it turned out, during China's Cultural Revolution of the 1960s (Lacouture 1979).

Still another attack on Foucault appeared in the April 21 issue of *L'Express*, a mass-circulation centrist weekly. It was written by Bernard Ullmann, a well-known journalist who had covered the Indochina and Algerian wars and was now a member of *L'Express*'s editorial board. In his review of *Iran: The Revolution in the Name of God*, Ullmann wrote that Foucault's interview "did not have the same prudence" as the rest of the book in assessing the possible dangers of an Islamist regime in Iran. Foucault, he added, "deplores the absence of an 'immediate sympathy' among the thoughtful Left, for some aspects of the Revolution of the Mullahs. 'What struck me in Iran,' he writes with noble certitude, 'is that there is no struggle among different elements'" (Ullmann 1979). Ullmann also reported that two masked men had staged a physical attack on Foucault in his apartment building, during which they accused him of supporting the "veiling of Iranian women." Ullmann concluded in cynical liberal fashion: "These were certainly not his words. But after all, Michel Foucault is neither the first nor the last Western intellectual to hold illusions about the aftermath of a revolution, whether that of October 1917, the [1974] Revolution of the Carnations in Portugal, or that which knocked down the throne of the Pahlavis" (Ullmann 1979). Foucault never responded directly to these various attacks in the reviews of *Iran: The Revolution in the Name of God*, but he did publish two more articles on Iran, each of them more critical in tone and substance than his earlier ones.

Foucault's Final Writings on Iran and Their Aftermath, Including Rodinson's Posthumous Critique

By mid-April, a number of summary trials and executions across Iran filled the headlines in France. Foucault published an open letter to Prime Minister Mehdi Bazargan in the April 14 issue of *Le Nouvel Observateur*, the same number of the journal in which Lacouture's review appeared. Foucault began his open letter by recalling his meeting with Bazargan in September 1978 during the shah's repression of the revolutionary movement. At that time, Bazargan was president of the Committee for the Defense of Human Rights in Iran. To begin with, Foucault distanced himself from President Jimmy Carter's notion of human rights, which, he wrote, had "enlisted the shah as one of the defenders of human rights." Apparently referring to the criticisms by Millett, de Beauvoir, Halimi, Sebbar, and other feminists, Foucault also wrote that he could understand why "many Iranians are angry that they are being given such noisy lectures" from abroad ("Open Letter to Prime Minister Mehdi Bazargan," app., 261).

Foucault then noted that Bazargan had intervened to stop several executions in March 1979. Next he discussed some of the substance of their conversation in September 1978, which he said Bazargan had recently mentioned publicly. Foucault recalled three reasons that Bazargan had given him in their September conversation to show that an avowedly Islamic regime could be compatible with human rights.

First, Bazargan had said, having a spiritual dimension in politics did not mean a "government of mullahs" ("Open Letter," app., 261). Second, Bazargan had argued that Islam could address questions that neither communism nor capitalism had been able to resolve. Here Foucault sounded the most sympathetic, "not seeing in the name of what universality Muslims could be prevented from seeking their future in an Islam whose new face they will have to shape with their own hands." Such a rejection of universals was of course vintage Foucault, but the stress on spiritual politics and Islamism was the new feature that had emerged in his Iran writings. What if the Iranian "Muslims," or at least their dominant leaders, decided to impose their version of Islam in such a way as to oppress non-Muslim minorities, such as Baha'is and Jews, as well as non-Shi'ite Muslims or even different tendencies within Shi'ism? Foucault did not seem to have anticipated this. More important, even now, Foucault had a hard time accepting that such developments had occurred. He added: "Concerning the expression 'Islamic government,' why cast immediate suspicion on the adjective 'Islamic'? The word 'government' suffices, in itself, to awaken vigilance" (ibid.).[12]

Third, Foucault suggested that, rather than leading to new forms of oppression, the injection of religion into government might have the opposite effect: "You said that by invoking Islam, a government would thereby create important limitations upon its basic sovereignty over civil society, due to obligations grounded on religion." Foucault added that although this idea "seemed important," he "was somewhat skeptical" as to whether governments could so limit themselves ("Open Letter," app., 261–62). Why was he only *somewhat* skeptical? Apparently because government, especially the modern centralized state, was the major danger to human dignity and autonomy. This had certainly been the theme of his today well-known 1978 essay, "Governmentality," which had been concerned with issues such as "reason of state" and the development of the modern state as a whole. The problem was that the modern state was "governed according to *rational principles* that are intrinsic to it and cannot be derived from natural or *divine laws* or the principles of wisdom and prudence" (Foucault 2000b, 212–13; emphasis added). Thus, it would seem that even a state justifying itself by "divine laws" was less a danger than a religiously neutral but therefore more autonomous modern state.

After these preliminaries, Foucault began his critique of the Islamic Republic, writing that "the trials taking place in Iran today do not fail to cause concern" ("Open Letter," app., 262). He went on to ask if those on trial had been given their full rights to defend themselves, noting that in a situation where a defendant is hated by the public, this is especially difficult. Foucault then expressed the wish that Bazargan would hear his plea, despite the fact that Iranians were tired of having Westerners tell them what to do.

Seen in the context of the discussions in France at the time over Iran, Foucault's criticisms were rather mild and hesitant. This was probably because this letter was addressed to the Iranian prime minister rather than the French public. But it could hardly have satisfied Foucault's critics very much, since he never called into question the overall project of an Islamist government.

The closest Foucault came to a reply to his now numerous critics, still without naming any of them, was in his article "Is It Useless to Revolt?" which was published on the front page of *Le Monde* on May 11, 1979. Foucault began with some general comments on revolutionary uprisings, mentioning not only Iran, but also the 1943 Warsaw Ghetto Uprising against the Nazis:

> Uprisings belong to history, but in a certain way, they escape it. The movement through which a lone man, a group, a minority, or an entire people say, "I will no longer obey," and are willing to risk their lives in the face of a power

> that they believe to be unjust, seems to me to be *irreducible*. This is because no power is capable of making it absolutely impossible. Warsaw will always have its ghetto in revolt and its sewers populated with insurgents. ("Is It Useless to Revolt?" app., 263; emphasis added)

Here again, as in his fall 1978 articles, Foucault was using the term *irreducible* to describe the Iranian uprising. At least in part, this seemed to mean that it was so elemental that it could not be reduced to any smaller constituent elements, such as parties, tendencies, or factions.

In the *Le Monde* article, Foucault also focused on the themes of death, dying, and martyrdom, with which he continued to be fascinated: "The man in revolt is ultimately inexplicable. There must be an uprooting that interrupts the unfolding of history, and its long series of reasons why, for a man 'really' to prefer the risk of death over the certainty of having to obey." In a dig at liberalism, he added that this type of sentiment is "more solid and experiential than 'natural rights'" ("Is It Useless to Revolt?" app., 263). Many revolts across history had therefore expressed themselves in religion, he argued:

> Because it is in this way both "outside of history" and in history, because each person stakes his life and his death, one can understand why uprisings have been able to find their expression and their drama so readily in religious forms. For centuries, all of these promises of the hereafter or of the renewal of time, whether they concerned the awaited savior, the kingdom of the last days, or the reign of the absolute good, did not constitute an ideological cloak. Instead, they constituted the very manner in which these uprisings were lived, at least in those places where the religious forms lent themselves to such possibilities. (Ibid., 264)

Thus, religion seemed indeed to be Marx's "spirit of spiritless times," but not his "opium of the people."

Here, in rejecting any notion of religion as an ideology, Foucault argued that the Iranian experience moved outside the paradigms that had defined similar social movements ever since 1789:

> Then came the age of "revolution." For two centuries, it hung over history, organized our perception of time, and polarized hopes. The age of revolution has constituted a gigantic effort to acclimate uprisings within a rational and controllable history. "Revolution" gave these uprisings a legitimacy, sorted

> out their good and bad forms, and defined their laws of development. For uprisings, it established preliminary conditions, objectives, and ways of bringing them to an end. Even the profession of revolutionary was defined. By thus repatriating revolt into the discourse of revolution, it was said, the uprising would appear in all its truth and continue to its true conclusion. This was a marvelous promise. Some will say that the uprising thus found itself colonized by *realpolitik*. Others will say that the dimension of a rational history was opened to it. ("Is It Useless to Revolt?" app., 264)

The experience of Iran could thus be a turning point for the world. It could free uprisings from the paradigms dominant since 1789, whether liberal democratic or socialist.

However, Foucault's attempt to link the Iranian Revolution to premodern, elemental mass revolts was harder to swallow, even if one left aside the secular, leftist, and feminist tendencies. With its clandestine committees under the control of a religious hierarchy and its use of the then cutting-edge technologies of communication such as cassette tapes, the Islamist movement was as meticulously organized from above as the most Stalinized vanguard party, something that was becoming more evident by the day. Foucault, in his utter and sometimes nihilistic rejection of modern Western forms of state power, seemed unable to grasp that an anti-Western, religiously based system of power could be in the process of creating a state that would prove to be every bit as oppressive as Stalinist or fascist totalitarianism. Similar to fascism, this new state was in the process of combining many modernist features with an antimodernist ideology.

To Foucault, the events in Iran seemed outside the Western paradigm of revolution. Further, they were perhaps even outside history itself, part of a timeless "political spirituality" that the modern concept of revolution had tried vainly to supplant:

> They inscribed, on the borders of heaven and earth, in a dream-history that was as religious as it was political, all their hunger, their humiliation, their hatred of the regime, and their will to bring it down. They confronted the Pahlavis, in a game where each one staked his life and his death, a game that was also about sacrifices and millennial promises. Thus, came the celebrated demonstrations, which . . . unfold according to the rhythm of religious ceremonies, and finally refer to a timeless drama in which power is always accursed. This drama caused a surprising superimposition to appear in the middle of the twentieth century: a movement strong enough to bring down a

> seemingly well-armed regime, all the while remaining in touch with the old dreams that were once familiar to the West, when it too wanted to *inscribe the figures of spirituality on the ground of politics*. ("Is It Useless to Revolt?" app., 264–65; emphasis added)

Here again, Foucault spoke of political spirituality, a dream that had been abandoned by the West but could be reborn as a result of the Iranian Revolution.

Finally, Foucault began to address some of the problematic features of post-revolutionary Iran: "At this stage, the most important and the most atrocious mingle—the extraordinary hope of remaking Islam into a great living civilization and various forms of virulent xenophobia, as well as the global stakes and the regional rivalries. And the problem of imperialisms. And the *subjugation of women, and so on*" ("Is It Useless to Revolt?" app., 265; emphasis added). This passing reference to women was the only time in over eight months of discussion of Iran that Foucault had mentioned women's oppression. It was an offhand, almost grudging acknowledgment, without any elaboration. At no point, however, did he mention the summary executions of gay men that were continuing as he was writing these very lines.

Foucault now swerved once again toward the themes of death and martyrdom, as he sought to separate the martyrs of 1978 from the regime: "The spirituality of those who were going to their deaths has no similarity whatsoever with the bloody government of a fundamentalist clergy" ("Is It Useless to Revolt?" app., 265). This seemed like a strong critique, and in some sense, it was. But why the focus on 1978, rather than May 1979, the time of this writing? What about the nonspirituality of those Iranians who wanted to live, to experience freedom in *this* world, especially the women of March 8 and their allies? There was no room in Foucault's binary schema for them, any more than there had been for the dissent of "Atoussa H." five months earlier. He concluded with a defiant refusal to acknowledge any errors in his writings on the Iranian Revolution: "It is certainly not shameful to change one's opinions, but there is no reason to say that one's opinion has changed when one is against hands being chopped off today, after having been against the tortures of the SAVAK yesterday" (ibid., 266).

As a whole, this article seemed to set out what can only be described as a new concept of revolution that attempted to go beyond both liberalism and Marxism. Just as most Marxists regarded the 1917 Russian Revolution as a new type of revolution that had gone beyond the perspectives of 1789, so Foucault seemed to see a new epoch unfolding in Iran in 1979, one that could reduce the two centuries from 1789 to 1979 to a modernist parenthesis amid something far deeper and more permanent, the phenomenon of the elemental or irreducible religious uprising. And like the more intelligent and critical-minded of his Marxist predecessors, Foucault's support for the new wave of Islamist uprisings that started in Iran in 1978, what he called this "powder keg" set against the dominant global powers, was not entirely uncritical. Yet it was fundamentally a stance of support. If his aim was to set out a new theory of revolution that could be widely embraced, his essay was an utter failure. It gained him no followers. And he lapsed into silence on Iran from May 1979 until his death in 1984, making no public declarations of any kind as the Iranian people suffered terribly under a regime for which he had helped to build support.[13]

Alongside Foucault's May 11 article on Iran, there appeared that same day in *Le Monde* one entitled "Corrupter of the Earth," an analysis of the current situation by Brière and Blanchet. Again, as in their earlier interview with Foucault, they were more forthright than he was in condemning the repression inside Iran, beginning their article with a detailed account of the consequences of Khomeini's injunction to "cut off the hands of the rotten ones." They described the heart of the Islamic revolution as directed against Westernization and modernization, and its social base as the clergy, the bazaar merchants, and the ordinary people. The mass executions being carried out in the spring of 1979 were not only a form of vengeance against the past oppression by the shah's regime, but also and more importantly, an effort to "purify" the country of its Westernized corruption, in blood if necessary (Brière and Blanchet 1979b). At the same time, Brière and Blanchet acknowledged, more than Foucault had ever done, a multiplicity of tendencies and currents within the 1978–79 Revolution. They pointed out that the masses had cried not only "Long live Khomeini," but also "Azadi!" (Freedom). Here they referred to secular as well as religious opposition groups. They noted as well that even the Islamic leadership was hardly unanimous, citing objections to the repression ordered by Khomeini that was coming from Ayatollahs Shariatmadari and Taleqani as well as Prime Minister Bazargan. However, they concluded that Khomeini had the upper hand and that therefore, unfortunately, "Islamic fundamentalism has Iran in its grip and this can engender only dictatorship and war" (Brière and Blanchet 1979b).

While the May 11 *Le Monde* article was Foucault's last word on Iran, his critics did not allow the issue to die. A few months later, the political theorist Pierre Manent published a lengthy critique, devoted entirely to the *Le Monde* article. He did so in the liberal journal *Commentaire*, which had been founded by Raymond Aron. Manent zeroed in on the looseness of the criteria Foucault had used in explaining his support for the Islamist movement in Iran. In particular, Manent focused on the metaphysical, spiritual dimension of Foucault's theory and ethics of revolution, especially his evident fascination with martyrdom and death: "Michel Foucault wants to close off all discussion, even the possibility of a discussion, on the well-foundedness of this or that uprising, by stressing the unassailable fact . . . of one who 'stakes his life.' . . . The irreducibility of this act is supposed to close off any inquiry into its reasons or justifications" (Manent 1979, 372). To Manent, a decided nihilism seemed to lurk behind Foucault's political spirituality.

In a coda to the controversy, in 1993, nearly a decade after Foucault's death, Rodinson made public the fact that his articles in *Le Monde* and *Le Nouvel Observateur* during the Iranian Revolution had been aimed mainly at Foucault. He did so in a lengthy essay accompanying their republication,[14] where he wrote: "A very great thinker, Michel Foucault, part of a line of radically dissident thought, placed excessive hopes in the Iranian Revolution" ("Critique of Foucault on Iran," app., 270). In part, Rodinson attributed this to Foucault's lack of knowledge concerning the Islamic world. He criticized not only Foucault's enthusiastic reports in the fall of 1978 on a new "political spirituality" and the prospects for an "Islamic government." He also took issue with Foucault's April 1979 open letter to Bazargan, which had been somewhat critical of the outcome of the Revolution. Additionally, Rodinson suggested that when Foucault's open letter had defended the principle of an Islamic government against those who expressed suspicion about the adjective "Islamic," this was a criticism directed at Rodinson's own writings on the revolution: "To the extent that I was myself the target of Foucault's open letter, I will respond that if I cast suspicion on the adjective 'Islamic,' it was the same thing concerning every adjective that denoted an attachment to an ideal doctrine, whether religious or secular" (ibid., 275). Relying heavily on Weber's theory of charismatic domination, Rodinson wrote that "religious charisma reveals itself to be much more effective than all types of secular charisma" (ibid., 272). Foucault, however, Rodinson concluded, had "yielded" to "the banal and vulgar conception of the spiritual" that "shrank from questioning the foundations" of a "dissident" movement like Iranian Islamism (ibid., 276).

Rodinson detailed a number of brutal and destructive features of the Islamic Republic, referring to Khomeini's notorious hanging judge, the cleric Sadeq Khalkhali. He recalled his February 1979 response to Foucault, where he had suggested that, rather than something similar to the English revolutionary Cromwell (as Foucault had written), what might be in store for

Iran was the Spanish Grand Inquisitor Torquemada. Now he wrote that Khalkhali's actions were "eclipsing" those of the "terrible Spaniard" ("Critique," app., 269). In addition to a lack of knowledge about Islam and Iran, Rodinson pointed to another source of Foucault's misperceptions of Iranian Islamism—the fact that he was a philosopher by training. "Philosophically formed minds, even and perhaps especially the most eminent, are among the most vulnerable to the seductions of theoretical slogans. . . . They have . . . a tendency to minimize the obstacles and the objections that stubborn reality puts in the way of conceptual constructs" (ibid., 269–70). Elsewhere, Rodinson generalized his critique of the philosophical approach to politics: "To understand the social world and its dynamics, it is more worthwhile to have closely studied a society, a series of events, or a complex of concrete phenomena than to have spent months or years on achieving a good understanding of [Hegel's] *Phenomenology of Spirit*" (Rodinson 1993b, 11).

Rodinson ended on a note of Gallic humanism, making reference to his own earlier and stubbornly held illusions about the Soviet Union:

> Those who, like the author of these lines, refused for so long to believe the reports about the crimes committed in the name of the triumphant socialism in the former Tsarist Empire, in the terrible human dramas resulting from the Soviet Revolution, would exhibit bad grace if they became indignant at the incredulity of the Muslim masses before all the spots that one asks them to view on the radiant sun of their hope.
>
> Michel Foucault is not contemptible for not having wanted to create despair in the Muslim world's shantytowns and starving countryside, for not having wanted to disillusion them, or for that matter, to make them lose hope in the worldwide importance of their hopes. ("Critique," app., 277)

This concession of course carried a double edge, suggesting that Foucault had fallen into problems similar to the very Marxist dogmatism he had so frequently attacked.

While we find many of Rodinson's critiques of Foucault compelling, we certainly cannot agree with his argument for the advantages of a purely socioeconomic approach to the realm of the political over a philosophical one. In this study, we have argued that there were particular aspects of Foucault's philosophical perspective that helped to lead him toward an abstractly uncritical stance toward Iran's Islamist movement. If a philosophical perspective per se were the problem, how then could equally philosophical feminist thinkers like de Beauvoir and Dunayevskaya have succeeded in arriving at a more appropriately critical stance toward the Iranian Revolution? The male philosopher Jean-Paul Sartre also expressed alarm in conversations with members of the Iranian community in France.[15] What's more, how could so many Iranian leftist men, imbued with notions of the primacy of the socioeconomic interests over "idealist" ones like religion or gender, have ended up supporting the Khomeini regime in its early years, precisely because, despite its oppressive features, it was firmly anti-imperialist?

Foucault biographer David Macey acknowledged that "his articles on Iran cost him . . . friends, and had done his reputation little good, and the resultant controversy had put a sudden end to his collaboration with *Corriere della sera*" (1993, 423). As we have shown, even among those French intellectuals who had voiced uncritical enthusiasm for the revolutionary movement in Iran, Foucault stood out in his celebration of its dominant Islamist wing, including the latter's rejection of Western Marxist and liberal notions of democracy, women's equality, and human rights.[16]

It is relatively easy, from the vantage point of the twenty-first century, when militant Islamist movements have caused immense destruction not only in Iran, but also in Algeria, Egypt, Afghanistan, and the United States, to see substantial flaws in Foucault's writings on Iran. Were Foucault's almost totally uncritical assessments of Islamism in Iran an aberration for a theorist usually concerned with the critique of systems of power and control? Were they, as Rodinson suggested, an example of a European theorist making ill-informed judgments on a non-European society about which he had little knowledge? Recall that Foucault himself had once criticized Sartre for attempting to be a "spokesman of the universal." In that 1977 critique of Sartre, Foucault had said that what was needed, instead of a great humanist philosopher speaking on all relevant political issues, was "the 'specific' intellectual as opposed to the 'universal' intellectual" (1977b, 68), one who spoke on the basis of a particular expertise, such as Foucault's own on the prison, or others on nuclear weapons, or the environment.

In this study, we have argued that something deeper than ignorance of Iranian history and culture, something more organic to Foucault's core theoretical stance, was at work in creating the deep flaws that marked his writings on Iran. Foucault's positions on Iran are not only rooted in his better-known writings, but they also accentuate some of the problematic consequences of his overall theoretical enterprise. Did not a post-structuralist, leftist discourse, which spent all of its energy opposing the secular liberal or authoritarian modern state and its institutions, leave the door wide open to an uncritical stance toward Islamism and other socially retrogressive movements, especially when, as in Iran, they formed a pole of opposition to an authoritarian state and the global political and economic order?

In 1984, just before his death, Foucault penned an essay entitled "What Is Enlightenment?" on the two-hundredth anniversary of Immanuel Kant's famous article with the same title. As Steven Best and Douglas Kellner (1991) and David Ingram (1994) have written, here Foucault seemed to alter somewhat his stance toward both the Enlightenment and humanism. We believe that the tragic outcome of the Iranian Revolution formed part of the background to this essay. Foucault now acknowledged that many philosophical questions formulated by the Enlightenment "remain for us to consider" and that, therefore, one does not have "to be 'for' or 'against' the Enlightenment" (Foucault 1984, 43). He even called for a more nuanced attitude toward the concept of humanism. He pointed out that there had been a variety of forms of humanism, such as Christian humanism, scientific humanism, Marxist humanism, and Existential humanism, as well as claims to humanism by fascists and Stalinists. Foucault seemed to take back some of his earlier attacks on humanism: "From this we must not conclude that everything that has been linked with humanism is to be rejected, but that the humanistic thematic is in itself too supple, too diverse, too inconsistent in itself, to serve as an axis of reflection." Still, he maintained that it was "dangerous to confuse" humanism with the Enlightenment (44).

Finally, Foucault reformulated his longtime preoccupation with the local and the particular versus the universal in a sharp critique of any "global or radical" solutions:

> The historical ontology of ourselves must turn away from all projects that claim to be global or radical. In fact *we know from experience* that the claim to escape from the system of contemporary reality so as to produce the overall programs of another society, or another way of thinking, *another culture*, another vision of the world, has led only to the *return of the most dangerous traditionalism*. (1984, 46; emphasis added)

It is quite likely that the points above concerning his "experience," "another culture," and "the most dangerous traditionalism" were directed at his own earlier writings on the Iranian Revolution. In this 1984 essay, Foucault also altered his well-known formulation that critique had to be aimed at the knowledge/power axis. He now added the concept of ethics, referring to "the axis of knowledge, the axis of power, and the axis of ethics." Ethics was also the subject of the last two volumes of *The History of Sexuality*, which dealt with the "ethics of love" in the ancient Greco-Roman world. And so we turn to Foucault's later writings on ethics—and their relationship to his Iran writings—in our last chapter.

Chapter 5

Foucault, Gender, and Male Homosexualities in Mediterranean and Muslim Societies

There has been much speculation about Foucault's sudden interest in the Greco-Roman world, the focus of the last two volumes of *The History of Sexuality*, subtitled *The Uses of Pleasure* and *The Care of the Self*, both published in 1984. Eribon suggested there was a "personal crisis and an intellectual crisis" in Foucault's life in the years after the 1976 publication of the first volume of *The History of Sexuality*, which received mixed reviews, and the negative reception to his writings on Iran (Eribon 1991, 277). Others have criticized Foucault for turning to a period and a region outside his area of expertise, instead of continuing with his ground-breaking critique of modernity. But was this in fact the case? David Halperin argued that Foucault was still speaking to our present concerns with sexuality, even though the subject matter was the ancient Mediterranean world. Foucault went back to the Greeks because of his concern with the here and now and in order to "discover a new way of seeing ourselves and possibly to create new ways of inhabiting our skin" (Halperin 1990, 70).[1] Mark Poster wrote that Foucault "undermined the unquestionable legitimacy of the present by offering a recreation of a different past." Poster argued that this re-creation of the past was not a nostalgic one and that the "rupture between the past and the present generates the space for critique" (1986, 209).

We suggest that contemporary concerns lay behind Foucault's late writings in a different way. As we argued in chapter 1, Foucault's Orient was not a geographical concept; rather, it included the Greco-Roman world, as well as the modern Middle East and North Africa. With this in mind, the last two volumes of *The History of Sexuality* suddenly become more relevant to today, specifically in relation to his writings on Iran. There is some evidence that, in his explorations of male homosexuality in ancient Greece and Rome, Foucault may have been looking for parallels to contemporary sexual practices in the Middle East and North Africa. Indeed, if one reads the last two volumes of *The History of Sexuality* alongside some recent scholarship on male homosexuality in the Muslim world, one finds a similar pattern of social relations and customs. For this reason, Foucault's late writings on gender and sexuality in the ancient Greco-Roman world deserve more attention from readers concerned with the implications of his thought for contemporary Middle Eastern and Mediterranean societies.

This chapter begins with an analysis of Foucault's scattered remarks on gender and male homosexuality in the Muslim world, suggesting that he saw a continuity between ancient Greek homosexuality and male homosexual relations in contemporary North African and Middle Eastern societies. Next, we explore Foucault's writings on sexuality in the last two volumes of *The History of Sexuality* and suggest that Foucault's Orientalism extended itself to this realm as well. Recalling that Foucault lumped together premodern Western societies and modern Oriental ones, we explore his idealized notion of an ethics of love in the ancient Mediterranean societies that was practiced by a small group of elite Greek and Roman men. In the last section we return to the subject of male homosexuality in the Muslim Middle East and suggest that the issues of gender and sexuality occupied a nonobvious but undeniably crucial site in the revolutionary discourse in Iran.

Finally, we inquire into the ramifications of these writings of Foucault for the modern gay and lesbian movement in the Muslim world. Up to a point, Foucault was correct in his observation that Muslim societies have remained somewhat flexible on same-sex relations. But such a limited form of acceptance, which involves a total closeting, is not the same as the recognition sought by the modern gay and lesbian rights movement. Indeed, while several aspects of Foucault's thought can be quite useful for the study of the Middle East, his position on sexuality and gender rights comes into conflict with the aspirations of both the feminist and the gay and lesbian rights movements in the region. To this day, legal rights for homosexuals in Middle Eastern Muslim societies are nonexistent, and there are no centers or laws in these societies that are aimed at protecting the rights of those who engage in open, consensual gay relationships.

Imagining the Natives

Edward Said wrote that the colonies offered more than raw materials to the colonial metropolis: "Just as the various colonial possessions—quite apart from their economic benefit to metropolitan Europe—were useful as places to send wayward sons, superfluous populations of delinquents, poor people, and other undesirables, so the Orient was a place where one could look for sexual experience unobtainable in Europe" (1978, 190). Sexual tourism influenced the literary discourse of numerous European writers as well. By the nineteenth century, reading about "Oriental sex" had become part of mass culture: "Virtually no European writer who wrote on, or traveled to, the Orient in the period after 1800 exempted himself or herself from this quest: Flaubert, Nerval, 'Dirty Dick' Burton, and Lane are only the most notable. . . . What they looked for often—correctly, I think—was a different type of sexuality, perhaps more libertine and less guilt-ridden" (190).[2]

Foucault's stint as a visiting professor of philosophy in Tunisia from 1966 to 1968 was not entirely free of such attitudes.[3] Two themes emerge from his experience in Tunisia that may have prefigured some of his later attitudes toward the Iranian Revolution. The first is his strong admiration for those who sacrificed themselves for a cause, especially when there was a risk of death or harsh punishment. Foucault had great respect for the Tunisian leftist students who, in 1967–68, faced severe government repression against their protest movements.[4] A decade later, in a discussion of Marxism when he was at the height of his enthusiasm for the Iranian Revolution, Foucault referred to this experience as what had influenced him to become more politically engaged. He stated that he was "profoundly struck and amazed by those young men and women who exposed themselves to serious risks for the simple fact of having written or distributed a leaflet, or for having incited others to go on strike" (1991, 134). He also suggested that there was something deeper about the Tunisian student movement than the more risk-free situation of the French student rebels of May 1968. While he acknowledged that the Tunisian students considered themselves Marxists, he described the role of what he called "political ideology" as "secondary" to a more "existential" commitment to self-sacrifice:

> What on earth is it that can set off in an individual the desire, the capacity, and the possibility of an absolute sacrifice without our being able to recognize or suspect the slightest ambition or desire for power or profit? That is what I saw in Tunisia. The necessity for a struggle was clearly evident there on

> account of the intolerable nature of certain conditions produced by capitalism, colonialism, and neo-colonialism. (136–37)

As we saw earlier, a similar fascination with sacrifice and death appears throughout his Iran writings.

The second theme in his attitude toward Tunisia never became explicit in Foucault's Iran writings but likely formed a backdrop to them. He seemed to have formed an impression that homosexual men enjoyed greater sexual freedom there than in France. His biographer David Macey noted that "gay men from France had long known that North Africa was an agreeable holiday destination," and mentioned that Foucault did not hesitate to avail himself of a number of young Arab male lovers during those years in what he evidently perceived as a society permeated with homoeroticism (1993, 184–85).

The Tunisian sociologist Fathi Triki, who studied with Foucault from 1966 to 1968, points out that Foucault was part of the French tourist culture and shared similar assumptions about the openness of Arab and Middle Eastern culture on homosexuality. Like many other French gay men who came to North Africa for recreation and often found sexual partners within both the French tourist colonies and the Arab community, Foucault was excited by the culture he witnessed in the Maghreb and what he regarded as the open homoeroticism of the Arab Mediterranean. Moreover, in this admiration for the Mediterranean/Muslim world, Foucault avoided addressing the sexism or homophobia of these cultures. It was true that, while in Tunisia, Foucault did frequent a women's cultural center; the Club Culturel Tahar Haddad, a café run by the feminist activist and writer Jalila Hafsia.[5] Perhaps Foucault's frequent lectures at Hafsia's café were at least an indirect expression of support for women's rights, as Triki has suggested (personal communication, March 3, 2002). Triki also commented on Foucault's rather naïve view of homosexuality in the Muslim world:

> I believe that Foucault was very subjective and at the same time very naïve. He knew well that his privileged situation permitted deviations. What's more, in a society whose economy is founded on tourism (like Tunisia), sexuality (homo and hetero) was part of the landscape, and Foucault availed himself of it. It is probably true that this situation influenced his opinions on homosexuality in Islam and in Iran. French intellectuals are very exacting concerning specialized knowledge, except on Islam. One can all of a sudden become a specialist on Islam. (Personal communication, March 27, 2002)

Foucault expressed a similar sentiment during a 1976 conversation in Paris with his friends Claude Mauriac and Catherine von Bülow. Mauriac and Foucault began by joking about the "satin beauty" of a young Arab acquaintance they had seen at a Paris demonstration against the expulsion of Pakistani immigrants. As recorded in Mauriac's diary, von Bülow complained at this point about the sexism of Middle Eastern men at the march. She stated that she had been "flabbergasted" by an Arab man who had told her to separate herself from the men at the demonstration (Mauriac 1986, 235). Foucault responded very forcefully. He shifted the issue from the treatment she had received to one of sympathy for a culture marked by an underlying homoeroticism. His remarks seemed to stun Mauriac, who recorded them at some length, perhaps with Foucault's later Iran episode in mind:

> They live among men. As men, they are made for men, with the fleeting bedazzlement, the brief reward of women. One has succeeded in denying, in breaking that fundamental bond that was, for a long time, that of the Spanish army: groups of ten men who never left one another, depended upon and responded to each other, fought and defended themselves together, and took responsibility for the families of those who were killed. To be sure, those fraternal cells were based on a subtle mixture of friendship and sensuality. And sexuality (later denied and rejected so constantly) had its place there. (235)

Expressed only two years before his 1978 visits to Iran, Foucault's remarks exemplified what from Said's perspective could be termed a Romantic Orientalism. Here, Foucault may have merged homoeroticism with gender-segregated customs in Muslim societies and a different sense of cultural taboos, as in the case of men commonly holding hands or kissing.

In his Iran writings, Foucault reacted in a similar manner to criticisms of gender roles in a future Islamist-run Iranian society. As we saw earlier, in his visits in 1978 and even after the revolution, Foucault made little criticism of the "separate but equal" doctrine on women's rights of Iran's religious authorities. He also accused "Atoussa H.," an Iranian feminist who attacked his stance on Iran, of harboring Orientalist sentiments.

When he arrived in Iran in 1978, Foucault seemed to believe that Iranian Islamism would also display a greater acceptance of homosexuality than the modern West. Two decades later, the sociologist Ehsan Naraghi, who had met with Foucault during one of his visits to Iran, recalled their conversation in an interview with the well-known journalist Ibrahim Nabavi:

> IBRAHIM NABAVI: What was the story about Michel Foucault in the early period of the revolution? I heard Michel Foucault suddenly sided with the Iranian Revolution and defended it, and that it was for this reason that he was ostracized in France. EHSAN NARAGHI: You know that Michel Foucault was a homosexual, and this issue had an important influence on his ideology and his thinking. Well, I knew him from our days at the Collège de France. We were friends and went a long way back. About three or four months before the victory of the revolution—I do not remember if it was the first or the second time he had come to Iran—he called me one day and said he would like to speak with revolutionaries. I said, "Very well, come to my house tonight." He agreed but said he was not alone and would bring a young student who was his secretary. I understood what he meant, but I did not tell my wife, since she was sensitive about [homosexuals]. . . . Several devout Muslims came . . . and my wife [Angel Arabshaybani] was also in the meeting. Foucault was very curious and very sensitive about the issue [of homosexuality], and suddenly he asked, "What would the position of Islam and this future Islamic government be toward those we call minorities?" My wife and the other two said, "In Islam, respect for minorities is required, and several religions such as Judaism, Christianity, and Zoroastrians may exist." They did not understand the meaning of Foucault's question, although I immediately understood what he meant. Foucault said, "I mean the attitude toward those whom society calls abnormal and such other things . . ." My wife realized what he was talking about. . . . She got up and brought a French translation of a Quranic verse, placed it in front of Michel Foucault, and said, "Execution!" Foucault was dumb-founded. He was upset and left that night. This was the first denunciation he received from Islam, because until then he did not know Islam. He believed that Islam approved of homosexuality. I know from other sources that he insisted a great deal on justifying this issue. Two or three weeks after the revolution, when Khalkhali hanged several homosexuals, my wife said to me, "Give me the address of this friend of yours so I could tell him that that idealistic society where you thought homosexuality would be approved, is this!" She wanted to send him a newspaper clipping where an account of the execution of homosexuals was printed. (Nabavi 1999, 124–25)

Later, Naraghi said he was simply baffled by Foucault's ignorance. Despite his great respect for Foucault, Naraghi wondered how such an enormously erudite man, a friend of Muslims and Arabs, nevertheless was so ignorant on same-sex relations in the Muslim world (personal communication from Ehsan Naraghi, April 10, 2001).

What do we know about homosexuality in the Muslim world, and to what extent was Foucault correct in his assumptions about male homosexuality in more traditional Muslim societies? His Iranian acquaintances were certainly correct to caution Foucault about his naïveté concerning the harsh views of the Quran on homosexuality. But perhaps the situation here is more complex than they thought, at least concerning covert homosexuality. We return to these questions in the last part of this chapter. First we need to look at Foucault's writings on homosexuality in the Greco-Roman world.

Moderation or Misogyny? The Ethics of Love in the Ancient Mediterranean World

The last two volumes of Foucault's *The History of Sexuality* centered on the Greco-Roman world, from the fourth century BCE to roughly the second century CE. Foucault's interest here lay principally in the following important question: "How, why, in what form was sexuality established as a moral domain?" (Foucault 1985, 10). In other words, at what point in history, and under what circumstances, did sex become equated with sin and evil? Unlike some of his earlier works, *The History of Sexuality*, especially volumes 2 and 3, was concerned with the issue of subjectivity and the "history of desiring man." However, a close reading of these last two volumes suggests that he was almost exclusively interested in the point of view and history of the elite men of the Greek academy and the Roman aristocracy. Conflicting voices of marginalized others—women, young boys, slaves, or noncitizens—were almost never heard in Foucault's narrative, even when they could be found in ancient philosophy, poetry, or comedy. In addition, Foucault scarcely questioned the classic discourses he reproduced and often read normative, prescriptive texts as descriptive ones.

Amy Richlin has argued that Foucault's history of antiquity omits significant discussions not only of women, but also of numerous other marginalized groups: "Foucault has reproduced for his readers an antiquity without Jews . . . without Africans, Egyptians, Semites, northern Europeans; without children, babies, poor people, slaves. All the 'Greeks' are Athenians and most of the 'Romans' are Greeks" (Richlin 1998, 139; see also Foxhall 1998).

Foucault's selective reading of classical Greco-Roman texts followed a binary pattern similar to that of his earlier genealogical studies. At first, he seemed to be emphasizing a certain continuity in the discourse on sex from the ancient Greeks and Romans, to the medieval Christians, and to modern Western society. A closer examination, however, shows that he was again privileging, older, idealized, and self-imposed ethical forms in contrast to newer institutionalized ones. While acknowledging a plurality of discourses on love in the classical Greek period, Foucault singled out the rituals of love associated with a small group of elite, Athenian, male citizens and lamented the gradual loss of these rituals by the time of the Roman Empire.

Foucault argued that certain rituals of courtship were observed in the relations between adult men and adolescent boys and that these rituals constituted the first recorded ethics of love in the Western world. These rituals were followed because Greek society had a problem. Boys were expected to take their place as adult citizens of the state and their reputation as adolescents would affect their future status. The Greek ethics of male love revolved around how to treat the boys as sexual objects without reducing them to the low status of women. Foucault was aware that this ethics of love was practiced in a society where misogyny was overwhelming. Throughout the text and elsewhere, he pointed to the subordinate position of women as well as the ethics of male love, but ultimately failed to relate the two issues in a coherent, systematic way. His ethics of love was clearly in a dialectical tension with the pervasive Greek male contempt for women and a taxonomy that relegated women, slaves, and noncitizens to the bottom rungs of the social ladder. As we shall see, Foucault recognized the fact that the Greek concepts he so valorized—the models of ethicality, moderation, self-mastery, and even health and diet concerns—were all built on a gendered subtext. Nonetheless, he dismissed the ramifications of this link for his "aesthetics of existence." We may therefore legitimately ask: Is the new space that Foucault created between the old and the new worlds hospitable to feminist concerns?

The Economy of Marriage

According to Foucault, sex in the ancient Greco-Roman world was seen as neither bad nor a sin.[6] In fact, it was the most natural activity, restoring men to the highest state of being (Foucault 1985). The Greeks drew a distinction between sex according to nature (between a man and women for procreation), and sex that was against nature and for pleasure. But in a society that prided itself on "triumph over nature," going against nature was not necessarily equated with immorality.[7] Propriety and ethics in sex were defined by two other Aristotelian concepts: (1) According to the principle of moderation, sex was a natural desire, similar to that for food or drink. One partook of it to satisfy a need; more than that was excessive and hence improper. (2) According to the principle of position, there was a significant distinction between the active adult lover, the *erastes*, and the passive adolescent boy, the *paidika*. Hence, "for a man, excess and passivity were the two forms of immorality in the practice of the *aphrodisia*" (Foucault 1985, 47).

Likewise, ethical behavior in the ancient world was different from that of the modern West, since marriage was an economic and political affair negotiated between the father of the bride and the male suitor. Elite married men often kept mistresses, concubines, and paidikas.[8] Foucault placed the blame for the lack of reciprocity between husband and wife on the institution of marriage. He argued that marriage prevented the husband from desiring reciprocity with his wife. But since there were no "institutional constraints" in the man/boy relationship, here we found "reciprocal independence," Foucault concluded (1985, 203). He surmised that the notion of "conjugal pleasure" was irrelevant to both the Greco-Roman and the medieval Christian worlds. In Greece, pleasure was experienced outside marriage, often in erotic relations with boys, while under Christianity sexual pleasure was not an ideal (144). In Greek marriage there was a "reciprocal" relationship though not a "symmetrical" one. The husband trained his usually younger wife, who was expected to stay indoors and to manage the household and the children. In return for the wife's fidelity, the husband might agree not to humiliate her. Justice meant not doing things that seriously compromised the woman's position, such as engaging in public extramarital liaisons, openly maintaining regular concubines, or producing illegitimate children, activities that nevertheless took place (179).

Foucault was not interested in women's voices or how their resistance was reflected in literary works such Homer's *Odyssey* or Euripides's *Medea*, works that showed women's rage toward unfaithful men and their desire for greater reciprocity.[9] With regard to such omissions, Foxhall writes, "I would not argue that women in classical Greece were not oppressed, but I would maintain they resisted suppression" (1998, 137). Richlin suggests that even the most misogynistic texts of antiquity considered women as erotic beings, and points out that "the absence of the female from *The History of Sexuality* is pervasive, going beyond a simple choice of subject matter" (1998, 139). Richlin asks how Foucault's works would have looked if he had included the female subject. She provides outlines of accounts and events that were inexplicably left out of Foucault's work, including many details on female prostitution, slavery, and lesbian relations. She reaches the conclusion that Foucault's account of sexuality in the ancient world is "even more male-centered than what his sources present" (148).[10]

Eros, or Love of Boys

Foucault was not concerned with the alternative visions of gender relations explored by ancient philosophers and writers.[11] Nor was he interested in exploring the technologies through which women were dominated and domesticated as wives. A key question, then, is whether he was interested in the technologies of power that defined same-sex relations among men in the ancient world. The answer is that he was not interested in that subject either. *The Uses of Pleasure* celebrates the man/boy ethics of love, or in Foucault's words, "*true love*" (as against the presumed false love of women). This male ethics was composed of a set of courting rituals between the erastes and the paidika, the purpose of which was to guard the boy's public reputation, since he was eventually to become an adult citizen and take his place in public affairs of the state. While having a boy as a lover was an acceptable practice in ancient Greece, the reputation of the boy during these adolescent years could determine his future political status. Foucault celebrated this sexual ethics as an "aesthetics of existence" and emphasized the concern of the lover for the beloved, as well as certain self-imposed "forms of austerity" observed by the older lover (1985, 253).[12]

Foucault's interpretation of eros was markedly different from that of several leading scholars of the ancient world and Greek homosexuality, especially Kenneth J. Dover (1989) and David M. Halperin (1990). Dover, an eminent scholar in the field, whose *Greek Homosexuality*[13] had an important influence on Foucault's own work, stresses that certain modes of behavior were regarded as honorable, others as dishonorable.[14] The erastes used a variety of customary gifts to court the young adolescent. The erastes also promised the boy social contacts that would advance his future career, advised and trained him in the art of manhood, and ultimately introduced him to "philosophical truths." The paidika was expected to refuse, resist, flee, or escape. Eventually, he might agree to mutual masturbation but was never to permit "penetration of any orifice in his body." When he agreed to engage in amorous relations, it was supposed to be out of a sense of admiration, gratitude, and affection for the erastes, as well as the desire to please him, not because of the paidika's own sexual feelings (Dover 1989, 103). Greek society publicly maintained the fiction that these adolescent boys were still incapable of experiencing any sexual pleasure or sensation. Xenophon wrote that "the boy does not share in the man's pleasures in intercourse, as a woman does; cold sober, he looks upon the other [who is] drunk with sexual desire" (cited in Dover 1989, 52). Other cardinal rules were that a paidika should never submit for money, which reduced him to the level of a prostitute, nor should he initiate a sexual liaison, which was regarded as shameful. Once he grew a beard and became an adult, the relationship was expected to end, and usually did. The young man then took his place as a citizen in the city-state, entered a respectable marriage, and might cultivate his own string of paidikas (224).[15]

Foucault did not explore the "division of labor" in which the senior lover was assumed to be in the active position. A theorist who was known for his keen and incisive observations on the knowledge/power axis, an author who had endlessly reminded us that the body is a site for minute articulations of power, and the location upon which domination is established, entirely missed the boat when the knowledge/power axis was the Greek academy, which was operated by elite older men, and where the bodies upon which they took their pleasure were those of its adolescent students. Where were Foucault's ruminations on the minute operations of power in the academy, the assembly, the family, the popular culture (such as the bitter satire of Aristophanes),[16] or on the "economy" of this highly asymmetrical relationship?

Dover, in contrast, pays a great deal of attention to the class, ethnic, and gender subtexts of Greek society. His work, together with a close reading of some of the texts used by Foucault, suggests that Foucault's emphasis on an ethics of love that was self-regulated and stemmed from a desire for moderation was seriously questionable. This is because the relationship between the erastes and the paidika was regulated by a set of technologies of power, backed by laws and class prerogatives.

Greek philosophers and artists referred to the inequality between the two partners in same-sex male relations, or what Dover calls the "fundamental contradiction within the Greek homosexual ethos" (1989, 137). Plato's *Symposium* includes a discussion of this customary double standard. The friends of the erastes admired him for his dogged pursuit of the young boy and found his seemingly irrational efforts to win the heart of the boy amusing. The father of the young paidika, however, was disturbed by the possibility of sex between his boy and the erastes in the academy. If the father was wealthy, he employed slaves to watch the boy like a hawk. More important, the boy's same-age friends admonished and "reproached" him if anything was going on between the young paidika and his erastes (82). Foucault touched on this subject without exploring the fact that the relationship between the erastes and the paidika fit a common pattern of dominant/subordinate human relations.

Eros played a significant role in political power games as well. The comedies of Aristophanes often centered on older male citizens, who were resentful of younger ones who ran for office, assumed lucrative posts, and took over the assembly. Sometimes, the older men expressed their resentment by accusing the younger citizens of having engaged in homosexual conduct when they were boys (Dover 1989, 141). Also, sometimes young aspirants tried to assure future success by courting the sexual favors of the right people; hence, they used sex in jockeying for position and in order to secure powerful patrons. Sex was therefore a powerful political weapon that was used regularly in Athenian society, not just in marriage and heterosexual relations, but also in same-sex relations where the political stakes were high. And yet the uses of eros in the game of politics hardly appeared in Foucault's text.

Foucault suggested that the relationship between the erastes and the paidika was regulated by a self-imposed moderation rather than by law. But in fact, Greek society had developed a detailed juridical structure through which proper and improper same-sex relations (as well as heterosexual relations) were examined, tried, and punished. A legal distinction was made between legitimate and illegitimate eros. Slaves often endured nonconsensual sexual relationships. They also were barred from using the gymnasium and were prohibited from "being in love with a boy of free status or following him" (Dover 1989, 46). Rape of a paidika incurred severe penalties. In addition, a paidika who had received money in return for sexual favors could not address the public assembly or hold office as an adult citizen. If he did, and if a jury proved charges of "prostitution" against him, he could be executed. The unethical father or guardian of a boy of free status who hired him out for sexual services was also punishable by law (27). In legal disputes, juries discussed the extent of such transgression and explored the circumstances when reaching a verdict (36). Greek society also had its own version of congressional impeachment. Timarkhes, the Athenian politician who had opposed the peace treaties with Philip II of Macedonia, was tried in 346 BCE on charges of having prostituted himself as a boy. The accusations almost certainly stemmed from efforts by his political enemies to remove him and his friends from office (Dover 1989).

There was also an economic dimension to the relation of the erastes to the paidika. Foucault correctly pointed out that it was customary to give gifts to the young boy. But at what point did a "gift" become a "monetary compensation," relegating the boy to the status of a "prostitute"? The cost of winning over a desired person by expensive gifts was high. One also needed a great deal of leisure time to watch the boy in the gymnasium and follow him around. Furthermore, "many conversations about art and war and life were needed in order to make oneself admirable and interesting in the eyes of a boy." Virtually all the personages we meet in Plato's dialogues belong to a leisure class, some of them from the high aristocracy (Dover 1989, 150). Greek comedians were aware of this class distinction and used it as material for their satire. In contrast to Foucault, who called the relationship between the erastes and the paidika "true love" and the relationship between husband and wife "reciprocal" though "not symmetrical," Dover pointed out that in Greek society neither heterosexual nor same-sex relations involved the "reciprocated sentiments of equals but . . . the pursuit of those of lower status by those of higher status. The virtues admired in an eromenos [paidika] are the virtues which the ruling element in a society (in the case of Greek society, adult male citizens) approve in the ruled (women and children)" (84). These technologies of power, law, and economics show that the position of the paidika was that of a subordinate, yet desired and pursued object of sexual conquest.

Finally, Foucault never devoted more than a few brief lines to the subject of lesbian relations (Foucault 1986, 202, 206). Dover explored the life and poems of Sappho, the Greek lesbian poet of the sixth century BCE, and other female same-sex issues. He pointed out that in Sappho's poetry we come across the same themes that existed between the erastes and the paidika—that is, pursuit, fleeing, gifts, and ultimately love—so that male and female same-sex relations paralleled each other in some areas, though lesbian relations were more reciprocal than male homosexual ones (Dover 1989, 177).

In this society, therefore, the erastes played the traditional dominant role, and the paidika played the traditional subordinate one. In societies with complex social class hierarchies, dominant groups have access to a society's culture and overall outlook in literature, philosophy, and the law. They usually legitimize the unequal relationships and incorporate them into the society's guiding principles. Dominant groups define the subordinates by assigning one or more acceptable roles to them. They might assume that the subordinates have some innate mental or moral defect. Dominant groups also encourage subordinates to develop psychological traits that are pleasing to them. When subordinates break through these assigned roles and show assertiveness and initiative, the dominant group defines them as abnormal. Finally, dominant parties perceive the way things are as "right" and "good" for themselves as well as for the subordinates and see little reason for change (Miller 2001).

All of these patterns appeared in the relationship between the erastes and the paidika, as the adult lovers tried to confine the paidika to the passive position in sexual relations. They assumed that the paidika was physically incapable of experiencing any sensations (pleasure or trauma) during sex. Young adolescent boys were not expected to initiate sexual relations or ask for monetary compensation. Those who did so were branded prostitutes. In the academy, the erastes legitimized this unequal relationship as one of the guiding principles of society, and developed a set of courtship practices around it. They also made such courtship a necessary component of attaining philosophical truth. The erastes seemed to have convinced themselves that this relationship was of great value to the paidikas, who were trained in the art of manhood and helped to develop valuable social connections. How is it that Foucault never critiqued or questioned the difference in power in these relations and instead celebrated the point of view of the erastes?

What Is the Gender of Moderation?

As we saw, the Greeks were ostensibly concerned with two modalities, position and moderation, which we discuss briefly below. The Greek male's disdain for passivity was linked to a disdain for femininity: "In Greek eyes the male who broke the 'rules' of legitimate eros detached himself from the rank of male citizenry and classified himself with women and foreigners" (Dover 1989, 103). By dancing around the actual definition of "passivity" in Greek homosexuality throughout the text, Foucault played down the hypocrisy of a culture where same-sex relations were prevalent but boys who submitted to physical penetration (by force or by consent) were vilified for life.

But what about moderation? What did the Greeks mean by moderation? And what did excess imply to them? Moderation was a matter of self-control and self-mastery. It was an internal, rather than an external, limitation and hence, in Foucault's eyes, a more highly-regarded concept. The notion of moderation, as used by the ancients, was summed up most comprehensively in Aristotle's *Nicomachean Ethics*. A well-known example was Aristotle's notion of courage. The virtue of courage was a mean, bounded at one extreme by recklessness and at the other by cowardice. Virtue was the ability to express one's feelings to a moderate degree, neither too strongly nor too weakly and as pertaining to a particular situation. Moderation was not a gender-neutral concept, for being able to conceptualize and apply the ideal of moderation implied reason, something Aristotle saw as lacking in women. Women, he argued, were incapable of exercising political rule in a moderate, reasoned manner and when given political power, they all too easily lost self-control and fell into excess. This had happened at times in Sparta, undermining the state.[17]

Hence, both moderation and passivity stemmed from the male/female opposition. Foucault admitted this himself:

> [The fact] that moderation is given an essentially masculine structure has another consequence. . . . Immoderation derives from a passivity that relates to its femininity. To be immoderate was to be in a state of nonresistance with regard to the force of pleasures, and in a position of weakness and submission; it meant being incapable of that virile stance with respect to oneself that enabled one to be stronger than oneself. In this sense, the man of pleasures

> and desires, the man of non-mastery (*akrasia*) or self-indulgence (*akolasia*) was a man who could be called feminine. (Foucault 1985, 84–85)

Woman, who was associated with nature, was immoderate and weak, while a true man was one who had gained self-mastery. In *The Care of the Self*, Foucault reiterated the relationship between masculinity and self-mastery: "The penis thus appears at the intersection of all these games of mastery: self-mastery" (Foucault 1986, 34).

There was also a gendered subtext to moderation in matters of health, food, and exercise. Since it was assumed that one spent vital and much-needed energy during the sexual act, philosophers and physicians provided detailed advice on the age of the partners, season of the year, time of day, and frequency of sexual activities. Self-imposed moderation, rather than religious and state-imposed prohibitions, defined the ethics of sexual activity in this era as well (Foucault 1985, 114). Moderation was advised with regard to exercise, food, drink, and seasons of the year when, depending on the severity of the weather, one engaged in certain activities or abstained from others, all with an eye toward maintaining optimum sexual health. The male-centered nature of this ethics of health was revealed especially in the interpretations of the act of coitus. In the Greek view, men's secretion of semen depleted their vital life force. Ejaculation was a "small death." Excessive sex and great indulgence in sexual pleasures could supposedly lead to death (126–33). Sex was beneficial to women for the opposite reason, however. Women not only experienced orgasm, but they also literally benefited from the secretion of men's semen. In this dried-sponge view of women's sexuality, the male's fluids improved a woman's health. The womb was moistened, preventing it from drying up and causing contractions and extreme pain: "For the woman's body, penetration by the man and absorption of sperm are the primary source of the equilibrium of its qualities and the key stimulus for the necessary flow of its humors." The semen that was evidently life-giving to the woman was life-draining for the man (129, 137).[18]

Foucault concluded that in the three areas where Greeks questioned themselves about sexual behavior as an ethical problem, namely health and diet, marriage, and love of boys, they cultivated an "aesthetics of existence" (1985, 253). As the preceding discussion has shown, this art of living, which demarcated the boundary between acceptable and unacceptable lifestyles, was founded on subtle (and sometimes flagrant) gendered assumptions. It is true that the techniques that defined this lifestyle—moderation, self-mastery, and health—were not based on a code of law of supposedly divine origin. They did, however, stem from an inherent devaluation of passivity, of women and of their subordinate position. Greek society defined itself in sex, economy, law, and politics through an invisible feminine subtext.[19] Foucault's reading of Greek homosexuality was problematic because he ignored the theoretical ramifications of this gendered subtext of the ancient (male) ethics, which defined the sexual relations between men and women, and between men and boys. In Foucault's genealogies of the modern world, we have docile bodies but not resisting subjects; in his nostalgic pursuit of an ethics of love in Greek antiquity, we have desiring subjects whose power games and techniques of domination are hardly scrutinized.

The Care of the Self

In *The Care of the Self*, volume 3 of *The History of Sexuality*, Foucault admitted that the status of women in marriage improved in the Hellenistic and Roman eras, compared to their status in classical Athenian society.[20] However, the language he chose to discuss this change betrayed his sentiments. We know that marriage became more and more a voluntary agreement between partners. The father had less authority in deciding his daughter's marriage. The wife gained certain economic and legal rights. Women sometimes collected their inheritance, owned property, and could dispose of their guardians. Women's sexual obligations remained the same, while men's rights were now more limited. Women could specify in a marriage contract that there be no regularly maintained concubines in a separate house and no recognized children outside marriage (Bridenthal, Koonz, and Stuard 1987). But Foucault wrote that Roman society "threw off the economic and social purposes that had invested [marriage] with value. . . . It became more and more restrictive for spouses [*sic*] . . . a stronger force for binding conjugal partners and hence a more effective one for isolating the couple in a field of other social relations" (1986, 77). Foucault clearly took a dim view of these changes. The earlier economic and social purposes of marriage had made the institution valuable. Stripped of these purposes, marriage was now disadvantageous. Apparently, the more rights women gained in marriage, the less valuable as a whole the institution became![21] Marriage, Foucault agreed, "isolated" the couple from other social relations. In fact, however, women's social relations outside the home substantially increased in the Hellenistic and Roman eras.

Plutarch (45–125 CE) summarized many of these new ways of thinking. Sex was no longer a man's absolute right in marriage; it now involved affection, attention, and reciprocity. There was also a questioning of adult male love for boys, on new moral and ethical grounds. Plutarch, who had been a member of Plato's academy, argued that pederasty often involved force and violence. What was lacking in the relationship to the *paidika* was *charis*, or consent.[22] The Roman rhetorician Marcus Fabius Quintilian (35–95 CE) had likewise called for new standards in the academy. The teacher, he argued, must "adopt the attitude of a parent toward his pupils and consider that he is taking the place of those who entrust their children to him" (cited in Foucault 1986, 190).

In *The Care of the Self*, Foucault did not respond to Plutarch or Quintilian's keen observations that consent was lacking in most man/boy relations. Instead, he lamented the fact that as marital love and better communication between husband and wife become cherished goals, "one begins to question, in an increasingly doubtful mode, the privileges that used to be granted to the love of boys" (Foucault 1986, 185). A bit further on, Foucault wrote: "Everything that the erotics of boys was able to claim as properly belonging to that form of love (*in opposition to the false love for women*) will be re-utilized here, not only to the fondness for women, but to the conjugal relationship itself" (203). Furthermore, Foucault wrote that Plutarch "has borrowed from the erotics of boys its fundamental and traditional features in order to demonstrate that they can be applied not to all forms of love, but to the conjugal relationship alone" (205). While many readers today would sympathize with Foucault's lament, they would find his rejection of reciprocity more troubling.

Elsewhere, in a conversation with Paul Rabinow, Foucault was even more blunt in distinguishing his "ethics" from any notion of reciprocity:

> *L'Usage du plaisir* is a book about sexual ethics; it's not a book about love, or about friendship, or about reciprocity. And it is very significant that when Plato tries to integrate love for boys and friendship, he is obliged to put aside sexual relations. Friendship is reciprocal, and sexual relations are not reciprocal; in sexual relations, you can penetrate or you are penetrated . . . If you have friendship, it is difficult to have sexual relations. (Foucault 1983, 344)[23]

Foucault's ethics of love in antiquity shared some of the problems of the Aristotelian ethics on which it was based, without exhibiting many of its positive attributes. As Ruth Groenhout (1998), Linda Hirshman (1998), and Martha Nussbaum (1998) have argued, the problem with Aristotelian ethics was that it upheld many existing traditions, including social and religious ones that subordinated women. Aristotle set up a hierarchical notion of social organization, where women occupied the bottom rungs of intellectual life, rationality, and humanity. However, despite all of his limitations, Aristotle at least emphasized what he considered to be the reciprocity inherent in friendship as a key ethical issue.[24]

The sad truth about Foucault's analysis is that in the end he was not wrong to look at love relations in the ancient Greco-Roman world in his attempt to explore a new ethics for modern male homosexuality. Indeed, a more critical and dialectical reading of the gradual transformation of this relationship in the ancient world could have led to an ethics of love that more effectively addressed contemporary concerns. Foucault could have concluded that the absence of *charis*, or consent, in same-sex relations of the classical Greek society, the prevalent hypocrisy regarding the relationship between the erastes and the paidika, the re-creation of male/female gendered patterns of subordination, and the overall misogyny of Greek society ultimately undermined the false ethics of Greek love. What has made the contemporary gay/lesbian movement such a historic breakthrough is that it has incorporated a number of new feminist ethical principles in its discourse, such as mutual consent of the partners, public recognition for the relationship, and alliances across racial, ethnic, class, and gender divides. In this way, the gay/lesbian movement has moved far beyond the aristocratic male ethics of love in ancient Greece to a more inclusive and modern ethics of care.

Homosexuality in the Muslim World

Let us now look at homosexuality in Middle Eastern and Muslim societies in order to explore possible affinities with earlier practices in Greco-Roman societies.[25] The three major religions of the Abrahamic tradition explicitly termed homosexuality an abomination, at times punishable by death, but their implicit stances were usually less stringent. Both the Old Testament (Leviticus 18:22 and 20:33) and the Talmud prohibit male homosexuality on several grounds.[26] Punishment could take the form of banishment or even death (Leviticus 18:29 and 20:13). Most scholars, however, suggest that these harsh penalties were seldom enforced, since Jews in the Diaspora seldom had the authority to impose the death penalty. Furthermore, ritualistic repentance was possible to avoid divine punishment (Eron 1993, 117). Likewise, Christianity regarded homosexuality as a sin, an argument that was based on both the Old Testament and on passages in the New Testament (Romans 1:26–27; 1 Corinthians 6:9; 1 Timothy 1:10). However, Christianity was also influenced by Greco-Roman culture, which had greater tolerance for homosexuality, and it was not until the twelfth century that it developed a much stricter attitude toward same-sex relations (Carmody and Carmody 1993, 142).

Similarly, there were strict injunctions against both male and female homosexuality in the Quran (26:165–66; 15:73–74) and the *hadiths* (reports about what the prophet Muhammad said or did). Status-defined homosexuality between unequal partners pre-dated Islam in the Middle East and North Africa. Herodotus claimed that the Persians had learned it from the Greeks (Roscoe 1997, 61). Islam, like Judaism, approves of sexual desire, but maintains that it must be fulfilled within marriage. To prove that a sexual transgression has taken place, the legal system of the shariat demands solid evidence (four adult men observing the violation) before punishment could be meted out to the offenders. In practice, therefore, substantial leverage has been exercised if the relationship did not become a "public nuisance" (Duran 1993, 183). Both female and male same-sex relations have been ignored, tolerated, or even accepted so long as they were not flaunted and hierarchy between the two partners was maintained.

In a survey of male homosexuality in the Muslim world, Stephen Murray argues that it adopted the policy of "don't ask, don't tell, don't pursue," centuries before the U.S. military did under President Bill Clinton. Sexuality was not divided along the lines of homosexuals versus heterosexuals, but between those who took pleasure and those who submitted to pleasure (Murray 1997, 41–42). These sexual practices are reflected in everyday life, and in religious and even in military discourses, where a distinction is maintained between the active and passive sides of a relationship. A subtle gendered structure underlies social interactions. From time to time, one comes across a veiled theological discourse that defines the relations between Muslims and non-Muslims in an allegorical erotic language. "Initiation" and "submission" take place through the sword of jihad. The active/passive status-differentiation thus also defines relations between Muslims and non-Muslims (Wafer 1997a, 91).

Classical Persian literature, the poems of Attar (d. 1220), Rumi (d. 1273), Sa'di (d. 1291), Hafez (d. 1389), Jami (d. 1492), and even those of the twentieth-century Iraj Mirza (d. 1926) are replete with homoerotic allusions, as well as explicit references to beautiful young boys and to the practice of pederasty (Iraj Mirza 1972; Baraheni 1977).[27]

One of the best sources on homoerotic relations is the study by Cyrus Shamisa, who writes that "Persian literature is essentially a homosexual literature" (2002, 10). Elsewhere, Annemarie Schimmel has noted that many Sufis "directed their admiration to young boys, disciples, or foreigners, and the books from the Abbasid period are bound with love stories of this kind. The handsome boy of fourteen, radiant like the full moon, soon became the ideal of human beauty, and as such is praised in later Persian and Turkish poetry" (Schimmel 1975, 289). As in the Greek tradition, the early budding of hair on the youth's face was deemed a great tragedy, since it meant that the courtship would soon be over. Persian poets such as Sa'di and Hafez used many metaphors to refer to this stage of a young man's life (between the ages of fifteen and eighteen) when his faint mustache was likened to a violet or budding meadow (Shamisa 2002, 52).

Some of the famous love relationships celebrated by classical poets were between kings and male slaves. The beloved could also be the slave of another more powerful person. Many erotic Persian love poems, in which the lover describes the secret and sporadic nocturnal visits of the beloved, refer to such situations. Outside the royal court, homosexuality and homoerotic expressions were tolerated in numerous public places, from monasteries and seminaries to taverns, military camps, bathhouses, and coffee houses. In the early Safavid era (1501–1722), male houses of prostitution (*amard khaneh*) were legally recognized and paid taxes. Bathhouses and coffee houses were also common locations for illicit sex. John (Jean) Chardin, the seventeenth-century Huguenot traveler, recalled large coffeehouses where young male prostitutes entertained customers. Customers could procure the services of the boys, and the most popular coffee houses were those that had the best-looking ones (Ravandi 1989, 7:493).

Remnants of an ethics of homoerotic love, with similarities to that of ancient Greece, continue to be reported by Western travelers. In the case of Afghanistan, much of which was part of Iran until the late nineteenth century, gender practices remained more traditional than in Iran. In the nineteenth century, ethnic Pashtuns from Afghanistan serving in the British colonial army sang odes in praise of the young boys they loved.[28] In the late twentieth century, the predominantly Pashtun city of Kandahar, Afghanistan, was referred to by some as "the gay capital of South Asia," and the practice of homosexuality was found at all levels of Sunni Pashtun society, both rich and poor. A local joke in Kandahar was that "birds fly over the city using only one wing, the other shielding their tail feathers" (*The Times* [London], January 16, 2002).

Anthropologist Charles Lindholm observed that in the Pashtun culture, a man's object of love was often a boy or a handsome young man. Before the advent of modernity, guests were entertained by dancing boys: "No aspersions were cast on men who had sexual intercourse with a bedagh [passive homosexual]. . . . Men who are bedaghs are laughingstocks, but they also marry and are not socially ostracized" (Lindholm 1982, 224). Dancing boys were likewise quite common in Iran, a tradition that continued into the early twentieth century.

Modernity gradually brought about a sense of shame regarding homosexuality among the more educated sections of society, but the practice continued. In the 1970s, "dancing girls had replaced dancing boys, and transvestites had become rare. Nonetheless, the first sexual experience of many, if not most boys, is with one of their passively inclined peers, or with an older man who is a confirmed bedagh. Older men still may cultivate a handsome young protégé who will accompany them everywhere, though the practice is hardly universal. . . . Pakhtun [Pashtun] poetry is often frankly homoerotic, following the Persian model" (Lindholm 1982, 225).

As we saw earlier, Foucault had argued that sex and friendship were mutually incompatible. Likewise, Lindholm writes, "In sexual union the Pakhtun see domination and subordination. This duality destroys the essence of the hoped-for-relation, that is complete mutuality. For this reason, unlike the Greek case, friendship is never mingled with homosexual love affairs, since sex affirms separateness. Lovers cannot truly be friends" (Lindholm 1982, 226–27).

In the 1990s, after Soviet forces had left Afghanistan, and U.S.-armed Mujahedeen divided the country into fiefdoms, Kandahar warlords violated the ethics of courting in the most flagrant way. They simply kidnapped and raped the boys (or girls) they desired rather then pursuing them: "Boys couldn't come to the market because the commanders would come and take away any that they liked" (Smith 2002, A4). In 1994, Mullah Omar, the future leader of the Taliban, became a local hero in Kandahar when he challenged the warlords and promised to bring an end to the abductions. But in place of the feuding warlords, the Taliban instituted a brutal regime of its own that punished any publicly known homosexual activity, sometimes burying homosexuals alive under a mud wall. Still, covert homosexuality continued to be practiced in the *madrasas* (seminaries) and among the Taliban warriors.

After the ouster of the Taliban regime by the United States in late 2001, the ancient ethics of love resurfaced in the streets of Kandahar. The sight of so many men pursuing young boys outraged the new government of Hamid Karzai, which "issued a directive barring 'beardless boys'—a euphemism for under-age sex partners—from police stations, military bases, and commanders' compounds" (Smith 2002, A4). At twenty-nine, Muhammad Daud, who in 1995 at the age of twenty-two fell in love with twelve-year-old Fareed in an auto repair shop and courted him for months, described the routine to a

Western journalist: "If you want a haliq—a boy for sex—you have to follow the boy for a long time before he will agree. . . . At first [Fareed] was afraid, so I bought him some chocolate and gave him a lot of money. . . . I went step by step and after about six or seven months, he agreed." Fareed told the Western observer that while he hid the relationship from his older brothers and parents he did "not regret being lured into a relationship by his older friend." Now that he was nineteen, he "would do the same to a young boy" and was in fact looking for a suitable lover (A4). By 1995, it should be noted, Kandahar was already under Taliban rule.

The prevalence of these forms of homosexuality in Afghanistan, Iran, and elsewhere in the Middle East means that, despite explicit prohibitions of homosexuality in the Quran, a certain degree of latitude can also be found in many religious treatises reflecting both a degree of cultural tolerance and the lived experience of Muslims. Shi'ite Muslim manuals define the daily conduct of the believers and their mandatory rituals of purification. They might state explicitly that homosexuality is a sin, but many of these manuals also include a brief section outlining the necessary rituals of cleansing for men (either partner) who have engaged in sodomy or bestiality.

Ayatollah Khomeini's 1947 manual, *Risaleh-yi Towzih al-masa'il* (Explanation of problems), is a case in point. Article 349 of this book states that "if a person has sex and [his organ] enters [the other person's body] to the point where it is circumcised [corona] or more, whether he enters a woman or a man, from behind or the front, an adult or pre-adult youngster, and even if no semen is secreted, both persons will become ritually polluted (najes)." But ritual impurity can always be cleansed away through the observance of rules stated in the same manual. Likewise, under the category of incest, Khomeini makes a distinction between "sodomy" with a man/boy who is related to a woman one intends to marry (her son, brother, or father), in which case that marriage may not take place (Article 2405), and sodomy with the same man after marriage to his female relative, in which case the marriage is still valid. "In the case of a person who marries the mother, sister, or daughter of a man and after marriage has sodomite relations with that man [his wife] will not become unlawful to him" (Article 2407). Similar statements appear in the manuals of Ayatollahs Montazari and Golpaygani. Persons who have engaged in such sexual acts can achieve ritual cleansing by performing a ten-point guideline of ablution (*ghosl-i Janabat*) and observing penitence in the form of fasting and giving alms to the poor (Khomeini 1947, articles 357–66). Here we see that some Shi'ite theologians are quite accommodating of what are officially seen as sexual transgressions, provided proper rituals of cleansing and penance are performed. Moreover, unlike Roman Catholicism,

Islam does not require an oral confession, a repentance through verbalization of all sinful thoughts. In Shi'ite Islam, penitence is achieved through a series of rituals that involve the body or the giving of alms. No one need know what has transpired, why someone is fasting, or why he is feeding the poor. For the most part, one's thoughts are also exempt. Sexual transgression can remain a secret between the individual and God.

Despite the commonly held view of Muslim societies as puritanical, they can therefore be more tolerant of (status-defined) homosexuality, provided the relationship is not flaunted. But such tolerance is not the same as recognition of civil rights and legal equality. As in the earlier Greco-Roman and Persian societies, in modern Muslim countries, including Iran, the boy in a same-sex relationship is assumed to be the passive object of the relationship and might be rewarded with money and gifts for accepting this role. Once a boy is labeled passive, he is fair game for others and is regarded as a "prostitute." If his activities are kept private, he is expected to outgrow his status, to marry and to produce children. If as an adult he enters a same-sex relationship, he is assumed to be the active partner in the affair. Homosexual behavior is socially tolerated if the man maintains a family and does not flaunt his activity. Pederasty and adult male homosexuality are prevalent practices, but "demanding respect for identities based on homosexuality (demanding respect for being gay or lesbian)" is completely unacceptable in any Islamic society (Murray 1997, 17). Rape of a man, if it becomes public knowledge, can destroy the victim's reputation. Rape remains a brutal, physical, psychological, and political expression of humiliation and repudiation. As in the ancient Greek world, the contemporary Muslim Middle East remains uncompromising toward the junior partner. The prevalence of certain forms of same-sex relations in the region, therefore, should not be equated with recognition for a gay lifestyle.

Since the late nineteenth century, when a new women's rights discourse gained ground in the region, supporters of women's rights have been among the vocal opponents of traditional homosexuality in Iran. One of the first modern criticisms of pederasty and male homosexuality appeared in the late nineteenth-century treatise of an Iranian feminist, Bibi Khanom Astarabadi, called *Vices of Men* (Javadi, Marashi, and Shekarloo 1992). She complained bitterly about the lives of women trapped in loveless marriages with men whose objects of passion were other men. During the 1906–11 Constitutional Revolution, Transcaucasian and Iranian social democrats, such as Jalil Mamed Qolizadeh, editor of *Molla Nasreddin* (Tiflis), and Ali Akbar Dehkhoda, editor of *Sur-i Esrafil* (Tehran), criticized the practice of pederasty, as well as child marriage and polygamy. Pederasty and consensual adult homosexuality were lumped together as discredited, premodern traditions that had to be replaced with the more modern ideal of monogamous marriage based on mutual love.

In the latter part of the twentieth century, as a result of greater contact with Western culture and sexual practices, a new discourse developed in Iran and many other Middle Eastern countries. The West was branded as "immoral" for ostensibly two reasons: female nudity and open adult male homosexuality. In part, this new discourse was the result of an expansion of the tourist industry and increased exposure to Western media. Parts of North Africa—Morocco, Tunisia, Turkey, and the Muslim Coast of Kenya—became favorite tourist spots for European men and women.[29] Such overt conduct by Western homosexuals made the task of local gay and human rights activists more difficult in the traditional Middle East. Homosexuality and pederasty remain significant cultural practices, but members of Middle Eastern communities would not dare declare themselves gay. There are homosexual men in high positions—ministers, deputies, Islamist leaders—who remain married, have families, and maintain same-sex relations outside the home. The community ostracizes those who stop camouflaging their homosexuality.

There is also a long tradition in nationalist movements of consolidating power through narratives that affirm patriarchy and compulsory heterosexuality, attributing sexual abnormality and immorality to a corrupt ruling elite that is about to be overthrown and/or is complicit with foreign imperialism (Hayes 2000, 16). Not all the accusations leveled against the Pahlavi family and their wealthy supporters stemmed from political and economic grievances. A significant portion of the public anger was aimed at their "immoral" lifestyle. There were rumors that a gay lifestyle was rampant at the court. Prime Minister Amir Abbas Hoveyda was said to have been a homosexual. The satirical press routinely lampooned him for his meticulous attire, the purple orchid in his lapel, and his supposed marriage of convenience. The shah himself was rumored to be bisexual. There were reports that a close male friend of the shah from Switzerland, a man who knew him from their student days in that country, routinely visited him. But the greatest public outrage was aimed at two young, elite men with ties to the court who held a mock wedding ceremony.[30] Especially to the highly religious, this was public confirmation that the Pahlavi house was corrupted with the worst kinds of sexual transgressions, that the shah was no longer master of his own house. These rumors contributed to public anger, to a sense of shame and outrage, and ultimately were used by the Islamists in their calls for a revolution. Soon after coming to power in 1979, Ayatollah Khomeini established the death penalty for homosexuality. In February and March 1979 there were sixteen executions for crimes related to sexual violations.[31]

At the same time, in the new, sex-segregated Islamic Republic, the greatest transgression became dating and sexual relations between unmarried or unrelated men and women. To this day, hundreds of such "criminals" are arrested, flogged, tormented, forced to pay a penalty, and sometimes held in prison each year. In a culture where kissing, hugging, and holding hands between men and between women are perfectly acceptable social customs, traditional covert homosexuality has continued to exist and is even protected by sex-segregated institutions and public spaces.[32]

Foucault's Orientalist impressions of the Muslim world, his selective reading and representation of Greco-Roman texts, and his hostility to modernity and its technologies of the body, led him to prefer the more traditional Islamic/Mediterranean culture to the modern culture of the West. Perhaps he hoped that the revival of traditional culture in Iran under an Islamist government could lead to a less restrictive counterdiscourse on bodies and sexualities. This may have happened, at least to an extent, with traditional, covert, same-sex relationships. As we saw, there are indications that, by 1984, Foucault had begun to reconsider some of his earlier attacks on the Enlightenment project; however, the last two volumes of *The History of Sexuality* retained the dualism from his earlier work that had privileged ancient and premodern cultures over modern ones. This suggests that Foucault's theoretical direction retained a substantial continuity until his death in 1984.

Epilogue

From the Iranian Revolution to September 11, 2001

Radical Islamist Politics since 1979

Radical Islamism is a diverse movement. This diversity is both ideological and political. Ideologically, there is not only a divide between Sunnis and Shi'ites, but also among various Sunni influences, from Wahabbism on the Arabian Peninsula to the Deobandi School of South Asia. At a political level, the Iranian Islamist regime almost went to war with the Afghanistan's Taliban in 2001. Nonetheless, like fascism earlier, which had German, Italian, Spanish, Romanian, and many other varieties, radical Islamism has enough common features to discern it as general phenomenon.[1] Below we outline very briefly some of the key elements in its development since it emerged as a global phenomenon during the Iranian Revolution, up through September 11, 2001, and its immediate aftermath.

As we have seen, in Iran in 1979, the newly established regime of Ayatollah Khomeini moved quickly to repress feminists, ethnic and religious minorities, liberals, and leftists—all in the name of Islam.[2] Moreover, Khomeini outflanked the anti-imperialist politics of the Iranian Left by encouraging his youthful followers to occupy and take hostages at the U.S. Embassy in Tehran. This fourteen-month confrontation gave Iran's brand of radical Islamism a surge of popularity throughout the Muslim world, easily crossing the divide between Shi'ites and Sunnis. Khomeini's humiliation of the United States also played a significant role in the election to the U.S. presidency in November 1980 of the ultra-conservative Ronald Reagan, who promised to make America strong again. By the end of his eight-year presidency, Reagan had helped to realign global politics in several major ways. The new conservative Western leaders, who notably included Britain's Margaret Thatcher as well, began to speak in a type of unyielding language not heard in over a generation toward the very idea of international cooperation, toward labor, toward the welfare state, and especially toward the new social movements of the 1960s, whether those for feminism, gay and lesbian rights, or ethnic minority rights. The Reaganites and the Iranian Islamists fed on each other. At an international level, each claimed to defend a sacred way of life against hostile enemies. At home, each propagated what it called traditional values, especially concerning gender and sexuality. During this same period, forms of politicized religious fundamentalism grew dramatically, from Hindu revivalism, to extreme right-wing Zionism and Christian fundamentalism.

In February 1989, as he was nearing death, Khomeini issued a *fatwa*, or religious ruling, sentencing Salman Rushdie to death for blasphemy and apostasy. Rushdie, a British subject born to a Muslim family in Bombay (Mumbai), had published *The Satanic Verses*, a novel that supposedly defamed the Prophet through a fictional character many believed stood for Muhammad. With this unprecedented attempt to extend Islamic law into a predominantly non-Muslim country, Britain, Khomeini again placed himself at the head of militant Islam at a global level, just as he had during Iran's takeover of the U.S. Embassy in 1979. Iran put its money and its intelligence service behind attacks on Rushdie and his publishers and translators. Within weeks, Abdullah al-Ahdal, a Muslim cleric in Belgium who had opposed the Khomeini's *fatwa* as inapplicable outside the Islamic world, was shot to death. Then, in July 1991, Hitoshi Igarashi, who had translated *The Satanic Verses* into Japanese, was stabbed to death. Ettore Caprioto, the book's Italian translator, survived a similar attack that same month.

While it galvanized radical Islamists around the world, this dramatic attempt to punish artistic expression led at the same time to a wave of support for Rushdie, a man of the Left who had previously published a novel sympathetic to Nicaragua's Sandinistas. That support came not only from Western liberals and leftists, but also from more secular or more tolerant Arab and Muslim intellectuals, who took far greater risks in speaking out. In 1992, for example, a group of fifty Iranian intellectuals and artists living in exile condemned the *fatwa* as "odious and barbaric." They also noted that Rushdie was only the best known among the many victims of Islamist repression, declaring that "Iranian writers, artists, journalists, and thinkers living in Iran suffer every day from religious censorship and that the number of Iranians executed or imprisoned on the pretext of 'blasphemy' is far from negligible" ("Appel des artistes" 1992). By 1993, such prominent figures as the Egyptian Nobel Laureate Naguib Mahfouz, the Palestinian-American literary critic Edward Said, and the Palestinian poet Mahmoud Darwish spoke out in a joint statement against Khomeini's *fatwa*.

A second nation that experienced radical Islamist rule was Afghanistan, where conditions eventually became even more repressive than in Iran. As is well known, in the 1980s, the United States, Pakistan, and Saudi Arabia supported the Islamist mujahedeen against a Russian-installed regime, motivated by Cold War politics. Among these mujahedeen were the Saudi billionaire Osama bin Laden and others from what was to become the Al Qaeda network. During the years 1992–96, after their victory over Russian troops, various mujahedeen factions vied for power, conducting a second civil war, while at the same time continuing to restrict the rights of women severely. In 1996, the Taliban, a still more dogmatic Islamist faction, came to power, again with substantial support from Pakistan and Saudi Arabia, as well as U.S. acquiescence. The Taliban oppressed women even more harshly than had the mujahedeen, forbidding them to attend school, to work outside the home, or even to walk the streets without a male relative. Courageous underground women's groups ran clandestine schools for women and girls, and also smuggled out video footage of the public execution of a woman for "adultery," which to the Taliban could mean simply talking with an unrelated person of the opposite sex. Despite protests from most governments, including Muslim ones, the Taliban also destroyed as "idols" the giant Buddhist statues at Bamyan that had stood for over a thousand years. The United States never seriously opposed the Taliban until September 11, 2001, even after Al Qaeda moved its bases there in 1996, despite the fact that Al Qaeda was linked to the 1993 attack on the World Trade Center. The unbridled joy with which the population of Kabul greeted the fall of the Taliban in late 2001 shocked many Islamists, as well as those Western leftists and progressives who had taken a culturally relativist position toward Afghanistan.

Sudan was the only other country to experience direct rule by militant Islamists, but here they came to power via a series of military coups. Since independence from Britain in 1956, the predominantly Christian and animist South has vainly sought autonomy from the mainly Muslim North, which has responded with terrible violence. After the 1990–91 Gulf War, however, a new military ruler, General Hassan al-Bashir, together with the Islamist theologian and politician Hassan al-Turabi, sought not only to crush the South, but also to project Sudan as a global center of radical Islamism. It was during this period that Sudan's long civil war reached genocidal proportions, with some two million deaths from starvation, disease, and war in the South, whose people were also the victims of a massive slave trade. (The genocide was also racial, in the sense that the "Arab" North looked down on the "black" South, as well as on the Muslim "blacks" of Darfur.) Bin Laden and Sheikh Omar Rahman of Egypt, later imprisoned in the United States for orchestrating the first World Trade Center bombing in 1993, were allowed to base themselves in Sudan for a time. In 1996, Sudan's military rulers pulled back somewhat, expelling bin Laden that year and sidelining al-Turabi in 1999. After September 11, the regime attempted to placate the United States, which sponsored peace negotiations with the southern resistance.

While radical Islamists never came to power in Algeria, they fought a lengthy and extremely brutal civil war in the 1990s that claimed more than a hundred thousand lives. In the late 1980s, Islamist parties were gaining headway as the National Liberation Front (FLN), which had led Algeria to independence from France in 1962, attempted to move toward a multiparty system. By 1992, the newly formed Islamic Salvation Front (FIS) seemed poised to win the national elections. In response, elements within the FLN and the military seized power in a coup, canceling the elections, banning the FIS, and imprisoning thousands of Islamists. The Armed Islamic Group (GIA), whose core consisted of Algerian men who had participated in the Afghanistan jihad, now took up arms. While the GIA was able to mount serious attacks on the regime, its extreme brutality toward civilians included the massacre of whole villages and the kidnapping and rape of village women and girls. The GIA also assassinated intellectuals, labor activists, secular leftists, feminists, and even women who dared walk the streets in anything less than the GIA's definition of proper clothing. Such tactics lost it the support of all but the most extremist Islamists.[3] This gave an opening to the military regime, which reformed itself somewhat, succeeding by 1999 in legitimating its rule through an election that, although essentially an authoritarian plebiscite, nonetheless seemed to reflect popular revulsion at the Islamists.

By the early 1980s, Egypt had also begun to experience Islamist terrorism, albeit on a far smaller scale than in Algeria, with about a thousand deaths resulting from both the terror and the government repression against it. Still, the crucial importance of Egypt as a center of Muslim culture meant that the actions of the Islamist movement there had a very wide impact. Earlier, in the 1970s, as he moved away from the left-wing and pro-Soviet policies of Gamel Abdel Nasser, President Anwar Sadat had courted the Islamists as a counterweight to leftist groups that opposed his realignment toward the United States. However, Sadat's separate peace with Israel in 1979 outraged the Islamists, who broke with him completely. Their movement also gained strength in the aftermath of the Iranian Revolution, and in 1981 Islamists assassinated Sadat in a suicide attack.

For the next two decades, a small-scale war was fought between an increasingly repressive Egyptian state under Sadat's successor, Hosni Mubarak, and Islamist terrorists. The Islamists were not without a real base in some sectors of society, not only taking over professional associations of lawyers, doctors, and engineers, but also setting up social aid programs in the slums, as for example in the wake of the 1993 earthquake. During the same period, armed Islamist fanatics attacked secular, leftist, or feminist students and intellectuals, driving many of them from the campuses. In 1994, they nearly assassinated Naguib Mahfouz, the first Egyptian to have won the Nobel Prize for Literature. In an act of desperation as the state began to defeat them, the Islamists alienated much of the population by targeting a core part of the economy, tourism, killing a number of Western tourists in 1996 and 1997. After the main Islamist groups called off their war against the Egyptian state, members of the movement's most fanatical wing, led by Ayman al-Zawahiri, joined with bin Laden in 1998 and became a core element of the leadership of Al Qaeda, first in Sudan and then Afghanistan. The Egyptian state has also placated Islamists by allowing them to preach on the airwaves, to censor literature, and to harass secular and feminist intellectuals.

By the end of the 1990s, the radical Islamist movement had lost much of its organizational strength and to some extent, even its mass base, especially in Iran. In Egypt and Algeria, after some Islamist leaders accepted compromise or defeat, small groups split away, vowing to continue the fight. It was this wing, the fringe of a fringe, that joined with bin Laden to form the Al Qaeda movement, with Taliban-ruled Afghanistan its most secure base of operations.

The September 11, 2001, attacks, which killed three thousand civilians in the heart of the world's sole remaining superpower, unleashed an equally profound global realignment. First and most obvious was the new stage reached by Islamist terrorism, which until 2001 had succeeded in attacking mainly outposts of the United States abroad, with the exception of the relatively low-impact 1993 World Trade Center bombing. Unlike the Iranian Islamists of 1978–79, who had a considerable mass base, the secretive Al Qaeda network was cut off from direct contact with the populations it claimed to represent. Nonetheless, as with the 1979 hostage-taking in Iran, a surge of support around the Muslim world gave their brand of radical Islamism an ideological victory, making bin Laden and Al Qaeda heroes in many quarters for having taken on the widely hated United States government.

The Bush administration was initially caught off guard by September 11, but, like the Reagan administration earlier, it took advantage of the new challenge from radical Islamism to implement its own very conservative agenda, both abroad and at home. The administration responded with what it called a global war on terrorism, initiating a level of military-security buildup not seen since the Vietnam War, as well as massive and indiscriminate arrests of Arab and Muslim immigrants at home. Having toppled the Taliban in a matter of weeks, but unable to capture bin Laden or other top Taliban and Al Qaeda leaders, the Bush administration then decided on a course of confrontation with the brutal, but decidedly not Islamist, regime of Saddam Hussein in Iraq. The administration's aggressive unilateralism severely undermined what had been a rather broad alliance in 2001 and early 2002 against Al Qaeda, one that had involved such disparate players as Western Europe, Japan, Russia, China, India, and more reluctantly, Pakistan, Saudi Arabia, as well as several other Middle Eastern governments. The Bush administration's war in Iraq also outraged the Arab and Muslim world, swelling the ranks of radical Islamism. Within Iraq itself, the toppling from without of the somewhat secular Ba'athist regime opened the way for the rise of radical Islamism, both Sunni and Shi'ite.

Western Leftist and Feminist Responses to September 11

Until September 11, 2001, the rise of radical Islamism had received little attention from Western progressives and leftists, who were unsure how to characterize a movement that outbid the older Marxist Left in its anti-imperialism, but also advocated a rejection of Western culture (but not technology), the repression of women, and forms of politics that seemed to have more in common with fascism than the discourses of the Left. As we saw in chapter 3, Rodinson had termed the new militant Islamism a "type of archaic fascism" as early as December 1978 in a critique of Foucault's writings on Iran. However, most of the Left tended to view Islamism through the lens of Cold War politics, attributing its rise to "blowback" from the U.S. and Saudi Arabian-backed war against the Russians in Afghanistan. Some also viewed Islamism through the lens of the Arab-Israeli conflict, again pointing to U.S. responsibility in arming and financing Israel. Others took a more culturally relativist position, arguing that Westerners had no right to judge other cultures. A few noted that the United States and the regimes it supported had worked to destroy secular leftist movements throughout the region, thus opening space for Islamism. Even fewer people spoke about gender and Islamism, and those that did sometimes faced accusations of cultural insensitivity or even cultural imperialism.

These attitudes formed the backdrop to the discussions after September 11 by leftists and progressives in the United States and Western Europe. As had occurred briefly in March 1979 during the debate over Iranian women, but now on a far larger scale, the question of how to respond to the challenge of radical Islamism became a core political issue of the day. Now everyone, or nearly everyone, took a position. The anti-imperialist U.S. writer Noam Chomsky quickly became the most prominent critic on the Left of official responses to September 11, especially the Bush administration's war on Al Qaeda and Afghanistan. Within days of September 11, Chomsky had "contextualized" the Islamist attacks by connecting them to the broader anti-imperialist struggles of the twentieth century. The uniqueness of the September 11 attacks, which he duly denounced as "horrifying atrocities," lay not in the reactionary and misogynist political ideology of the terrorists, but in the fact that this time the victims of imperialism had struck back at the heart of global power: "European powers conquered much of the world with extreme brutality. With the rarest of exceptions, they were not under attack by their foreign victims. England was not attacked by India, nor Belgium by the Congo, nor Italy by Ethiopia, nor France by Algeria" (Chomsky 2001, 11, 12). The leftist historian Howard Zinn took a similar position, putting perhaps a bit more emphasis on the "murderous fanatical feeling" that in his view "motivated" the September 11 attacks, but again tying the terrorists to a broader, anti-imperialist sentiment: "You might say there is a reservoir of possible terrorists among all those people of the world who have suffered as a result of U.S. foreign policy" (2002, 17).

What such arguments failed to answer was why movements similar to Al Qaeda had not developed in Latin America or Central Africa, areas of the world that had suffered very deeply from Western imperialism and particularly U.S. intervention. Thus, they ignored the specific social and political context in which Al Qaeda arose, that of two decades of various forms of radical Islamist politics, beginning with the Iranian Revolution. In terms of its social vision, Islamism was far closer to fascism than to the socially progressive politics of a Sandino, a Fanon, a Lumumba, a Mandela, or even a Gandhi. Bracketing out these uncomfortable facts, including especially the gender politics of Al Qaeda and the Taliban, allowed Chomsky and Zinn to employ a type of anti-imperialist discourse that had arisen in a quite different context, the wars in Vietnam, Nicaragua, and El Salvador. Chomsky and Zinn refrained from expressions of admiration or support for the attacks themselves, seeming to regard them as understandable, but nonetheless criminal. This did not prevent crude attacks by right-wing groups like Campus Watch, which accused these critics, and university faculty generally, of supporting terrorism. Such

McCarthyite tactics led many leftists and progressives to close ranks, making the needed critique of positions like those of Chomsky and Zinn harder to carry out.

Some anti-imperialists went even further, such as the French postmodernist philosopher Jean Baudrillard. In a long opinion piece published in *Le Monde* on November 3, 2001, Baudrillard not only developed a justification of the nineteen suicide attackers, but also seemed to express a certain admiration for them. He wrote that September 11 "represents both the high point of the spectacle and the purest type of defiance" and that therefore, "it could be forgiven" (2001). In Baudrillard's essay, Al Qaeda represented the "other" of the U.S.-led global system of domination, with nary a word about the various forms of domination that it and its co-thinkers had established, from Iran and Afghanistan to Sudan. Baudrillard also attempted to link September 11 to the anti-globalization movement:

> When the situation has been so thoroughly monopolized, when power has been so formidably consolidated by the technocratic machine and by one-dimensional thought [*pensée unique*], what means of turning the tables remains besides terrorism? In dealing all the cards to itself, the system forced the Other to change the rules of the game. And the new rules are ferocious, because the game is ferocious. *Terrorism is the act that restores an irreducible singularity to the heart of a generalized system of exchange.* All those singularities (species, individuals, cultures), which have paid with their deaths for the establishment of a global system of commerce ruled by a single power, avenge themselves by transferring the situation to terrorism. (Baudrillard 2001; emphasis added)

This article produced a pungent retort a few days later from the liberal writer and *Le Monde* editor Alain Minc, who instead linked "Islamic fundamentalism" to "fascism," accusing Baudrillard of "a morbid fascination for the terrorists" and pointing as well to his long-standing philosophical "anti-humanism" (Minc 2001). As mentioned in our introduction, Minc went on to link Baudrillard's stance to that of Foucault during the Iranian Revolution: "After Michel Foucault, advocate of Khomeinism in Iran and therefore in the theory of its exactions, here is Baudrillard, philosopher of the terrorist model" (2001). Even some of Baudrillard's language, especially the sentence about the "irreducible singularity" of the September 11 suicide attacks, echoed Foucault's descriptions of the Iranian Islamism in 1978–79, which, as we have seen, he regarded as a form of "irreducible" opposition to Western modernity.

Not all voices on the Left were as one-sided as those of Chomsky or Zinn, let alone Baudrillard. The U.S. literary theorist Michael Bérubé, who has written in the postmodernist vein, emphasized the social agenda of the Islamists:

> So, faced with an enemy as incomprehensible and as implacable as bin Laden, much of the left checked the man's policy positions on women, homosexuality, secularism, and facial hair, and slowly backed out of the action. They didn't move right, as so many Chomskian leftists have charged; they simply decided that the September 11 attacks were the work of religious fanatics who had no conceivable contact with anything identifiable as a left project save for a human-rights complaint about the sanctions against Iraq. As Marx himself observed, there are a number of social systems more oppressive than that of capitalism. Al Qaeda and the Taliban are good cases in point. (2002)

Some U.S. feminist intellectuals also took account of radical Islamism's threat to women's rights and human rights more generally.[4] Writing in November 2001, the well-known feminist writer Barbara Ehrenreich focused not on imperialism, but on misogyny, attributing Islamist misogyny to a "crisis of masculinity" brought about by the ways in which some aspects of modernity, especially the paid employment of women, had undermined patriarchal values. She also noted the radical disjuncture between the ideology of Islamism and the earlier anti-colonialist movements:

> The mystery of fundamentalist misogyny deepens when you consider that the anti-imperialist and anti-colonialist Third World movements of 40 or 50 years ago were, for the most part, at least officially committed to women's rights. Women participated in Mao's Long March; they fought in the Algerian revolution and in the guerrilla armies of Mozambique, Angola, and El Salvador. The ideologies of these movements—nationalist or socialist—were inclusive of women and open, theoretically anyway, to the idea of equality. Bin Laden is, of course, hardly a suitable heir to the Third World liberation movements of the mid-20th century, but he does purport to speak for the downtrodden against Western capitalism and militarism. Except that his movement has nothing to offer the most downtrodden sex but the veil and a life lived indoors. (Ehrenreich 2001)

Other feminist intellectuals developed similar themes.

Writing in the *Nation* in December 2001, the culture critic Ellen Willis stressed the global struggle between fundamentalism and secular feminism: "Opponents of the 'clash of civilizations' argument are half right. There is such a clash, but it is not between East and West. The struggle of democratic secularism, religious tolerance, individual freedom, and feminism against authoritarian patriarchal religion, culture, and morality is going on all over the world—including the Islamic world, where dissidents are regularly jailed, killed, exiled, or merely intimidated and silenced" (Willis 2001, 373). Willis also criticized the way that the Left, from the Iranian Revolution onward, had espoused versions of anti-imperialism and cultural pluralism in ways that excused repressive religious measures against women:

> Except for feminists, the American left, with few exceptions, enthusiastically supported the revolution and brushed off worries about the Ayatollah, though he had made no secret of his theocratic aims: The important thing was to get rid of the Shah—other issues could be dealt with afterward. Ten years later, on the occasion of the fatwa against Salman Rushdie . . . an unnerving number of liberals and leftists accused Rushdie and his defenders of cultural imperialism and insensitivity to Muslim sensibilities. Throughout, both defenders and detractors of our alliance with "moderate" Saudi Arabia have ignored Saudi women's slavelike situation, regarding it as "their culture" and none of our business. . . . It's as if, in discussing South Africa, apartheid had never been mentioned. (Willis 2001, 376)

A number of other feminists also took issue with the Chomskian position of much of the Left. Such voices were heard as well among Iranian feminists, to whom we now turn.

Transcending Islamism: Iranian Dissident Responses Today

During the last decade, the Iranian regime has been challenged from within by a group of moderates, led by President Muhammad Khatami, and by many more secular and feminist students and intellectuals throughout the nation. For several years after his election by a landslide in 1997, Khatami held a small and mainly symbolic measure of political power, but the main levers of power, including the army, the intelligence service, the police, the judiciary, and foreign policy, remained in the hands of religious conservatives. Since then, a new generation of Iranian women has emerged in the vanguard of the reform movement. It has been demanding a more liberal reading of Islamic law; new civil liberties that clearly demarcate the boundaries between religion, state, and the individual; a more egalitarian concept of gender relations; and a new relationship to the outside world and the complex phenomenon of modernity.

Women's support was crucial to the election of Khatami in 1997. He was reelected in 2001 with close to 76 percent of the vote, despite his limited success against the hardliners. Women voters also prevented the election of many conservative deputies to the sixth *majlis* in 2000 and sent reform candidates to that body instead. In 1999, many women ran as candidates for election to urban and provincial councils. In fifty-six cities they attained first place, and in fifty-eight, they gained second place in the leadership of the councils. A significant number of women in many remote locations were also elected to leadership posts in the village councils.[5]

In many other Middle Eastern countries, governments aligned themselves with the United States after September 11, 2001, but much of the public sympathized with bin Laden. The reverse was true in Iran. The dominant conservative part of the government around Ayatollah Ali Khamenei condemned U.S. actions against bin Laden, but many Iranians (and President Khatami) publicly expressed their contempt for the terrorist attacks of September 11 and their solidarity with the American people. This message was first expressed that September in a moment of silence in memory of the victims at the national soccer stadium, to the discomfiture of the more conservative clerics. In the years that followed, however, the public became disillusioned with Khatami and the reformers, because they brought little real change.

Where is the place of Michel Foucault in the political and intellectual ferment in Iran? Foucault and postmodern thought are vigorously discussed in Iran, both by Islamists and their opponents (Khatami 2003). Islamists sometimes argue that postmodernists are the best critics of modernity. They use postmodern arguments concerning the disciplinary practices of the modern state to justify their own rejection of Western cultural institutions. Iranian Islamists also refer to the concept of cultural diversity to defend some of the retrogressive practices that they have imposed in society, especially on women.

A strong response to these arguments emerged from Tehran's dreaded Evin Prison, where many executions have taken place. One of Evin's many political prisoners, Akbar Ganji, a courageous journalist and former Islamist, has written a thought-provoking series of essays on postmodernism. Ganji was imprisoned because in the late 1990s he published a series of articles in major newspapers proving that the government was behind a number of assassinations of dissidents. From Evin, where he languishes in harsh conditions, Ganji has written on Foucault and Lyotard, as well as Rorty and Habermas. He is read enthusiastically both in Iran and in the Iranian diaspora.

In one of Ganji's essays on Foucault, "The Prison-Like Archipelago"—its title adapted from Alexander Solzhenitsyn's *Gulag Archipelago* and Foucault's *Discipline and Punish*, he wrote,

> In our society, nostalgic fundamentalists are happy to use postmodern thought in their attempts to reject modernity. They use postmodern criticisms of rationality, individualism, fear of the future, and nostalgia for the past, as an intellectual resource for their own views. But we need to remember that postmodernists are uttering their ideas in more tolerant democratic societies, whereas our fundamentalists are applying these ideas to a society that has yet to experience rationalism, individualism, pluralism, human rights, freedom of expression, and so forth. . . . [Our] "Prison-Like Archipelago" is a police state that does not recognize human rights and destroys those who think differently. Opposition to modernity stems from a certain "nostalgia" for the past. However, fundamentalists use the most modern instruments to destroy a modern civilization (attacking the Twin Towers with an airplane). And they use the most modern technologies to control [our] society, to abolish freedom, to remove those who think differently, and to establish an all-seeing panopticon rule, over everyone and everywhere. (2002, 290–91)

While highlighting some useful concepts from postmodern thought, Ganji suggested nevertheless that the Iranian dissident movement needed to be more cautious in its appropriation of postmodern thought: "Whether bad or good, postmodernism is born out of the Enlightenment. However here [the Middle East] it is used to revive traditions that existed prior to the Enlightenment" (2002, 291).

Foucault is in fact read creatively by some Iranian intellectuals who wish to apply his criticisms of modernity to the Islamist state. Many are interested in Foucault's writings on the nature of power, the view that the operations of power are all-pervasive, that power games define all social, political, and economic relations. They find some of Foucault's theories liberating, since he attacked dogmatic Marxist interpretations, where power was defined exclusively in class terms. Those who lived through the revolutionary period, and who remember the highly authoritarian leftist organizations of the time, whether Stalinist or Maoist, sometimes turn to Foucault and postmodern thought to reveal power relations within the Left itself. Dissidents are also interested in Foucault's keen insight that "power creates knowledge." Through such uses of Foucault, they attempt to undermine the vast body of highly dogmatic Islamist doctrine taught in schools and colleges (Jahangard 2004). This aspect of Foucault resonates well with Iranian dissidents, since resistance to Islamism is not only political, but also social and cultural. By creating "multiple sites of resistance," this new generation hopes to undermine the hegemonic control of the state.

Indeed, battles for a more tolerant society are being fought in numerous sites. The partisans of this new democratic movement include journalists, lawyers, fashion designers, actresses and film directors, college students, literary writers, and ordinary housewives.

1. Fashion is a feminist issue in contemporary Iran. Young secular women, in contrast to their parents' generation, leftist radicals who abhorred bourgeois decadence, express their defiance of the morality police by wearing makeup, streaking their hair in vibrant colors (the bit they can show from under their colorful scarves). Before the eyes of the clerics and police authorities on the streets, they claim the public arenas with elegant capes in creative designs that meet the minimum requirement of the morality police, but are nowhere near the drab black veils recommended by them.

2. Sports stadiums have also become sites for expressions of democracy. There has been a push to open the soccer stadiums to women, from which they have been barred since the revolution.

3. Yet another ideological arena is religious deconstruction. Iranian women and men are trying to take back their religion from Islamists who have reduced it to a set of puritanical and intolerant laws. After twenty-five years under a theocratic regime, women have also become well versed in arcane religious legalisms, and have learned to reinterpret religious texts either to give them a feminist reading or to provide ample ambiguity about the origins of the more sexist statements. Hence, they have both de-legitimated the authenticity of such statements and provided an alternative reading to that of the orthodox clerics.

4. Other more secular writers have argued that the needs of our modern world require us to move beyond these regulations. This latter argument is pursued not only by secular lawyers and advocates of human rights, but also by some religious thinkers, such Mojtahed Shabastari and Seyyed Mohsen Saidzadeh, who was jailed briefly for his writings.

5. Feminist discourses permeate higher education, the arts, and the cultural arena. In recent years, more women than men have passed the national entrance exams to the universities. There are more than 72 women's publishers in Iran. Iranian cinema, which has achieved world recognition, has also become a feminist arena. Both male and female filmmakers have probed difficult issues in the Iranian and Islamic patriarchal cultures, from polygamy and repudiation (easy, male-initiated divorce) to rape and other forms of violence against women.

6. There has also been an attempt to move beyond the binary debate on universalism and cultural relativism. Feminist writers such as Mehrangiz Kar,

Shahla Sherkat, Nooshin Ahmadi, and Parvin Ardalan point to the limits of cultural relativism as it is currently argued in the West. They are calling for adherence to a set of strategic universals to be reached through dialogue and consensus among women of the East and the West. Iranian feminists want to strengthen the authority of organizations like the United Nations and documents like the UN Charter on Human Rights or the Beijing Charter on Women's Rights. Since the conservative Islamists have institutionalized sexism and other forms of discrimination in the name of culture, the reformist opposition now calls for adherence to internationally recognized codes of human rights. A strategic universalism instead of a limited cultural relativism provides more opportunities for creating tolerant societies in the Middle East, they argue (Afary 2004b).

Shirin Ebadi, winner of the 2003 Nobel Peace Prize, is a representative of this generation. Ebadi, who is a practicing Muslim, is also a staunch advocate of the separation of religion and state. The first woman to have been appointed as a judge under the Pahlavi regime, she was removed from her post by the Khomeini regime, barred from practicing law, and demoted to a clerk in the new religious courts. Gradually Ebadi, as well as her colleague Mehrangiz Kar, were allowed to practice law again. They distinguished themselves by taking up the cases of abused women and children, as well as political dissidents. The author of eleven books, Ebadi has defended the rights of women against domestic violence, "honor killings," and repudiation. She has also worked to gain child custody and financial compensation for divorced women. Additionally, Ebadi has called for the release of all those, like Akbar Ganji, who are imprisoned for political reasons, and has stated, "I am proclaiming the Iranian people's message of peace and friendship to the world. We are a peace-loving people. We hate violence. We condemn terror. We are not hostile toward other religions." Upon her return to Iran after the announcement of the prize, tens of thousands of people lined the streets of Tehran to welcome her home. A smaller crowd of ten thousand greeted her jubilantly in the airport, showering her with white flowers.

These are all elements of a new feminist and more tolerant and democratic politics in Iran, sentiments that are shared by a number of women's rights organizations and feminist intellectuals in Afghanistan, Pakistan, Turkey, Lebanon, Morocco, Algeria, and Tunisia, and can be cultivated elsewhere in the Middle East. Perhaps those who essentialize the women and men of the region should expand their definitions of feminism and human rights to encompass the voices of feminists such as Shirin Ebadi and Mehrangiz Kar. Not every misogynist interpretation of religion is authentic or indigenous, nor is every tolerant and progressive reading Western or foreign-influenced and therefore inauthentic. This type of labeling has been the tactic of Islamist movements in their efforts to gain power. It is now being challenged in the region by intellectuals and women's rights activists, individuals whose voices need to be heard more widely.

APPENDIX

Foucault and His Critics, an Annotated Translation

Translated by

Karen de Bruin, Kevin B. Anderson, Alan Sheridan, Roger Hardy, Thomas Lines, Janet Afary, and Marybeth Timmerman

Annotated by

Janet Afary and Kevin B. Anderson

Contents

Introductory Note

The order of the texts in this appendix generally follows that of their original publication. Unless otherwise indicated, Foucault is the author. Foucault's writings and interviews on Iran were first published between September 1978 and May 1979, a period that spanned the Iranian Revolution and its immediate aftermath. They took the form of newspaper reports, interviews, opinion pieces, and letters to the editor. Most of the material included here consists of newspaper articles that Foucault published in the leading Italian newspaper *Corriere della sera*, which had sent him to Iran as a special correspondent in the fall of 1978. Although *Corriere della sera* datelined the articles "Tehran," Foucault actually wrote them in France upon his return from two trips to Iran, the first from September 16 to September 24 and the second from November 9 to November 15, 1978. Since *Corriere della sera* translated the articles into Italian, they did not appear in French at the time. However, Foucault published a smaller but not insignificant portion of his writings on Iran in several French publications, including the left-of-center weekly *Le Nouvel Observateur* and the leading newspaper *Le Monde*. From June 1979 until his death in 1984, Foucault never referred publicly to Iran. In addition, one of the texts included here, a September 1978 dialogue between the Iranian writer Baqir Parham and Foucault, was first published in Persian in the spring of 1979 in *Nameh-yi Kanun-i Nevisandegan* (Publication of the Center of Iranian Writers). Except for this interview, the original French versions of all of Foucault's writings and interviews on Iran appeared in French some fifteen years later, in volume 3 of *Dits et écrits*, a four-volume collection edited by Daniel Defert and François Ewald, with Jacques Lagrange (Foucault 1994b). Most of Foucault's writings on Iran (up to February 1979) were later translated into Persian and published by Hussein Ma'sumi Hamadani (Foucault 1998).

This appendix also contains a number of critiques of Foucault. With one exception, they were also published in 1978 or 1979. The longest of these are two responses to Foucault by the noted Middle East scholar Maxime Rodinson, published in late 1978 and early 1979 in *Le Monde* and *Le Nouvel Observateur*. Rodinson's revealing 1993 preface to a reprint of them is also translated here and is the sole item from after 1979. In addition to the Rodinson critiques, we have included three other short texts by authors other than Foucault, all translated from the French. The first is a brief November 1978 letter to the editors of *Le Nouvel Observateur* criticizing Foucault and signed "Atoussa H.," the pseudonym of an Iranian feminist. The second is the March 1979 speech by the French feminist philosopher Simone de Beauvoir in support of the women of Iran on the eve of the departure from Paris of an international women's delegation to Iran. De Beauvoir's short text, while not a direct response to Foucault, provides context for the debate over Foucault and Iran in France. The third is a March 1979 article by the journalists Claudie and Jacques Broyelle attacking Foucault's stance on Iran, published in March 1979 in the leftist newspaper *Le Matin*. Finally, we have translated from the Persian the statement that Iranian feminists issued on March 10, 1979, during their demonstrations against Khomeini's order for women to re-veil themselves. It was reprinted in Matin-Daftari 1990.

Note on the Translations and the Annotation

Unless otherwise indicated, Karen de Bruin and Kevin B. Anderson carried out the translation from the French of these writings. The rest were translated as follows: (1) Foucault's interview with the leftist journalists Claire Brière and Pierre Blanchet was translated from the French by Alan Sheridan. (2) Roger Hardy and Thomas Lines translated Rodinson's "Islam Resurgent?" from the French. (3) Marybeth Timmerman translated de Beauvoir's speech from the French. (4) Janet Afary translated Foucault's September 1978 dialogue with Parham in *Nameh-yi Kanun-i Nevisandegan* and the Iranian women's March 10, 1979, statement, both from the Persian. Throughout this appendix, unless otherwise indicated, the notes are by Afary and Anderson.

Dialogue between Michel Foucault and Baqir Parham

Conducted in September 1978 and published in *Nameh-yi Kanun-i Nevisandegan* (Publication of the Center of Iranian Writers), no. 1 (Spring 1979): 9–17.

PREFACE BY PARHAM: Michel Foucault, the famous French thinker and philosopher, was recently in Iran. He came to visit the country, to travel around, and to write several articles on it. His trips apparently took him to Qom,[1] where he spoke with some of the Grand Ayatollahs. Although Foucault is not well known in Iran, he has an immense reputation in the world of philosophy. By first analyzing the field of medicine and its history, he initiated a unique and penetrating study of reason, of the structure and organization of knowledge. He has a number of valuable works, such as *Madness and Civilization, The Archaeology of Knowledge*, and *The Order of Things*. Foucault's short trip to Iran was an occasion to have a conversation with him about structuralism and some other key issues. Perhaps, in a search for an answer to them, he has come to this end of the world. This interview was conducted on Saturday, September 23, 1978, in Tehran.

PARHAM: Philosophy has a claim to objectivity in its worldview. How do you, as a philosopher, see the question of political commitment?

FOUCAULT: I do not think that we could give a definition of an intellectual unless we stress the fact that there is no intellectual who is not at the same time, and in some form, involved with politics. Of course, at certain points in history, there have been attempts to define the intellectual from a purely theoretical and objective angle. It is assumed that intellectuals are those who refuse to become involved in the issues and problems of their own societies. But in fact, such periods in history have been very rare, and there are very few intellectuals who have adopted such a premise.

If we look at Western societies, from the very first Greek philosophers up to today's intellectuals, we see that they all had ties in some form to politics. They were involved in politics, and their actions had meaning only insofar as they concretely affected their societies. At any rate, this is a general principle. Therefore, to the question, "Should an intellectual interfere in the political, social, economic life of his or her country," I respond that it is not a matter of should or ought. Being an intellectual requires this. The very definition of an intellectual comprises a person who necessarily is entangled with the politics and major decisions of his society. Thus, the point is not whether or not an intellectual has a presence in political life. Rather, the point is what should the role of an intellectual be in the present state of the world, in order that he or she [*u*][2] would reach the most decisive, authentic, accurate results. I am, of course, only dealing with the society of which I am a part. Later, in comparison to your experiences, we shall see what are the differences between our situation in the West and yours.

In France and in Europe in general, ever since the French Revolution, the intellectual has played the role of a prophet, a foreteller of the future society. In other words, the intellectual was one whose responsibility was to deal with general and universal principles for all of humanity. But in our Western societies something important has happened. The role of science, knowledge, technique, and technologies has perpetually increased, and so has the significance of these issues for politics and the organization of society. Engineers, lawyers, doctors, healthcare workers and social workers, researchers in the humanities, all form a social layer in our society whose numbers, as well as whose economic and political significance, are constantly increasing. Therefore, I think that the role of the intellectual is perhaps not so much, or maybe not only, to stand for the universal values of humanity. Rather, his or her responsibility is to work on specific objective fields, the very fields in which knowledge and sciences are involved, and to analyze and critique the role of knowledge and technique in these areas in our present-day society. In my opinion, today the intellectual must be inside the pit, the very pit in which the sciences are engaged, where they produce political results. Thus, working with intellectuals—mostly doctors, lawyers, psychiatrists, and psychologists—has paramount importance to me.

PARHAM: In response to my first question, you also partly answered my second question.

FOUCAULT: No problem, ask it again. Maybe in this way I could answer your first question!

PARHAM: Very well. You see, we have witnessed a closeness between philosophy and political reality. I wanted to ask you, with regard to this proximity between philosophy and politics, do you see any basic change in the philosophical worldview of our time? And if so, what is its foundation and its nature?

FOUCAULT: If again we keep in mind the West, I think we should not forget two grand and painful experiences we had in our culture in the last two centuries. First, throughout the eighteenth century, philosophers—or it is better to say, intellectuals in France, England, and Germany—attempted to rethink society anew, according to the vision and principles of good government as they perceived it. The impact of this type of thinking can be seen, to a great extent, in the revolutions and in the social and political changes in France, England, and Germany. In actuality, out of this philosophical vision—the vision of a non-alienated, clear, lucid, and balanced society—industrial capitalism emerged, that is, the harshest, most savage, most selfish, most dishonest, oppressive society one could possibly imagine. I do not want to say that the philosophers were responsible for this, but the truth is that their ideas had an impact on these transformations. More importantly, this monstrosity we call the state is to a great extent the fruit and result of their thinking. Let us not forget that the theory of the state, the theory of the all-powerful state, the all-powerful society vis-à-vis the individual, the absolute right of the group against the right of the individual, can be found among French philosophers of the eighteenth century and the German philosophers of the late eighteenth and early nineteenth centuries. This is the first painful experience.

The second painful experience is the one that emerged not between the philosopher and bourgeois society, but between revolutionary thinkers and the socialist states we know today. Out of the visions of Marx, the visions of socialists, from their thoughts and their analyses, which were among the most objective, rational, and seemingly accurate thoughts and analyses, emerged in actuality political systems, social organizations, and economic mechanisms that today are condemned and ought to be discarded. Thus, I think both of these experiences were painful ones, and we are still living through the second one, not just in thought but also in life.

I can give another example that is both most interesting and tragic for Western intellectuals—that of Vietnam and Cambodia. One felt that there was a people's struggle, a struggle that was just and right at its foundation, against vicious American imperialism. One anticipated that out of this remarkable struggle a society would emerge in which one could recognize oneself. By "ourselves," I do not mean the Westerners, since this was not their battle. I mean a society in which the face of revolution could be recognized. But Cambodia, and to some extent Vietnam, present us with a face from which freedom, a classless society, a non-alienating society, were absent.

I think we live at a point of extreme darkness and extreme brightness. Extreme darkness, because we really do not know from which direction the light would come. Extreme brightness, because we ought to have the courage to begin anew. We have to abandon every dogmatic principle and question one by one the validity of all the principles that have been the source of oppression. From the point of view of political thought, we are, so to speak, at point zero. We have to construct another political thought, another political imagination, and teach anew the vision of a future. I am saying this so that you know that any Westerner, any Western intellectual with some integrity, cannot be indifferent to what she or he hears about Iran, a nation that has reached a number of social, political, and so forth, dead ends. At the same time, there are those who struggle to present a different way of thinking about social and political organization, one that takes nothing from Western philosophy, from its juridical and revolutionary foundations. In other words, they try to present an alternative based on Islamic teachings.

PARHAM: In my first two questions, the topic of discussion was mostly philosophy, science, and especially the humanities. Now, with your permission, I would like to speak of something that is closer to our particular situation in Iran, that is, religion. Could you please tell us what your opinion is of the role of religion as a world perspective and in social and political life?

FOUCAULT: One of the statements I have heard repeatedly during my recent stay in Iran was that Marx was really wrong to say, "Religion is the opium of the people." I think I must have heard this statement three or four times. I do not intend to begin anew a discussion of Marx here, but I do think that we ought to reexamine this statement of Marx. I have heard some supporters of an Islamic government say that this statement of Marx might be true for Christianity, but it is not true for Islam, especially Shi'ite Islam. I have read several books on Islam and Shi'ism, and I totally agree with them because the role of Shi'ism in a political awakening, in maintaining political consciousness, in inciting and fomenting political awareness, is historically undeniable. It is a profound phenomenon in a society such as Iran. Of course, there have at times been proximities between the state and Shi'ism, and shared organizations have existed. You had a Safavid Shi'ism,[3] and against it you have tried to resurrect an Alavid Shi'ism.[4] All of this is accurate. But on the whole, and despite changes that occurred in the nature of religion due to the proximity between Shi'ism and state power in that period, religion has nevertheless played an oppositional role.

In the Christian centers of the world, the situation is more complicated. Still, it would be naïve and incorrect if we said that religion in its Christian form was the opium of the people, while in its Islamic form it has been a source of popular awakening for the people. I am astonished by the connections and even the similarities that exist between Shi'ism and some of the religious movements in Europe at the end of the Middle Ages, up to the seventeenth or eighteenth centuries. These were great popular movements against feudal lords, against the first cruel formations of bourgeois society, great protests against the all-powerful control of the state. In Europe in the late eighteenth and early nineteenth centuries, before they adopted a directly political form, all such movements appeared as religious movements. Take for example the Anabaptists, who were allied to such a movement during Germany's Peasant Wars.[5] It was a movement that rejected the power of the state, government bureaucracy, social and religious hierarchies, everything. This movement supported the right to individual conscience and the independence of small religious groups, which wished to be together, have their own organizations, without hierarchy or social stratification between them. These were all extremely important social movements that left their mark on the religious and political consciousness of the West. In England, during the bourgeois revolutions of the seventeenth century, underneath the bourgeois and parliamentary revolutions as such, we have a complete series of religious-political struggles. These movements are religious because they are political and political because they are religious, and are very important. I therefore think that the history of religions, and their deep connection to politics, ought to be thought anew.

In actuality, the type of Christianity that was the opium of the people was the product of political choices and joint tactics by the states, or the government bureaucracies, and the church organization during the nineteenth century. They said we ought to bring the rebellious workers back to religion and make them accept their fate. In Marx's time, religion was in fact the opium of the people, and Marx was right for this reason, but only in the context of his own time. His statement ought to be understood only for the time period in which he lived, not as a general statement on all eras of Christianity, or on all religions.

PARHAM: Precisely. Now I come to my last question, which, unlike my other questions, is more academic. I wanted to use this opportunity to ask you about philosophical structuralism. You have been known as one of the most authentic representatives of this form of thought. Could you please tell me what the issues are exactly?

FOUCAULT: Very well, but let me first say that I am not a structuralist. I never have been. I never made such a claim. And I have always clearly said that I am not a structuralist, but such terms, such labels, are out of necessity both correct and incorrect. There is a truthful dimension to them and an untruthful one. In actuality, what is known as structuralism is a methodology used in linguistics, sociology, history of religions, comparative mythology, and so forth. These make up a group of scientific fields that use the structuralist method. In other words, their analysis is based more on systems of relations than on explorations of elements and contents. Structuralism in this meaning has no relationship to my work, none.

Beyond this, there is the fact that in the 1960s in the West, especially in France, a change took place in the form of analysis and philosophical thinking. Briefly, without wishing to enter a debate, the issue is this: From the time of Descartes until now, the point of origin of philosophical thought was the subject, and the foundational subject of philosophy was to determine what is the subject, what is self-consciousness? Is the subject free? Is self-consciousness absolute self-consciousness? In other words, is it aware of itself? In sum, can self-consciousness, as Hegel said, become worldly?

Around the 1960s, after the world became more connected with technique and technical knowledge, I believe that a rethinking at the point of origin of philosophical thought began. That is, it seemed better to begin with contents, with things themselves. In other words, and very simply, this meant to begin with things that exist positively and to analyze them. It meant to see how the subject could be placed within this content, which is the only role that the subject can play, focusing on how the subject is determined by outside elements. In other words, the principal change is not to privilege the subject as against the objective reality from the very beginning. Rather the objects, the relation between the objects, and the comprehensibility of objects within themselves are what we explore. That is, we pay more attention to the comprehensibility of things in their own right than to the awareness of the subject.

From this point of view, we can understand why some types of research are called structuralist research. For example, look at the problem of psychoanalysis. Lacan tried to discuss the subject on the basis of the unconscious, whereas Sartre and Merleau-Ponty began with subject and tried to see if they could reach the unconsciousness or not, and they never, of course, reached it. Lacan begins with the unconscious, the principle of the unconscious that appears in the process of psychoanalytical probing, and asks the question: Given the existence of this unconscious, what would the subject be?

Now I turn to myself, since your question was for me. My first book was called *Madness and Civilization*, but in fact my problem was rationality, that is, how does reason operate in a society such as ours? Well, to understand this issue, instead of beginning with the subject moving from awareness to reason, it is better if we see how, in the Western world, those who are not the subjects of reason, those who are not considered reasonable, that is, those who are mad, are removed from the life process. Starting with this practice, with constellations of real practices, and finally, a process of negation, we reach the point where we can see the place of reason. Or we find out that reason is not just the movements and actions of rational structures, but the movements of the structures and the mechanisms of power. Reason is what sets aside madness. Reason is what gives itself the right and the means to set aside madness.

From such analyses that do not start with the subject, I reached the point of how one could question various manifestations of power and analyze them. In general, we can say that a philosophy based on self-consciousness is necessarily related to the idea of freedom. And this is very good, but the philosophy or thinking whose subject matter is not self-consciousness, but real practice or social practice, relates to the theory of power. In other words, instead of self-consciousness and freedom, we reach practice and power.

I do not mean to say that power, from my point of view, is a foundational, unconquerable, absolute entity that one has to kneel before. Rather, the purpose of all of my analyses is that, in light of them, we find out where are the weak points of power, from which we can attack it. When we speak of the relationship between reason and madness, when we show that reason exercises its power on madness, this is not to justify reason. Rather, it is to show how reason as a system of power can be questioned and fought against. Thus, my analyses are in fact strategic analyses and are meaningful only in relation to strategies.

My studies on the issues of youth crime and prison are of a similar nature. I want to show what are the existing mechanisms of power that separate the criminal from the noncriminal. What are the points of weakness of this system or the historic points in between which the system has taken shape, so that we could objectively and practically challenge them? Many regard structuralism as an analysis of mechanisms that are undefeatable and imperishable, whereas the opposite is true. They say that structuralism is about analyzing relations that are part of the nature of the objects and cannot be changed. The opposite is true. I want to explain relations that have been tied together through the power of human beings and for this very reason are changeable and destructible. Therefore, from my point of view, structuralism is more a philosophy or a manual of combat, not a document of impotence. My problem is not to explore my self-consciousness to see if I am free or not. My problem is to analyze reality to see how one can free oneself.

The Army—When the Earth Quakes

First published in *Corriere della sera*, September 28, 1978.

Tehran—On the edge of the two great salt deserts that stretch across the middle of Iran, an earthquake has just occurred. Tabas and forty villages have been annihilated.

Ten years ago to the day, Ferdows, in the same region, was wiped out. On this ruined land, two rival towns were born, as if in the shah's Iran the same misfortune could not give rise to the same renewal. On one side, there was the town of administration, the Ministry of Housing, and the notables.

But a little further away, the artisans and the farmers rebuilt their own town, in opposition to all these official plans. Under the direction of a cleric, they collected the funds, built and dug with their own hands, laid out canals and wells, and constructed a mosque. On the first day they planted a green flag.[6] The new village is called Islamiyeh. Facing the government and against it, Islam: already ten years old.

Who will rebuild Tabas today? Who will rebuild Iran after the earthquake of Friday, September 8,[7] right under the treads of the tanks? The fragile political edifice has not yet fallen to the ground, but it is irreparably cracked from top to bottom.

In the torrid heat, under the only palm trees still standing, the last survivors of Tabas work away at the rubble. The dead are still stretching their arms to hold up walls that no longer exist. Men, their faces turned toward the ground, curse the shah. The bulldozers have arrived, accompanied by the empress; she was ill received. However, mullahs rush in from the entire region; and young people in Tehran go discreetly from one friendly house to another, collecting funds before leaving for Tabas. "Help your brothers, but nothing through the government, nothing for it," is the call that Ayatollah Khomeini has just issued from exile in Iraq.

The earth that shakes and destroys things can also bring men together; it divides the politicians and demarcates the adversaries more clearly than ever. The state believes that it is possible to divert the immense anger from the Black Friday massacre—anger that is now congealed into shock, but not disarmed—toward this natural disaster. It will not succeed. The dead of Tabas will lie down next to the victims of Djaleh Square and make demands on the latter's behalf. A woman posed the question publicly: "Three days of national mourning for the earthquake, that's good; but does it mean that the blood that was shed in Tehran was not Iranian as well?"

In Tehran's hotels, journalists coming back from Tabas the other night were confused. Evidently, the soldiers stood by impassively and let civilian men and women dig up the earth themselves in order to turn up their dead. Instructions? Incompetence? Ill will? The enigma of the army, here as everywhere.

On Monday, September 4, the crowd throws gladiolas at the soldiers; they fraternize and they cry. On Thursday, September 7, the immense demonstration rolls into the streets of Tehran; a few centimeters away from the machine guns, pointed at them but silent. On Friday, September 8, machine guns and perhaps bazookas were fired throughout the day; the troops sometimes had the methodical coldness of a firing squad.

From the first days of Islam, and especially for the Shi'ites ever since the assassination of Ali, the murder of a Muslim by another Muslim—and God knows that this has occurred—still has the impact of a religious scandal, both politically and juridically.

As a stopgap measure, they answered with myth: "Those who fired on us do not belong to our people; they had long hair and spoke a foreign tongue: Israelis, therefore, brought in the day before by cargo planes." I asked an oppositionist, who because of his own situation is very familiar with what happens in the army, about this. "Yes," he responded to me, "there is technical cooperation with the Israeli army; yes, the anti-guerrilla forces had, in the beginning, Israeli advisers; but nothing, absolutely nothing, allows one to say that our dead in Tehran were killed by foreigners."[8]

Is real power now in the hands of the army? The army, for the moment, holds back the immense revolt of the people against the shah, who is abandoned by everyone, even the privileged. In the coming weeks, will the army be a decisive force, as many Western observers are saying?

It seems not. Iran has what is apparently the fifth largest army in the world. One out of every three dollars of its oil revenue is dedicated to this precious toy. However, a budget, good equipment, jet fighters, and hovercrafts—this is not yet an army. It is sometimes even the case that arms hamper the formation of an army.

First, there is not *one* army in Iran, but four: the traditional army,[9] responsible for the tasks of surveillance and administration for the whole territory; the shah's Praetorian guard, a closed body of Janissaries,[10] with its recruitment, its schools, its living quarters, some of which were constructed by a French company; the combat army,[11] with armaments that are sometimes more sophisticated than those available to the American army. And then thirty or forty thousand American advisors.

Furthermore, they were careful not to create something that would resemble a veritable general staff. Each one of the principal units of these armies is directly linked to the shah. An internal police controls them. No high-ranking officer can move about without the personal authorization of the shah: "One of my colleagues," one of them said to me, "had reproached the shah for having gotten himself named a general in the English army; he thought that this time the gewgaw [*hochet*][12] felt a little too much like something from the Victorian age. This man, who had supported the shah against Mossadeq,[13] found himself in prison for three years."

In the Iran of oil and poverty, the army occupies a very important place. Four million people (one out of six Iranians) live off of it, according to economists. But this is not enough to give it a coherent social base, or even to oblige it to participate in economic development. Most of its weaponry is purchased abroad. There are of course economic consequences. For the generals, these include commissions on contracts. At the lowest level, the military is a small manual labor force recruited largely from among the unemployed. Iran lacks a solid economic-military structure.

Nor is there an army ideology. Never in the history of Iran has the army been allowed to take on the role of molding the nation or of developing the type of political project that can be found in the South American armies since the wars of independence. The Iranian army has never liberated anything. It has been marked successively with Russian, English, and then American insignia. The army protected its rulers and stood guard side by side with foreign troops, around the foreign concessions. It never had the opportunity to identify with Iran. Nor did it want to take charge of the country's destiny. One day a general seized power, but he commanded the Cossack legion and was pushed forward by the English. He was the father of the current king.[14]

Of course, things can happen again. The American ambassador can replay the Ironside *coup* that allowed Reza Khan to substitute himself for the Qajars,[15] or at least impose an ironhanded general on the shah as prime minister. But this would only be a temporary solution. It would not be a military dictatorship under the direction of a caste of officers showing internal solidarity despite personal rivalries. The Pinochet or Videla formulas seem to be off the agenda.[16]

Thank heavens.

Let us say, thanks to Allah.

One day, twenty-four Iranian officers were executed for communism. The next day, the shah laid down his crown at the feet of a statue of Lenin. The victims of the earlier bloodbath were never replaced.[17]

The army's anti-Marxism stems from two sources. Among those who are inclined toward the opposition, it is justified by the Soviet Union's policies and its at least tacit support, since the fall of Mossadeq, of the shah's policies. A lot of physical, intellectual, and moral courage would be necessary today in order to be a nationalist oppositionist and at the same time a Soviet-type Marxist. For these people, anti-Marxism undergirds nationalism. And for the simple-minded, there is of course government propaganda. I was shown internal army circulars that said one must never kill women or children, except of course if they are communists.

Because it is so solidly anti-Marxist, is it not possible that the army would intervene forcefully in national life, as unrest spreads and as the government blames this unrest on "international communism"?

Some friends arranged for me, in a well-scrubbed place on the outskirts of Tehran, a meeting with high-ranking officers, all from the opposition.

The more the disturbances increase, they told me, the more the government, in an attempt to maintain order, is being forced to call on soldiers who lack both training and the willingness to follow orders. And these troops have the opportunity to discover that they are not dealing with international communism, but rather with the street, with the bazaar merchants, with workers, with the unemployed, men like their brothers, as they themselves would be if they were not soldiers: "We can make them shoot once, but not twice; in Tabriz eight months ago,[18] it was necessary to change the entire garrison; and even though we brought regiments to Tehran from remote corners of the provinces, it will still be necessary to change them rapidly." It was confirmed to me that on Black Friday at least one officer had been killed by his soldiers when he gave the order to shoot at the crowd, and also that some of the soldiers had committed suicide the next day.

As agitation develops under the banner of this Islam, to which the whole army adheres,[19] the soldiers and the officers discover that they do not have enemies in front of them, but rather masters above them. And when an army learns, at the moment of combat, that instead of enemies it has masters, what does it do?

"Does not a Nasser or a Qaddafi emerge from its ranks?"

The officer hesitates a second.

"If this Qaddafi is patriotic, legalist, democratic, and religious, I would accept him, and I believe that we would accept him."

"Yes, of course, he would be all of that on the day he comes to power. But the next day?"

"As popular as he is, his popularity would cease at the very instant that he became a dictator."

And he added: "Do not forget that there is nothing in the army that is intended to make it popular. We would accept a democratic leader that would emerge from it, but not a dictatorship emanating from it."

I remembered, then, what lots of others had said to me, that the large size of the Iranian army could not be justified by national defense. Apparently, it would be swept away by a Soviet attack within eight minutes. Its sole task, according to this hypothesis, would be to practice a scorched-earth strategy—in other words, to destroy the country. Therefore, such a disproportionately large force only has meaning insofar as it ensures internal order or policing at the regional level. One of its most recent military interventions was in Afghanistan shortly after the coup d'état.[20] It has the potential to attack from the rear the entire battlefield of the Middle East. It is a regional intervention force throughout Southwest Asia. In short, it is too brittle and divided to impose, with or without the shah, the American order in Iran; it is also a gendarme that is too obviously turned against its Muslim neighbors to ensure, with widespread agreement, a national "restoration." It is a question of troops equipped in the American manner, but not of an Americanized army.

I asked one of these army representatives what, according to him, was the biggest danger to Iran: the United States or the USSR. This time he said, without any hesitation:

"The United States, because it is the Americans who are dominating us."

To me, these words seemed to carry a lot of weight, because I knew that the man to whom I was talking had been far from hostile to the actions of the Americans twenty-five years earlier, when they restored the shah to the throne.

The army does not seem, therefore, to have within it the power to carry out a political intervention. It is true that the shah cannot subsist without it, but it is besieged, or rather crisscrossed, by forces that threaten *him.*

It can permit or block a solution, but it can neither propose nor impose one that it develops itself. It is a keyhole instead of a key. And of the two keys that claim to be able to turn it, the one that seems the best adapted at the moment is not the American one of the shah. It is the Islamic one of the people's [*populaire*][21] movement.

The Shah Is a Hundred Years Behind the Times

First published in *Corriere della sera*, October 1, 1978.[22]

Tehran—When I left Paris, I was told over and over again: "Iran is going through a crisis of modernization. An arrogant monarch, clumsy and authoritarian, is attempting to compete with the industrialized nations and to keep his eyes fixed on the year 2000, but the traditional society, for its part, cannot and does not want to follow. Wounded and hurt, it comes to a halt. It folds itself back onto its own past and, in the name of millenarian beliefs, it seeks shelter among a retrograde clergy."

How many times have I also heard intelligent observers ask with all seriousness what political form will be able to reconcile the deepest layers of Iranian society with the country's needed modernization. Would that be a liberal monarchy, a parliamentary system, or a strong presidential one?

I arrived in Tehran with these questions in mind. I have asked them twenty times and I have received twenty responses: "Let the king reign, but not govern." "Let us go back to the 1906 Constitution."[23] "Let us establish a regency for a while, before making definitive decisions." "The shah must totally or partially step back." "The Pahlavis should leave the country and never be heard from again." But always, underlying all these responses, there is the same *leitmotif*: "At any rate, we want nothing from *this regime*." I have advanced very little.

One morning, in a big empty apartment where closed curtains let through only the almost unbearable noise of the cars passing by, I met an oppositionist who was described to me as one of the country's astute political minds. He was wanted by the police. He was a very calm, very reserved man. He made few gestures, but when he opened his hand, one could see large scars. He had already had encounters with the police.

— Why do you fight?

— To bring down despotism and corruption.

— Despotism first, or corruption?

— Despotism sustains corruption, and corruption supports despotism.

— What do you think of the idea, often put forward by the shah's entourage, that it is necessary to have a strong power in order to modernize a still backward country, that modernization cannot help but lead to corruption in a country that lacks a cohesive administration?

— The modernization-despotism-corruption combination is precisely what we reject.

— In short, that is how you characterize "this regime."

— Exactly.

A small detail that struck me the day before when I visited the bazaar, which had just reopened after a strike that had lasted more than eight days, suddenly came back to me. Incredible sewing machines, high and misshapen, as can be seen in the advertisements of nineteenth-century newspapers, were lined up in the stalls. They were adorned with patterns of ivy, climbing plants, and budding flowers, roughly imitating old Persian miniatures. These unfit-for-use Western objects, under the sign of an obsolete Orient, all bore the inscription: "Made in South Korea."

I then felt that I had understood that recent events did not signify a shrinking back in the face of modernization by extremely retrograde elements, but the rejection, by a whole culture and a whole people, of a *modernization* that is itself an *archaism*.

The shah's misfortune is to have espoused this archaism. His crime is to have maintained, through a corrupt and despotic system, that fragment of the past in a present that no longer wants it.

Yes, modernization as a political project and as a principle of social transformation is a thing of the past in Iran.

I do not mean that mere mistakes and failures have doomed the recent forms that the shah wanted to give to modernization. It is true that all the great efforts undertaken by the regime since 1963 are now rejected, by all social classes.[24] It is not only the big property owners who are discontented with the agrarian reform, but also the small peasants, who fall into debt as soon as they are granted a parcel of land, and are then forced to emigrate to the city. The artisans and the small manufacturers are discontented, because the creation of an internal market benefited mainly foreign products.[25] The bazaar merchants are discontented because the current forms of urbanization suffocate them. The wealthy classes, who counted on a certain level of national industrial development and who can now only imitate the governing caste by placing their capital in California banks or in Parisian real estate, are also discontented.

"Modernization," which is no longer desired, is this series of stinging failures. But "modernization" is also something older that sticks to the current monarch, and that is his *raison d'être*. It is something that is the basis not only of his government, but also of his dynasty.

In 1921, when Reza Khan, the head of the Cossack Brigade, was brought to power by the English, he presented himself as a disciple of Ataturk.[26] No doubt this was a usurpation of the throne, but he also had three objectives borrowed from Mustafa Kemal: nationalism, secularism, and modernization. The Pahlavis were never able to reach the first two objectives. As to nationalism, they neither could, nor knew how to, loosen the constraints of geopolitics and oil wealth. The father placed himself under English domination in order to stave off the Russian threat. The son substituted American political, economic, and military control for the English presence and for Soviet penetration. For secularism, things were equally difficult. Because it was the Shi'ite religion that in fact constituted the real principle of national consciousness, Reza Shah, in order to dissociate the two, tried to propagate a notion of "Aryanness," whose sole support was the myth of Aryan purity that reigned elsewhere. In the eyes of the people, what did it mean to discover one fine day that they were Aryans? It was nothing more than seeing the two-thousand-year-old monarchy being celebrated today on the ruins of Persepolis.

Out of the whole Kemalist program, international politics and the internal situation left to the Pahlavis only one bone to chew on, that of modernization. This modernization is now utterly rejected, not only because of the setbacks that have been experienced, but also because of its very principle. With the present agony of the regime, we witness the last moments of an episode that started almost sixty years ago, the attempt to modernize the Islamic countries in a European fashion. The shah still clings to this as if it were his sole *raison d'être*. I do not know if he is still looking toward the year 2000,[27] but I do know that his famous gaze dates from the 1920s.[28]

There are in Iran as in Europe certain technocrats, whose function is to correct the errors of the previous generation of technocrats. They speak of measured growth, of development, but also of the environment. They speak of the social fabric with respect. One of them explained to me that everything could still be straightened out, that a "reasonable" modernization could occur, which would take "cultural identity" into account, but on condition that the king abandon his dreams. Turning around, he showed me a huge photo on the wall where a small, disguised man was strutting in front of a gem-studded throne, as a way of saying, in the manner of de Tocqueville: "This is the man with whom we will have to govern Iran."

Even now, this ambitious man and several others with him would like to continue to save "modernization" by limiting the shah's powers and by neutralizing his dreams. They have not understood that in Iran today it is modernization that is a dead weight.

I have always regretted that corruption, which attracts so many unscrupulous people, interests honest people so little. Do you know of a treatise on political economy, or of sociology or history books, that offers a serious and detailed analysis of the speculation, corrupt practices, embezzlement, and swindling that constitute the veritable daily bread of our trade, our industry, and our finances?

In Tehran, I at last met my man, an austere economist with malicious eyes.

"No," he told me, "corruption was not the misfortune that compromised the country's development, nor has it been the dynasty's weakness. It has always been the dynasty's way of exercising power and a fundamental mechanism of the economy. Corruption is what held despotism and modernization together. Please consider that it is not a vice that is more or less hidden. It is the *regime*."

I then had the privilege of hearing a superb presentation on "Pahlavi corruption." The clever professor knew a lot. By birth, he was well enough connected to the traditional wealth of his country to be familiar with the old-time ruses, and his expertise had helped him to understand today's procedures well.

He showed me how Reza Shah, this unknown who came to power with only foreign support, had immediately inscribed himself on the economy of the country as a result of predatory conquests—confiscation of a few great feudal treasures and then of great stretches of fertile land on the shores of the Caspian. He then explained to me the system of the current team. They use modern methods, such as government loans, banking associations, lending institutions such as the Pahlavi Foundation,[29] as well as very archaic forms, where it is a question of concessions granted to a family member, of revenues accorded to a favorite: "To one of the brothers, the real estate; to the twin sister, the drug traffic; to her son, the trade in antiquities; the sugar to Félix Agaian; the arms trade to Toufanian; the caviar for Davalou."[30] Even the pistachio trade was parceled out. All this "modernization" has led to a gigantic appropriation. Thanks to the Omran bank, the benefits of the agrarian reform ended up in the hands of the shah and of his family. New construction projects in Tehran were distributed like spoils.

A very small clan of beneficiaries weaves the right of conquest into the initiatives of economic development. If we add that the government disposes of the whole oil revenue left to it by foreign companies, that it can therefore acquire "its" police, "its" army, and sign fabulous and fruitful contracts with Westerners, how could we not understand that the Iranian people see in the Pahlavis a regime of occupation? It is a regime that has the same form and comes from the same age as all the colonial regimes that have subjugated Iran since the beginning of the century.

Therefore, I beg of you, do not tell us any more about the fortunes and misfortunes of a monarch who is too modern for a country that is too old. What is old here in Iran is the shah. He is fifty years old and a hundred years behind the times. He is of the age of the predatory monarchs. He has the old-fashioned dream of opening his country through secularization and industrialization. Today, it is his project of modernization, his despotic weapons, and his system of corruption that are archaic. It is "the regime" that is the archaism.

Tehran: Faith against the Shah

First published in *Corriere della sera*, October 8, 1978.[31]

Tehran—Tehran is divided in two, along a horizontal axis. The wealthy part of the city, in the middle of enormous construction sites, slowly climbs the foothills, toward the cool air. The villas with their gardens are enclosed by high walls and solid metal doors. In the south are the bazaar, the old city center, and the poor suburbs. At the periphery, very low, barrack-type buildings blend dustily into the plains, as far as the eye can see. A little further away, the city collapses, for over the centuries, enormous excavations have been dug for the clay needed to build Tehran. Five or six hundred meters below the level of the royal palace and the Hilton Hotel, the city left its empty molds. Here, above the holes, red and black tarps have been stretched to create dwellings.

There, where the city ends and where one can already feel the desert, two opposite waves have met, peasants forced from their homes because of the failure of agrarian reform and city dwellers forced out because of the triumphs of urbanization. This is a phenomenon that characterizes the whole of Iran, for in ten years the urban population has increased from nine to seventeen million.

Today, like every Friday, the two halves of the city, side by side during the week, have separated. The North went further north, toward the beaches of the Caspian. The South went further south, toward Shahr-e Rey and the old sanctuary where the [great-grand-]son of Imam Reza lies.[32] All around the mausoleum there is stamping and jostling. The European is probably wrong to seek to discern what part is village fair and what part devotion. The present monarch has tried indeed to harness some of this current. Very close to here, he erected the tomb of his own father. The father, Reza Shah, also laid out a large avenue and designed concrete platforms where there had been only vegetable gardens. He threw parties and received foreign delegations, all for naught, for in the rivalry between the dead, the [great-grand-]son of the imam wins, every Friday, over the father of the king.

"At this point, what else do they have left?" is a frequent question. "They have been cut off from their traditional existence. To be sure, their life was narrow and precarious. However, by tearing them away from their farms and their workshops, by promising them a salary that can only be found in earth-moving or construction (and this only sporadically), one exposes them to permanent unemployment. Displaced in this manner, what refuge do they have except the one they can find in the mosque and the religious community?"

But those who stay at home undergo a similar but unseen "transplantation." There are attempts to develop agribusiness where there used to be individual plots of land. There are attempts to create export crops, while products that used to be farmed onsite are now imported. There are attempts to put new administrative structures in place. Several months ago, on a deserted road, a sign welcomed arriving motorists to Meybod. One searched in vain, but there was no trace of Meybod. People of the area, when questioned, did not understand what was being asked. This inquiry revealed that a town that existed only for bureaucrats had been created from five scattered hamlets, undoubtedly for some land speculator. At the moment, no one yet cared about this city, which was thrown on the ground like a rootless geography,[33] but soon these people were going to be governed differently, forced to live otherwise, connected to each other by other relations, and maybe displaced.

Where can protection be sought, how can what one is be found, if not in this Islam, which for centuries has regulated everyday life, family ties, and social relations with such care? Have not its rigor and its immobility constituted its good fortune? A sociologist told me of its "value as a refuge."[34] It seems to me, however, that this man, who knew his country well, erred (out of discretion, perhaps, in front of the European that I am) by an excessive Westernness.

Let us remember that the commemoration of the victims of the uprising took place eight days ago in Tehran's immense cemetery, which carries the name "Paradise."[35] Where the dead sleep in shallow ground under a thin layer of cement, the families, the friends of the dead, and people by the thousands were praying. They wailed, raising up their arms. But early in the afternoon, around the black and gray robes of the mullahs, discussion had already begun, and with such violence! Overthrow the shah, immediately or later? Chase out the Americans, but how? Take up arms or keep waiting? Support or denounce the opposition deputies who, by attacking the regime in parliament, give the world the impression that freedom is back? Late in the evening, groups formed, broke apart, and re-formed around the clerics. In the political excitement, the dead were not forgotten, but given the veneration to which they were entitled.

Moreover, eight days earlier, thousands of demonstrators, bare-handed in front of armed soldiers, had streamed into the streets of Tehran, shouting "Islam, Islam!"; "Soldier, my brother, why shoot your brother? Come with us to save the Quran"; "Khomeini, heir to Hussein, Khomeini, we follow in your footsteps." And I know more than one student, "left-wing" according to our categories, who had written in big letters, "Islamic Government," on the placard on which he had written his demands and that he was holding up with outstretched arms.

It is necessary to go back even further. Throughout this whole year, revolt ran throughout Iran, from celebrations to commemorations, from worship, to sermons, to prayers. Tehran honored the dead of Abadan, Tabriz those of Isfahan, and Isfahan those of Qom. White, red, and green lanterns were lit up after nightfall on big tree branches in front of hundreds of houses.[36] It was the "wedding bed" of the boys just killed.[37] In the mosques during the day, the mullahs spoke furiously against the shah, the Americans, and the West and its materialism. They called for people to fight against the entire regime in the name of the Quran and of Islam. When the mosques became too small for the crowd, loudspeakers were put in the streets. These voices, as terrible as must have been that of Savonarola in Florence, the voices of the Anabaptists in Münster, or those of the Presbyterians at the time of Cromwell,[38] resounded through the whole village, the whole neighborhood. Many of these sermons were recorded, and the tapes circulated throughout Iran. In Tehran, a writer who was not at all a religious man let me listen to some of them. They seemed to evoke neither withdrawal nor a refuge. Nor did they evoke disarray or fear.

I did not even have to ask him whether this religion, which alternately summons the faithful to battle and commemorates the fallen, is not profoundly fascinated with death—more focused, perhaps, on martyrdom than on victory. I knew that he would have responded: "What preoccupies you, you Westerners, is *death*. You ask her to detach you from life, and she teaches you how to give up. As for us, we care about *the dead*, because they attach us to life. We hold out our hands to them in order for them to link us to the permanent obligation of justice. They speak to us of right and of the struggle that is necessary for right to triumph."

Do you know the phrase that makes the Iranians sneer the most, the one that seems to them the stupidest, the shallowest? "Religion is the opium of the people."[39] Up to the time of the current dynasty, the mullahs preached with a gun at their side in the mosques.

Around 90 percent of Iranians are Shi'ites. They await the return of the Twelfth Imam, who will create the reign of the true order of Islam on earth.[40] While this creed does not announce each day that the great event will occur tomorrow, neither does it accept indefinitely all the misery of the world. When I met Ayatollah Shariatmadari (he is undoubtedly the highest spiritual authority in Iran today), one of the first sentences he uttered to me was: "We are waiting for the Mahdi, but each day we fight for a good government." Shi'ism, in the face of the established powers, arms the faithful with an unremitting restlessness. It breathes into them an ardor wherein the political and the religious lie side by side.

First, it is a matter of belief. For the Shi'ites, the Quran is just because it expresses the will of God, but God himself wanted to be just. It is justice that made law and not law that manufactured justice. Of course, one must find this justice in "the" text dictated by God to the Prophet. However, one can also decipher it in the life, the sayings, the wisdom, and the exemplary sacrifices of the imams, born, after Ali, in the house of the Prophet,[41] and persecuted by the corrupt government of the caliphs, these arrogant aristocrats who had forgotten the old egalitarian system of justice. While also waiting for the Twelfth Imam, who, by becoming visible, will reestablish the egalitarian system in its perfection, it is necessary, through knowledge, through the love of Ali and of his descendents, and even through martyrdom, to defend the community of believers against the evil power.

Consequently, it is a matter of organization. Among the Shi'ite clergy, religious authority is not determined by a hierarchy. One follows only the one to whom one wants to listen. The Grand Ayatollahs of the moment, those who, in facing down the king, his police, and the army, have just caused an entire people to come out into the streets, were not enthroned by anybody. They were *listened to*. This is true even in the smallest communities, where neighborhood and village mullahs gather around themselves those attracted by their words. From these volunteers comes their subsistence, from them comes what is necessary to support the disciples they train, and from them comes their influence. But from them also comes the unrelenting plea to denounce injustice, to criticize the government, to rise up against unacceptable measures, and to mete out blame and to prescribe. These men of religion are like so many photographic plates on which the anger and the aspirations of the community are marked. If they wanted to go against the current, they would lose this power, which essentially resides in the interplay of speaking and listening.

Let us not embellish things. The Shi'ite clergy is not a revolutionary force. Since the seventeenth century, it has administered the official religion. The mosques and the tombs of the saints have received valuable donations. Considerable goods have been accumulated in its hands, leading to conflicts as well as complicities with the people in power. This has also led to many oscillations, even if it is true that the mullahs, especially the most humble ones, have been most often on the side of the rebels. For example, Ayatollah Kashani was at the peak of his popularity during the time that he supported Mossadeq. After he changed sides, he was forgotten.[42]

The mullahs are not at all "revolutionary," even in the populist sense of the term. But this does not mean that the weight of inertia is the only thing that the Shi'ite religion can put forth in opposition to the government and to the detested modernization. This does not mean that it constitutes an ideology that is so widespread among the people that true revolutionaries are forced for a time to join it. It is much more than a simple vocabulary through which aspirations, unable to find other words, must pass. It is today what it was several times in the past, the form that the political struggle takes as soon as it mobilizes the common people. It transforms thousands of forms of discontent, hatred, misery, and despairs into a *force*. It transforms them into a force because it is a form of expression, a mode of social relations, a supple and widely accepted elemental organization, a way of being together, a way of speaking and listening, something that allows one to be listened to by others, and to yearn for something with them at the same time as they yearn for it.

Persia has had a surprising destiny. At the dawn of history, it invented the state and government. It conferred its models of state and government on Islam, and its administrators staffed the Arab Empire. But from this same Islam, it derived a religion that, throughout the centuries, never ceased to give an irreducible [*irréductible*][43] strength to everything from the depths of a people that can oppose state power.

What Are the Iranians Dreaming [*Rêvent*] About?

First published in *Le Nouvel Observateur*, October 16–22, 1978.[44]

"They will never let go of us of their own will. No more than they did in Vietnam." I wanted to respond that they are even less ready to let go of you than Vietnam because of oil, because of the Middle East. Today they seem ready, after Camp David,[45] to concede Lebanon to Syrian domination and therefore to Soviet influence, but would the United States be ready to deprive itself of a position that, according to circumstance, would allow them to intervene from the East or to monitor the peace?

Will the Americans push the shah toward a new trial of strength, a second "Black Friday"? The recommencement of classes at the university, the recent strikes, the disturbances that are beginning once again, and next month's religious festivals, could create such an opportunity. The man with the iron hand is Moghadam, the current leader of the SAVAK.[46]

This is the backup plan, which for the moment is neither the most desirable nor the most likely. It would be uncertain: While some generals could be counted on, it is not clear if the army could be. From a certain point of view, it would be useless, for there is no "communist threat": not from outside, since it has been agreed for the past twenty-five years that the USSR would not lay a hand on Iran; not from inside, because hatred for the Americans is equaled only by fear of the Soviets.

Whether advisers to the shah, American experts, regime technocrats, or groups from the political opposition (be they the National Front or more "socialist-oriented" men),[47] during these last weeks everyone has agreed with more or less good grace to attempt an "accelerated internal liberalization," or to let it occur. At present, the Spanish model is the favorite of the political leadership.[48] Is it adaptable to Iran? There are many technical problems. There are questions concerning the date: Now, or later, after another violent incident? There are questions concerning individual persons: With or without the shah? Maybe with the son, the wife? Is not former prime minister Amini,[49] the old diplomat pegged to lead the operation, already worn out?

The King and the Saint

There are substantial differences between Iran and Spain, however. The failure of economic development in Iran prevented the laying of a basis for a liberal, modern, westernized regime. Instead, there arose an immense movement from below, which exploded this year, shaking up the political parties that were being slowly reconstituted. This movement has just thrown half a million men into the streets of Tehran, up against machine guns and tanks.

Not only did they shout, "Death to the Shah," but also "Islam, Islam, Khomeini, We Will Follow You," and even "Khomeini for King."

The situation in Iran can be understood as a great joust under traditional emblems, those of the king and the saint, the armed ruler and the destitute exile, the despot faced with the man who stands up bare-handed and is acclaimed by a people. This image has its own power, but it also speaks to a reality to which millions of dead have just subscribed.[50]

The notion of a rapid liberalization without a rupture in the power structure presupposes that the movement from below is being integrated into the system, or that it is being neutralized. Here, one must first discern where and how far the movement intends to go. However, yesterday in Paris, where he had sought refuge, and in spite of many pressures, Ayatollah Khomeini "ruined it all."

He sent out an appeal to the students, but he was also addressing the Muslim community and the army, asking that they oppose in the name of the Quran and in the name of nationalism these compromises concerning elections, a constitution, and so forth.

Is a long-foreseen split taking place within the opposition to the shah? The "politicians" of the opposition try to be reassuring: "It is good," they say. "Khomeini, by raising the stakes, reinforces us in the face of the shah and the Americans. Anyway, his name is only a rallying cry, for he has no program. Do not forget that, since 1963, political parties have been muzzled.[51] At the moment, we are rallying to Khomeini, but once the dictatorship is abolished, all this mist will dissipate. Authentic politics will take command, and we will soon forget the old preacher." But all the agitation this weekend around the hardly clandestine residence of the ayatollah in the suburbs of Paris, as well as the coming and going of "important" Iranians, all of this contradicted this somewhat hasty optimism. It all proved that people believed in the power of the mysterious current that flowed between an old man who had been exiled for fifteen years and his people, who invoke his name.

The nature of this current has intrigued me since I learned about it a few months ago, and I was a little weary, I must confess, of hearing so many clever experts repeating: "We know what they don't want, but they still do not know what they want."

"What do you want?" It is with this single question in mind that I walked the streets of Tehran and Qom in the days immediately following the disturbances. I was careful not to ask professional politicians this question. I chose instead to hold sometimes-lengthy conversations with religious leaders, students, intellectuals interested in the problems of Islam, and also with former guerrilla fighters who had abandoned the armed struggle in 1976 and had decided to work in a totally different fashion, inside the traditional society.[52]

"What do you want?" During my entire stay in Iran, I did not hear even once the word "revolution," but four out of five times, someone would answer, "An Islamic government." This was not a surprise. Ayatollah Khomeini had already given this as his pithy response to journalists and the response remained at that point.

What precisely does this mean in a country like Iran, which has a large Muslim majority but is neither Arab nor Sunni and which is therefore less susceptible than some to Pan-Islamism or Pan-Arabism?

Indeed, Shi'ite Islam exhibits a number of characteristics that are likely to give the desire for an "Islamic government" a particular coloration. Concerning its organization, there is an absence of hierarchy in the clergy, a certain independence of the religious leaders from one another, but a dependence (even a financial one) on those who listen to them, and an importance given to purely spiritual authority. The role, both echoing and guiding, that the clergy must play in order to sustain its influence—this is what the organization is all about. As for Shi'ite doctrine, there is the principle that truth was not completed and sealed by the last prophet. After Muhammad, another cycle of revelation begins, the unfinished cycle of the imams, who, through their words, their example, as well as their martyrdom, carry a light, always the same and always changing. It is this light that is capable of illuminating the law from the inside. The latter is made not only to be conserved, but also to release over time the spiritual meaning that it holds. Although invisible before his promised return, the Twelfth Imam is neither radically nor fatally absent. It is the people themselves who make him come back, insofar as the truth to which they awaken further enlightens them.

It is often said that for Shi'ism, all power is bad if it is not the power of the Imam. As we can see, things are much more complex. This is what Ayatollah

Shariatmadari told me in the first few minutes of our meeting: "We are waiting for the return of the Imam, which does not mean that we are giving up on the possibility of a good government. This is also what you Christians are endeavoring to achieve, although you are waiting for Judgment Day." As if to lend a greater authenticity to his words, the ayatollah was surrounded by several members of the Committee on Human Rights in Iran[53] when he received me.

One thing must be clear. By "Islamic government," nobody in Iran means a political regime in which the clerics would have a role of supervision or control. To me, the phrase "Islamic government" seemed to point to two orders of things.

"A utopia," some told me without any pejorative implication. "An ideal," most of them said to me. At any rate, it is something very old and also very far into the future, a notion of coming back to what Islam was at the time of the Prophet, but also of advancing toward a luminous and distant point where it would be possible to renew fidelity rather than maintain obedience. In pursuit of this ideal, the distrust of legalism seemed to me to be essential, along with a faith in the creativity of Islam.

A religious authority explained to me that it would require long work by civil and religious experts, scholars, and believers in order to shed light on all the problems to which the Quran never claimed to give a precise response. But one can find some general directions here: Islam values work; no one can be deprived of the fruits of his labor; what must belong to all (water, the subsoil) shall not be appropriated by anyone.[54] With respect to liberties, they will be respected to the extent that their exercise will not harm others; minorities will be protected and free to live as they please on the condition that they do not injure the majority; between men and women there will not be inequality with respect to rights, but difference, since there is a natural difference. With respect to politics, decisions should be made by the majority, the leaders should be responsible to the people, and each person, as it is laid out in the Quran, should be able to stand up and hold accountable he who governs.

It is often said that the definitions of an Islamic government are imprecise. On the contrary, they seemed to me to have a familiar but, I must say, not too reassuring clarity. "These are basic formulas for democracy, whether bourgeois or revolutionary," I said. "Since the eighteenth century now, we have not ceased to repeat them, and you know where they have led." But I immediately received the following reply: "The Quran had enunciated them way before your philosophers, and if the Christian and industrialized West lost their meaning, Islam will know how to preserve their value and their efficacy."

When Iranians speak of Islamic government; when, under the threat of bullets, they transform it into a slogan of the streets; when they reject in its name, perhaps at the risk of a bloodbath, deals arranged by parties and politicians, they have other things on their minds than these formulas from everywhere and nowhere. They also have other things in their hearts. I believe that they are thinking about a reality that is very near to them, since they themselves are its active agents.

It is first and foremost about a movement that aims to give a permanent role in political life to the traditional structures of Islamic society. An Islamic government is what will allow the continuing activity of the thousands of political centers that have been spawned in mosques and religious communities in order to resist the shah's regime. I was given an example. Ten years ago, an earthquake hit Ferdows. The entire city had to be reconstructed, but since the plan that had been selected was not to the satisfaction of most of the peasants and the small artisans, they seceded. Under the guidance of a religious leader, they went on to found their city a little further away. They had collected funds in the entire region. They had collectively chosen places to settle, arranged a water supply, and organized cooperatives. They had called their city Islamiyeh. The earthquake had been an opportunity to use religious structures not only as centers of resistance, but also as sources for political creation. This is what one dreams about [*songe*] when one speaks of Islamic government.

The Invisible Present

But one dreams [*songe*] also of another movement, which is the inverse and the converse of the first. This is one that would allow the introduction of a spiritual dimension into political life, in order that it would not be, as always, the obstacle to spirituality, but rather its receptacle, its opportunity, and its ferment. This is where we encounter a shadow that haunts all political and religious life in Iran today: that of Ali Shariati, whose death two years ago gave him the position, so privileged in Shi'ism, of the invisible Present, of the ever-present Absent.

During his studies in Europe, Shariati, who came from a religious milieu, had been in contact with leaders of the Algerian Revolution, with various left-wing Christian movements, with an entire current of non-Marxist socialism. (He had attended Gurvitch's classes.)[55] He knew the work of Fanon and Massignon.[56] He came back to Mashhad, where he taught that the true meaning of Shi'ism should not be sought in a religion that had been institutionalized since the seventeenth century, but in the sermons of social justice and equality that had already been preached by the first imam. His "luck" was that persecution forced him to go to Tehran and to have to teach outside of the university, in a room prepared for him under the protection of a mosque. There, he addressed a public that was his, and that could soon be counted in the thousands: students, mullahs, intellectuals, modest people from the neighborhood of the bazaar, and people passing through from the provinces. Shariati died like a martyr, hunted and with his books banned. He gave himself up when his father was arrested instead of him. After a year in prison, shortly after having gone into exile, he died in a manner that very few accept as having stemmed from natural causes. The other day, at the big protest in Tehran, Shariati's name was the only one that was called out, besides that of Khomeini.

The Inventors of the State

I do not feel comfortable speaking of Islamic government as an "idea" or even as an "ideal." Rather, it impressed me as a form of "political will." It impressed me in its effort to politicize structures that are inseparably social and religious in response to current problems. It also impressed me in its attempt to open a spiritual dimension in politics.

In the short term, this political will raises two questions:

1. Is it sufficiently intense now, and is its determination clear enough to prevent an "Amini solution,"[57] which has in its favor (or against it, if one prefers) the fact that it is acceptable to the shah, that it is recommended by the foreign powers, that it aims at a Western-style parliamentary regime, and that it would undoubtedly privilege the Islamic religion?

2. Is this political will rooted deeply enough to become a permanent factor in the political life of Iran, or will it dissipate like a cloud when the sky of political reality will have finally cleared, and when we will be able to talk about programs, parties, a constitution, plans, and so forth?

Politicians might say that the answers to these two questions determine much of their tactics today.

With respect to this "political will," however, there are also two questions that concern me even more deeply.

One bears on Iran and its peculiar destiny. At the dawn of history, Persia invented the state and conferred its models on Islam. Its administrators staffed the caliphate. But from this same Islam, it derived a religion that gave to its people infinite resources to resist state power. In this will for an "Islamic government," should one see a reconciliation, a contradiction, or the threshold of something new?

The other question concerns this little corner of the earth whose land, both above and below the surface, has strategic importance at a global level. For the people who inhabit this land, what is the point of searching, even at the cost of their own lives, for this thing whose possibility we have forgotten since the Renaissance and the great crisis of Christianity, a *political spirituality*. I can already hear the French laughing, but I know that they are wrong.[58]

An Iranian Woman Writes

by "Atoussa H."

First published as a letter in *Le Nouvel Observateur*, November 6, 1978.[59]

Living in Paris, I am profoundly upset by the untroubled attitude of French leftists toward the possibility of an "Islamic government" that might replace the bloody tyranny of the shah. Michel Foucault, for example, seems moved by the "Muslim spirituality" that would advantageously replace, according to him, the ferocious capitalist dictatorship that is tottering today. After twenty-five years of silence and oppression, do the Iranian people have no other choice than that between the SAVAK and religious fanaticism? In order to have an idea of what the "spirituality" of the Quran, applied to the letter under Ayatollah Khomeini's type of moral order, would mean, it is not a bad idea to reread the texts. [. . .][60] Sura 2: "Your wives are for you a field; come then to your field as you wish."[61] Clearly, the man is the lord, the wife the slave; she can be used at his whim; she can say nothing. She must wear the veil, born from the Prophet's jealousy toward Aisha![62] We are not dealing here with a spiritual parable, but rather with a choice concerning the type of society we want. Today, unveiled women are often insulted, and young Muslim men do not themselves hide the fact that, in the regime that they wish for, women should behave or else be punished. It is also written that minorities have the right to freedom, on the condition that they do not injure the majority. At what point do the minorities begin to "injure the majority"? [. . .]

Spirituality? A return to deeply rooted wellsprings? Saudi Arabia drinks from the wellspring of Islam. Hands and heads fall, for thieves and lovers. [. . .] It seems that for the Western Left, which lacks humanism, Islam is desirable . . .[63] for other people. Many Iranians are, like me, distressed and desperate about the thought of an "Islamic" government. We know what it is. Everywhere outside Iran, Islam serves as a cover for feudal or pseudo-revolutionary oppression. Often also, as in Tunisia, in Pakistan, in Indonesia, and at home, Islam—alas!—is the only means of expression for a muzzled people. The Western liberal Left needs to know that Islamic law can become a dead weight on societies hungering for change. The Left should not let itself be seduced by a cure that is perhaps worse than the disease.

Foucault's Response to Atoussa H.

First published as a letter in *Le Nouvel Observateur*, November 13, 1978.

Mme. Atoussa H. did not read the article she criticizes. This is her right. But she should not have credited me with the idea that "Muslim spirituality would advantageously replace dictatorship." Since people protested and were killed in Iran while shouting "Islamic government," one had an elementary obligation to ask oneself what content was given to the expression and what forces drove it. In addition, I pointed out several elements that did not seem to me to be very reassuring. If there had been in Mme. H.'s letter only a misreading, I would not have responded to it. But it contains two intolerable things: (1) It merges together all the aspects, all the forms, and all the potentialities of Islam within a single expression of contempt, for the sake of rejecting them in their entirety under the thousand-year-old reproach of "fanaticism." (2) It suspects all Westerners of being interested in Islam only due to scorn for Muslims. What could we say about a Westerner who would scorn Islam? The problem of Islam as a political force is an essential one for our time and the coming years. In order to approach it with a minimum of intelligence, the first condition is not to begin by bringing in hatred.

A Revolt with Bare Hands

First published in *Corriere della sera*, November 5, 1978.

Tehran—The kings of the last century were after all quite accommodating. One could see them in the early morning fleeing their palaces in big black sedans after having abdicated to a worried and courteous minister. Were the people in power more timorous than today, less attached to power, more sensitive to hate, or perhaps simply not as well armed? The fact remains that governments fell easily when the people went into the streets.

In the twentieth century, in order to overthrow a regime, more than "emotions" are needed. Arms, a military command, organization, preparation, and so forth are necessary. What is happening in Iran is enough to worry today's observers. In it they recognize not China, not Cuba, and not Vietnam,[64] but rather a tidal wave without a military leadership, without a vanguard, without a party. Nor can they find in it the movements of 1968.[65] This is because the men and women who protest with banners and flowers in Iran have an immediate political goal: They blame the shah and his regime, and in recent days they are indeed in the process of overthrowing them.

When I left Tehran a month ago, the movement was thought to be irreversible, but it was still possible to think that it would grow more slowly. Sudden obstacles could have emerged. There could have been a bloodbath if the movement became more intense; efforts to break it up if it spread; or a slowing down, if it showed that it was incapable of developing a program. None of this has happened, and things have developed very quickly.

Look at the first paradox and the first cause of its intensification. For ten years, the population has opposed a regime that is one of the best armed in the world, with a police force that is among the most powerful on earth. They have done so with bare hands, without resorting to armed struggle, with a determination and a courage that are in the process of immobilizing the army, which, little by little, freezes and hesitates to fire on them. Two months ago, the army killed three to four thousand in Djaleh Square. Yesterday, two hundred thousand people marched in front of soldiers, who did not react. The government is reduced to sending in provocateurs, to no avail. As the final crisis looms, recourse to violent repression seems less and less possible. The uprising of a whole society has choked off the possibility of civil war.

The second paradox is that the revolt spread without splits or internal conflicts. The reopening of the universities could have put into the forefront the students, who are more westernized and more Marxist than the mullahs from the countryside. The liberation of over a thousand political prisoners could have created a conflict between old and new oppositionists. Finally and most important, the strike by the oil workers could have, on the one hand, worried the bourgeoisie of the bazaar and, on the other hand, started a cycle of strictly job-oriented demands. The modern industrialized sector could have separated itself from the "traditional" sector (by immediately accepting pay raises—the government was counting on this). But none of this happened. What's more, the striking workers gave a tremendous economic weapon to the movement. The shutdown of the refineries dried up the government's sources of revenue and gave an international dimension to the Iranian crisis. For Iran's trading partners, the shah became an obstacle to their oil supply. This is a fitting response to those who had in an earlier period overthrown Mossadeq and reestablished the monarchy, the better to control the oil.

The third paradox is that the absence of long-term objectives is not an indication of weakness. On the contrary, because there is no plan for a government and because the slogans are simple, there can be a clear, obstinate, almost unanimous popular will.

Iran is currently experiencing a generalized political strike, which is really a strike *in relation to* politics. This has two aspects. There is a refusal to sustain in any manner the current system, to allow its apparatus, its administration, or its economy to function. But there is also a refusal to step aside in favor of a political battle over a future constitution, over social issues, over foreign policy, or over the replacement of officials. To be sure, these issues are discussed, but in such a way that these questions cannot give rise to political manipulation by anyone. All of these spines, the Iranian people, transform themselves into a hedgehog.[66] The Iranian people's political will is to prevent politics from gaining a foothold.

It is a law of history that the simpler the people's will, the more complex the job of the politicians. This is undoubtedly because politics is not what it pretends to be, the expression of a collective will. Politics breathes well only where this will is multiple, hesitant, confused, and obscure even to itself.

For the moment, two solutions have been offered to give a political form to a whole people's desire for a change of regime. There is the proposal of Ali Amini, the shah's former prime minister, a man of compromise. Amini's proposal assumes that it is only a matter of rejecting, almost fondly, the shah and his method of governance. If the sovereign disappears, if the regime is liberalized, the political maneuvering would be able to start again. Karim Sanjabi, the leader of the National Front and a former member of the Mossadeq government, shows greater foresight by proposing that the rejection of the dynasty take the form of a referendum. This would be a way of pushing the shah aside even before the vote took place, since the very process of organizing it would call into question the power he inherited thirty-five years ago. Even before the official demise of the monarchy, a referendum campaign would create the opportunity for a full renewal of political life, including the political parties. The day after such a referendum, whose outcome would be certain, Iran would find itself without a ruler, and perhaps without a constitution, but with a political scene already solidly in place. Everything suggests that the National Front will give a green light to Amini's proposal only on condition that latter commit himself to organizing a referendum on the fate of the dynasty.

Here there is a problem, however. Ayatollah Khomeini and the clerics who follow him want to force the shah's departure solely through the strength of the people's movement that they have organized, unconnected to the political parties. The clerics have forged, or in any case sustained, a collective will that has been strong enough to hold at bay even the most police-ridden monarchy in the world. They are certainly not very anxious to have a referendum that would transform this collective will into a political coalition. But it is certainly very difficult to reject all forms of electoral consultation in the name of the people's will. This is why Khomeini has just this very morning proposed a different type of referendum. It would be held after the shah is forced out solely by the pressure of the ongoing movement, and it would center on the establishment of an "Islamic government." The political parties would then find themselves in a very embarrassing position. These parties would either have to reject one of the essential themes of the people's movement. (The politicians would then be opposed to the religious leaders and would certainly not win.) Or they would have to bind their own hands in advance by accepting a form of government under which the political parties would have precious little room for maneuver. At the same time, the ayatollah brandished two threats: that of civil war if the shah would not leave and that of expelling from the movement any person or party that would accept even temporarily the preservation of the dynasty, even if deprived of power. It is a way of reviving openly the slogan of a "strike against politics."[67]

The question today is no longer whether or not Muhammad Reza will leave. Except in the unlikely case of a complete turnabout in the political situation, he will leave. Instead, it is a question of knowing what form this naked and massive will would take, this will that for a long time has said no to its ruler and which has finally disarmed him. It is a question of knowing when and how the will of all will give way to politics. It is a question of knowing if this will wants to do so and if it must do so. It is the practical problem of all revolutions and the theoretical problem of all political philosophies. Let us admit that we Westerners would be in a poor position to give advice to the Iranians on this matter.

The Challenge to the Opposition

First published in *Corriere della sera*, November 7, 1978.[68]

Tehran—Two events set the stage for what happened this weekend in Tehran:

1. The entire opposition has just regrouped behind Ayatollah Khomeini. A way out supported by the Americans called for the shah's semiretirement and a progressive liberalization, but this presupposed that the main opposition parties would remain neutral. During the day on Friday, Karim Sanjabi,

the leader of the National Front, had finally accepted the first point of the ayatollah's declaration, to the effect that the shah's monarchy is illegitimate and illegal. His abdication and departure had thus become a prerequisite for the reconstitution of political life. By Friday evening, the monarch lacked even indirect support anywhere among the opposition, leaving him without any room to maneuver. For its part, the opposition was totally ready and organized.

2. The day before, the official Soviet press had termed the demand for an Islamic government in Iran "dangerous." It was, on the one hand, a way of signaling to the Americans that the USSR did not object to a solution, even a "vigorous one," that would block the way for an opposition movement under Khomeini. It was also, on the other hand, a way of signaling to the shah that in case of a long and violent struggle, the opposition would find no support in the USSR, or in the arms-supplying people's democracies,[69] or in those Middle Eastern governments sponsored by the Russians. Therefore, on the international side, it was the shah who on Friday evening was completely ready and armed, while the opposition was completely isolated.

The shah had only one card left to play. It consisted of getting these international facts to play on the domestic stage.

The opportunity was given by a student riot. Whether it was provoked and by whom will be a topic of discussion for a long time to come. Was it provoked by gunfire from soldiers on Saturday, or by their retreat on Sunday? The word "provocation" always bothers me, because there is no action that is unprovoked.[70] The problem is to know what makes someone susceptible to provocation. Why did the students switch this weekend to a type of action different from that of previous months, one that was probably not desired by even the most radical leaders of the opposition? Maybe it was because of the rivalry between the political and the religious groups. There was on everybody's mind a sort of mutual challenge between revolutionary radicalism and Islamic radicalism, neither of which wanted to seem more conciliatory and less courageous than the other. For this reason and because of a situation that had greatly evolved, the student milieu revealed itself as much more "explosive" than the rest of the population, alongside whom these same students had demonstrated a few weeks ago.

Now the army has occupied Tehran, and top military officers are running the country. Is this the seizure of power by the military that some had predicted? For the moment, it seems not.

Indeed, the generals, now government ministers, did not impose themselves on the shah. They are the king's men, designated by him long ago to occupy the highest positions. On the other hand, the shah declared this very morning that the new government was in place only for a short time, and that if order were reestablished, liberalization would recommence immediately. I do not think that a lot of Iranians believe him, but it is a way of telling the opposition, "You declared that I was illegal, and you wanted to liberalize *after me*. You will not be able to do it *without me*, not only because I have the power to stay, but also because I have political legitimacy." It is also a way of telling the Americans and their man, Ali Amini: "You wanted me to disappear for the benefit of my big clown of a son, but as you can see, I am more indispensable than ever to the liberalization of the regime."

In short, the army intervened today neither to carry out a large-scale repression of the opposition, nor to eliminate for its own benefit both the king and his adversaries. The shah caused the army to move in order to divide the opposition and to guarantee himself a strong hand at a time when he would have to negotiate with the moderate opposition. One can imagine—but it is on my part pure speculation—that the shah pulled off this trick with the help of the Americans, who train on site a large part of his army. However, he may have done so in order to resist Carter and those who saw the need for him to go.[71]

In order for the shah's calculations to prove correct, however, the country would have to remain as quiet as Tehran is this morning. The army, or at least the most reliable part of the army, is strong enough to hold the big cities. But can it maintain a hold over the country—I mean not only the whole territory but also the whole population? Can it control the workers, the civil servants, and the bazaar merchants, who for months and months have been on strike and have paralyzed the various sectors of society? For it is here that the shah finds himself up against the religious leaders, the mullahs, and the irreducible ayatollah. They could continue to organize the resistance, which could take many forms other than riots, or could move to a completely different level of effectiveness. The shah has responded to the mass political strike of last week, which aimed to topple him, by staging a noisy return. He reappeared as a man of law and order. He can impose order on the street, but definitely not on society. Were he to attempt the latter, the army might crumble in his hands. One fine morning, an officer could consider the idea of making a pact with this religious movement, which is certainly not ready to give in to the shah, even if he takes refuge behind his tanks. The religious movement, which has finally absorbed the entire political opposition, could well break up the apparent unity of the army by forming an alliance with one of its factions. Order has its dangers.

The Revolt in Iran Spreads on Cassette Tapes

First published in *Corriere della sera*, November 19, 1978.[72]

Tehran—In Iran the religious calendar sets the political schedule. On December 2, the Muharram celebrations will begin.[73] The death of Imam Hussein will be celebrated. It is the great ritual of penitence. (Not long ago, one could still see marchers flagellating themselves.) But the feeling of sinfulness that could remind us of Christianity is indissolubly linked to the exaltation of martyrdom for a just cause. It is a time when the crowds are ready to advance toward death in the intoxication of sacrifice. During these days, the Shi'ite people become enamored with extremes.

It is said that order is slowly being reestablished in Iran. In fact, the whole country is holding its breath. An American advisor sounds hopeful: "If we hang on during Muharram, everything can be saved. Otherwise . . ." The State Department is also awaiting the anniversary of the martyred imam.

Between the demonstrations in September during Ramadan and the impending great mourning, what is to be done? At first, there was the mild response under Sharif-Imami.[74] Prisoners were freed, political parties legalized, and censorship abolished. There was an attempt to decrease political tensions in order to prevent them from feeding the religious fervor. Then on November 5 came a harsh response, with the military coming to power. It is now up to the army to occupy the country with enough force to limit the effects of Muharram, but also in a fashion measured enough to avoid an explosion of despair.

It is said that this change of direction was suggested to or imposed on the shah by a small lobby: General Oveisi, manufacturers like Khayami (automobiles) and Reza'i (copper), politicians like Fouroud (former mayor of Tehran) or Massoudi (from the 1953 coup).[75] Perhaps. But if a sudden decision had been made to change the leadership team in order to prepare for Muharram "the hard way," it is due to the situation in the country as a whole. Specifically, it is because of the strikes that have spread from one province to another like a prairie fire. There are strikes in the oil sector, the steel mills, the Minoo factories,[76] public transport, Iran Air, and public administration. Most surprisingly, there were work stoppages in customs houses and tax bureaus, where work is not easily stopped, given the fact that its remuneration is increased tenfold or a hundredfold by smuggling and bribery. In a regime like that of the shah, if corruption itself goes on strike . . .[77]

I wanted to know what this strike movement, its magnitude hidden by censorship, is made of. In Tehran, I met some of the more "privileged" strikers, a crew from Iran Air. They had an elegant apartment, teak furniture, and

American magazines. A thousand kilometers to the south, I met the "hard ones," those from the oil sector. What European has not dreamed about Abadan, the biggest refinery in the world, producing six million barrels a day? It is a surprise to find it to be so huge, yet rather old-fashioned, surrounded by corrugated iron, with British-style management buildings, half-industrial and half-colonial, that one can glimpse above the flares and the chimneys. It is a colonial governor's palace, modified by the austerity of a big Manchester spinning mill. But one can see that it is a powerful institution, respectable and rich, by the tremendous misery it has created on this island of sand between two yellowish rivers. The misery starts around the factory with a sort of subtropical mining village, then very quickly one enters the slums where children swarm between truck chassis and heaps of scrap iron, and finally one arrives at the hovels of dried mud bathed in filth. There, crouching children neither cry nor move. Then everything disappears in the grove of palms that leads to the desert, which is the front and the rear of one of the most valuable properties in the world.

There are amazing similarities between the Iran Air strikers, who meet you in their living rooms, and those of Abadan, whom one must meet in secret after mysterious arrangements have been made. There is this one, if no other. They were on strike for the first time, the former because they had not had the desire, the latter because they had not had the right. Furthermore, all these strikes graft political issues directly onto economic demands. The workers from the refinery received a 25 percent raise last March. After October 23, the beginning of the strike, they obtained, without too many discussions on labor issues, first a 10 percent wage increase, then a 10 percent "factory bonus." ("Wording had to be found to justify this raise," said a management representative.) Then they were given a hundred rials every day for lunch.[78] It seems as though the Abadan strikers could continue indefinitely. At any rate, like the pilots of Iran Air who cannot complain about their salaries, what they want is the abolition of martial law, the liberation of all political prisoners, the dissolution—some say—of the SAVAK, and the punishment of thieves and torturers.

Neither the Iran Air workers nor the oil workers—and this seemed to me a little strange at the time—asked for the departure of the shah or the "end of the regime." Each, however, claims to want it. Caution? Perhaps. The fact is that, first and foremost, they believe that it is up to the entire people to formulate this demand and, when the time comes, to impose it. It suffices for the moment that the old saint in exile in Paris asks for this on their behalf, without faltering. Today, they are all conscious of participating in a political strike, because they are doing so in solidarity with the entire nation. An Iran

Air pilot explained to me that during the flight he is responsible for the *safety* of the passengers. If he does not fly today, it is because he has to watch over the *safety* of the country. In Abadan, the workers say that production has never been totally stopped and that it has been partially started again because domestic needs must be met. The thirty-eight tankers lying offshore in the bay will still have to wait. Are these simple declarations of principle? Probably. Nevertheless, these declarations indicate the mood of these scattered strike movements. They do not constitute a *general* strike, but each one sees itself in *national* terms.

This is why these strikes can so easily support each other. The teachers of Abadan and the oil workers declared complete solidarity with one another. On November 4, the workers of Iran Nippon, of the Iran-Japan Petroleum Company, and of the petrochemical complex united with those from the refinery in a joint meeting. This is also why there has been a continual call for foreigners to leave, whether American technicians, French air hostesses, or Afghan laborers: "We want our country to be nationalized." How to transform these strikes with national ramifications into a general strike? This is the current problem. No single party has the necessary strength to achieve this. (The nationwide strike endorsed by some politicians for November 12 did not fail, as was said, but simply never took place.) On the one hand, the extraordinary strength of the movement leans locally on a few clandestine and diffuse organizations. (They stem from old Islamic or Marxist guerrilla movements, like that of Ettehadieh Communist that I heard about in Abadan.)[79] On the other hand, however, the point of connection is found outside of the country, outside of the political organizations, outside of all possible negotiations. This is in Khomeini, in his inflexible refusal to compromise and in the love that everyone individually feels for him. It was impressive to hear a Boeing pilot say in the name of his workmates: "You have in France the most precious thing that Iran has possessed for the last century. It is up to you to protect it." The tone was commanding. It was even more impressive to hear the strikers of Abadan say: "We are not particularly religious." "Whom do you trust then? A political party?" I asked. "No, no one." "A man?" I asked. "No, no one, except Khomeini, and he alone."

The first task undertaken by the military government was to bring the strikes to a halt, a classic expedient and thus uncertain. The SAVAK, the political police that had been the shame of the regime, has instead become its most embarrassing failure. Its agents, who returned to their previous vocation of brawlers, are sent everywhere to provoke, burn, and use their truncheons. Everything is then attributed to the strikers and the demonstrators, running the risk that such a provocation would only add fuel to the fire and create an authentic explosion, as in Tehran. Even the army has moved into the Abadan refinery, leaving behind wounded people in its wake. It remains behind the factories with its armored vehicles. The soldiers have entered the workers' homes in order to lead them by force to the refinery. But how can they force them to work?

During the two months of the Sharif-Imami government, the news transmitted every day by the once again free press had "kindled" the strikes, one after the other. The military had to reestablish censorship, to which the journalists responded by refusing to publish the newspapers. They knew very well that they were making way for an entire network of information, a network that fifteen years of obscurantism had allowed people to perfect—that of telephones, of cassette tapes, of mosques and sermons, and of law offices and intellectual circles.

I was able to observe the functioning of one of these "grassroots cells" of information. It was near one of the Abadan mosques, with the usual backdrop of great poverty, except for a few carpets. The mullah, his back against a bookshelf filled with religious books and surrounded by a dozen of the faithful, was seated next to an old telephone that was constantly ringing—work stopped in Ahwaz, several deaths in Lahijan, and so forth. At that very moment, when the public relations director of the National Iranian Oil Company was manufacturing for journalists the "international truth" of the strike (economic demands that had been satisfied, absolutely no political demands, general and continued resumption of work), I heard the mullah, in his corner, manufacturing the "Iranian truth" of the same event: there were no economic demands at all and all of them were political.

It is said that De Gaulle was able to resist the Algiers putsch, thanks to the transistor.[80] If the shah is about to fall, it will be due largely to the cassette tape. It is the tool *par excellence* of counterinformation. Last Sunday, I went to the Tehran cemetery, the only place where meetings are tolerated under martial law. People stood behind banners and laurel wreaths, cursing the shah. Then they sat down. One by one, three men, including a religious leader, stood up and started talking with great intensity, almost with violence. But when they were about to leave, at least two hundred soldiers blocked the gates with machine guns, armored vehicles, and two tanks. The speakers were arrested, as well as all those who had tape recorders.

But one can find, outside the doors of most provincial mosques, tapes of the most renowned orators at a very low price. One encounters children walking down the most crowded streets with tape recorders in their hands. They play these recorded voices from Qom, Mashhad, and Isfahan so loudly that they drown out the sound of cars; passersby do not need to stop to be able to hear them. From town to town, the strikes start, die out, and start again, like flickering fires on the eve of the nights of Muharram.

The Mythical Leader of the Iranian Revolt

First published in *Corriere della sera*, November 26, 1978.[81]

Tehran—Iran's year-long period of unrest is coming to a head. On the watch-face of politics, the hand has hardly moved. The semi-liberal September government was replaced in November by a half-military one. In fact, the whole country is engulfed by revolt: the cities, the countryside, the religious centers, the oil regions, the bazaars, the universities, the civil servants, and the intellectuals. The privileged rats are jumping ship. An entire century in Iran—one of economic development, foreign domination, modernization, and the dynasty, as well as its daily life and its moral system—is being put into question. It is being totally rejected.

I cannot write the history of the future, and I am also rather clumsy at foreseeing the past. However, I would like to try to grasp *what is happening right now*, because these days nothing is finished, and the dice are still being rolled. It is perhaps this that is the work of a journalist, but it is true that I am nothing but a neophyte.

Iran was never colonized. In the nineteenth century, the British and the Russians divided it into zones of influence, according to a precolonial model. Then came oil, two World Wars, the Middle East conflict, and the great confrontations in Asia. At one stroke, Iran moved to a neocolonial position within the orbit of the United States. In a long period of dependency without direct colonization, the country's social structures were not radically destroyed. These social structures were not completely overturned, even by the surge of oil revenue, which certainly enriched the privileged, favored speculation, and permitted an over-provisioning of the army. The changes did not create new social forces, however. The bourgeoisie of the bazaars was weakened, and the village communities were shaken by the agrarian reform. However, both of them survived enough to suffer from dependency and the changes that it brought, but also enough to resist the regime that was responsible for these changes as well.

This same situation had the opposite effect on the political movements. In the half-light of dependency, they too subsisted, but could not sustain themselves as real forces. This was due not only to repression, but also to their own choices. The Communist Party was tied to the USSR, was compromised by the occupation of Azerbaijan under Stalin, and was ambiguous in its support of the "bourgeois nationalism" of Mossadeq.[82] With respect to the National Front, heir of this same Mossadeq, it has been waiting for fifteen years, without making a move, for the moment of a liberalization that it did not believe to be possible without the permission of the Americans.[83] During this time, some impatient cadres from the Communist Party were becoming technocrats for the regime. They were dreaming of an authoritarian government that would develop a nationalist politics. In short, the political parties had been victims of the "dependent dictatorship" that was the shah's regime. In the name of realism, some played the card of independence, others that of freedom.

Because of, on the one hand, the absence of a colonizer-occupier and, on the other, the presence of a national army and a sizable police force, the political-military organizations, which elsewhere organized the struggle for decolonization and which, when the time came, found themselves in a position to negotiate independence and impose the departure of the colonial power, could not emerge. In Iran, the rejection of the regime is a massive social phenomenon. This does not mean that the rejection is confused, emotional, or barely self-conscious. On the contrary, it spreads in an oddly effective manner, from the strikes to the demonstrations, from the bazaars to the universities, from the leaflets to the sermons, through shopkeepers, workers, clerics, teachers, and students. For the moment, however, no party, no man, and no political ideology can boast that it represents this movement. Nor can anyone claim to be at its head. This movement has no counterpart and no expression in the political order.

The paradox, however, is that it constitutes a perfectly unified collective will. It is surprising to see this immense country, with a population distributed around two large desert plateaus, a country able to afford the latest technical innovations alongside forms of life unchanged for the last thousand years, a country that is languishing under censorship and the absence of public freedoms, and yet demonstrating an extraordinary unity in spite of all this. It is the same protest, it is the same will, that is expressed by a doctor from Tehran and a provincial mullah, by an oil worker, by a postal employee, and by a female student wearing the chador. This will includes something rather disconcerting. It is always based on the same thing, a sole and very precise thing, the departure of the shah. But for the Iranian people, this unique thing means *everything*. This political will yearns for the end of dependency, the disappearance of the police, the redistribution of oil revenue, an attack on corruption, the reactivation of Islam, another way of life, and new relations with the West, with the Arab countries, with Asia, and so forth. Somewhat like the European students in the 1960s, the Iranians want it all, but this "all" is not a "liberation of desires." This political will is one of breaking away from all that marks their country and their daily lives with the presence of global hegemonies. Iranians also view the political parties—liberal or socialist, with either a pro-American tendency or a Marxist inspiration—or, it is better to say, the political scene itself, as still and always the agents of these hegemonies.

Hence, the role of this almost mythical figure, Khomeini. Today, no head of state, no political leader, even one supported by the whole media of his country, can boast of being the object of such a personal and intense attachment. These ties are probably the result of three things. Khomeini *is not there.* For the last fifteen years, he has been living in exile and does not want to return until the shah has left. Khomeini *says nothing,* nothing other than no—to the shah, to the regime, to dependency. Finally, Khomeini *is not a politician.* There will not be a Khomeini party; there will not be a Khomeini government. Khomeini is the focal point of a collective will. What is this unwavering intransigence seeking? Is it the end of a form of dependency where, behind the Americans, an international consensus and a certain "state of the world" can be recognized? Is it the end of a dependency of which the dictatorship is the direct instrument, but for which the political maneuvers could well be the indirect means? It is not only a spontaneous uprising that lacks political organization, but also movement that wants to disengage itself from both external domination and internal politics.

After I left Iran, the question that I was constantly asked was, of course: "Is this revolution?" (This is the price at which, in France, an entire sector of public opinion becomes interested in that which is "not about us.") I did not answer, but I wanted to say that it is not a revolution, not in the literal sense of the term, not a way of standing up and straightening things out. It is the insurrection of men with bare hands who want to lift the fearful weight, the weight of the entire world order that bears down on each of us, but more specifically on them, these oil workers and peasants at the frontiers of empires. It is perhaps the first great insurrection against global systems, the form of revolt that is the most modern and the most insane.

One can understand the difficulties facing the politicians. They outline solutions, which are easier to find than people say. They range from a pure and simple military regime to a constitutional transformation that would lead from a regency to a republic. All of them are based on the elimination of the shah. What is it that the people want? Do they really want nothing more? Everybody is quite aware that they want something completely different. This is why the politicians hesitate to offer them simply that, which is why the situation is at an impasse. Indeed, what place can be given, within the calculations of politics, to such a movement, to a movement that does not let itself be divided among political choices, a movement through which blows the breath of a religion that speaks less of the hereafter than of the transfiguration of this world?

Islam Resurgent?

by Maxime Rodinson

First published on the front page of *Le Monde*, December 6–8, 1978.

Are we witnessing a revival of Islamic fundamentalism? This is an interpretation suggested to many people by a host of recent events and developments: the fate of Mr. Bhutto, Pakistan's former prime minister;[84] the applications of Quranic laws, with certain spectacular excesses, in Libya and Saudi Arabia; the leading role played by the Shi'ite ayatollahs in Iran's vast opposition movement; the vigor of the anti-Kemalist reaction in Turkey; anti-Coptic troubles in Egypt, the Maschino Affair in Algeria, . . .[85] and so on.

A revival of fundamentalism? "It has never lost its sway," sighs one nominal Muslim in exile from the Muslim world, a woman who could not tolerate the dead weight of social constraint imposing religious observance and, above all, conformity with traditional customs, in her own country. There are many others in her position. Does this not seem to confirm the strong reputation for fanaticism which has clung to Islam since the nineteenth century, in European eyes? In the seventeenth and eighteenth centuries Islam was well known for its tolerance. Before that, if Islam as an ideological and political enemy was detested, the piety of its followers was, to a degree, admired. The priests made good use of this to shame the Christians for their halfheartedness.

Where God Is Not Dead

The facts are there, and they are real enough. But are they part of a trend, whether broken or continuous? Are they linked to the essence of Islam and hence destined to indefinite renewal? Or is this trend perhaps not what it seems? Is it, as the ideologists and apologists of the Third World suggest, just an insidious campaign mounted by "imperialism"—elusive but omnipresent—to bring into disrepute an element in the forefront of the developing world? These are questions that need to be answered. I shall base my argument and my examples on the central domain of Islam: the Arab countries, Turkey, and Iran.

There are many different things at stake. But equally, there are common factors and common trends that link them. What links them for Europeans is the common appeal to religious tradition and religious regulations, even when by European standards they have nothing to do with that tradition. This is why many people have borrowed the label of *intégrisme* from recent Catholic history.[86] The term is relatively appropriate if we are talking about the desire to use religion to solve all social and political problems and, simultaneously, to restore full obedience to dogma and ritual.

Such an appeal is plausible enough in the House of Islam [*Dar al-Islam*] because Muslim societies still have social foundations of a type characterized as "traditional" (albeit too summarily, but this is not the place for a fuller analysis). This term means, among other things, that religious law remains the supreme authority in the eyes of the masses, even if in practice they neglect or by-pass it. Practices which have other origins are legitimized by being linked, in a derivative and artificial way, to religious law. The weight of social constraint, imposing conformity and punishing transgression, has remained considerable.

Its Primordial Character

From the beginning these Muslim societies have differed from traditional Christian societies. Christianity, at the outset a small, isolated sect within a vast and powerful empire, gradually succeeded in becoming a force to be reckoned with in that empire, and then in becoming adopted by it as the state ideology. But it always had to coexist with the state and its juridical, social, and cultural structures, which plainly had other origins.

In contrast, Islam has never ceased to be in some sense *intégriste*. Born in a society where each elementary group and tribe had political functions and formed a micro-state, the community of the faithful, if it wished to survive and grow, had to assume such functions too. God himself, in the Quran, gave that community not a comprehensive code, it is true, but at least certain precepts of social organization.

These precepts were supplemented with multiple traditions of various origins, borrowed from the different nations and peoples whom the Muslims conquered. But they were all legitimized through being linked, directly or indirectly, with the word of God, in accordance with the fundamental principle that the law of Islam was responsible for the whole shaping of the social order. No such copyright, or even underwriting, has ever been attributed to Jesus regarding Roman or Germanic law, the Scottish feud or the Corsican vendetta, or the economic and philosophical thought of Aristotle. But copyright of this kind has been attributed to the Prophet of Allah, thanks to the immense body of *hadith*, or traditions, which became more or less codified in the ninth century A.D.

The passage of time only accentuated this initial divergence. Certainly, whatever the extent of its realm, religion remained for a long time the primary ideological authority and the object of widespread popular belief, as much in the Christian as in the Muslim world. Both suffered serious erosion as far back as the Middle Ages because of the multiplicity of schisms and of associated tendencies to challenge the religious leaders—the men of religion linked to power—sometimes even crossing the boundaries of the prevailing religion. But this evolution, which continued and grew in Christian countries, was only brought to a halt within Islam in the eleventh century by the vigorous Sunni reaction, whose success was favored by the internal evolution of Islamic societies and by changes in their situation vis-à-vis the outside world.

Thus loyalty to the faith remained strong. The calm monopoly of truth left little room for doubt. For a long time in the Sunni world, the few remaining tolerated sects became closed communities, like the other monotheistic religions, with no wish to proselytize and hence tolerable as minorities, as if they were some sort of established foreign caste. The conversion of Iran to Shi'ite Islam in the seventeenth century stabilized the principal heresy, giving it a state base and dominance in its own domain. As in Europe at this time, the principle of *cuius regio, eius religio* maintained the established order.[87]

Thus for a long time Islam experienced none of the challenges to its "ecclesiastical" institutions, its dogma and ritual, which were so marked and so deeply rooted in Europe. The masses were not deeply affected, to the point of abandoning religion, by the "disenchantment of the world" which industrialization produces.[88] The Islamic world has not witnessed the death of God following the death of the angels and demons, and the general disbelief in miracles, including those which are regularly renewed in the common rite. Pietist moralism, attributing misfortune and misrule to the lack of faith and consequent immorality of rulers, has not on the whole yielded either to this general disbelief or to an extension of the ideology of moral freedom affecting every level of society.

On the contrary, belief has always been reinforced by an old obsession: the constant dread of a great shift toward a rival religion, existing at the very heart of Muslim society and at the same time finding vital support outside.

The Christians, assured of an ideological monopoly in their own world (with the exception of the tiny Jewish minority, which had no external support and presented little risk of spreading its spiritual contagion), have seldom had cause to fear that an infidel army from without would join forces with its accomplices within. This fear, present in Islam early in the Middle Ages and reinforced by the Crusades and the Mongol invasion, could only grow in the face of stronger and stronger aggression by Europe's imperial powers in the nineteenth and twentieth centuries. It reached paroxysms that can only be compared either with Catholic paranoia in the nineteenth century in the face of the increasing decline of religion (supposedly inspired by the Jewish-Protestant-Masonic conspiracy, led by Satan) or with the analogous fears and obsessions felt by the communist world.

A Period of Political Occultation

As elsewhere, a universalist faith, a particular national identification of the community of believers (in colonial Algeria, as in Poland or Ireland), a supranational identification of Muslims as Muslims—each of these has reinforced the other in varying degrees of emphasis which have assured the permanence of general loyalty to the ancestral belief.

Industrialization and a degree of modernization have had the effect of pushing limited sections of society toward skepticism, religious liberalism, and freedom of behavior, beneath the theoretical umbrella of an Islam reinterpreted in this light, or of a vague deism, or even atheism. But the conversion of these people to such Westernizing trends has reinforced the attachment to Islam, in its most rigidly traditional form, among the larger masses. The poor, driven to the limit of famine or wretched subsistence, direct their anger and recrimination against the privileges of the rich and powerful—their ties with foreigners, their loose morality, and their scorn of Muslim injunctions, the most obvious signs of which are the consumption of alcohol, familiarity between the sexes, and gambling. For them, as Robespierre put it so well, atheism is aristocratic: and so is that "subatheism" which is (supposedly) betrayed by the slightest ungodliness or departure from orthodox morality. These are not, as once was the case here, old-fashioned priests or pious old maids railing against short skirts and kisses on the cinema screen; but angry crowds who indiscriminately attack shops selling luxury goods, hotels where the rich and the foreigners get their drink and debauchery, and (sometimes) the places of worship of "heretics" or non-Muslims.

If there is an apparent revival of fundamentalist Islam, it is because we are witnessing—provisionally perhaps—the end of an epoch in which the crystallization of such attitudes (a process briefly described above) has been partially hidden from view.

Throughout a whole era, beginning in the middle of the nineteenth century, the elites of the Muslim world have been seduced by new ideologies. First, secular nationalism of the type that developed in Europe after a long evolution and that offered the most suitable answer to the ideological exigencies of the region. Later, to a greater or lesser extent, this nationalism was colored by socialist ideals, and socialism in a universalist form even emerged at certain points.

These Muslim elites succeeded in channeling the feelings and aspirations of the masses into these ideologies, transforming them into support for political mobilization. One must notice, however, that the masses reinterpreted these ideas in their own way. It happened that foreign domination was the work of infidels and that the exploiters were infidels or else one's fellow countrypeople in the pay of infidels. No one in the lowest social strata, where nothing had shaken the faith in Islam, could fail to notice this. Nor could skilled and perceptive leaders fail to add this singularly effective weapon to their arsenal of strictly national and social means of mobilization.

However, the masses, being inundated with propaganda, were little by little conditioned to formulate slogans of the modern sort. Members of the popular classes were, moreover, genuinely influenced by these ideas. In areas of the Arab East where there were religious minorities, the national and social struggle was often waged jointly by Muslims, Christians, and even (until quite recently) Jews. In Turkey, a prestigious national leader, who scarcely concealed his basic lack of belief, could draw a large following and carry out militantly secular measures.

In Iran, certain elements, even outside the elite, could be seduced by a nationalism which celebrated the glories of Iran in the Zoroastrian era and which considered the conversion to Islam a mere cultural and national regression brought about by barbarous Arab conquerors (and Sunni, too!).[89] In the Maghreb, emigrants proletarianized in France were exposed in large numbers to the influence of a social climate that linked militancy with (at the very least) indifference toward religion.

None of these modernizing tendencies has been forgotten. But they have all lost part of that power to arouse enthusiasm which gave them supremacy and relegated religion to the status of an auxiliary, everyday morality, and which at the same time could call into question practices and dogmas at variance with modern ideologies and the ideology of modernization.

Politics According to the Quran

Marxist-inclined nationalism of the Nasserist variety, identifying the basic enemy not as the foreigner per se, nor as the infidel, but as "imperialism," has not managed to achieve any great success. Its alliance with the supposed coalition between the oppressed of the world and the self-styled socialist states has by no means allowed it to get the better of the Israeli challenge. It has been called into disrepute by the policies of the new class in power, scarcely more seductive than those of its predecessors. This nationalism was, in part, the heir to Westernizing Jacobin liberalism. The mobilization which it preached was to remain secular and mulitconfessional. But the struggle against Israel had already made it almost impossible to include Jews in this. The prevailing reactions of the Christians in Lebanon have reinforced the old fears arising from both the Crusades and the historical links with imperialist Europe, to make all Christian Arabs increasingly suspect.[90] The realities of national independence have proved less exhilarating than the slogans that mobilized the masses in the cause of liberation.

Nowhere, moreover, has this type of nationalism resulted in an escape from economic dependence and underdevelopment. The only achievements of the great Arab nation in the field of power politics and national prestige have been the work of the oil potentates—the most fundamentalist and conservative of Muslims—in selling their oil with the haggling of skilled businessmen and technocrats (but whose kaffiyahs, agals, and abayahs enable them to be associated with Bedouin tradition).[91] As for the ideal of the united Arab nation, it has grown ever harder in the face of the evident development of regional nationalisms (Egyptian, Algerian, Moroccan, and so on) to maintain that its realization is hampered only by the "plots" of Israel and "imperialism."

A Muslim Nationalism

In Turkey, as in Iran, it has become difficult to direct the nation's hatred against a Muslim enemy, even if the three main peoples of the Middle East are always ready to denigrate each other. The anti-Arab ideology of part of the Turkish and Iranian nationalist elites does not exert enough leverage—as an irredentist territorial conflict might—to arouse the serious mobilization of populations which are indifferent to the pre-Islamic glory of the celestial Turks of Orkan, or of Cyrus and Khosroe.[92] The perceived enemies are still non-Muslim: the atheist Russians, who oppress the Turkic and Iranian Muslims of Central Asia, and whose hidden hand is everywhere suspected;

Christian Europeans and Americans, who clearly manipulate local leaders, imposing their will through financial and technological supremacy, sapping and corrupting Islam by means of their impious morality, their debauchery and drunkenness. Last but not least, their bad example regarding the equality of the sexes, if not indeed female domination (may my feminist friends forgive me—it is simply that it often looks that way from the outside), gives the indigenous women dangerous ideas.

Thus pure nationalism becomes more and more strongly a Muslim nationalism, a nationalizing Islam. The exceptions are the ethnic minorities that consider themselves oppressed by other Muslims, such as the Kurds, or those Arabs most sensitive to Palestinian irredentism and the Israeli challenge: Syrians, Iraqis, and above all Palestinians; among the latter the significant participation of Christians in the Palestinian movement strengthens the reluctance to give a purely Islamic coloring to the ideology of struggle.

As for socialism, in those states where a regime claiming to be socialist has been established, it has not been slow in making its heavy, oppressive character felt and in demonstrating its deficiencies of all kinds—even if it has also achieved positive results. External models are no more encouraging, as becomes increasingly clear, especially in those countries which have been slow to respond to post-Stalinist demystification. The exceptions are provided by elements of the working class, in places where they are of some importance, and by certain intellectuals or semi-intellectuals who were formerly inspired by the Marxist spirit and who remain under its spell, either through faith, misty vision, ignorance, or hardening of the arteries.

The same disappointments have made themselves felt in Europe. Here, too, the desperate desire to find an outlet for unchanneled fervor has sometimes provoked a return to the old, indigenous, local, national religion. But here Christian belief, for all the mystical or devotional individualism of the quest for salvation, or of organized charity, scarcely offers opportunities of mobilization which is at the same time uplifting and specific. On the one hand are parties and movements which are conservative or boringly gradualist, and reactionary movements whose program of restoring the City of God is hardly convincing when they revere one whose kingdom was not of this world and who rendered unto Caesar what was Caesar's. On the other hand, progressive or revolutionary movements, largely comprising (and in any case initiated by) unbelievers, are tendencies to which Christians can only subscribe when also inspired by other motives.

In the Islamic countries, by contrast, the appeal of the national religion is for many people accessible, stimulating, credible, and alive. Islam, as I have said, has not suffered either internal erosion or the challenge which has gradually sapped Christianity's power of attraction. It has been kept intact among people whose daily culture it has provided and whose aspirations and humble ethics it has sanctified. Throughout the epoch which has witnessed the prestige of nationalism and socialism, the idea has been propagated that Islam defended and incorporated the same values that they did. But it became more persuasive to fight for such ideals under the banner of Islam than to tie oneself ideologically to foreigners whose motives were suspect—as was the case with Marxist-inclined nationalism as well as with socialism.

Even outside the Muslim world, Islam has acquired the prestige of being, now and in the past, unflagging in the forefront of the resistance to a Christian Europe which was expansionist, proselytizing, and imperialist; or simply of being in the vanguard of the anti-European struggle. But henceforth the enemies who direct the greatest hatred against them are the Europeans and the Americans, and the Europeanized strata of the societies at the periphery of the capitalist world. Thus all these enemies can be identified as either non-Muslims, anti-Muslims, or their fellow travelers. It would appear that in the furthest recesses of the House of Islam there may be an awareness of this worldwide polarization, that Islam proudly receives the title of universal champion of good against evil without ever yielding to anyone the banner of the avant-garde.

Muslims make themselves different images of Islam according to the social strata to which they belong, the sort of education they have received, their political affiliation, and even their individual temperaments. But everywhere the dominant, almost unchanging image is of Islam as guardian, guarantor, surety, and protector of traditional morality. Analogous to the image that Christian fundamentalism makes of Christianity—the image of Christianity that it alone (or almost alone) conceives—this image is almost universal in Muslim society. Christian faith is sometimes a fundamentalist faith in a tradition rigidified at a certain period, sometimes a faith which, while rooted in the message of Jesus, is not afraid of the constant revision of tradition. Publicly professed examples of such revisionism are rare in Islam: the message of the founding father is (for the moment) more difficult to extricate from the dead weight of tradition.

Fondness for the advantages of tradition is partly responsible for the male tribe's religious faith, which cuts across political beliefs and classes. As with Latin Catholicism in the past, for example, religious tradition can be exploited in order to dominate the sex which males unquestioningly consider weak and subordinate, even if the vengeance awaiting them in hearth and home, and in the conjugal bed, often deters them from taking full advantage of it. Without needing opinion polls, rulers and would-be rulers were well aware of these inclinations among their people and took good account of them.

Qaddafi and Others

Some leaders genuinely want to translate into reality the social and political precepts of Islam, having learned at school that such precepts existed and were alone capable of building a harmonious society. Such were the leaders who established the Saudi state and such, today, is Libya's Qaddafi.

When put to the test by taking office, most of these leaders are (or become) convinced—depending how far their ideological intoxication has conditioned them to reject the lessons of reality—that they cannot achieve very much in this spirit. They end up discovering how right Nasser was when he declared that he failed to see how anyone could govern a state solely with the laws of the Quran. From that moment they realize that they are disappointing those who have come to expect great things from the application of Quranic law. In order to maintain a broad consensus among their subjects, they must concentrate essentially on symbolic measures—on what I would call Muslim "gesticulation"—and on the visceral faith in a Muslim identity whose various springs and sources I have in part outlined.

In sum, the problem is not fundamentally different from that faced, for example, by the Soviet leaders. Stalin and Khrushchev, each in his own way, were highly expert in Marxist "gesticulation." But the depth and breadth of belief in the virtues of Marxism were much less great; the Gulag policies have largely discredited it; the symbolism of Marxism is much less rich; the rationalism of its doctrine is far less metaphysically satisfying; and other beliefs, however clandestine and persecuted, have always been available to the Soviet peoples.

Almost alone, Qaddafi ingenuously pursues his project for a Muslim state, by definition free and egalitarian and (also in the name of Islam) opposed to American plutocracy. Persistently he theorizes and refines, straining to specify the right methods in his Green Books and his Libyan policies. Besides the sneers of professional cynics and the cold comfort of those of his countrypeople who have the means to enjoy their pleasures abroad, he earns the frowns of clerics who are shocked by his novel interpretations, his rejection of codified tradition, and his criticism of bigots and hypocrites.

Much more numerous among Muslim leaders are and were those who, whatever the depth of their personal conviction, have known all along that they could carry out only a few of Islam's ideals. They knew that they must govern essentially with nonreligious prescriptions and could hope for, at most, a superficial and limited moral and religious transformation.

They have resigned themselves to achieving little and—for all the world like cynical manipulators only after their own power—have reaped their reward with a more or less clear conscience. They have all realized that they must at least hold Islam and its functionaries in some respect. Or they can go further and get good results through Islamic "gesticulation." The building of a mosque can put a gloss on certain unsavory aspects of reality.

Besides the leaders, there are the would-be leaders and, in the sole case of Turkey—where there is at least a recurring, if not peaceful, alternation of power—a third category: those who govern from time to time and, when out of office, can at least stay in business without having to go underground.

Political parties and groups all display a minimum of respect for Islam. Those who are most suspected of being against religion—previously the communists—have shown the most zeal in displaying their respect for performing painful feats of reconciliation (but not, after all, more painful than for the French Communist Party in identifying itself with Joan of Arc). However, in the midst of this chorus of reverence, certain groups are prominent by their insistence on the defense of Islam.

Authentically Religious Groupings

The Turkish Democratic Party is one. Its leaders seem on average neither more nor less devout than their Republican counterparts, but they draw on the religious faith of the peasant masses in order to combat the attenuated Kemalism of the Republican Party and the Westernizing modernism which has spread among the military, the technocrats, and elsewhere.

Apart from this type of demagoguery, there exist groups which are authentically religious in the sense that their leaders, whether sincerely or not, declare that they want to construct a Muslim state. One could make fine distinctions about the sincerity of such leaders' faith, the image they project of this Muslim state in relation to their social origins, to their culture and temperament, and to the degree of radicalism in their practical politics—often going to the extreme of terrorism. Here, moreover, these sects can benefit not only from international example, but from a specifically Islamic tradition, that of the medieval sect of Hashishiyin—those fedayeen who bequeathed to European languages the word "assassin." Some in all sincerity seek power in order to apply Islam, while others choose Islam as an instrument with which to gain power. But in politics such distinctions are only of occasional importance. The results are often the same.

One of these groups is the vast clandestine movement of the Muslim Brotherhood. The extent of its membership is unknown, but the fluctuating numbers of its sympathizers are certainly considerable. It is hard to ascertain the different trends which run through the ranks of this organization. But the dominant trend is certainly a type of archaic fascism. By this I mean a wish to establish an authoritarian and totalitarian state whose political police would brutally enforce the moral and social order. It would at the same time impose conformity to religious tradition as interpreted in the most conservative light. Some adherents consider this artificial renewal of faith to be the first priority, while others see it as a psychological aid, sweetening the pill of reactionary social reform.

There also exist similar movements, for example in Turkey, to the right of the Democratic Party. But it is in Iran that there is something more akin to a religious party. Its strength has been all too apparent in recent months.

Between Archaism and Modernity

The phenomenon of the political influence of the Iranian *ulama* (the men of religion), who constitute a sort of religious party, has astonished everyone. The apologists, whether Muslim or pro-Muslim, and those who come fresh to the problem in an idealistic frame of mind[93]—as is usual with questions of religion (of even of ideology, to judge from the French "new philosophers")—are quick to attribute this, at least in part, to the nature of Shi'ite doctrine. But it is more complex than this. It is true that the foundations of Shi'ite doctrine, in the first centuries of Islam, were elaborated among opposition groups stubborn in challenging the legitimacy of those in power. The ideology preserved this imprint. But doctrines are always susceptible to interpretation. There is never a shortage of theologians and theoreticians capable of reversing doctrine at the dictates of changing circumstances. (With regard to Islam, see Cahen 1977.)

As Nikki Keddie has admirably demonstrated, it was the evolution of the respective strengths of the state and the leading ulama that shaped the growing power of the latter in Iran and, in contrast, the decline of their power (a power which could also be doctrinally founded) within Sunni Islam. (See especially Keddie 1962; Keddie 1966; and Keddie 1969.) The Safavid dynasty (1500–1722), which converted Iran to Shi'ite Islam, cooperated with Shi'ite ulama, which it had to import from Arab countries. Their interdependence was given a theoretical base. But, roughly speaking, the state gradually lost its power later on, while the advantages conceded to the ulama were institutionalized, legitimized, and strengthened. The struggles of the eighteenth century enhanced the flexibility of doctrine and the independence of judgment of each *'alim* (the singular of *ulama*), based on foundations which were medieval. Their financial autonomy and security, assured by the Safavids, could not be shaken by weak governments that were afraid of opposition. Their leaders knew how to increase their power by choosing to stay outside the frontiers of the kingdom, near holy sanctuaries.

The apparently paradoxical alliance between the men of religion and the secular reformers or revolutionaries was formed in the nineteenth century, in opposition to the Qajar dynasty's concessions to the West, and cemented during the "constitutional revolution" of 1905–1911. The two parties were already afraid of modernization from above, which in their eyes could only augment the authoritarian power of a dynasty supported by foreign powers. The religious leaders above all dreaded the consequences for their autonomous power of the secularizing implications of modernization. The secular modernizers within the opposition feared the strengthening of absolute power. Both groups directed their struggle against domination by powers which were both foreign and infidel. The alliance won the vote for the Constitution of 1906, a compromise between the two tendencies, which greatly limited the power of the shah. The religious leaders, shocked by the institution of civil tribunals alongside religious tribunals, and by the whole idea of interconfessional equality, as well as other measures, were for the moment appeased by the insertion of an article stipulating that no law could contradict sacred law—which was to be determined by a committee of mujtahids (the most learned ulama). (See the penetrating analysis of the constitution in Ann Lambton 1965.)

The alliance was broken off in the second phase of the revolution, after most of the ulama had discovered its underlying dangers. But some of them continued to participate in the revolutionary coalition.

The strengthening of authoritarian power under the two Pahlavi monarchs, since 1925, has resulted in the renewal of the alliance. The modernizing democratic nationalists, shocked by the foreign policy of the shah, by the degree of repression and the blatant profiteering, have rediscovered, as they did under the last of the Qajars, the advantages of alliance with the ulama. The latter, sharing the general dislike of these same policies, and adding to it their fear of modernization and Westernization, are able to tap this dissatisfaction, enjoying as they do the veneration of the crowds and the impregnability of the pulpit—rather as the Polish clergy do.

An Islamic Government?

The events of 1978 are the result of the escalation set in motion by the Ayatollah (literally, "sign"—i.e., proof—"of God," the honorary title of the most important mujtahids) Khomeini as early as June 1963, when he publicly compared the shah to Yazid, the Umayyad caliph who ordered the murder of Hussein, grandson of the Prophet. His imprisonment, with some thirty other ulama, caused large-scale demonstrations, from which, this time, the secular nationalists dissociated themselves. The subsequent repression resulted in at least a hundred deaths.

As they had done in the past, the ulama could give the word for the establishment of an Islamic state (and it could gain acceptability by virtue of what we have said above). In the restoration of the 1906 Constitution they saw, above all, in addition to the limitation of the shah's authoritarianism, that one crucial article, never applied in the past, which could put legislation under their control.

So there came into being a provisional alliance against one form of despotism which usually numbered among its members people dreaming of another form of despotism. Similarly in Egypt, between 1952 and 1954, the Muslim Brothers joined the communists and the liberals, led by Naguib, in calling for the return to a parliamentary system. In both cases a hated brand of authoritarianism was to be overthrown in order to set up a regime in which the people could be mobilized in the cause of another brand of authoritarianism. I am not saying that the Iranian ulama are all authoritarian. Their political views are probably diverse and in many cases characterized by a notable fluidity and naïveté.

Since they have difficulty in applying and defining programs setting out concrete measures, political leaders, as I have said, have recourse to symbols—whether they proclaim them, demand them, or actually put them into effect. The vexing thing for their image in the West is that these symbols are archaic. This is the other side of the coin, the price to be paid for the advantage gained by including in a political program a few precepts taken from the Quran regarding social organization, and many others to be found in the Tradition.

In the Christian world one can call for a minimum (revisionist) fundamentalism by invoking the holy texts only so as to prohibit divorce and contraception. Some Catholic fundamentalists, unwilling to reinterpret their traditions to this extent, want the Latin liturgy and the cassock to be restored. This certainly gives grounds for complaint! But, by contrast, the minimum

Muslim fundamentalism, according to the Quran, requires the cutting off of a thief's hand and the halving of a woman's inheritance. In returning to tradition, as the men of religion require, anyone caught drinking wine must be whipped, and an adulterer either whipped or stoned. A spectacular piece of archaism indeed—though perhaps a little less spectacular, it is true, than the symbolism of orthodox Judaism. But then, the latter is often impossible to put into effect and, when it is, affects only a tiny community and thus startles fewer observers.

Will the future see any great change in this situation? It does not look like it. Certainly the panacea of Islamic government may be discredited in future among larger sections of Muslim society. Whatever may be said in Islamic countries or elsewhere, neither Islam itself, nor Muslim tradition, nor the Quran provides any magic guarantee either of fully satisfactory government or of social harmony. Islam is confined to offering precepts regarding only limited sectors of social life, legitimizing certain antiquated types of social and political structure, at best achieving small improvements, and, like all universalist, and some other, religions, it encourages people (beneficially moreover) to wield power and wealth with charity and moderation.

A Spiritual Enrichment

Muslim government in itself means nothing. A ruler can declare the state to be Muslim by satisfying certain minimal conditions which are easily fulfilled: the proclamation of adherence to Islam in the constitution; the institution, or reinstitution, of archaic laws; conciliation of the ulama (which is easy among Sunnis, more difficult among Shi'ites). But over and above this minimum, the scope is vast. The term can cover different, even diametrically opposed, regimes. Governments can make mutual accusations of the betrayal of the "true" Islam. Nothing is easier or more dangerous than this time-honored custom of dubbing your adversary an "enemy of God." Mutual recriminations, often incorporated in contradictory fatwas (legal consultations) issued by obliging authorities, are hardly designed to strengthen one's confidence in a state's supposedly Islamic character.

At any rate, is it not possible for one of these states to be genuinely Muslim and to inject some spiritual enrichment into the government of human affairs? Some people hope so, or say they do, whether militant revolutionaries because Muslim, or vice-versa, or else Europeans convinced of the vices of Europe and hoping to find elsewhere (why not in Islam?) the means of assuring a more or less radiant future.[94]

It is astonishing, after centuries of common experience, that it is still necessary to recall one of the best-attested laws of history. Good moral intentions, whether or not endorsed by the deity, are a weak basis for determining the practical policies of states. The best example is undoubtedly the weak influence of Christ's nonviolent anarchism—however often it may be invoked in writing, and revered, and memorized—with regard to the behavior of Christian states (and, for that matter, of the majority of their subjects). Muslim spirituality may exert a beneficial influence on the style of practical politics adopted by certain leaders. It is dangerous to hope for more.

Islam, according to its followers, is still superior to Christianity in demanding less of human virtue, in resigning itself to society's imperfections and prescribing or justifying repressive laws to deal with them. But in so doing, it can be said, it encourages people to expect more from these legal structures. Power can only disappoint. But it will disappoint the more if it promises more, if it pretends to be endowed more than any rival with the power to satisfy. This disappointment can only recoil on the doctrine which made use of it. If the magic potion is ineffective, one loses confidence not only in the sorcerer but in sorcery itself.

Waves of disenchantment may thus spread within the Muslim world as they have within Christian society. It is indeed unwise that so many regimes have declared themselves Islamic.

Spiritual malaise of this kind can already be detected among many of the people who have left Muslim societies and are free to express their disenchantment once they are outside. Heavy social constraint resulting from a stifling moral piety is, moreover, an important factor in the (noneconomic) emigration from these countries. The women are especially bitter. In Paris they have recently been declaiming their hatred of Islam—a hatred which owes nothing to "imperialism." One might say they are wrong to link Islam proper—the spiritual force of its gospel—with particular oppressive laws which are only contingent upon it. This is true. But who made the link before they did, and who continues to do so?

This is as pertinent inside Muslim countries as outside, but it is much more difficult to express such feelings from within. Industrialization, as it slowly develops, and the seductive forces of the way of life in secularized countries—as seen on film and television—will probably increase the challenge not only to regimes but to the religion which they have taken up as their banner, as long as this religion is still invoked to justify repression.

Under the pressure of such disaffection it is quite possible that, one day, the men of religion will present a rather more modern, concrete, and persuasive form of Islam. There might then develop a leftist Islamic ideology—and not simply an Islam challenging a particular regime—just as a leftist Christian ideology has developed. This will perhaps be slow in coming. Certainly, loyalty to a community long under attack, communal "patriotism" with its customary paranoia and narcissism, and pride in leading the Third World will still play their part. But this may not always be so.

For the moment, this leftist Islam is quite far off. One must make do, at best, with an Islam which retrospectively legitimizes anti-American, anti-Western postures, while exerting pressure to maintain an archaic moral order. One can call this "left-wing" if one wishes. Among their opponents, the shah and his followers are now (for tactical reasons) discovering "Islamic Marxists." They are not entirely wrong insofar as the implicit ideology of the Third World revolt has let both the people and a wide variety of intellectuals adopt or rediscover militant aspects of Marxism. Some people do so by presenting such tendencies as part of the "essential" Islam. They are wrong, but these are nevertheless universal tendencies which were present in medieval Islam. If they make reference to Islam, it is often to enable them to combine the politically progressive with social reaction.

It is this combination of the modern-revolutionary with the social-archaic that characterizes Qaddafi, who almost alone after coming to power has maintained the vitality of militant rebellion. For their part, the Saudi rulers combine the technologically modern with the politically and socially archaic, and their anxious ulama on the Right reproach them for it as Qaddafi does from the Left. Mixtures of this type are unstable, as are alliances between the men of religion and socialists or liberals, at least until the former have brought their outlook up to date. We shall probably see the alliance broken off once again in Iran (and elsewhere), as it was in 1907.

But humankind continually poses problems which it cannot solve, or poses them in terms which make them insoluble. Renewed despair is echoed by renewed hope. One will always find imperfections in existing regimes, whether seen in the light of "true" Islam or of "true" Marxism. For a long time to come, the attempt will still be made to correct "errors" by returning to the lost fundamentalism of hallowed tradition. There is still a future for Muslim fundamentalism—and for the fresh recoveries and fresh challenges that lie ahead of it.

A Powder Keg Called Islam

First published in *Corriere della sera*, February 13, 1979.

Tehran[95]—On February 11, 1979, the Iranian Revolution took place. I have the impression that I will read this sentence in tomorrow's newspapers and in the history books of the future. It is true that in the strange series of events that have marked the past twelve months of Iranian politics, a known figure finally appears. This long succession of festivities and mourning, these millions of men in the street invoking Allah, the mullahs in the cemeteries proclaiming revolt and prayer, these sermons distributed on cassette tapes, and this old man who, every day, crosses the road in a suburb of Paris in order to kneel down in the direction of Mecca; it was difficult for us to call all this a "revolution."

Today, we feel as though we are in a more familiar world. There were the barricades; weapons had been seized from the arsenals; and a council assembled hastily left the ministers just enough time to resign before stones began shattering the windows and before the doors burst open under the pressure of the crowd. History just placed on the bottom of the page the red seal that authenticates a revolution. Religion's role was to open the curtain; the mullahs will now disperse, taking off in a great flight of black and white robes. The decor is changing. The first act is going to begin: that of the struggle of the classes, of the armed vanguards, and of the party that organizes the masses, and so forth.

Is this so certain?

One did not have to be a great prophet in order to notice that the shah, last summer, was already politically dead, nor in order to realize that the army could not constitute an independent political force. It was not necessary to be a seer in order to ascertain that religion did not constitute a form of compromise, but rather a real force, one that could raise a people not only against the monarch and his police, but against an entire regime, an entire way of life, an entire world. But things today seem rather clear, permitting a retracing of what needs to be called the strategy of the religious movement. The long demonstrations—sometimes bloody, but incessantly repeated—were as much juridical as political, depriving the shah of his legitimacy and the political personnel of their representativeness. The National Front bowed out. Bakhtiar,[96] on the contrary, wanted to resist and to receive from the shah a legitimacy that he would have deserved for having guaranteed the shah's irrevocable departure. In vain.

The second obstacle, the Americans, seemed formidable. They yielded, however, due to powerlessness and also by calculation. Rather than support at arm's length a dying regime, with which they were all too compromised, they prefer to allow the development of a Chilean-type situation, to allow the sharpening of the internal conflicts and then to intervene. And perhaps they think that this movement, which, deep down, worries all of the regimes of the region, will accelerate the realization of an agreement in the Middle East. This was what the Palestinians and the Israelis at once felt, with the former appealing to the ayatollah for the liberation of all the holy places and the latter announcing one further reason not to give up anything.

With respect to the obstacle of the army, it was clear that it was paralyzed by the political currents running through it. But this paralysis, which constituted an advantage for the opposition as long as the shah was still in power, became a danger, since each current felt free, in the absence of all state power, to have its own way. It was necessary to unite the army sector by sector, without breaking it up too soon.

But the clash occurred much faster than was expected. Whether from provocation or accident, it did not matter. A cell of "hard-liners" attacked the part of the army that had joined with the ayatollah, precipitating between that part of the army and the crowd a rapprochement that went well beyond merely marching side by side. Quickly thereafter came the distribution of arms, the pinnacle *par excellence* of all revolutionary uprisings.

It is solely this distribution of arms that made everything seesaw back and forth, avoiding a civil war. The military command realized that a major part of the troops was escaping its control and that in the arsenals there were enough weapons to arm tens of thousands of civilians. It was better to go over as a bloc before the population took up arms, perhaps for years. The religious leaders immediately returned the compliment: they gave the order to hand back the arms.

Today, we are still at this point, in a situation that has not come to a head. The "revolution" showed, at certain moments, some of its familiar traits, but things are still astonishingly ambiguous.

The army, which went over to the religious leaders without ever having been really broken up, is going to weigh heavily. Its different currents are going to confront each other in the shadows in order to determine who will be the "new guard" of the regime, the one that protects it, enables it to hold on, and takes hold of it.

At the other extreme, it is certain that all will not give up their arms. The "Marxist-Leninists," who played no small role in the movement, probably think that it is necessary to move from the unity of the masses to the class struggle. Also, not having been the "vanguard" that rallies and rouses, they will want to be the force that settles the ambiguity and that clarifies the situation: "outflanking," the better to divide.

This nonviolent uprising of a whole people that overthrew an all-powerful regime—an incredibly rare outcome for the twentieth century—faces a decisive choice. Maybe its historic significance will be found, not in its conformity to a recognized "revolutionary" model, but instead in its potential to overturn the existing political situation in the Middle East and thus the global strategic equilibrium. Its singularity, which has up to now constituted its force, consequently threatens to give it the power to expand. Thus, it is true that, as an "Islamic" movement, it can set the entire region afire, overturn the most unstable regimes, and disturb the most solid ones. Islam—which is not simply a religion, but an entire way of life, an adherence to a history and a civilization—has a good chance to become a gigantic powder keg, at the level of hundreds of millions of men. Since yesterday, any Muslim state can be revolutionized from the inside, based on its time-honored traditions.

Indeed, it is also important to recognize that the demand for the "legitimate rights of the Palestinian people" has hardly stirred the Arab peoples. What would happen if this cause experienced the dynamism of an Islamic movement, something much stronger than the effect of giving it a Marxist, Leninist, or Maoist character? Additionally, how strong would Khomeini's "religious" movement become, if it were to put forward the liberation of Palestine as its objective? The Jordan no longer flows very far from Iran.

Khomeini and the "Primacy of the Spiritual"

by Maxime Rodinson

Originally published in *Le Nouvel Observateur*, February 19, 1979.

Jacques Julliard made intelligent use of the events in Iran in order to reexamine the conventional wisdom of the European Left. (See Julliard 1978.)[97] He boldly questions a basic judgment inherited from our venerable intellectual ancestors: Religion is organically tied to obscurantism and oppression. Nothing good can come of it. Freeing oneself from it is "pulling the mind out of the dungeon," as the good Communard Pottier expressed it in verse.[98] This, at least, is a first step toward total liberation. What irony that the transcendence of this conception, at the very least a simplistic one, takes place under the influence of the most archaic men of religion, the Iranian mullahs and the Orthodox popes, whose message is conveyed, it is true, by the eloquent Solzhenitsyn.

Do we need to invert Voltaire, as Marx inverted Hegel? Is it religion that liberates and philosophy that oppresses? Julliard does not think so, and he is right. Things are more complex. Here, I would only like to suggest a few lines of reflection inspired by a degree of familiarity with the ideological histories of the East and the West.

Neither philosophy nor religion is under consideration here. The content of an ideology does not necessarily play a decisive role in the movements that that ideology supports with its authority. In the beginning, Christianity preached submission to Caesar, and Marxism, revolt against all oppression. This did not prevent radical revolts, like those of the Anabaptists, from legitimizing themselves through the Christian scriptures, nor Marxism from canonizing submission to renewed oppressions. Religious and secular theorists are immensely skilled at interpreting an apparently very clear principle in infinitely different ways, occasionally opposite to its most evident meaning.

Revolt is first; it is (up to now) eternal, as seems to be the desire to establish (even to live in) a stable and inevitably (until now) inegalitarian order. So too is the necessity to justify the one and the other. The protest against an unfavorable situation, just like the authority that wants to disarm and repress that revolt, is always seeking a source of ideological legitimation. Religions, philosophies, sects, schools, parties, and even vague, barely conscious tendencies can all serve to attain this objective. Clearly, at certain moments, in certain circumstances, some are more suitable than others for producing the anticipated legitimations.

A few categories and some examples will suffice here. Against an ideology used by government, one can mobilize in the name of a prior, rival ideology, one that has been defeated but continues to exist. Ideological victories are not always total, nor are they irreversible. Consolidation depends on many things: the institutions established by the new or renewed government, the depth of their penetration into the different social or national layers, the structural transformations achieved; this without neglecting, far from it, the conjuncture, the circumstances.

Shortly after the triumph, there is often hesitation. Christianity, victorious in the Roman Empire after Constantine, was still poorly consolidated forty years later. Julian's pagan reaction, based on the elites, resulted in neither a strong resistance nor a mobilizing enthusiasm.[99] However, it took many centuries and much skill, in order even superficially to Christianize the peasant masses (*paganus* [pagan] signifies "peasant"), which remained passive.

Disputes soon arose among the new Christian tendencies, which battled each other ferociously. The last of the pagan elite were reduced to deploring the triumph of those they bitterly called the preponderants.

Three centuries later, the Berbers, who relentlessly resisted Arab Islam, did not waste any time in imbuing their protest with dissident Muslim "heresies." After the same Arab victory in Iran, the Iranians followed the divergent paths of the defeated Zoroastrian ideology, of Muslim "heresies" more or less penetrated by the musty odor of Zoroastrianism, or of those ideologies formerly persecuted by the defeated Zoroastrian state, Manichaeism or communist Mazdakism.[100] Or the Iranians simply fought under the banner of purely Muslim tendencies (of Arab origin) like Shi'ism, among others.

In the Soviet Union, the victorious ideology was connected to the radical transformation of society. Society was indeed transformed, and the state ideology penetrated all sectors. However, alongside other ideological outlets, discontent found a way to express itself through the defeated Russian Orthodoxy. The latter seemed moribund after the collapse of its political and social base, and after the persuasive and largely justified denunciation of undesirable growths on the Church, which it had sanctified.

Recourse is always available. It takes the form of spontaneous ideological tendencies, unorganized and eternal, despite shorter or longer periods of eclipse. Thus, nationalisms and egalitarianism are always ready to flower again after periods of resignation to the requisite hierarchy. Religious yearning also seems like a somewhat universal tendency. It can lead, it is true, to indifference to the social order in a quest for individual salvation or mystical ecstasy. But it frequently serves to shape an organized movement, often violent, of national or social protest.

Mobilizing ideologies can be autochthonous or can seek the authority of foreign "prophets." The role of intellectuals, with their preoccupations and their own interests, should not be minimized. There is always a layer of intellectuals (in general neither the most learned nor the most profound, nor especially the most disinterested) seeking an important (even if painful) role as guide, or as defender or oppressor of the people, often successively or both at the same time.

In particular, the "ideological movements" (I have tried elsewhere to specify this category),[101] especially when they have taken power, resemble the catch-all parties. Under the veil of an artificial unity, contradictory variants of their ideology subsist or develop. The leaders never succeed in totally imposing their interpretation of the common doctrine on all of their "faithful" followers. Tendencies crystallize and often organize. They can go as far as to push for a revolt against the new establishment in the name of faithfulness to the very values that the latter extols. This is often seen in Christianity, Islam, and elsewhere.

Everywhere, Islam, Sunni or Shi'ite, is again suited to the maximum degree (after the obvious failure of other doctrines) to serve as the banner or as the "foundational doctrine" for those who want to translate (translation, treachery!) generalized aspirations. One can find in the innumerable precepts that its more or less sacred texts contain (as well as in texts that are Christian, Jewish, etc.) enough to justify social protest. The humiliations of a situation of national dependence make attractive the ancestral religious identity, a historic enemy of the current dominant forces. The fervent faith of the masses has been lessened only slightly: God is not dead; the machines have not killed him. Islam, which does not possess very many concretely applicable political and social prescriptions, has always proclaimed itself, in contrast to Christianity, qualified to establish equitable institutions on its own, rather than merely preaching the moralization of the mainsprings of society and of iniquitous or indifferent men.[102] This is still widely ascribed to it.

Islamic doctrine is by no means sufficient, but it can help. Shi'ism has more often been in the minority, thus persecuted and dissident. Its founding myths exalt resistance to oppression and to reasons of state.

The Iranian elites and masses were horrified by the arbitrary authoritarianism of the shah, the repressive actions of an omnipresent and cruel police, and the modernization imposed from above with its attendant corruption, injustice, and misery. No charismatic secular leader was available. Moreover, secular heroes always fade before religious guides, who can add holiness to ordinary forms of charisma. In contrast to the Sunni *ulama*, the Shi'ite mullahs, also at the grassroots level close to the people, constitute a self-governing force. They form a "church," whose own wealth makes it independent of the state, which allows it to support or to attack the state.[103] Hence, Khomeini's success as an irreconcilable and sacred leader at the apex of a powerful, rich, and untouchable hierarchy, for a people who no longer wanted reconciliation.

There is neither improbability nor scandal in revolutionary mobilizations that take place in the name of religion. They can succeed better than others. However, it is necessary to be vigilant toward their victories. It is also necessary to maintain a critical attitude toward both the propaganda of the intellectuals within these movements and the credulity of those outside them. A revolutionary tendency can easily continue to be put forward under the banner of Islam. But what superior facilities religion has for those who want to smother society with conservative and reactionary options! Religions are not dangerous because they preach belief in God, but rather because the only remedy they have at their disposal concerning the inherent evils of society is moral exhortation. The more they seem to have such remedies at their disposal, the more they make sacred the social *status quo* that more often than not suits their clerics. In power, they succumb more often than not to the temptation of imposing, in the name of moral reform, an order of the same name.

Khomeini does not have the necessary capacities, even at an illusory level, to be a Robespierre or a Lenin. They were not archbishops. He could be a Savonarola or, if power inspires him with some politically practical ideas, a Calvin or a Cromwell. Let us hope for the Iranian people that he does not reveal himself to be a Dupanloup tending toward a Torquemada.[104]

Statement by Iranian Women Protestors

Read out during a demonstration at the Ministry of Justice, Tehran, March 10, 1979.

Whereas all human beings are created free, and the gift of freedom has been granted to them equally, regardless of gender, color, race, language, and opinion;

Whereas half of the population of Iran is composed of women, whose influence on the education of the next generation, as well as their own participation in social, educational, political, and economic matters, is undeniable;

Whereas women's selfless participation in the opposition to imperialism and despotism has been an important dimension of the Iranian Revolution, and their contribution to the victory of the revolution has been admitted and accepted by all active sectors of the revolution;

Whereas in the very difficult days of this nation, politically active women made many sacrifices that were recognized by the leader of the revolution;

Whereas according to the messages, interviews, and statements of Ayatollah Khomeini, women were promised freedom, equality, and inclusion in all social and political rights, and were explicitly promised that they will not be forced back fourteen hundred years;

We Iranian women announce the following demands:

1. We women perform our social obligations for the nation alongside the men, and at home are responsible for the education of the future generation. We are fully capable and are quite aware of the need to maintain our dignity, character, and honor. Though we have strong convictions concerning the need to maintain women's dignity, we also believe that a woman's honor is not dependent on a particular form of covering. Rather, women's clothing must be left to them according to tradition, customs, and the needs of the environment.

2. Women's equality in civil liberties must be recognized, and all forms of prejudice in these laws and Family Rights Laws must be removed.

3. The political, social, and economic rights of women must be maintained and guaranteed without prejudice.

4. Women must be guaranteed security in the exercise of their legal rights and freedoms.

5. True access to principal freedoms such as freedom of the pen, freedom of expression, freedom of opinion, freedom of employment, and social freedoms must be guaranteed for men and women of the nation.

6. All inequalities between men and women in national law, such as in labor and employment law, must be removed.

7. Women's present employment must be maintained.

8. We express our gratitude to the government for its decision to reinstate the Family Protection Law, and we ask that the limits of the law be addressed so that women's rights are restored. We demand that the provisional government of Engineer Bazargan declare its view with regard to this statement by women.

Speech by Simone de Beauvoir

Delivered at a press conference in Paris on the eve of a trip to Iran by an international women's delegation, which departed on March 19, 1979.

We have created the International Committee for Women's Rights (CIDF) in response to calls from a large number of Iranian women. Their situation and their revolt have greatly moved us. We have decided to create this committee, which has set itself several tasks. The first one is information. It is a matter of becoming informed about the situation of women across the world, a situation that to a very, very great extent is extremely difficult, painful, and even odious. Therefore, we wish to inform ourselves, in very precise cases, of this situation.

We then wish to inform others of it; that is, to communicate the knowledge that we have gained by publishing articles. And finally, we wish to support the struggle of the women who fight against the situation that affects them. That is the general idea of the CIDF.

The first task we have taken up is a very, very burning one for today. It is the task of acquiring information concerning the struggle of the Iranian women, communicating that information, and supporting their struggle. We have received an appeal from a very large number of these women. We have also seen their struggles, their fights, and their actions. We have appreciated the depth of the utter humiliation into which others wanted to make them fall, and we have therefore resolved to fight on their behalf.

Thus, the first practical step that will make our call to action concrete is a specific one. We are sending a women's delegation to Tehran, in order to gather information. We have sent a telegram to M. Bazargan, asking him if he will see us. I say "we," although for personal health reasons, I am not going. But I have many women friends who are going to travel to Iran on Monday. We have asked him to receive the delegation, but even if he does not reply, we are going anyway! In that case, however, it would no longer be a dialogue with a head of state. It would solely be an effort to gather information. Unless, of course, they turn us away completely, which is still a strong possibility. It is very possible that the mission will fail, inasmuch as they might turn it away the moment it arrives. Nevertheless the die will have been cast, and it is important to have a demonstration—on the part of a very large number of Western women, French women, Italian women, and others—of solidarity with the struggle of Iranian women.

I reiterate, however, that this is essentially an effort to gather information, in order to put ourselves in contact with Iranian women, in order to know their demands and the ways in which they plan to struggle.

What Are the Philosophers Dreaming About? Was Michel Foucault Mistaken about the Iranian Revolution?

by Claudie and Jacques Broyelle

First published in *Le Matin*, March 24, 1979.

Editors' Note by *Le Matin*: What is the character of Ayatollah Khomeini's regime in Tehran? This is still an open question that provokes heated debates. Whereas the fall of the shah was welcomed with a sense of relief by Western opinion, the evolution of the Iranian Revolution has given rise to serious concerns. The philosopher Michel Foucault had foregrounded the spiritual dimension of the Islamic revolution. Claudie and Jacques Broyelle, whose book, *A Second Return from China*, caused a sensation two years ago, and who have just published the *Happiness of Stones* (Seuil),[105] criticize Michel Foucault's position unstintingly, calling upon him to "acknowledge his errors."

Returning from Iran a few months ago, Michel Foucault stated that he was "impressed" by the "attempt to open a spiritual dimension in politics" that he discerned in the project of an Islamic government.[106]

Today there are little girls all in black, veiled from head to toe; women stabbed precisely because they do not want to wear the veil; summary executions for homosexuality; the creation of a "Ministry of Guidance According to the Precepts of the Quran"; thieves and adulterous women flogged. Iran has had a narrow escape. When one thinks that after decades of ferocious dictatorship under the shah and the SAVAK, this country almost fell into the trap of a "Spanish-type" solution, of a democratic parliament, this news is proof enough of that country's good fortune.

October 1978: "The Saint," "the destitute exile," "the man who rises up with bare hands," "Ayatollah Khomeini" ruined it all. He sent out an appeal to the students . . . the Muslims . . . and the army to oppose, in the name of the Quran and in the name of nationalism, these ideas of compromise concerning elections, a constitution, and so forth. Thank God, the call was heard.

What form was this Islamic government supposed to have taken? "Absence of hierarchy in the clergy . . . importance of purely spiritual authority, a both echoing and guiding role that the clergy must play in order to sustain its influence . . ." Spiritual light "that is capable of illuminating from the inside, a law that is not made to be conserved . . ."—this is so stupidly the sign of "Western" democracies—". . . but to release over time the spiritual meaning that it holds." Pertinent: Shoot a homosexual, and you have revealed, it is true, the spiritual meaning of the law "in the Islamic fashion." "In the pursuit of this ideal" . . . (very old and "very far in the future" . . . a brighter future) . . . "distrust of legalism seemed essential to me." As a matter of fact, the Islamic government, each day, proves its illegalism by way of bullets. This "political will" therefore will have been "sufficiently intense to prevent itself from aiming toward a Western-style parliamentary regime."

This spirituality that disciplines and punishes allowed the people of Iran to rise up. Spontaneous armed groups, benevolent Islamic committees that "counterattack" and take immediate revenge, sweeping away the odious and stage-managed bourgeois courts with their well-known and oppressive trail of interrogations, investigations, witnesses, proofs, hearings, and supposedly neutral judges—this is the people's justice for which Michel Foucault passionately yearned, notably in "On Popular Justice: A Conversation with Maoists" (*Temps modernes*, no. 310 bis, 1972).[107]

No, the philosopher is not responsible for the blood that flows today in Iran. It is not he who invented Islam and the ayatollahs. It is not he who, sitting cross-legged in a mosque in Qom, fulminates his "firmans,"[108] like Mao, not long ago, with his "supreme directives." The philosopher contents himself with painting and offering images, holy images: the abridged illustrated imam, sequel to the hurried marabout of people's justice.[109] He is no more responsible than Léon Daudet for the Holocaust,[110] or than the Western communist intellectuals for the socialist gulags.

Also, no one is forced, with a gun to the head, to declare that Daudet,

Andrieu,[111] or Foucault have developed ideas "of genius." Consumers have some obligations, but they also have the right to submit the ideas that are put forward to the most elementary test of consumption, that of reality. This concerns especially ideas such as "the truth of justice is the police," or "revolution can only happen through the radical elimination of the judicial apparatus."[112] Also, when one realizes that all models on the Foucauldian scale carry the same anti- (bourgeois) democratic, anti-legalist, anti-judiciary label, one has the right to protest in the name of deceptive advertising. These articles cannot be sold under the label of "defense of human rights."

When one is an intellectual, when one works both on and with "ideas," when one has the freedom—without having to fight at the risk of one's life in order to obtain it—not to be a sycophantic writer, then one also has some obligations. The first one is to take responsibility for the ideas that one has defended when they are finally realized. The philosophers of "people's justice" should say today, "Long live the Islamic government!" and it would be clear that they are going to the final extreme of their radicalism. Or they should say, "No, I did not want that, I was mistaken. Here is what was wrong in my reasoning; here is where my thinking is in error." They should reflect. After all, that is their job.

Will there never then be any warranty for parts and for labor, or for pick-up and disposal, for the philosophies that are put on the market?

Foucault's Response to Claudie and Jacques Broyelle

First published in *Le Matin*, March 26, 1979, under the title "Michel Foucault and Iran."

Two weeks ago, *Le Matin* asked me to respond to M. Debray-Ritzen;[113] today, to M. and Mme. Broyelle. To him, I was anti-psychiatry. To them, I am "anti-judiciary." I will respond neither to the one nor the others, because throughout "my life" I have never taken part in polemics. I have no intention of beginning now. There is another reason, also based on principles. I am "summoned to acknowledge my errors." This expression and the practice it designates remind me of something and of many things, against which I have fought. I will not lend myself, even "through the press," to a maneuver whose form and content I detest.

"You are going to confess, or you will shout long live the assassins." Some utter this sentence by profession, others by taste or habit. I think that it is necessary to leave this order on the lips of those who utter it and to discuss it only with those who are strangers to such forms of conduct. I am, therefore, very anxious to be able to debate here and now the question of Iran, as soon as *Le Matin* will give me the opportunity. Blanchot[114] teaches that criticism begins with attention, good demeanor, and generosity.

Iran: The Spirit of a World without Spirit

This conversation with Foucault originally appeared as the appendix to Claire Brière and Pierre Blanchet, *Iran: la révolution au nom de Dieu* (227–41), first published in March 1979. Brière and Blanchet were the Iran correspondents of *Libération*, the leftist Paris newspaper. Their book is one of the more uncritical accounts of Iran's Islamic Revolution.

CLAIRE BRIÈRE: Could we begin with the simplest question? Like a lot of others, like you, I have been fascinated by what happened in Iran. Why?

MICHEL FOUCAULT: I would like to go back at once to another, perhaps less important question, but one that may provide a way in: What is it about what has happened in Iran that a whole lot of people, on the left and on the right, find somewhat irritating? The Iran affair and the way in which it has taken place have not aroused the same kind of untroubled sympathy as Portugal,[115] for example, or Nicaragua. I'm not saying that Nicaragua, in the middle of summer, at a time when people are tanning themselves in the sun, aroused a great deal of interest, but in the case of Iran, I soon felt a small, epidermic reaction that was not one of immediate sympathy. To take an example: There was this journalist you know very well. At Tehran she wrote an article that was published in Paris and, in the last sentence, in which she spoke of the Islamic revolt, she found that the adjective "fanatic," which she had certainly not written, had been crudely added. This strikes me as being fairly typical of the irritations that the Iranian movement has provoked.

PIERRE BLANCHET: There are several possible attitudes to Iran. There's the attitude of the classic, orthodox, extreme left. I'd cite above all the Communist League,[116] which supports Iran and the whole of the extreme left, various Marxist-Leninist groups, which say they are religious rebels, but that doesn't really matter. Religion is only a shield. Therefore we can support them unhesitatingly; it is a classic anti-imperialist struggle, like that in Vietnam, led by a religious man, Khomeini, but one who might be a Marxist-Leninist. To read *L'Humanité*, one might think that the PC [Communist Party] had the same attitude as the LCR [Trotskyist Revolutionary Communist League]. On the other hand, the attitude of the more moderate left, whether of the PS [Socialist Party] or that of the more marginal left around the newspaper *Libération*, is one of irritation from the outset. They would say more or less two things. First: Religion is the veil, an archaism, a regression at least as far as women are concerned; the second, which cannot be denied, because one feels it: If ever the clerics come to power and apply their program, should we not fear a new dictatorship?

MICHEL FOUCAULT: It might be said that, behind these two irritations, there is another, or perhaps an astonishment, a sort of unease when confronted by a phenomenon that is, for our political mentality, very curious. It is a phenomenon that may be called revolutionary in the very broad sense of the term, since it concerns the uprising of a whole nation against a power that oppresses it. Now, we recognize a revolution when we can observe two dynamics: one is that of the contradictions in that society, that of the class struggle or of social confrontations. Then there is a political dynamic, that is to say, the presence of a vanguard, class, party, or political ideology, in short, a spearhead that carries the whole nation with it. Now it seems to me that, in what is happening in Iran, one can recognize neither of those two dynamics that are for us distinctive signs and explicit marks of a revolutionary phenomenon. What, for us, is a revolutionary movement in which one cannot situate the internal contradictions of a society, and in which one cannot point out a vanguard either?

PIERRE BLANCHET: At Tehran University, there were—I have met several of them—Marxists who were all conscious of living through a fantastic revolution. It was even much more than they had imagined, hoped for, dreamt for, dreamt about. Invariably, when asked what they thought, the Marxists replied: "It's a revolutionary situation, but there's no vanguard."

CLAIRE BRIÈRE: The reaction I've heard most often about Iran is that people don't understand. When a movement is called revolutionary, people in the West, including ourselves, always have the notion of progress, of something that is about to be transformed in the direction of progress. All this is put into question by the religious phenomenon. Indeed, the wave of religious confrontation is based on notions that go back for thirteen centuries; it is with these that the shah has been challenged, while, at the same time, advancing claims for social justice, etc., which seem to be in line with progressive thought or action. Now, I don't know whether you managed, when you were in Iran, to determine, to grasp the nature of that enormous religious confrontation—I myself found it very difficult. The Iranians themselves are swimming in that ambiguity and have several levels of language, commitment, expression, etc. There is the guy who says "Long Live Khomeini," who is sincerely convinced about his religion; the guy who says "Long Live Khomeini, but I'm not particularly religious, Khomeini is just a symbol"; the guy who says "I'm fairly religious, I like Khomeini, but I prefer Shariatmadari," who is a very different kind of figure; there is the girl who puts on the *chador* to show that she is against the regime and another girl, partly secularized, partly Muslim, who doesn't put on the veil, but who will also say, "I'm a Muslim and Long Live Khomeini" . . . ;[117] among all these people there are different levels of thought. And yet everybody shouts, at one and the same time, with great fervor, "Long Live Khomeini," and those different levels fall away.

MICHEL FOUCAULT: I don't know whether you've read François Furet's book on the French Revolution.[118] It's a very intelligent book and might help us to sort out this confusion. He draws a distinction between the totality of the processes of economic and social transformation that began well before the revolution of 1789 and ended well after it, and the specificity of the revolutionary event. That's to say, the specificity of what people experienced deep inside, but also of what they experienced in that sort of theater that they put together from day to day and which constituted the revolution. I wonder whether this distinction might not be applied to some extent to Iran. It is true that Iranian society is shot through with contradictions that cannot in any way be denied, but it is certain that the revolutionary event that has been taking place for a year now, and which is at the same time an inner experience, a sort of constantly recommended liturgy, a community experience, and so on, all that is certainly articulated onto the class struggle: but that doesn't find expression in an immediate, transparent way. So what role has religion, then, with the formidable grip that it has on people, the position that it has always held in relation to political power, its content, which makes it a religion of combat and sacrifice, and so on? Not that of an ideology, which would help to mask contradictions or form a sort of sacred union between a great many divergent interests. It really has been the vocabulary, the ceremonial, the timeless drama into which one could fit the historical drama of a people that pitted its very existence against that of its sovereign.

PIERRE BLANCHET: What struck me was the uprising of a whole population. I say *whole*. And if you take, for example, the demonstration of the 'Ashura, add up the figures: take away young children, the disabled, the old and a proportion of women who stayed at home. You will then see that the whole of Tehran was in the streets shouting "Death to the king," except the parasites who, really, lived off the regime. Even people who were with the regime for a very long time, who were for a constitutional monarchy as little as a month before, were shouting "Death to the king." It was an astonishing, unique moment and one that must remain. Obviously, afterwards, things will settle down and different strata, different classes, will become visible.

MICHEL FOUCAULT: Among the things that characterize this revolutionary event, there is the fact that it has brought out—and few peoples in history have had this—an absolutely collective will. The collective will is a political myth with which jurists and philosophers try to analyze or to justify institutions, etc. It's a theoretical tool: nobody has ever seen the "collective will" and, personally, I thought that the collective will was like God, like the soul, something one would never encounter. I don't know whether you agree with me, but we met, in Tehran and throughout Iran, the collective will of a people. Well, you have to salute it; it doesn't happen every day. Furthermore (and here one can speak of Khomeini's political sense), this collective will has been given one object, one target and one only, namely, the departure of the shah. This collective will, which, in our theories, is always general, has found for itself, in Iran, an absolutely clear, particular aim, and has thus erupted into history. Of course, in the independence struggles, in the anticolonial wars, one finds similar phenomena. In Iran the national sentiment has been extremely vigorous: the rejection of submission to foreigners, disgust at the looting of national resources, the rejection of a dependent foreign policy, the American interference that was visible everywhere, have been determinants in the shah's being perceived as a Western agent. But national feeling has, in my opinion, been only one of the elements of a still more radical rejection: the rejection by a people, not only of foreigners, but of everything that had constituted, for years, for centuries, its political destiny.

PIERRE BLANCHET: We went to China in 1967, at the height of the Lin Biao period, and, at that time, too, we had the feeling that there was the same type of collective will. In any case, something very strong was taking place, a very deep desire on the part of the whole Chinese people, for example, concerning the relationship between town and country, intellectuals and manual workers, that is to say, about all those questions that have now been settled in China in the usual, traditional way. At Beijing, we had the feeling that the Chinese were forming a people "in fusion." Afterwards, we came to realize that we'd been taken in to some extent; the Chinese, too. It's true that, to an extent, we took ourselves in. And that's why, sometimes, we hesitate to allow ourselves to be carried away by Iran. In any case, there is something similar in the charisma of Mao Zedong and of Khomeini; there is something similar in the way the young Islamic militants speak of Khomeini and the way the Red Guards spoke of Mao.

MICHEL FOUCAULT: All the same, the Cultural Revolution was certainly presented as a struggle between certain elements of the population and certain others, certain elements in the party and certain others, or between the population and the party, etc. Now what struck me in Iran is that there is no struggle between different elements. What gives it such beauty, and at the same time such gravity, is that there is only one confrontation: between the entire people and the state threatening it with its weapons and police. One didn't have to go to extremes, one found them there at once, on the one side, the entire will of the people, on the other the machine guns. The people demonstrated, the tanks arrived. The demonstrations were repeated, and the machine-guns fired yet again. And this occurred in an almost identical way, with, of course, an intensification each time, but without any change of form or nature. It's the repetition of the demonstration. The readers of Western newspapers must have tired of it fairly soon. Oh, another demonstration in Iran! But I believe the demonstration, in its very repetition, had an intense political meaning. The very word *demonstration* must be taken literally: a people was tirelessly *demonstrating* its will. Of course, it was not only because of the demonstrations that the shah left. But one cannot deny that it was because of an endlessly demonstrated rejection. There was in these demonstrations a link between collective action, religious ritual, and an expression of public right. It's rather like in Greek tragedy, where the collective ceremony and the reenactment of the principles of right go hand in hand. In the streets of Tehran there was an act, a political and juridical act, carried out collectively within religious rituals—an act of deposing the sovereign.

PIERRE BLANCHET: On the question of the collective will, what struck me—I was both spellbound by Iran and, sometimes, too, somewhat irritated—is when, for example, the students came and said, "We are all the same, we are all one, we are all for the Quran, we are all Muslims, there's no difference between us. Make sure you write that, that we're all the same." Yet we knew perfectly well that there were differences, we knew perfectly well, for example, that the intellectuals, a section of the *bazaaris*, and the middle classes were afraid to go too far. And yet they followed. That's what needs explaining.

MICHEL FOUCAULT: Of course. There's a very remarkable fact in what is happening in Iran. There was a government that was certainly one of the best endowed with weapons, the best served by a large army that was astonishingly faithful compared with what one might think, there was a police that was certainly not very efficient, but whose violence and cruelty often made up for a lack of subtlety: it was, moreover, a regime directly supported by the United States; lastly, it had the backing of the whole world, of the countries large and small that surrounded it. In a sense, it had everything going for it, plus, of course, oil, which guaranteed the state an income that it could use as it wished. Yet, despite all this, a people rose up in revolt: it rose up, of course, in a context of crisis, of economic difficulties, etc., but the economic difficulties in Iran at that time were not sufficiently great for people to take to the streets, in their hundreds of thousands, in their millions, and face the machine-guns bare-chested. That's the phenomenon that we have to talk about.

PIERRE BLANCHET: In comparative terms, it may well be that our own economic difficulties are greater than those in Iran at the time.

MICHEL FOUCAULT: Perhaps. Yet, whatever the economic difficulties, we still have to explain why there were people who rose up and said: We're not having any more of this. In rising up, the Iranians said to themselves—and this perhaps is the soul of the uprising: "Of course, we have to change this regime and get rid of this man, we have to change this corrupt administration, we have to change the whole country, the political organization, the economic system, the foreign policy. But, above all, we have to change ourselves. Our way of being, our relationship with others, with things, with eternity, with God, etc., must be completely changed, and there will only be a true revolution if this radical change in our experience takes place." I believe that it is here that Islam played a role. It may be that one or other of its obligations, one or other of its codes exerted a certain fascination. But, above all, in relation to the way of life that was theirs, religion for them was like the promise and guarantee of finding something that would radically change their subjectivity. Shi'ism is precisely a form of Islam that, with its teaching and esoteric content, distinguishes between what is mere external obedience to the code and what is the profound spiritual life; when I say that they were looking to Islam for a change in their subjectivity, this is quite compatible with the fact that traditional Islamic practice was already there and already gave them their identity; in this way they had of living the Islamic religion as a revolutionary force, there was something other than the desire to obey the law more faithfully, there was the desire to renew their entire existence by going back to a spiritual experience that they thought they could find within Shi'ite Islam itself. People always quote Marx and the opium of the people. The sentence that immediately preceded that statement and which is never quoted says that religion is the spirit of a world without spirit. Let's say, then, that Islam, in that year of 1978, was not the opium of the people precisely because it was the spirit of a world without a spirit.[119]

CLAIRE BRIÈRE: By way of illustrating what you just said—"A demonstration there is really a demonstration"—I think we should use the word *witness*. People are always talking about Hussein in Iran. Now who is Hussein? A "demonstrator," a witness—a martyr—who, by his suffering, demonstrates against evil and whose death is more glorious than the life of his victor. The people who demonstrated with their bare hands were also witnesses. They bore witness to the crimes of the shah, of the SAVAK, the cruelty of the regime that they wanted to get rid of, of the evil that this regime personified.

PIERRE BLANCHET: There seems to me to be a problem when one speaks of Hussein. Hussein was a martyr, he's dead. By endlessly shouting "Martyr,

Martyr," the Iranian population got rid of the shah. It's incredible and unprecedented. But what can happen now? Everybody isn't just going to shout "Martyr, Martyr" until everybody dies and there's a military coup d'état. With the shah out of the way, the movement will necessarily split apart.

MICHEL FOUCAULT: There'll come a moment when the phenomenon that we are trying to apprehend and which has so fascinated us—the revolutionary experience itself—will die out. There was literally a light that lit up in all of them and which bathed all of them at the same time. That will die out. At that point, different political forces, different tendencies will appear, there'll be compromises, there'll be this or that; I have no idea who will come out on top, and I don't think there are many people who can say now. It will disappear. There'll be processes at another level, another reality in a way. What I meant is that what we witnessed was not the result of an alliance, for example, between various political groups. Nor was it the result of a compromise between social classes that, in the end, each giving into the other on this or that, came to an agreement to claim this or that thing. Not at all. Something quite different has happened. A phenomenon has traversed the entire people and will one day stop. At that moment, all that will remain are the different political calculations that each individual had had in his head the whole time. Let's take the activist in some political group. When he was taking part in one of those demonstrations, he was double: he had his political calculation, which was this or that, and at the same time he was an individual caught up in that revolutionary movement, or rather that Iranian who had risen up against his king. And the two things did not come into contact, he did not rise up against his king because his party had made this or that calculation.

CLAIRE BRIÈRE: One of the significant examples of this movement is what has happened in the case of the Kurds. The Kurds, a majority of whom are Sunnis, and whose autonomist tendencies have long been known, have used the language of this uprising, of this movement. Everybody thought they would be against it, whereas they have supported it, saying: "Of course we are Sunnis, but above all we are Muslims." When people spoke to them of their Kurdish specificity, their reaction was almost one of anger, or rejection. "What! We are Kurds!" they replied to you in Kurdish and the interpreter had to translate from Kurdish, "No, not at all, we are Iranians above all, and we share all the problems of Iran; we want the king to go." The slogans in Kurdistan were exactly the same as those in Tehran or Mashad. "Long Live Khomeini," "Death to the Shah."

MICHEL FOUCAULT: I knew some Iranians in Paris, and what struck me about a lot of them was their fear. Fear that it would be known that they were consorting with left-wing people, fear that the agents of SAVAK might learn that they were reading this or that book, and so on. When I arrived in Iran, immediately after the September massacres, I said to myself that I was going to find a terrorized city, because there had been four thousand dead. Now I can't say that I found happy people, but there was an absence of fear and an intensity of courage, or rather, the intensity that people were capable of when danger, though still not removed, had already been transcended. In their revolution they had already transcended the danger posed by the machine-gun that constantly faced all of them.

PIERRE BLANCHET: Were the Kurds still with the Shi'ites? Was the National Front still with the clerics? Was the intelligentsia still following Khomeini? If there are twenty thousand dead and the army reacts, if there's a civil war lurking below the surface or an authoritarian Islamic Republic, there's a risk that we'll see some curious swings back. It will be said, for example, that Khomeini forced the hand of the National Front. It will be said that Khomeini did not wish to respect the wishes of the middle classes and intelligentsia for compromise. All these things are either true or false.

MICHEL FOUCAULT: That's right. It will be true and, at the same time, not true. The other day, someone said to me, "Everything you think about Iran isn't true, and you don't realize that there are communists everywhere." But I do know this. I know that in fact there are a lot of people who belong to communist or Marxist-Leninist organizations—there's no denying that. But what I liked about your articles was that they didn't try to break up this phenomenon into its constituent elements; they tried to leave it as a single beam of light, even though we know that it is made up of several beams. That's the risk and the interest in talking about Iran.

PIERRE BLANCHET: Let me give you an example. One evening, we went out after the curfew with a very Westernized, forty-year-old woman, who had lived in London and was now living in a house in northern Tehran. One evening, during the pre-Muharram period, she came to where we were living, in a working-class district. Shots were being fired on every side. We took her into the back streets, to see the army, to see the ordinary people, the shouts from the rooftops. It was the first time she had been in that district on foot. It was the first time she had spoken with such ordinary people, people who cried out *Allah O Akbar*.[120] She was completely overcome, embarrassed that she was not wearing a *chador*, not because she was afraid that someone might throw vitriol in her face, but because she wanted to be like the other women. It wasn't so much the episode of the *chador* that is important, but what those people said to us. They spoke in a very religious way and always said at the end, "May God keep you" and other such religious expressions. She replied in the same way, with the same language. She said to us, "This is the first time I have ever spoken like that." She was very moved.

MICHEL FOUCAULT: Yet, one day, all this will become, for historians, a rallying of the upper classes to a popular, left-wing movement, etc. That will be an analytical truth. I believe it is one of the reasons why one feels a certain unease when one comes back from Iran and people, wanting to understand, ask one for an analytical schema of an already constituted reality.

CLAIRE BRIÈRE: I'm thinking of another interpretative grid that we Western journalists have often had. This movement has followed such an odd logic that, on several occasions, Western observers have ignored it. The day of the National Front strike, in November, which had been a failure. Or the fortieth day of mourning of Black Friday. Black Friday had been terrible. One could imagine how the fortieth day of mourning would be very moving, very painful. Now, on the fortieth day, many shops were reopened and people didn't seem particularly sad. Yet the movement began again with its own logic, its own rhythm, its own breathing. It seemed to me that in Iran, despite the hectic rhythm at Tehran, the movement followed a rhythm that might be compared with that of a man—they walked like a single man—who breathes, gets tired, gets his breath back, resumes the attack, but really with a collective rhythm. On that fortieth day of mourning, there was no great demonstration of mourning. After the massacre in Djaleh Square, the Iranians were getting their breath back. The movement was relaunched by the astonishing contagion of the strikes that began about that time. Then there was the start of the new academic year, the angry reaction of the Tehran population, which set fire to Western symbols.

MICHEL FOUCAULT: Another thing that struck me as odd was the way the weapon of oil was used. If there was one immediately sensitive spot, it was oil, which was both the cause of the evil and the absolute weapon. One day we may know what happened. It certainly seems that the strike and its tactics had not been calculated in advance. On the spot, without there being any order coming from above, at a given moment, the workers went on strike, coordinating among themselves, from town to town, in an absolutely free way. Indeed it wasn't a strike in the strict sense of a cessation of work and an interruption of production. It was clearly the affirmation that the oil belonged to the Iranian people and not to the shah or to his clients or partners. It was a strike in favor of national reappropriation.

CLAIRE BRIÈRE: Then, on the contrary, for it would not be honest to be silent about it, it must be said that when I, an individual, a foreign journalist, a woman, was confronted by this oneness, this common will, I felt an extraordinary shock, mentally and physically. It was as if that oneness required that everyone conform to it. In a sense, it was woe betide anyone who did not conform. We all had problems of this kind in Iran. Hence, perhaps, the reticence that people often feel in Europe. An uprising is all very fine, yes, but . . .[121]

MICHEL FOUCAULT: There were demonstrations, verbal at least, of violent anti-Semitism. There were demonstrations of xenophobia and directed not only at the Americans, but also at foreign workers who had come to work in Iran.

PIERRE BLANCHET: This is indeed the other side of the unity that certain people may find offensive. For example, once, one of our photographers got punched in the face several times because he was thought to be an American. "No, I'm French," he protested. The demonstrators then embraced him and said, "Above all, don't say anything about this in the press." I'm thinking, too, of the demonstrators' imperious demands: "Make sure you say that there were so many thousand victims, so many million demonstrators in the streets."

CLAIRE BRIÈRE: That's another problem: it's the problem of a different culture, a different attitude to the truth. Besides it's part of the struggle. When your hands are empty, if you pile up the dead, real and imaginary, you ward off fear, and you become all the more convincing.

MICHEL FOUCAULT: They don't have the same regime of truth as ours, which, it has to be said, is very special, even if it has become almost universal. The Greeks had their own. The Arabs of the Mahgreb have another. And in Iran it is largely modeled on a religion that has an exoteric form and an esoteric content. That is to say, everything that is said under the explicit form of the law also refers to another meaning. So not only is saying one thing that means another not a condemnable ambiguity; it is, on the contrary, a necessary and highly prized additional level of meaning. It's often the case that people say something that, at the factual level, isn't true, but which refers to another, deeper meaning, which cannot be assimilated in terms of precision and observation . . .[122]

CLAIRE BRIÈRE: That doesn't bother me. But I am irritated when I am told over and over again that all minorities will be respected and when, at the same time, they aren't being respected. I have one particularly strong memory—and I am determined all the same that it will appear somewhere—of the September demonstration when, as a woman, I was veiled. I was wearing a *chador*. They tried to stop me getting into the truck with the other reporters. I'd had enough of walking. When I was in the truck, the demonstrators who were around us tried to stop me standing up. Then some guy starting yelling—it was hateful—because I was wearing sandals without socks: I got an enormous impression of intolerance. Yet there were about fifty people around us saying:

"She's a reporter, she has to be in the procession, there's no reason why she can't be in the truck." But when people speak to you about Jews—it's true that there was a lot of anti-Semitic talk—that they will tolerate them only if they don't support Israel, when anonymous notes are sent out, the credibility of the movement is somewhat affected. It's the strength of the movement to be a single unity. As soon as it perceives slight differences, it feels threatened. I believe the intolerance is there—and necessary.

MICHEL FOUCAULT: What has given the Iranian movement its intensity has been a double register. On the one hand, a collective will that has been very strongly expressed politically and, on the other hand, the desire for a radical change in ordinary life. But this double affirmation can only be based on traditions, institutions that carry a charge of chauvinism, nationalism, exclusiveness, which have a very powerful attraction for individuals. To confront so fearsome an armed power, one mustn't feel alone, nor begin with nothing. Apart from the problem of the immediate succession to the shah, there is another question that interests me at least as much: Will this unitary movement, which, for a year now has stirred up a people faced with machine-guns, have the strength to cross its own frontiers and go beyond the things on which, for a time, it has based itself? Are those limits, are those supports going to disappear once the initial enthusiasm wanes, or are they, on the contrary, going to take root and become stronger? Many here and some in Iran are waiting for and hoping for the moment when secularization will at last come back to the fore and reveal the good, old type of revolution we have always known. I wonder how far they will be taken along this strange, unique road, in which they seek, against the stubbornness of their destiny, against everything they have been for centuries, "something quite different."

Open Letter to Prime Minister Mehdi Bazargan

First published in *Le Nouvel Observateur*, April 14, 1979.

Dear Mr. Prime Minister,

Last September, after several thousand men and women had just been machine-gunned in the streets of Tehran, you granted me an interview at the home of Ayatollah Shariatmadari in Qom. Around a dozen of those working for human rights had sought refuge in his house. Soldiers holding machine guns were guarding the entrance to the alley.

You were then President of the Committee for the Defense of Human Rights. You needed courage. You needed physical courage, for prison awaited you, and you already knew it. You needed political courage, for the American president had recently enlisted the shah as one the defenders of human rights.[123] Today, many Iranians are angry that they are being given such noisy lectures. As to their rights, they showed that they knew how to make them prevail, they alone. They also refused to think that sentencing a young black man in racist South Africa equals the sentencing of a murderer from the SAVAK in Tehran. Who would not understand them?

A few weeks ago you ordered a halt to summary trials and hasty executions. Justice and injustice are the sensitive point of any revolution. Revolutions are born from justice and injustice and it is because of these that often they get lost and die. Since you thought it appropriate to allude to it in public, I felt the need to remind you of the conversation that we had on this topic.

We discussed all the regimes that oppressed people while claiming to defend human rights. You expressed a hope that in the desire to form an Islamic government, so widely supported by Iranians at the time, a true guarantee for these rights could be found. You gave three reasons for this. A spiritual dimension, you said, pervaded the revolt of a people where each one risked everything for an entirely different world. (And for many, this "everything" was neither less nor more than themselves.) It was not the desire to be ruled by a "government of mullahs"—I believe that you indeed used this expression. What I saw, from Tehran to Abadan, did not contradict your words, far from it.

Concerning these rights, you also said that Islam, in its historical profundity and its contemporary dynamism, was capable of facing the formidable challenge that socialism had not addressed any better than capitalism, and that is the least that could be said. "Impossible," some say today, who pretend to know a lot about Islamic societies or about the nature of all religion.[124] I will be a lot more modest than them, not seeing in the name of what universality Muslims could be prevented from seeking their future in an Islam whose new face they will have to shape with their own hands. Concerning the expression "Islamic government," why cast immediate suspicion on the adjective "Islamic"? The word "government" suffices, in itself, to awaken vigilance. No adjective—whether democratic, socialist, liberal, or people's—frees it from its obligations.

You said that by invoking Islam, a government would thereby create important limitations upon its basic sovereignty over civil society, due to obligations grounded in religion. By virtue of its Islamic character, this government would be aware that it was linked to supplementary "obligations." It would also respect these links, because the people could use against the government this very religion that it shares with them. This idea seemed important to me.

Personally, I am somewhat skeptical concerning the extent to which governments will respect their obligations. However, it is good that the governed can rise up to remind everyone that they did not simply give up their rights to the one who governs, but that they are determined to impose obligations on him. No government can escape these fundamental obligations and, from this point of view, the trials taking place today in Iran do not fail to cause concern.

Nothing is more important in the history of a people than the rare moments when it rises up collectively in order to bring down a regime that it no longer supports. On the other hand, nothing is more important for the daily life of a people than those moments, so frequent, when the public authorities turn against an individual, proclaiming him their enemy and deciding to bring him down. Never do the public authorities have more essential obligations that they need to respect than in such moments. Political trials are always the touchstone, not because the accused are never criminals, but because here the public authorities operate without a mask. They submit themselves to judgment when they judge their enemies.

The public authorities always affirm that they need to be respected, and it is precisely here that they must be absolutely respectful. The right of defending the people that the public authorities invoke also gives them very heavy obligations.

It is necessary—and it is urgent—to give the one being prosecuted as many means of defense and as many rights as possible. Is he "obviously guilty"? Does he have the whole of public opinion against him? Is he hated by his people? This, precisely, confers on him rights, all the more intangible ones. It is the obligation of the one who governs to explain and to guarantee them to the accused. For a government, there can be no "vilest of men."

It is also the obligation of every government to show to all—that is, to the most humble, the most obstinate, the most blind of those it governs—under what conditions, how, and in the name of what authority it can claim for itself the right to punish in its name. Even though a punishment that one refuses to explain can be justified, it will still be an injustice, both toward the one who is sentenced and toward all those subject to trial.

Concerning this obligation by a government to submit itself to judgment when it claims to judge, I believe that it must accept it with respect to all men in the world. No more than I do, would I imagine that you would allow a principle of sovereignty that would have to justify itself only to itself. To govern is not self-evident, any more than to sentence, any more than to kill. It is good that a man, any man, even if he is on the other side of the world, can rise to speak because he no longer can stand to see another tortured or condemned. This is not about interfering in the internal affairs of a state. Those who protested on behalf of a single Iranian tortured in the depths of a SAVAK prison were interfering in the most universal matter of all.

Perhaps it will be said that the majority of the Iranian people shows that it has confidence in the regime that is being established and therefore also in its judicial practices. The fact of being accepted, supported, and voted for overwhelmingly does not attenuate the obligations of governments. Rather, it imposes stricter ones on them.

Evidently, Mr. Prime Minister, I do not have any authority to address myself in such a manner to you, except the permission that you gave me, by helping me understand, at our first meeting, that for you, governing is not a coveted right, but an extremely difficult obligation. You have to do what is necessary in order that the people will never regret the uncompromising force with which it has just liberated itself.

Is It Useless to Revolt?

First published on page one of *Le Monde*, May 11–12, 1979.

"To make the shah leave, we are ready to die by the thousands," Iranians said last summer. These days, the ayatollah says, "Let Iran bleed, to make the revolution strong."

There is a strange echo between these sentences, which seem to be linked. Does our horror at the second condemn the intoxication of the first?

Uprisings belong to history, but in a certain way, they escape it. The movement through which a lone man, a group, a minority, or an entire people say, "I will no longer obey," and are willing to risk their lives in the face of a power that they believe to be unjust, seems to me to be irreducible. This is because no power is capable of making it absolutely impossible. Warsaw will always have its ghetto in revolt and its sewers populated with insurgents.[125] The man in revolt is ultimately inexplicable. There must be an uprooting that interrupts the unfolding of history, and its long series of reasons why, for a man "really" to prefer the risk of death over the certainty of having to obey.

All the forms of freedom that are acquired or demanded, all the rights that are claimed, even concerning the things that seem to be of least importance, probably have a last point of anchor here, more solid and experiential than "natural rights." If societies persist and survive, that is to say if power in these societies is not "absolutely absolute," it is because behind all the consent and the coercion, beyond the threats, the violence, and the persuasion, there is the possibility of this moment where life cannot be exchanged, where power becomes powerless, and where, in front of the gallows and the machine guns, men rise up.

Because it is in this way both "outside of history" and in history, because each person stakes his life and his death, one can understand why uprisings have been able to find their expression and their drama so readily in religious forms. For centuries, all of these promises of the hereafter or of the renewal of time, whether they concerned the awaited savior, the kingdom of the last days, or the reign of the absolute good, did not constitute an ideological cloak. Instead, they constituted the very manner in which these uprisings were lived, at least in those places where the religious forms lent themselves to such possibilities.

Then came the age of "revolution." For two centuries, it hung over [*surplombé*][126] history, organized our perception of time, and polarized hopes. The age of revolution has constituted a gigantic effort to acclimate uprisings within a rational and controllable history. "Revolution" gave these uprisings a legitimacy, sorted out their good and bad forms, and defined their laws of development. For uprisings, it established preliminary conditions, objectives, and ways of bringing them to an end. Even the profession of revolutionary was defined. By thus repatriating revolt into the discourse of revolution, it was said, the uprising would appear in all its truth and continue to its true conclusion. This was a marvelous promise. Some will say that the uprising thus found itself colonized by *realpolitik*. Others will say that the dimension of a rational history was opened to it. I prefer the question that Horkheimer used to ask, a naïve question, and a little feverish: "But is it really so desirable, this revolution?"[127]

Concerning the enigma of the uprising, for those who sought in Iran not the "deep reasons" for the movement, but the manner in which it was lived; for those who tried to understand what was going on in the heads of these men and women when they risked their lives, one thing was striking. They inscribed, on the borders of heaven and earth, in a dream-history that was as religious as it was political, all their hunger, their humiliation, their hatred of the regime and their will to bring it down. They confronted the Pahlavis, in a game where each one staked his life and his death, a game that was also about sacrifices and millennial promises. Thus, came the celebrated demonstrations, which played such an important role. These demonstrations could, at the same time, respond concretely to the threat of the army (to the point of paralyzing it), unfold according to the rhythm of religious ceremonies, and finally refer to a timeless drama in which power is always accursed. This drama caused a surprising superimposition to appear in the middle of the twentieth century: a movement strong enough to bring down a seemingly well-armed regime, all the while remaining in touch with the old dreams that were once familiar to the West, when it too wanted to inscribe the figures of spirituality on the ground of politics.

After years of censorship and persecution, with a political class that was strung along, with political parties forbidden, and revolutionary groups decimated, on what, if not on religion, could the disarray and then the revolt of a population traumatized by "development," "reform," "urbanization," and all the other failures of the regime, lean on? This is true, but could the religious element be expected to quickly efface itself for the benefit of more substantial forces and less "archaic" ideologies? Probably not, and for several reasons.

First, there was the movement's quick success, which reinforced the form that it had taken. There was the institutional solidity of a clergy whose hold over the population was strong, and which had strong political ambitions. There was the whole context of the Islamic movement. Because of the strategic positions that Islam occupies, because of the economic importance that the Muslim countries hold, and because of the movement's power to expand on two continents, it constitutes, in the region surrounding Iran, an important and complex reality. As a result, the imaginary content of the revolt did not dissipate in the broad daylight of the revolution. It was immediately transposed onto a political scene that seemed totally willing to receive it but was in fact of an entirely different nature. At this stage, the most important and the most atrocious mingle—the extraordinary hope of remaking Islam into a great living civilization and various forms of virulent xenophobia, as well as the global stakes and the regional rivalries. And the problem of imperialisms. And the subjugation of women, and so on.

The Iranian movement did not experience the "law" of revolutions that would, some say, make the tyranny that already secretly inhabited them reappear underneath the blind enthusiasm of the masses. What constituted the most internal and the most intensely lived part of the uprising touched, in an unmediated fashion, on an already overcrowded political chessboard, but such contact is not identity. The spirituality of those who were going to their deaths has no similarity whatsoever with the bloody government of a fundamentalist clergy. The Iranian clerics want to authenticate their regime through the significations that the uprising had. It is no different to discredit the fact of the uprising on the grounds that there is today a government of mullahs. In both cases, there is "fear," fear of what just happened last fall in Iran, something of which the world had not seen an example for a long time.

Hence, precisely, the necessity of underscoring what is not reducible in such a movement and what is also profoundly threatening for all despotisms, those of today as well as yesterday.

It is certainly not shameful to change one's opinions, but there is no reason to say that one's opinion has changed when one is against hands being chopped off today, after having been against the tortures of the SAVAK yesterday.

No one has the right to say, "Revolt for me, the final liberation of each man hinges on it." But I do not agree with those who would say, "It is useless to revolt, it will always be the same." One does not dictate to those who risk their lives in the face of power. Is it right to rebel, or not? Let us leave this question open. It is a fact that people rise up, and it is through this that a subjectivity (not that of great men, but that of anyone) introduces itself into history and gives it its life. A delinquent puts his life on the line against abusive punishment, a madman cannot stand anymore being closed in and pushed down, or a people rejects a regime that oppresses it. This does not make the first one innocent, does not cure the second, and does not guarantee to the third the results that were promised. No one, by the way, is required to stand in solidarity with them. No one is required to think that these confused voices sing better than others and speak the truth in its ultimate depth. It is enough that they exist and that they have against them all that strives to silence them, to make it meaningful to listen to them and to search for what they want to say. A question of morality? Perhaps. A question of reality, certainly. All the disillusionments of history will not change this. It is precisely because there are such voices that human time does not take the form of evolution, but that of "history."

This is inseparable from another principle. The power that a man exerts over another is always dangerous. I am not saying that power, by nature, is evil. I am saying that power by its mechanisms is infinite (which does not mean that it is all-powerful, on the contrary). The rules limiting it will never be rigorous enough. Universal principles are never strict enough to take away from it all the opportunities that it seizes. Inviolable laws and unrestricted rights must always be opposed to power.

These days, intellectuals do not have a very good "press." I believe that I can use this word in a rather precise manner. Therefore, now is not the time to declare that one is not an intellectual. Besides, it would make you smile. I am an intellectual. If I were asked how I conceive of what I do, here is how I would answer. The strategist is a man who says, "How does this death, this outcry, or this uprising matter in relation to the needs of the whole and to such and such general principle in the particular situation in which we find ourselves?" It is all the same to me if this strategist is a politician, a historian, a revolutionary, or a partisan of the shah or of the ayatollah, for my theoretical ethics are on the opposite side. My ethics are "antistrategic." One must be respectful when a singularity arises and intransigent as soon as the state violates universals. It is a simple choice, but hard work: One needs to watch, a bit underneath history, for what breaks and agitates it, and keep watch, a bit behind politics, over what must unconditionally limit it. After all, this is my work. I am neither the first nor the only one to do it, but I chose it.

Critique of Foucault on Iran

by Maxime Rodinson

First published as the introduction to a reprint (Rodinson 1993a) of his "Khomeini and the 'Primacy of the Spiritual'" (also translated in this appendix, pp. 241–45). The present title was supplied by the translators.

"Khomeini and the 'Primacy of the Spiritual'" was intended as a clarification amid what I thought was a wave of confusion. At any rate, it still bears witness to the atmosphere among the leftist (and sometimes rightist) European and American intelligentsia, during and immediately after the period when the Iranian Revolution toppled the shah under the banner of Shi'ite Islam.

Gradually, as the revolt developed in Iran in 1977 and 1978 (see "Islam Resurgent?" app., 223–38), these leftist intellectuals had turned their attention in this direction, with greater and greater intensity. The hope for a world revolution that would abolish exploitation and the oppression of man by man, for a long time dead or moribund, resurfaced, timidly at first and then with more assurance. Could it have been that this hope now found itself incarnated in the most unexpected way in the Muslim Orient, up to now a not very promising location for it; and more precisely, in this old man lost in a universe of medieval thought?

High-flying intellectuals hurled themselves toward an Iran that was on fire. They wanted to see with their own eyes, to witness then and there this astonishing revolutionary process, to study it and to scrutinize it. Over there, Iranian intellectual friends, or friends of friends, took them in hand.

The latter were intoxicated by a struggle that was making gains every day. Soon, it would be the intoxication of victory. Every day brought new evidence of the mobilizing power of Islamic slogans and of the charisma of the one who embodied them most energetically, Ayatollah Khomeini. Under these slogans, barehanded crowds faced machine-guns and rifles.

Success leads to success. Increasingly, Iranian liberal democrats and Marxists asked themselves whether they had not made a mistake, whether they had not been wrong to dismiss their people's expressions of traditional religious fervor. Gaining more and more confidence in the efficacy of religious slogans, they increasingly sought to read into them at least a form of their own aspirations. They conferred on them a political and social meaning that corresponded to their expectations. They communicated their new confidence to their European visitors, who were impressed and even astonished, and who forced themselves to become familiar as quickly as possible with a mental climate of which they had been profoundly ignorant.

The establishment of the new government in February 1979 only increased the interest of Western intellectuals. Their trips to Iran multiplied, just as did, incidentally, the number of newspaper correspondents on the spot. The Iranian counterparts of these Western intellectuals exulted, intoxicated with their victory, but also found themselves gripped by the whirlwind of struggle and tensions that usually takes place in the aftermath of a revolution. The struggle for power was quickening, according to a most classic process: the effervescence of divergent or opposing ideas, of theses and antitheses, which must quickly lead to physical confrontations in the streets. This is a law.

Among contending forces, the eternal struggle for power often uses as its weapons conceptual tools that have been forged through theoretical virtuosity, whether these tools arose during the struggle or whether they were already there, available for such use. Those who love theory can be moved by the desire to place themselves deliberately in the vanguard, or (more rarely) by purely intellectual inclinations. Their creations are greedily seized upon, especially in this magma, by those who display forms of thought or speech capable of rousing the crowds and leading them to the next level. This convergence of personal ambitions and talents, even of virtuosity in the field of theoretical elaboration, normally produces rift upon rift, split upon split, opposition of options and programs, often very artificially, but often also as an expression of contradictory tendencies suggested in equal measure by one side or the other of social reality.

Alongside or ahead of Khomeini—and here differing with his traditional ideology—Iranian intellectuals had tried to develop a doctrine that was in practice oriented toward European notions of revolution, often socialist ones. At the same time, they integrated into this doctrine formulas that retained, unevenly, a fidelity to the Muslim religion. The sincerity of their attachment to Islam was also very uneven. In Machiavellian fashion, some of them saw, in the Muslim forms that had been retained, first and foremost a way to win the masses over to ideas unfamiliar to them. Others really believed that ideas drawn from European socialist, neo-Marxist, or liberal concepts were implied, even if only potentially and in a specific language that it was necessary to learn and decipher, in the heart of Islam's very foundations, or maybe (here a specifically Iranian variation) in those of Shi'ite Islam.

However, as early as the official inauguration of the new government in Tehran, the form that it took and the decisions that it made gave rise to worries among those who had struggled the most to clear a path for it. Little by little, they decided to communicate their concerns to their European friends. And the latter, moreover, were increasingly shaken by doubts themselves. Less and less could they blind themselves to the struggle for power at the top and its stakes, whose relationship to any ideals was very doubtful. Similarly, they were blinded less and less to the increasingly dangerous trends concerning values they cherished, trends that could be discerned more and more clearly among some of those whose mobilizing power or ascendancy over the controls of the new state was the most powerful, with Ayatollah Khomeini at the top. The ayatollah, who possessed many types of charisma, was not long in revealing completely his leanings toward the darkest forms of cultural archaism; toward traditional methods of government, concealed without very much intellectual honesty by the green coat of Islam; and by his serene indifference to the sufferings caused by his senile stubbornness and his vindictive fury. Writing at the beginning of February 1979 and still being cautious, I evoked Torquemada. These doubts were cleared up all too soon. A sadism that initially used as its alibi the idea of serving the supreme interest of his people or of humanity, or, with greater force, that of an avenging God, or of sending his victims as quickly as possible before divine justice, was increasingly visible in his truncated mental universe. With his blessing, his subordinates quickly rolled up their sleeves, torturing with pleasure the shackled bodies of those who had been imprisoned or condemned to death. A man of religion, Mullah Khalkhali,[128] quickly became an international celebrity in this way, worthy of eclipsing the centuries-old renown of the terrible Spaniard.

But it takes a long time to extinguish hope. For a long while, Iranian intellectuals, including the most open and the most liberal, held onto the conviction that the dynamics of the revolutionary process would end in the triumph of the conceptions that had guided those intellectuals when it began.

Philosophically formed minds, even and perhaps especially the most eminent, are among the most vulnerable to the seductions of theoretical slogans, which they can easily flesh out with magnificently elaborated justifications, with operations of dazzling profundity, taking advantage of their familiarity with the works of the great Occidental professionals of abstraction, from Plato onward. They are all the more vulnerable to this temptation because they have, professionally so to speak, a tendency to minimize the obstacles and the objections that stubborn reality places in the way of conceptual constructs.

A very great thinker, Michel Foucault, part of a line of radically dissident thought, placed excessive hopes in the Iranian Revolution. The great gaps in his knowledge of Islamic history enabled him to transfigure the events in Iran, to accept for the most part the semitheoretical suggestions of his Iranian friends, and to extrapolate from this by imagining an end of history that would make up for disappointments in Europe and elsewhere.

Observing in 1978 the "immense pressure from the people" that was exploding, justly doubting the explanations and prognostications of the secular and liberal Iranian "politicians" for whom Khomeini represented a mere epiphenomenon that the anticipated fall of the shah would allow to be pushed aside, Foucault went to make contact with Iran itself, going to Tehran and Qom in the days immediately following the great upheavals. Avoiding the "professional politicians," he passionately and sometimes for long periods of time conducted interviews with "religious leaders, students, and intellectuals interested in the problems of Islam, and also with former guerrilla fighters who had abandoned the armed struggle in 1976 and had decided to conduct their operations in a totally different fashion, inside the traditional society" (see "What Are the Iranians Dreaming About?" app., 205).

Most of his interlocutors, chosen in this way, spoke to him not of "revolution," but of "Islamic government." What did this signify? With good will, Foucault welcomed and repeated the explanations that liberal interpreters gave him, as in the case of Ayatollah Shariatmadari (see "Iranians Dreaming," app., 205). Already, in the beginning, Foucault said, "One thing must be clear. By 'Islamic government,' nobody in Iran means a political regime in which the clerics would have a role of supervision or control" (206). Apparently, Foucault had never heard of the theory already put forward by Khomeini at least thirty-four years ago, the *Velayat-i Faqih* (in Arabic *Wilayat al-Faqih*), which is the theory that the clerics are capable of governing.

It is necessary to recognize that Foucault received with some skepticism the "formulas from everywhere and nowhere" that were proposed to him concerning the deep meaning of the term "Islamic government": respect for the fruit of each one's labor, individual liberties, equality of the sexes, and so forth. It was explained to him that these were the ideas proposed at the outset by the Quran (a mythical representation strongly internalized and one that those oriented toward Islamism have heard a thousand times), of which the West had lost the meaning, but "Islam will know how to preserve their value and their efficacy" ("Iranians Dreaming," app., 207, 206).

Foucault felt embarrassed to speak of Islamic government as an "idea" or even an "ideal." But the slogan of an Islamic government seemed to express a "political will" that impressed him. According to him, it concerned, on the one hand, an effort to give the traditional structures of Islamic society (as they appeared in Iran) a permanent role in political life. He was given the example of grassroots associations that had formed spontaneously under religious direction, which had taken upon themselves social initiatives, as in the reconstruction of a town destroyed by an earthquake. On the other hand, and in another way, it expressed, here under the inspiration of Ali Shariati, a movement to introduce a spiritual dimension into the political, "in order that this political life would not be, as always, the obstacle to spirituality, but rather its receptacle, its opportunity, its ferment" ("Iranians Dreaming," app., 208, 207).[129]

Undeniably, the tendencies that Foucault uncovered existed at the heart of the Iranian revolutionary movement of the period. With a return to prudence, he asked himself if this "political will" was strong enough to be able, on the one hand, to prevent the establishment of a regime of compromise—conservative, parliamentary, and partially secular, with the shah maintained—or, on the other hand, to establish itself as a permanent fixture in the political life of Iran.

Only a little time passed before a positive response was given to the French philosopher's first question. He must have been very happy. But the course of events made an affirmative response to the second question more and more doubtful. At the very least, perhaps due to the deep-rootedness of his sentiments, Foucault wanted to announce the introduction of satisfactory political and social measures toward a humanist ideal,[130] due to the workings of the "political spirituality" in question.

Multiple cases of political spirituality have existed. All came to an end very quickly. Generally, they subordinated their earthly ideals, assumed in the beginning to flow from a spiritual or ideal orientation, to the eternal laws of politics, in other words the struggle for power. This is how I tried to respond to Foucault, already more or less implicitly in the article in *Le Monde* reprinted above ("Islam Resurgent?" app., 223–38), and then in a more precise and specific manner in the article in *Le Nouvel Observateur* ("Khomeini and the 'Primacy of the Spiritual,'" app., 241–45). Naturally, these articles made much less of an impression on Foucault than did the events in Iran, which markedly lowered his hopes. In April 1979, he decided to write to the head of the Iranian government, at that time Mehdi Bazargan. His "open letter" was published in *Le Nouvel Observateur* on Saturday, April 14 ("Open Letter," app., 260–63).

The philosopher rightly complained of the summary trials and the hasty executions that were increasing in revolutionary Iran, which had been proclaimed the Islamic Republic on April 2, following a plebiscite-referendum. He reminded Bazargan of their conversations in Qom in September 1978. At that time, Bazargan had explained to Foucault that the drive toward an Islamic government in Iran would truly guarantee fundamental human rights.

The unfortunate Mehdi Bazargan could only agree with Michel Foucault's complaints and worries. But despite his position as head of government, he had almost no power to correct the abuses and atrocities taking place in his country.

The "political spirituality" that had inspired the revolutionary movement—covering over the more material motives for the discontent and the revolt—had at a very early stage shown that it operated by no means in the humanist sense that had been attributed to it, very naively, by Foucault and Bazargan. One can mobilize the masses with ideas. However those who guide, orient, shepherd, or block the routes taken by this mobilization are people, and can only be people. Those who in the eyes of the masses seem to best embody this idea of protest and of restoration are those who, at least in the beginning, acquire the most power. Too bad if they use it poorly; too bad if they are fools, ignoramuses, those who have lost their way, or sadists; too bad if they are Torquemadas; too bad if they are Khomeinis.

The aftermath of revolution always favors the institution of a dual power. On the one hand, institutions framing the people's daily life continue to function in the old way, or are reformed, or new ones are put in place. On the other hand, the people and the structures that led the movement continue to benefit from a charisma that remains in effect for a long time. They cannot, at least for a while, simply be cast into the shadows. Quite often even, as in the case of Iran, their influence continues for a long time. Religious charisma reveals itself to be much more effective than all types of secular charisma.[131]

As happens in a lot of similar situations, an intense effervescence welled up from the depths of Iranian society. Individuals and groups that formulated different interpretations of the revolution—consequently envisaging, proposing, and advocating divergent paths to prolong it—multiplied rapidly. As usual, a cleavage separated the partisans of "everything is now possible," those who demanded radical measures in the direction of the objectives proclaimed at the time of the movement's development, from those who raised as an objection the necessities imposed by economic and political reality, both internationally and nationally. As is also customary, another cleavage, not exactly along the same lines, opposed those who invoked limitations due to humanistic and/or religious morality to those who scorned the latter in order to go all the way in their persecution, repression, and massacre of yesterday's enemy, whether due to simple feelings of hatred and vengeance, to personal interest, or to rational calculation: "Only the dead do not return," "No freedom for the enemies of freedom."

Revolutionary committees were set up throughout Iran—exacting, ordering, and repressing. But the spontaneity of the masses is never anything but a guided spontaneity. A revolt in the name of religion automatically gives special authority to clerics. No matter what the ideologues and their naive friends from the "stupid West" said, the Iranian clerics were for the most part conservative and even retrograde.

And it was above all Khomeini who supported them. The Revolutionary Council, whose composition was never officially revealed, supposedly for security reasons, was a lot more powerful than the Council of Ministers. The former convened in Qom, presided over by Khomeini. The old ayatollah, whose directives inspired this council and the primary revolutionary organizations—the Islamic Committees [*Komiteh*] and the Revolutionary Guards—was increasingly designated as the "imam." The term has many meanings and can designate, for example, the humble believer who, in advance of the others (the Arabic root expresses the idea of an anterior position) directs the gestures of the Muslim prayers several times a day. But in Shi'ite lands, one thinks irresistibly of the Prophet's descendent who exercises the right to function as the mystical leader of the community. For the Twelver branch of Shi'ism [*Ithna Ahshari*] that prevails in Iran, the twelfth of this lineage mysteriously disappeared toward the end of our ninth century. Dead or simply absent and supernaturally "occulted," he must reappear at the end of time in order to bring back, to an earth drenched in sin, the radiant period of the golden age just before the Last Judgment. The ambiguity that is maintained concerning the status of Khomeini, earlier promoted to ayatollah by his peers as a favor in order to shelter him from the shah's anger,[132] allowed the masses to attribute to him the supernatural powers of the mythical Savior.

His public proclamations, which settled the differences among multiple spiritual authorities, were also decisive. Generally, these proclamations leaned toward severity, cruelty, and archaism. In March 1979, Bazargan succeeded in obtaining from the imam the suspension of all trials and summary executions. But this pause lasted a very short time, and the trials and executions recommenced in April on an even greater scale, after the referendum.

Women, compelled to wear the specifically Iranian-style veil (the *chador*), forced into subordination and segregation, were less and less able to renew their March demonstrations in Tehran. Khomeini, who had to some extent hidden his opinions from Western journalists before taking power, covered the most archaic interpretations of traditional morality under the sacred cloak of Islam. It was useless to counterpose less constraining traditions to those he articulated. Even if they were his peers in the religious apparatus, his critics were increasingly silenced and pushed into retirement. It was already enough that Khomeini's need to conserve his prestige within the clergy allowed them to avoid torture and death.

The intolerant old mullah used the sacred texts. He both refrained from giving them an always-possible liberal interpretation and denounced the interpretations that had been in favor during preceding eras. Traditionally,[133] Christians and Jews (excluding militant Zionists) had been permitted certain rights and "protections," as second-class citizens. But supporters of the universalistic, innovating, ecumenical, and syncretic Baha'i religion, already discriminated against during the period of the shah, were now atrociously persecuted. Arguments of an anti-imperialist type were added to justify this persecution: the ties of some prosperous Baha'i businessmen with Western business and the fact that the chance operation of the vicissitudes of politics had placed the tomb of the founder, who died in 1892, on Israeli soil. These points were enough to win the support of many Western, far-left zealots.

Providentially for the imam, the ethnic minorities, which expressed autonomist claims to some degree, generally adhered to Sunnism, the other branch of Islam. This made it possible, in the name of patriotism, to create an identity between, on the one hand, upholding Persian-speaking, ethnic Iranian hegemony by force of arms, and on the other, support for the cause of "true Islam," in other words, Shi'ism.

Let us come back to the revealing open letter Michel Foucault addressed to Mehdi Bazargan, six months before the latter was definitively forced to offer the resignation of his government. It was "a knife without a blade," as Bazargan himself put it. The French philosopher refused to lose hope in the tenor of the possibilities that the Iranian politician had expressed to him the year before: "Concerning these rights, . . . Islam, in its historical profundity and in its contemporary dynamism, was capable of facing the formidable challenge that socialism had not addressed any better than capitalism, and that is the least that could be said" ("Open Letter," app., 261). Foucault added: "'Impossible,' some say today, who pretend to know a lot about Islamic societies or about the nature of all religion. I will be a lot more modest than them, not seeing in the name of what universality Muslims could be prevented from seeking their future in an Islam whose new face they will have to shape with their own hands. Concerning the expression 'Islamic government,' why cast immediate suspicion on the adjective 'Islamic'? The word 'government' suffices, in itself, to awaken vigilance" (261).

Indeed. But the "modesty" of the philosopher, so confident nonetheless of the value of his reason, is not the same as the modesty of the empirical specialist, whether historian, anthropologist, or sociologist. A philosopher should not exclude any possibility. Any factor unknown until now could have the same result as putting water on intense heat and its refusing to boil. The man or woman on the street, like the physicist, would rather rely on an experiment multiplied billions of times and on a studied analysis of the transformation of liquids into gases.

To the extent that I was myself the target of Foucault's open letter, I will respond that if I cast suspicion on the adjective "Islamic," it was the same thing concerning every adjective that denoted an attachment to an ideal doctrine, whether religious or secular. If the word "government" must by itself, as he precisely explained, arouse vigilance, it was even more correct on his part to say that "no adjective—whether democratic, socialist, liberal, or people's—frees it from its obligations" ("Open Letter," app., 261).

But if nothing allowed one to think that the adjective "Islamic" had less liberatory import than another adjective, nothing demonstrated either that it had more. Why, therefore, did Foucault not add adjectives such as "Christian," "Buddhist," "Jewish," "Islamic," and so on—in short, spiritual adjectives—to those that he was enumerating? Did he suppose that these terms referred only to a governmental structure impermeable to the usual vicissitudes of power?

A government that militantly proclaims itself Christian, Buddhist, Jewish, Islamic, and so on surely extols "political spirituality," an expression that this time Foucault is very careful not to repeat. Of course, it is Foucault who presupposes that such labels render the states to which they are applied magically capable of faithfully meeting the obligations to which the doctrine they venerate should commit them.

It is not we who, under the effect of some hidden anti-Muslim inclination, brushed aside the possibility (in reality, slight) that an Islamic government, as well as other so-called "spiritual" governments, could meet at least some of these obligations. Here, there was a slightly demagogic and accommodating wink at the Muslim states, at a time when the halo of the Algerian Revolution was marked with a sacred tint for the whole Far Left.

The philosopher's sarcasms about his adversaries' knowledge and their vain immodesty can only serve to mask a very clear fact. It is not necessary to have great familiarity, if not with the essence of religion ("the nature of all religion" ["Open Letter," app., 261], according to Foucault's very essentialist formulation), at least with the sociological facts concerning religion, with the history of religion, and even with the history of Islam, in order to understand that all of these "political spiritualities" escape only rarely from the usual laws of political struggle.

Spurred on by his political passions, Foucault, in many ways a brilliant and penetrating thinker, yielded to the banal and vulgar conception of the spiritual that had been declared taboo by virtue of millennia of forced deference. This is because he was interested in entirely different issues and shrank from questioning the foundations of a dissident fideism. It is also for this reason, I think, that elsewhere he diluted the notion of power, undermining the concept of political power by drowning it in a constellation of other powers, of micro-powers well-distanced from the extremely effective means that political power has at its disposal.

A few months later, history settled the question. It was more and more difficult to find people who were convinced that the Iranian Revolution had overcome, or was on a path toward overcoming, the oppressive potentialities of political power, or that it was on a path toward realizing an ideal, harmonious, and humane society.

Undoubtedly, the skepticism concerning the Iranian Revolution even went too far. Khomeini will die one day (written in 1988—he died on June 3, 1989), and his unfortunate influence will at least be weakened. The struggles for power, now very visible, at the heart of the corps of mullahs and beyond, will end by bringing to the top personalities who will not risk being more irrational and barbarous than this founding figure. One day, sooner or later, the deep-seated forces of Iranian civil society will insist on seeing their aspirations taken into account to a far greater extent than is allowed by oppressive frameworks in the grip of stultified tradition. During the period when Europe began to influence Iran, these aspirations became enriched with deep humanistic demands that were forgotten during periods of resignation. They are still alive. It is in neither the Quran nor the Sunna, no matter what one may think, that Khomeini found the inspiration to organize elections and to adopt a constitution. He was conscious, despite everything, that it was necessary to have the appearance of representativeness, in order to appease popular feelings.

Even under his regime, deep-seated reality created, at limited points, powerful pressures toward the adoption of reasonable measures. Some mullahs, placed in positions of responsibility, acquired technical competence and became successful administrators. To be sure, we are a long distance from the excessive hopes of Foucault, Bazargan, and those Iranians oriented toward freedom and progress. The human catastrophes were considerable. The old ayatollah sacrificed millions of Iranians, especially the youth, in a war he did not ask for, but also refused to end. (The war with Iraq ended in July 1988.)

What can one conclude, except that history continues, no matter what ideal banners the rulers brandish?

Finally, it is necessary to say that a whole sector of world opinion did not lose hope in the virtues of the Islamic Revolution. It is a question of millions of Muslims, Sunnis, and Shi'ites, who were influenced little by the unpleasant news put forth about Islamic Iran. Who spreads this news, if not journalists, press agents, and methods of mass dissemination controlled by Westerners, the developed world, the rich and powerful, those toward whom their resentment as poor and humiliated people is directed? Why have faith in them? Why not prefer the propaganda that comes from Tehran? Why not believe that the victims for whom the West is crying are conspirators, yesterday's well-to-do, now furious about their dispossession, perverse and harmful beings who oppose the founding of a new world of light; in short, enemies of God?

Those who, like the author of these lines, refused for so long to believe the reports about the crimes committed in the name of the triumphant socialism in the former Tsarist Empire, in the terrible human dramas resulting from the Soviet Revolution, would exhibit bad grace if they became indignant at the incredulity of the Muslim masses before all the spots that one asks them to see on the radiant sun of their hope.

Michel Foucault is not contemptible for not having wanted to create despair in the Muslim world's shantytowns and starving countryside, for not having wanted to disillusion them, or for that matter, to make them lose hope in the worldwide importance of their hopes. His immense philosophical talent contributed to this. As for me, I have always believed that more lucidity can be found in singers than in philosophers. I would rather find a conclusion in two lines of the good Communard Eugène Pottier, impregnated moreover with a blind confidence in the capacity of so-called spontaneous mass movements to translate their ideas into reality:

> It is not from a supreme Savior,
> Nor God, nor Caesar, nor Tribune.[134]

Millions of men and women enamored of justice have sung these lines and yielded to the unjustified confidence that the words expressed; this was truly the root of the problem. I see many who are beginning to understand that when the mullah, even if imbued with lofty, divine thoughts, enters the political process, he is never but a particular case of the Tribune.[135]

Notes

Introduction

1. In keeping with the current practice of most scholars of Islam and the Middle East, we have usually used the term "Islamism" to designate a number of more fundamentalist versions of Islam, as found in Khomeini's movement, the Afghan mujahedeen, and similar movements that have proliferated over the past three decades. The phrase "Islamic fundamentalism," used more commonly in journalistic accounts, has the advantage of making an obvious and sharp distinction between these versions of Islam and other more tolerant ones, while also allowing comparisons to other forms of religious fundamentalism, whether Christian, Hindu, or Jewish. However, "fundamentalism," which originated a century ago as a description of Protestant revivalism, has the decisive disadvantage of evoking a tendency by believers to return to the original sacred texts, supposedly unencumbered by interpretation. This is never the case with Islamism, whose adherents follow not only the original texts, but also a body of interpretation, much of it very recent. Another phrase sometimes used by scholars is "militant Islam," but this implies that the Islamists are merely advocating more forcefully what all Muslims believe, thus minimizing the distinction between Islamism and other versions of Islam.

2. See the appendix. All material included there is cited in this form in the text; "app." signifies the appendix to this volume.

3. Shortly before his death, Foucault spoke of plans for a new book on "technologies of the self." For his various essays between 1978 and 1984 on this issue, see Carrette 1999 and Martin, Gutman, and Hutton 1988.

4. Unless otherwise indicated, in-text translations from French or Persian sources are by the authors.

5. However, Cohen's attempt in this article to show that Michael Hardt and Antonio Negri's *Empire* (2000) also embraced militant Islamism is not very convincing. Tjark Kunstreich (2004) also paints with too broad a brush, while making some valid links to Heidegger's concept of authenticity.

6. We would like to thank Michael Löwy for helping us to clarify this point.

7. Georg Stauth (1991) has written that, rather than supporting the Iranian Islamists, Foucault was merely analyzing their movement (see also Olivier and Labbé 1991). Another Foucault supporter, Keating, pointed out that "Foucault turned out to be horribly wrong about the Iranian Revolution," but that, nonetheless, his Iran writings offered something important. This was because they revealed a "largely unarticulated theory of resistance" (Keating 1997, 181, 182). For very helpful critical analyses of the relationship of Foucault's thought to matters of cultural alterity involving Japan, Iran, and Islam, see Fuyuki Kurasawa (1999) and Ian Almond (2004).

Chapter 1

1. Of course, as discussed below, both Foucault and the Islamists deployed numerous elements of modernity. For the Islamists, this meant utilizing all the levers of power of a modern state after the revolution.

2. Two decades earlier, the neo-Marxist Herbert Marcuse expressed a somewhat similar view in his *Eros and Civilization*: "There is no freedom from administration and its laws because they appear as the ultimate guarantors of liberty. The revolt against them would be the supreme crime again—this time not against the despotic animal who forbids gratification but against the wise order which secures the goods and services for the progressive satisfaction of human needs. Rebellion now appears as the crime against the whole of human society and therefore as beyond reward and beyond redemption. However, the very progress of civilization tends to make this rationality a spurious one. The existing liberties and the existing gratifications are tied to the requirements of domination; they themselves become instruments of repression." Unlike Foucault, Marcuse believed that the system maintained itself through the manipulation of the individual's consciousness, including the promotion of "thoughtless leisure activities" and a relaxation of sexual taboos (1962, 85–86).

3. Foucault adopts two seemingly contradictory attitudes toward the concept of silence in volume 1 of the *History of Sexuality*. In one place, as above, he praises the premodern culture of silence, "where secrets of sex are not forced out" (1978a, 59), in contrast to the "regime of truth" established after the seventeenth century in Europe. In another place, however, he criticizes the silence imposed upon children concerning their own sexuality in the modern era, which results in parents and educators speaking *for* children in such matters (27). What he misses is that premodern silences are also imposed and forced, especially on women.

4. Michael Gillespie makes a valuable point when he writes that Heidegger's rejection of categorical reason in favor of pure intuitionism runs the danger of "mistaking the subrational for the suprarational" (1984, 174).

5. As we will see below, Foucault did explore the regulation of fertility in the West and the racist views about genetics and colonized peoples that accompanied it. Here again, his emphasis was on the West.

6. Foucault often leaves out facts that could undermine his thesis. For example, he does not mention that after the French Revolution, the penal code of 1791 decriminalized homosexuality and only recognized one type of sexual crime, the rape of a woman. France thus became the first European country to abrogate antisodomy laws. This did not mean

that all of the penalties against homosexuality disappeared, let alone the stigma attached to it (Sibalis 1996). The same penal code also removed some of the sanctions against suicide, even though leaders of the French Revolution condemned suicide and regarded the body of a suicide as the property of the state.

7. The new emphasis on the written word and the shift away from the spoken word had a gendered subtext as well. The spoken word now became "merely the female part of language." The active intellect was associated with writing, and the passive intellect, with speaking. "Writing was the 'male principle' of language" and contained the "Truth" (Foucault 1973, 39). Luce Irigaray and other post-structuralist French feminists have developed this point further.

8. For a probing critique of the empirical, historical, and scientific assumptions and observations of Foucault, which shows that his chronology was off by a century in most cases, see Rousseau 1972–73.

9. Foucault's relationship to Marxism, perhaps the dominant perspective of French intellectuals from the late 1940s to the mid-1970s, should also be mentioned in the context of his Iran writings. While he had briefly joined the Communist Party in his youth, by 1966 Foucault was writing about Marx's limitations in *The Order of Things*: "Marxism exists in nineteenth century thought like a fish in water: that is, unable to breathe anywhere else" (1973, 261). Jean-Paul Sartre, who had declared himself a Marxist a decade earlier, launched an attack on Foucault, accusing him of "rejection of history" and being trapped in a structuralist "succession of immobilities," calling the argument in his book "the last resort the bourgeoisie can enact against Marx" (cited in Macey 1993, 175). However, such public polemics masked more subtle affinities between Foucault's thought and some varieties of Marxism, at least through the 1970s. This is because the division among postwar French intellectuals between humanists and antihumanists was probably as important as that between Marxists and non-Marxists. On the humanist side, both existentialist and Marxist, stood Sartre, Simone de Beauvoir, Henri Lefebvre, and Lucien Goldmann, while on the antihumanist side, the side of Foucault, one found structuralists and post-structuralists like Claude Lévi-Strauss, Gilles Deleuze, Jacques Lacan, Louis Althusser, and Pierre Bourdieu. (For discussions, see Dosse 1991–92 and Anderson 1995.) Foucault retained some ties to Althusserian Marxism until at least 1977, when he began to attack and dismiss the Marxist notion of ideology, because in his view it implied not only a rigid dichotomy between truth and falsehood, but also "something of the order of a subject" (1977b, 60) This statement was a rejection not only of Marxism in general, but specifically of Althusserianism, which Foucault now pronounced guilty of the very concept that Althusser had labored so hard to remove from Marxism, subjectivity. (For a study of how newer structuralist and post-structuralist thinkers have tended to accuse previous ones of still holding onto forms of humanism and the subject, see Soper 1986.) In Foucault's 1978–79 Iran writings, one can discern the implicit use of the Marxist concepts of class or imperialism, even amid the explicit rejection of Marxism as a modernist ideology. For a more general exploration of implicit Marxist dimensions in Foucault's thought, including the many places he used Marx without naming him, see Paolucci 2003.

10. Diamond and Quinby suggest another point of convergence in that both feminism and Foucault criticize the claims to universalism in the proclamations of the Western male elite on truth, freedom, and human nature (1988, ix–xxii). However, we have

argued that Foucault's discourse can also be regarded as a metanarrative, one that attempts to compete with the Enlightenment tradition and establishes its own rituals of truth.

11. On this point, our thanks to Nancy J. Holland for her unpublished paper "Truth as Force: Michel Foucault on Religion, State Power and the Law."

12. In addition, MacCannell and MacCannell reject Foucault's notion that technologies of power are neutral and "can be open to all even when [they] appear to be held by a few." Instead they point out that those who exercise power have historically presented themselves as neutral in order to "justify their use of violence" (1993, 204). They also take issue with Foucault's view that we are experiencing a historical decline in physical violence, which is being replaced by a capillary power, a power that operates at the minute levels of the body and is internalized by the subject. Instead, they suggest that violence has not subsided and that when the subject offers resistance to legal, penal, administrative, or patriarchal powers, violence is sure to follow (212).

13. Foucault rejects the Freudian notion that a prudish and repressive morality was dominant in Europe before the twentieth century. Instead, he argues that since the seventeenth century, there has been a near-explosion of discourses on the subject of sex (1978a, 17–35). Roy Porter takes issue with Foucault here, noting that a lot of talk about sex does not mean equal access to the discourse of sex. Porter, who was writing in the 1980s in the midst of the anti-apartheid movement, brings an example from his time. He points out that we could not say South African blacks were not oppressed just because there was "so much talk about freedom in South Africa." Foucault does not tell us "*who* was permitted to say *what*, and *who* was prohibited and dissuaded from saying *what*, and *who* had *what* kinds of powers to enforce the taboos" (1991, 67).

14. Both Kate Soper (1993) and Amy Richlin comment on the tone of this section. Richlin mocks Foucault's sympathetic portrait of the farmer and points out that the subject positions of the little girl and her guardians are entirely left out of Foucault's account. She adds sarcastically that a clearer statement than the bucolic expression "playing the familiar game called 'curdled milk'" would have been to say "he obtained what is commonly known as a 'hand job'" (1998, 141).

15. This will be discussed in chapter 5. Ann Stoler also points to an unexplored implication of Foucault's discourse for colonized societies. European parents, especially those living in the colonies, feared sexual relations between their children and their servants. In the colonies it was not just sexual desire for native bodies that they feared, but personal and political identification with the native culture (1995, 159).

16. This issue remains hotly contested in gay and lesbian studies. The notion that sexuality is socially constructed has become widely accepted. At the same time, social and legal recognition for a homosexual lifestyle (marriage, child custody, inheritance) remains high on the agenda of gay, lesbian, bisexual, and transgender (GLBT) activists. Significant victories have been achieved in certain countries in this arena, a direction that during his lifetime Foucault neither pursued nor supported (Nye 1996). Foucault, of course, was not the only one who advocated such a polymorphism at the time. Herbert Marcuse (1962) did something similar. Part of the conflict between the feminist movement of the early 1970s and this type of sexual politics, advocated in the 1960s, was that these masculinist forms of sexual liberation proved not so liberating for women.

17. The novelist Maurice Clavel, a friend of Foucault, suggested that the "man whose death was proclaimed in *Les Mots et les choses* [The order of things] was 'man without God'" (cited in Carrette 1999, 15).

18. Up to a point, this was correct. Thomas Aquinas wrote of the human being's "natural inclination to virtue," which was of course corruptible by "sin." However, Aquinas deemed homosexuality to be against nature, a "perversion [that] stood in need of correction" (1953, 41, 52).

19. Foucault's criticism of psychoanalysis is quite nuanced. He recognizes, for example, Freud's challenge to biologically based racist theories (Foucault 1978a, 150), but he does not acknowledge the extent to which many of his own ideas were initially raised by Freud. For example, Freud readily acknowledged that human beings had an "unmistakably bisexual disposition" (Freud 1989, 61), that civilization normalized human sexuality, that child sexuality was suppressed, that polymorphous forms of sexuality were prohibited, that all sexual activity was channeled into heterosexual, monogamous relations, and that this constituted a tremendously damaging psychological trauma resulting in neurosis. Unlike Foucault, Freud believed that such restrictions were a necessary price to be paid in order to establish modern civilization, to attain a measure of peace and security, and to control the aggressive drives.

20. For another discussion of Freud and Foucault, see Stoler 1995. Earlier, Nietzsche had intoned against "that will toward self-tormenting, that repressed cruelty of the animal-man made inward and scared back into himself, the creature imprisoned in the 'state' so as to be tamed" (1967, 92).

21. Recently, some scholars have attributed *Disasters* to Goya's son, but the evidence is inconclusive.

22. For a discussion of the visual representation of these symbolic roles, see Chelkowski and Dabashi 1999.

Chapter 2

1. On July 13, 2002, a Shi'ite passion play, or Ta'ziyeh, was performed at Lincoln Center in New York. The performance was preceded by a daylong conference on "Ta'ziyeh: Performing Iran's Living Epic Tradition," at the Asia Society and Museum, with leading scholars in the fields of performance and Iranian studies. This chapter has benefited from the performance and the papers at these events.

2. A few years after the revolution, these same newspapers were filled with pictures of martyrs who had lost their lives in the jails of the Islamic Republic. Even Iranian student organizations in the United States drew their political legitimacy from the number of martyrs they had given to the cause. On these issues see especially Abrahamian 1999.

3. The phrase "the Karbala paradigm," used below, was coined by Michael Fischer (1980).

4. Shi'ites of Iran also refer to designated leaders of the Friday prayers as *imam jom'eh*. In Sunni Islam, the term *imam* is used more routinely and can refer to any high cleric (Richard 1995, 27–29).

5. *The Garden of the Martyrs* (Rowzat al-Shohada) was one of the first such accounts

in the Persian language and was written by Va'ez Kashefi (d. 1504/1505), who was actually a Sunni Muslim (Momen 1985, 118–19).

6. Self-flagellation in public, with chains and other sharp instruments that draw blood, is an exclusively male tradition. Women beat their chests rhythmically at indoor *rowzeh khvani* gatherings of Muharram, but their shedding of blood is abhorred (Hegland 1983).

7. For the best discussion of these rituals in Iran, see Chelkowski 1979. For a treatment of Muharram in India see Pinault 1992. For a fascinating discussion of the evolution of Muharram processions into "Hosay" festivals in Trinidad, see Thaiss 1994.

8. The first month of the Jewish calendar is called Tishri, and the tenth day of this month is Yom Kippur, a day of observance and fasting. The tenth day of the first month of the Muslim calendar (Muharram) is Ashura; hence the suggestion that there is a Jewish origin for the Shi'ite Muslim holiday.

9. When the actors move on the stage in a straight line, they are performing in real time, but when they circle the platform (often mounted on horses), they are traveling long distances (Beeman 2002).

10. Mary Hegland describes the situation in Peshawar, Pakistan, where Shi'ite women were unable to voice resistance through direct verbal discourse, but "they developed and expressed gender resistance implicitly through the body and specifically through its engagement in ritual activity." In this way "women formed, transformed, and subtly contested, meaning, identity and gender" (Hegland 1998, 242, 252).

11. Our thanks to Ahmad Sadri for this information.

12. In the Qajar period, young girls under the age of maturity were given certain minor roles in the play. The princess Qamar al-Saltaneh and other elite women of the harem sponsored Ta'ziyeh performances in which women played the lead roles, and male eunuchs played the musical instruments. Women characters appeared without the veil in these "women only" performances; they carried swords and rode on horses, and also played the "lead male characters in drag and with applied facial hair" (Mottahedeh 2002).

13. Many religious leaders criticize over-zealous acts of self-flagellation. For the clergy's reasons for sanctioning such rituals, see Mahjub 1979, 151.

14. Hegland also points out that in the course of the Iranian Revolution this interpretation of Hussein as "intercessor" lost ground to a new one that called for viewing Hussein as an "example" of courage, bravery, and defiance of death (Hegland 1983, 221).

15. Here, as in many other areas of his work, Foucault reverses Freud, who had regarded public penance as an "original infantile stage of [individual] conscience" and human civilization (Freud 1989, 88). But, as mentioned before, it would be wrong to assume that Foucault's project is entirely hostile to psychoanalysis. Also, Foucault's interest in nonverbal rituals is not so far from Kristeva's discussion of semiotics (Kristeva 1997).

16. Throughout the play, the performers reach out to the audience. They call on God to intercede on behalf of those who are sick, have a weakness, or wish to make a vow. Often one of the actors circulates a large bag among members of the audience, who are asked to write their vows on a piece of paper and drop it in the bag (with some money). It is hoped that Hussein will carry these vows to his maker after his (imaginary) death in the play.

17. Needless to say, there are also some differences, since Christians regard Jesus as divine, while Shi'ites consider Hussein a mortal designated by God as the leader of the community (Browne 1956, 4:172–94).

18. Some royalist sources have even suggested that he was financially supported by Nasser and other opponents of the shah (Hashemi 1994).

19. Estimates of the dead have varied. The Islamists published the names of four martyrs, but claimed that several thousand had died. The government admitted that eighty-six people were killed, and the U.S. Embassy estimated the number at around two hundred (Cottam 1988, 129).

20. This book has some resemblance to Frantz Fanon's *Black Skin, White Masks: The Experiences of a Black Man in a White World* (1967). Like Fanon, Al-Ahmad linked indigenous men's intermarriage with white Europeans to a desire to adopt Western culture. However, Al-Ahmad remained oblivious to what Fanon, in another book, *Wretched of the Earth*, famously termed "the pitfalls of national consciousness" (1968, 148). Al-Ahmad also singled out Western scholars of the Orient for harsh criticism and regarded them as agents of imperialism, somewhat in the manner of Edward Said's later *Orientalism*. Several English translations of his book exist, with the title sometimes translated as "Westoxication." On the influence of Western philosophy, including that of Heidegger, in Iran in this period, see Boroujerdi 1996 as well as Gheissari 1998; Mirsepassi 2000; and Vahdat 2002.

21. Another writer who helped construct a new narrative about Muharram was Khomeini's student Ne'matollah Salehi Najafabadi. His *Shahid-i Javid* (Eternal martyr) created heated debates in Iran's religious circles. At the end of his account of Karbala, Najafabadi concluded: (1) Rulers who impose an illegal (un-Islamic) form of government on their people must be opposed. (2) This should be done in consultation with the people, and with adequate military preparation. (3) If military victory is not possible, then the righteous leaders must wait until such time when they have the proper force to propagate true Islam. (4) If the leader of the rebellion is surrounded by the enemy, then he should fight back, and even face martyrdom, rather than submit to a humiliating death (Najafabadi 1982, 361–66). As can be seen from the above, the language of the lay theologian Shariati was much harsher.

22. Already in 1970, a series of his lectures had appeared under the title "Islamic Government," wherein he presented the outlines of an Islamic theocracy and his theory of *Velayat-i Faqih* (Rule of the Jurists). Drawing on the earlier Usuli principles of Shi'ism, which claimed legal and religious authority for the *mojtahed* (high-ranking clerics), Khomeini stated in unequivocal terms that "it was the duty of the religious scholar to establish an Islamic government" (Khomeini 1970, 37).

Chapter 3

1. On gender and culture in twentieth-century Iran see Sanasarian 1982; Vatandoust 1985; Haeri 1989; Kar 1987; Moghadam 1991; Tohidi 1991; Friedl 1991; Najmabadi 1993; Paidar 1995; Moghissi 1996; Matin-Daftari 2001; and Afkhami 2002.

2. For studies of the Constitutional Revolution, see Martin 1989; Bayat 1991; and Afary 1996. On its impact on European diplomacy, see Bonakdarian 1991.

3. For an overview of the Reza Shah period, see Banani 1961 and Niyazmand 1996. On military reforms in this period see Cronin 1997. For clothing and gender reforms, see Chehabi 1993 and Amin 2002.

4. For the role of the clerics before the Islamic Revolution, see Fischer 1980; Arjomand 1984a; Akhavi 1980; Floor 1983; Kazemi 1999; Richard 1995; and Keddie 2003.

5. For overviews of the years 1941–53, see Abrahamian 1982; Bill and Louis 1988; Katouzian 1993; Atabaki 1993; and Tavakoli-Targhi 2001. For detailed accounts of the 1953 coup, see Gasiorowski 1987 and Kinzer 2003.

6. For an overview of the Pahlavi era see Keddie 2003. On the educational reforms of the Muhammad Reza Shah period, see Menashri 1992 and Matthee 1993; on land reform, see Hooglund 1982 and Ashraf 1996; on trade unions, see Ladjevardi 1985; on minorities, especially Jews, see Sarshar 2002; on the practice of torture, see Abrahamian 1999.

7. Many of the speeches and writings of Ayatollah Khomeini can be found in Khomeini 1999. For an English translation of his major works see Khomeini 1981. On the rise of Khomeini and the origins of the revolution, see Abrahamian 1982, 1993; Ashraf and Banuazizi 1985; Sick 1985; Arjomand 1984b, 1988; Bakhash 1990; Milani 1994; Chelkowski and Dabashi 1999; and Martin 2000.

8. For a class analysis of the 1979 Revolution, see Parsa 1989. For a discussion of leftist political parties during the Revolution, see Behrooz 2000; Matin-Asgari 2001; and Shahidian 1994. For a personal account of gender politics within the Fedayeen, see Moghissi 1996.

9. For details, see Afary 1996, chap. 8.

10. In Tunis, Matzneff became friendly with Jalila Hafsia, the proprietor of a literary café who, as we discuss in chapter 5, was also close to Foucault during his stay in Tunisia during the 1960s. See Hafsia 1981, where she records her conversations about politics and culture with Foucault, Matzneff, Maxime Rodinson, Georges Balandier, Anaïs Nin, and other noted intellectuals who passed through her café.

11. For details on these differences with Khomeini, see especially Richard's contribution to Keddie 1981. See also Hussain 1985. In an October 1978 interview with an American reporter, Shariatmadari showed some hostility toward women's equality, but also a degree of tolerance toward minority religions (Kraft 1978).

12. Likely Ehsan Naraghi, who is discussed later in this chapter and in chapter 5.

13. The full flavor of Khomeini's religious intolerance could be seen in earlier essay, "Islamic Government" (1970): "We must shout and make people aware that the Jews and their Western supporters are opposed to the very principal of Islam and want to form a Jewish government in the world. Because they are a malicious and industrious people, I am afraid, that God forbid, they might reach their objective someday. In other words, our weakness might bring a day when a Jewish governor rules us, may God never bring such a day! . . . In our Tehran, Christian, Zionist, and Baha'i missionary centers are formed that divert the people from the teaching of Islam. Is it not our responsibility to destroy such centers that hurt Islam?" (153).

14. Jean Daniel's memoirs attest to his close intellectual and personal ties to Foucault, who was among those he "consulted the most" on difficult issues (Daniel 2002, 77). In

1979, Foucault wrote a preface for one of Daniel's books. After Foucault's death, Daniel wrote the preface to a 1989 reprint of *The Order of Things*.

15. Apparently a reference to oil deposits.

16. This was not the first time that Foucault had used the phrase "political spirituality." In a relatively unnoticed May 1978 roundtable on *Discipline and Punish* with a group of French historians, he had mentioned "political spirituality" as an alternative to the hyper-rationality of the modern disciplinary apparatus (1978c, 30).

17. Recall that its top editor, Jean Daniel, was a personal friend of Foucault.

18. As was revealed later, Khomeini had since 1965 organized from abroad a fairly large underground movement based on ten-person Hay'at cells, which operated in a classically vanguardist manner.

19. In France, Foucault was not alone in discounting the worries some were expressing about the character of the anti-shah movement and its clerical leadership. In a November 8 *Le Monde* article, for example, the noted scholar of religion Jacques Madaule attacked political "realists" who "have excluded God and the Iranian people from their calculations" (Madaule 1978; see also Chazi 1978; Albala 1978).

20. The statement about "love" by "everyone" for Khomeini seems astounding at first. But it becomes less so when considered in light of earlier accounts by some Western leftists of the adulation of Stalin by the Russians or of Mao by the Chinese.

21. As we will see in the next chapter, Foucault later expressed some reservations on this issue.

22. For more discussion of Sartre and Foucault, see chap. 1, n. 9.

23. Sadly, Maxime Rodinson (1915–2004) died just as our book neared completion. For more background on the life and work of this remarkable scholar of the Muslim world, see the following tributes to him upon his death: Alaoui 2004; Coroller 2004; Johnson 2004; and Harbi 2004. For additional background, see Vidal-Naquet 1993, 1998. On the Palestinian question, see also Daniel 2002.

24. An English translation appeared in Rodinson 1981. It is reprinted in the appendix to this volume. The original French title was "Reveil de l'intégrisme musulman?" See also Rodinson's introduction to the 1980 reprint of the English edition of *Muhammad*, where he makes a similar but less pointed analysis of the Iranian Revolution and the rise of Islamism more generally. A quarter of a century later, the prominent Iran scholar Yann Richard testified to the importance of Rodinson's *Le Monde* series. "He was the only one who was truly able to outline the dangers that were brewing; the Iranians themselves, mesmerized by the wish to get rid of the shah, were not able to anticipate this new form of ideological totalitarianism" (Richard, personal communication, January 28, 2004).

25. Criticizing one's opponents without naming them has been quite common in French intellectual discourse, as can be seen in the writings of Sartre or Althusser.

26. Rodinson reported that André Fontaine, *Le Monde*'s editor, had asked him some months earlier to write an article on Islamism (1993a, 261).

27. One of the authors of this volume heard Keddie speak on the events in Iran at City University of New York Graduate Center in December 1978. Like Rodinson, Keddie

poured cold water on the enthusiasm of the largely leftist student audience, both Iranian and American, for the uprising in Iran. She suggested pointedly that people should read Khomeini's 1963 statements against women's rights rather than crediting his vague 1978 ones implying democracy and pluralism.

Chapter 4

1. As mentioned earlier, in Sunni Islam, an imam is simply the prayer leader at a mosque, while in Shi'ism, the title is reserved for the original leaders of the faith. Using the term in 1979 implied that Khomeini might be the Mahdi (Messiah), who is to arrive when the world is at an end.

2. We will mention some of the most important contributions and controversies, focusing especially on French intellectual debates, but occasionally referring as well to the international feminist discussion.

3. As Rodinson indicated when reprinting this article in 1993, he had responded to Foucault "more or less implicitly" in his December 1978 *Le Monde* article, but here in *Le Nouvel Observateur*, his intention had been to do so "in a more precise and specific manner" ("Critique of Foucault on Iran," app., 271).

4. For a discussion of this issue from a theoretical standpoint, see Afary 1997.

5. Millett's account is not without its factual errors, some of them amusing. At one point for example, she gives the name of the relatively tolerant Ayatollah Taleqani with unintended humor as "Ayatollah Tolerani." Here and below, we also rely on the analyses of these events provided by Tabari and Yeganeh (1982); Azari (1983); and Afary (1983), as well as contemporary sources.

6. For more on the role of Islamist women during this period, see Afary 2001.

7. We would like to thank Hélène Bellour, who worked with *Histoires d'elles* during this period, for providing us with copies of the journal and for valuable background information on French feminist responses to the Iranian Revolution.

8. A briefer version of this article was reprinted in Dunayevskaya 1996.

9. These issues also affected rural Iran. For a discussion of village women during and after the revolution, see Friedl 1991.

10. Personal observation of one of the authors in June 1979.

11. Unfortunately for him, Franceschini had used, as part of his evidence against Foucault, a quotation that turned out to be from Brière rather than Foucault. Apparently under pressure from Foucault, *Le Monde*'s editors ran an unsigned but fairly lengthy correction two days later in which the newspaper admitted its factual error, adding that the review "intended in no way to question Michel Foucault's support for human rights in Iran." They stated further that, far from justifying "totalitarianism" in Iran, "in the entire interview" with Brière and Blanchet, Foucault had "insisted on the dangers of anti-Semitism and xenophobia" (Editors' Note, 1979). That may have been the view that Foucault now wished to attribute to himself, but if so, he did not expand upon it in his subsequent writings on Iran.

12. These two sentences seemed to be a response to Rodinson's earlier critique. This in any event was Rodinson's view, as we will see below. However, as with his other

opponents over Iran, including feminists, Foucault did not name any of them, in keeping with a common practice in French intellectual discourse mentioned earlier.

13. Bani-Sadr reported to us that Foucault quietly helped individual Iranians, however (personal communication, December 11, 2002).

14. Internal evidence suggests that this essay was written in 1988.

15. We owe this observation to Zahra Khanlari, a member of the distinguished Amirshahi literary family, who worked as one of Sartre's assistants during this period (interview, July 9, 1994).

16. Because of this, we cannot agree with Macey that Foucault's views "were in fact little different" from those expressed by many others on the Left. Nor can we agree entirely with Macey that it was "his visibility" rather than his actual views that made Foucault the target of so much criticism when the Iranian Revolution quickly turned into a harsh theocratic despotism (1993, 423).

Chapter 5

1. David Halperin supports our view (and Foucault's) that there may be a relationship between Middle Eastern/Mediterranean sexualities and those of ancient Greece, at least as far as Mediterranean societies are concerned: "Contemporary Mediterranean sexual practices continue to afford us a promising avenue of inquiry into the conventions of classical Athenian pederasty" (1990, 61). On the reception of Said in Middle East studies, see Lockman (2004). It should also be noted that when Foucault discusses ancient Greece he is frequently referring to Athens, since most of our knowledge comes from Athenian culture.

2. Ronald Hyam argues that the colonies were a location for the "revenge of the repressed," a place for ejaculations that European males were denied at home (1990, 58). See also Stoler 1995, 175, and Aldrich 2003. Joseph Boone has explored this issue in greater detail and writes, "For many Western men the act of exploring, writing about, and theorizing an eroticized Near East is coterminous with unlocking a Pandora's box of phantasmic homoerotic desire" (1995, 93).

3. Robert Young explores this period in a different way. He points out that Foucault wrote much of *The Archaeology of Knowledge* in Tunis. Young suggests that his distance from France and Europe provided him "with perhaps with a more effective ethnology of the West and its mechanisms of power." It also made him alter his earlier views. Whereas in *Madness and Civilization*, Foucault had emphasized the way in which a society labeled someone as "the Other" to be excluded and silenced, he now came to "radically reconceptualize the role of the 'other' and alterity in his work" (Young 2001, 397–98).

4. During the 1968 student protests, Foucault, who was not yet very politically involved, took some small actions to support his students as they faced long prison sentences, resulting in his being roughed up by the police one night as he drove one of his young Arab lovers home. Edward Said (2000b) argues that Foucault was deported because of homosexual relations with students, but these would likely have been tolerated had he not been involved in supporting the student protestors. Initially, however, Foucault was very critical of the Tunisian student movement, referring in a private letter to one of his former professors to what he called a "pogrom," in which hundreds of Jewish-owned

shops and a synagogue had been ransacked during unrest over the 1967 Middle East War. He seemed particularly outraged by the involvement of leftist students in the anti-Semitic violence and concluded "nationalism plus racism adds up to something ghastly" (cited in Eribon 1991, 192–93). However, as Rachida Triki (forthcoming) points out, Foucault later modified this critique, when he found out that the leftist students had been one of the first Arab political groups anywhere to recognize Israel's right to exist and that the attacks on Jews had been manipulated by the government and, in any case, not carried out by the leftist students.

5. As mentioned earlier, Hafsia recounted her conversations with a number of intellectuals, including Foucault, Rodinson, and Matzneff (Hafsia 1981). Macey notes that she also "confessed to having been forlornly in love" with Foucault (1993, 189). Hafsia's book also contained a conversation with the American author Anaïs Nin, known for her erotic novels and stories.

6. In *The Uses of Pleasure,* Foucault places the discussion of marriage and household under the title "Economics" and the discussion of love of boys under "Erotics," thus reproducing the categories not only of classical Greek texts, but also those of medieval Persian advice books.

7. This triumph over nature could also take the form of man's triumph over woman, who was equated with the natural world. For further clarification on this issue see Arthur 1987, 83.

8. "Mistresses we keep for the sake of pleasure, concubines for the daily care of our persons, but wives to bear us legitimate children and to be faithful guardians of our households" (cited in Foucault 1985, 143). This statement has been attributed to Demosthenes. See also Arthur 1987, 87.

9. Even when Foucault makes a brief mention of the "betrayed" Medea, he insists that her sadness is caused *only* by her loss of status as a result of the appearance of the royal bride (1985, 164).

10. For example, Foucault does not discuss Plato's treatment of lesbian relations in the *Symposium,* focusing only on that of male homosexuality (Plato 1961).

11. Chapter 5 of Plato's *Republic,* perhaps the best-known argument of the period for a form of gender equality, also receives only brief attention (Foucault 1985, 181). Regardless of what we might think of Plato's ideal society, which would abolish the family and place children under the care of communal nurses, we have to agree that Plato was the first major philosopher to understand the socially constructed nature of gender and sex roles in Greek society. Moreover, Plato could imagine a different set of social relations, in which at least a few women were regarded as equal in potential to men and, as philosophers, qualified to become military leaders and rulers of the state (Plato *Republic* 455 d).

12. Sometimes *true love* meant renouncing passion and practicing "strict austerities," as in Plato's *Symposium,* where Socrates rejects the amorous invitations of the beautiful Alcibiades. See Alcibiades's eulogy of Socrates, also in the *Symposium* (lines 216–22).

13. Here we will be using the 1989 revised edition of Dover's book, which was first published in 1978.

14. James Davidson has suggested that, especially in his later writings, Dover was influenced by contemporary homosexual practices in European and Mediterranean societies, which he then read back into Greek society (2001, 29; see also Davidson 1997).

15. Aristotle describes a king who was overthrown by two of his young male lovers, after the king broke his promises to allow one of them to marry his daughter and to support the other's return to power in his city of origin. To Aristotle, the king's political error lay not in the relationships themselves, but in his flouting of the rule of reciprocity, which humiliated the young men. This lack of moderation and reciprocity in pursuing one's desires was attributed to *hubris* (*Politics* 1311a39).

16. Foucault discusses Aristophanes, but only to show that he regarded same-sex relations as normal. For Aristophanes as viewed by Plato, see his *Symposium* (lines 189–93).

17. These statements by Aristotle on gender are part of an attack on the greater gender equality within the elite, as proposed in Plato's *Republic*. For some recent discussions of Plato and gender, see the essays in Tuana 1994.

18. This "life-giving" quality of the semen defined the relationship between the erastes and the paidika as well. The erastes not only had sex with the paidika, but he also transmitted the phallus (i.e., virility and authority) to the paidika through his semen, although this was not openly acknowledged. This old archetype whereby authority/life/power/virility is transferred from the active to the passive partner appears in the ancient myths of many cultures. We thank Houman Sarshar for pointing out this connection.

19. As Suzanne Pharr has argued, a great deal of opposition to homosexuality stems from misogyny: Misogyny gets transferred to gay men with a vengeance through the fear that their "feminine" sexual identity and behavior could bring down the entire system of male dominance and compulsory heterosexuality (Pharr 2001, 148).

20. Here Foucault skips a few centuries and looks at the changes that took place during the first two centuries CE within the Roman context, when a growing sexual austerity (for men) became more normative. Even more than in the classical Greek period, there was a concern in medical texts about health risks involved with sex; hence the title of Foucault's book, *The Care of the Self*. Fidelity to one's wife became a more highly regarded attribute, and love of boys came to be seen as less dignified. Still, Foucault makes a distinction between this Roman period and later Christianity, because once more, he argues, the new limitations on sex in the Roman era were self-imposed.

21. The early twentieth-century German feminist Marianne Weber made an argument that differed sharply from Foucault's on this point (1998, 215).

22. Plutarch (1957) assumed that consent always existed in marriage, but not in relations between men and boys.

23. Rabinow objects to this and asks, "Why does sex have to be virile? Why couldn't women's pleasure and boys' pleasure be taken account of without any big changes to the general framework? Or is it that it's not just a little problem, because if you try to bring in the pleasure of the other, the whole hierarchical, ethical system would break down?" At this point, Foucault finally admits that this is in fact the case (1983, 346).

24. See also Freeland 1998. Martha Nussbaum points out that according to Aristotle the basic needs of all human beings had to be provided for in an ethical social order, a notion that she says is entirely absent from Foucault's work (1998, 249).

25. We do not have much information about homosexuality in the Middle Eastern/Muslim world, since scholarship on this subject is in its very early stages. Therefore we have had to rely at times on materials by writers who are not specialists in this field. Our statements about homosexual practices in these societies are thus highly tentative, and much more work is needed in this area.

26. According to the texts, these are (1) the man is not fulfilling the Biblical commandment to procreate, (2) he is not fulfilling his sexual duties to his wife, and (3) he is indulging in a practice whose sole purpose is the gratification of his desire (Eron 1993, 115).

27. In the manner of Eve Sedgwick (1985), Afsaneh Najmabadi suggests that even some heterosexual Persian poetry, where an older women expresses desire for a younger man, reflects homoerotic attraction between the male reader and the object of his desire in the literary text, a desire that is expressed via the mediation of a woman (Najmabadi 2000).

28. One indication of the historical link between this region and ancient Greek culture is that, after centuries of Muslim rule, Kandahar retains its original name, based on a local pronunciation of the Greek word for Alexandria.

29. Khalid Duran discusses the colonial subtext to these sex tours (1993, 189).

30. Keyvan Khosravani was an architect, a painter, and a designer. He had a famous boutique in Tehran called "Number One" and was the designer of Queen Farah's Bakhtiari and traditional dresses. His companion was Bijan Saffari. Although the ceremony was ostensibly in jest, the feelings of the partners were apparently sincere. After a photojournalist took pictures of the event and sold them to the newspapers, however, the public outrage became too much to handle. Saffari denied any homosexual relationship and ended his friendship with Khosravani, who left for Italy soon after the revolution. (Thanks to Houman Sarshar and Homa Sarshar for this information.)

31. Some of this information is based on an e-mail exchange with Goudarz Eghtedari (Iran). For a discussion of this issue, see Sanasarian 2000 and various issues of the journal *Homan* (1999–2001). For more information on the Iranian GLB movement, see the website for Homan: The Group to Defend the Rights of Iranian Gays and Lesbians, www.homan.cwc.net. For literature on Iranian lesbians, see www.geocities.com/khanaeye-doost. According to Duran, "homosexual assault is frequently used by the police of repressive regimes, such as the SAVAK during the reign of the Shah of Iran or its successor, SAVAMA, the dreaded security organ of the Khomeini government" (1993, 187).

32. Comments by Norma Moruzzi on her visits to Iran at the Trans/national Sexualities Symposium, University of Illinois, Chicago, November 18, 2002.

Epilogue

1. Kepel (2002) provides the best empirical survey of the various radical Islamist movements. For an overview of Islamism and gender, an issue Kepel tends to minimize, see Afary 1997, 2004a. See also the informative discussions of Islamism's social context by Fred Halliday (2002) and John Esposito (2002), and of Islamism and totalitarianism by Paul Berman (2003).

2. For overviews of the human rights situation since 1979, see Mayer 1995; Sanasarian 2000; Afshari 2001; and Afary and Afshari 2001.

3. Throughout the 1990s, there was also evidence that some of the worst outrages by the GIA had been orchestrated by the military regime itself, which had deeply infiltrated their movement.

4. For a good collection of recent essays by feminists on religious fundamentalism, with an emphasis on the challenge of Islamism, see Reed 2002, a volume that we draw upon below.

5. Information provided by the Iranian feminist and human rights activist Mehrangiz Kar in a November 2001 lecture at Purdue University.

Appendix

1. This city is the Shi'ite religious center of Iran.

2. In Persian, the pronoun *u* can be male or female.

3. The shahs of the Safavid Dynasty (1501–1722) were the first Iranian rulers to make Shi'ism the country's official religion.

4. Literally, the Shi'ism of Ali. Imam Ali was Prophet Muhammad's cousin and son-in-law, as well as the fourth caliph (656–661 CE). This notion of returning to an original, supposedly uncorrupted Shi'ism, for which martyrdom was the supreme virtue, was developed by the lay Muslim theologian Ali Shariati. Shariati, who had a doctorate from the Sorbonne, died in 1977 while living abroad. At the time, the Iranian government was blamed for his sudden death. His writings had a dramatic impact on a whole generation of Iranian activists. At the time of the revolution, his picture was carried alongside that of Khomeini in the demonstrations.

5. During the years 1524 to 1534, in the aftermath of Martin Luther's break with Rome, Germany experienced a series of radical peasant revolts, which are the subject of Frederick Engels's *Peasant Wars in Germany* (1852).

6. The green flag represents Islam.

7. On Friday, September 8, "Black Friday," the army massacred several hundred protestors at Djaleh Square in Tehran. The Tabas earthquake happened a few days later.

8. This unfounded rumor suggested that Iran's mainly Muslim army had not really carried out the September 8 massacre.

9. The traditional army was based on universal male conscription, similar in some ways to a national guard.

10. The Praetorian Guard were the bodyguards of the Roman emperors; the

Janissaries were elite slave soldiers recruited by the Ottoman sultans from among Balkan Christian boys. Foucault was in fact referring to the shah's Immortals (*Gard-i Javidan*), an elite unit of royal bodyguards named after an earlier one from the pre-Islamic period.

11. The combat army was composed of professional career soldiers, separate from the traditional army.

12. This could also be translated as "toy rattle" and refers to ridiculous or childish behavior.

13. In August 1953, the United States and the British helped organize a coup that overthrew the democratic and nationalist government of Muhammad Mossadeq, restoring Muhammad Reza Shah Pahlavi to absolute power.

14. The reference is to Reza Shah Pahlavi, who reigned from 1925 to 1941. A member of the British-led Cossack Brigade, he carried out a successful coup in 1921 with the support of the British. In 1925, the *majlis* (parliament) disbanded the Qajar dynasty, which had ruled since 1795, and Reza Shah (formerly Reza Khan) became the first monarch of the Pahlavi dynasty.

15. This refers to Major Edmund Ironside, commander of the British forces in Iran in 1921.

16. The brutal dictator General Augusto Pinochet took power in Chile in 1973 with U.S. support, ousting the democratically elected Marxist government of Salvador Allende; his counterpart General Jorge Videla held power in Argentina from 1976 to 1982.

17. In 1955, twenty-seven officers linked to the banned pro-Soviet Tudeh Party were executed, but in 1956, the shah was invited to the Soviet Union for an official visit.

18. The unrest started in Qom in February 1978, when soldiers killed several *talabehs* (seminarians), who were demonstrating against a scurrilous letter in the newspaper *Etela'at* attacking Khomeini. It soon spread to Tabriz.

19. While predominantly Muslim, the army included non-Muslims as well.

20. In April 1978, Afghanistan's ruler General Muhammad Daud was overthrown and killed in an uprising by the pro-Soviet People's Democratic Party.

21. The French term *populaire*, often counterposed to *bourgeois*, has several meanings, among them "popular," "of the people," "of the common people," and "people's." It became part of communist ideology in the sense, for example, of "people's war" (*guerre populaire*) as applied by Mao Zedong to his guerrilla campaigns in China. It was also used to refer to what were termed the "people's democracies" (*démocraties populaires*) of Eastern Europe.

22. According to the editors of *Dits et écrits*, the title proposed by Foucault was "The Dead Weight of Modernization." This article was almost immediately translated into Persian and pasted on the walls of Tehran University.

23. The 1906–11 Constitutional Revolution established a strong parliament within a constitutional monarchy. The Constitution, which included the principle of equality before the law of all male citizens, continues even today to be a point of reference for many nationalists, liberals, and leftists.

24. Foucault was referring to the shah's "White Revolution" of 1963, which initiated a limited land reform program and women's suffrage, but no opening toward democracy. Khomeini led his first political campaign against the referendum supporting the shah's

program, which passed in any case. The shah reacted by attacking the theological seminary where Khomeini was based. In an attempt to save Khomeini's life, several Grand Ayatollahs declared that Khomeini was a recognized theologian, one who merited the title of ayatollah. The shah then exiled Khomeini to Iraq, where he lived until 1978.

25. In this form of what the Left considered to be dependent development, the internal market purchased commodities that had been manufactured abroad rather than at home.

26. Mustafa Kemal Ataturk (1881–1938) was a World War I military leader and founder of modern Turkey. During his years in power, 1923–38, he established the most secular political system ever created in a predominantly Muslim country.

27. According to Muhammad Reza Shah, by 2000, Iran was to have joined the "great civilizations" of the world.

28. This is a reference to the shah's father. There are numerous accounts of Reza Shah's terrifying gaze, his incessant control of all details, and of his summary arrest and execution of those he regarded as personal enemies, or whom he deemed irresponsible and capricious in matters of state. "Gaze" is the same term that Foucault used in his well-known discussion of power in the form of "hierarchical observation" in *Discipline and Punish*: "The perfect disciplinary apparatus would make it possible for a single gaze to see everything constantly" (1977a, 173).

29. An ostensibly charitable organization supported by public and private contributions, the Pahlavi Foundation became enormously wealthy by the 1970s. In September 1978, under pressure from critics, the government launched an investigation into its finances.

30. Foucault is probably referring to Gholamreza Pahlavi (the shah's brother), Ashraf Pahlavi (the shah's sister), and Ashraf's son Shahram Shafiq. Princess Ashraf once successfully sued *Le Monde* after it published an article suggesting that she was engaged in drug trafficking. Felix Agaian was a senator representing the Armenian minority and a close confidant of the shah. Hasan Toufanian was an air force general who pocketed illegal monies from arms contracts. He became vice-minister of defense during the revolutionary upheavals. Davalou Qajar was a good friend of the shah, who in the late 1970s was accused of illegal drug trading by the Swiss government. The shah secretly whisked him out of Switzerland in his private plane, creating a scandal in the European press.

31. According to the editors of *Dits et écrits*, the title proposed by Foucault was "Waiting for the Imam." His discussion of Shi'ism was informed by a meeting with the Grand Ayatollah Kazem Shariatmadari in the religious city of Qom on September 20, 1978. Shariatmadari was the most important Shi'ite cleric inside Iran during the time Khomeini was in exile. More moderate than Khomeini, he was edged aside after 1979 and placed under house arrest.

32. Imam Ali Al-Reza was the eighth Shi'ite Imam (765–818 CE).

33. This suggested the notion of a geographer simply drawing lines on a map as part of a development plan, without taking account of local particularities or sensibilities.

34. Probably a reference to Ehsan Naraghi, whom Foucault visited in Iran, having known him previously in Paris.

35. This is the Paradise of Zahra Cemetery (*Behest-e Zahra*), at that time in an oasis in the desert about five miles south of Tehran.

36. White, red, and green are Iran's national colors.

37. In Islamic communities, there is a tradition of making a "wedding chamber" (*hajleh*) for unmarried boys who have died. Typically, it contains a large glass box decorated with pictures of the dead, lots of flowers, and lights.

38. Besides the seventeenth-century English Revolution of Oliver Cromwell, Foucault was here referring to the fifteenth-century Italian religious leader Girolamo Savonarola and the radical Protestant peasant uprising of the early sixteenth century in Münster.

39. This is a reference to Marx's famous statement (1843, 175).

40. The Twelfth, or Hidden, Imam is the Mahdi, or Messiah, whose concealment gives meaning to the Shi'ite esoteric and mystical tradition, as against the more statist Sunni one.

41. These are the sons and grandsons of Ali who, together with him, form the twelve imams (saints) of Shi'ite Islam.

42. Ayatollah Abulqasem Kashani turned against Mossadeq shortly before the 1953 coup, which he may have helped to facilitate.

43. This could also be translated as "uncompromising" or "stubborn."

44. This was the first of Foucault's articles on Iran to appear in French. There are two French verbs for "to dream," *rêver* and *songer*. The former conveys the sense of dreaming as something emotional or spontaneous, and is related to the English word "reverie." In the latter, dreaming is something based more on thought and reflection.

45. This is a reference to the Camp David Accords of September 1978, signed by Prime Minister Menachem Begin of Israel and President Anwar Sadat of Egypt, with the mediation of U.S. president Jimmy Carter. Egypt became the first Arab state to establish diplomatic relations with Israel, but nothing concrete was done concerning the rights of the Palestinians.

46. General Nasser Moghadam was appointed head of the SAVAK, the regime's notorious political police, in 1978. He was executed in 1979.

47. The National Front, which was founded in October 1949, was a secular nationalist party claiming the legacy of Mossadeq. In 1978 Karim Sanjabi represented the party.

48. After the death of dictator Francisco Franco in 1975, Spain made a rapid and relatively peaceful transition from fascist dictatorship to constitutional monarchy. The first free elections in forty years were held in 1977, when leftist parties won a parliamentary majority.

49. Ali Amini was a moderate politician, considered to be close to the United States. In September of 1978, he advised the shah to step back from direct governance and to allow a coalition government uniting all the opposition parties to take over.

50. Here Foucault probably intended to write "thousands."

51. Two parties were set up by the government in this period, the Mardom Party (People's Party) and the Iran-i Novin Party (New Iran Party).

52. The shah's clampdown on the guerrilla activities of the Marxist-Leninist Fedayeen

Khalq and the Islamic leftist Mujahedeen Khalq resulted in the death of more than three hundred of their members. Some then abandoned such politics, but others remained, allowing these groups to emerge in 1978–79, primarily within the student Left.

53. A group headed by Mehdi Bazargan, a prominent Islamist, who served as interpreter during this conversation between Foucault and Shariatmadari. In 1977, Bazargan and several others helped established the Iranian Committee for the Defense of Freedom and Human Rights, which became a key link between the secular human rights activists and the clerics. In 1979, he became Khomeini's first prime minister. Opposed to the taking of hostages at the American Embassy, he resigned in late 1979.

54. This is apparently a reference to oil deposits.

55. Georges Gurvitch (1894–1965) was a prominent French sociologist and founder of the journal *Autogestion* (Self-management).

56. Frantz Fanon (1925–61), Caribbean-born philosopher, journalist, and psychologist, is often considered the greatest thinker produced by the African liberation struggles of the 1950s and 1960s. Shariati translated some of his work into Persian. Louis Massignon (1883–1962), a leading French Orientalist, is known especially for his writings on the Sufis and other Islamic mystics.

57. This would mean making the moderate pro-U.S. politician Ali Amini prime minister.

58. According to the editors of *Dits et écrits*, at this point in the Italian version of this article Foucault inserted the phrase, "I who know very little about Iran."

59. We have been unable to trace the identity of this pseudonymous writer.

60. Here and below, the ellipsis points in square brackets were apparently inserted by the editors of *Le Nouvel Observateur*.

61. Sura 1 (The Cow), verse 2:223 states: "Your wives are a tilth for you, so go into your tilth when you like and do good beforehand for yourselves and be careful of your duty to Allah and know that you will meet Him, and give good news to the believers."

62. This refers to the fact that many of Muhammad's statements limiting women's freedom, including the call for more modest clothing, reflected his conflicts with his wives, particularly the youngest, Aisha. See sura 24 (The Light), verse 31; sura 30 (Allies), verse 32.

63. Ellipsis points apparently inserted by the author herself.

64. Foucault refers to three upheavals, each with a Marxist dimension, with the first and the third ones also having been led by Marxist-Leninist vanguard parties: the Chinese Revolution of 1949, the Cuban Revolution of 1959, and the Vietnamese national resistance, first against the French and then the United States, ending in 1975.

65. The massive, mainly student, revolts of 1968 took their most radical form in France.

66. This small animal has sharp spines on its back, which bristle when it is attacked.

67. This meant no political debates or negotiations with the regime, an absolutely uncompromising stance that was very popular with both the Islamists and the far left groups like the Fedayeen and the Mujahedeen.

68. According to the editors of *Dits et écrits*, Foucault had proposed two possible titles for this article, "Order Has Its Dangers" and "The Weekend of Tehran." The latter

referred to the weekend of November 4–5, when students attacked and burned symbols of the Pahlavi dynasty and the West.

69. Some of the Eastern European communist regimes, particularly in Czechoslovakia, had a history of supplying arms to various Third World liberation movements.

70. Here Foucault seems to be criticizing a frequent characterization of far leftist actions by the French Communist Party and its counterparts elsewhere, for example, in 1968.

71. The reference to U.S. president Jimmy Carter's having distanced himself from the shah.

72. This article was written during Foucault's second trip to Iran, from November 9 to November 16.

73. In the yearly Muharram festival, Shi'ites mourn the martyrdom of Imam Hussein, a son of Imam Ali. Hussein was killed in Karbala in 680 CE in a battle against forces sent by Yazid, son of Muawiyeh, the founder of the Umayyad dynasty.

74. Foucault wrote mistakenly, "Hamani." Ja'far Sharif-Imami, leader of the Senate, was a loyal royalist. In August 1978, an arson fire at the Rex Cinema in Abadan killed hundreds in an incident that was at the time wrongly attributed to the regime. (Later reports attributed the fire to the Islamists.) During the crisis that followed the fire, the shah appointed Sharif-Imami prime minister. His government lasted until November 1978, when General Gholamreza Azhari became prime minister.

75. General Gholam Ali Oveisi, born in Qom, and highly religious, was also fiercely loyal to the shah. After martial law was declared in November, he became the military commander in Tehran. In 1962, Mayor Fathollah Fouroud helped to orchestrate an attack by the army on Tehran University students, who were demanding free elections. Ahmad and Mahmoud Khayami ran the Paykan automobile company, the nation's largest. The Reza'i brothers owned copper mines in Kirman Province. Senator Abbas Massoudi established the daily newspaper *Ettela'at* in 1926 and used to have lunch with the shah on Wednesdays.

76. This large chain of factories produced foodstuffs.

77. Ellipsis points in original.

78. At the time, 100 rials equaled about $1.50 U.S., a significant sum for an Iranian worker.

79. Ettehadieh Communist (Communist Platform) Iran is a far left group with Maoist origins.

80. In 1961, when right-wing French generals staged a revolt at a time when De Gaulle was ready to negotiate independence for Algeria, he quashed the coup by appealing directly to rank-and-file soldiers over the radio.

81. According to the editors of *Dits et écrits*, the title proposed by Foucault was "Iran's Madness."

82. After World War II, when the Soviet army did not leave the northern province of Azerbaijan, the Tudeh (Communist) Party refused to condemn this action, thus losing considerable support. In 1953, it also undermined Mossadeq at a crucial point during his confrontation with the United States and Britain.

83. After 1961, the National Front lost much of its support, and the Islamist-oriented

Iran Liberation Movement, led by Mehdi Bazargan and Ayatollah Mahmud Taleqani, took its place as the most important internal opposition movement.

84. Zulfikar Ali Bhutto was at that time imprisoned by an Islamist military regime; he was hung in 1979.

85. Ellipsis points in original. In 1978, Dalila Zeggar, a woman of Algerian origin married to Dennis Maschino, a French schoolteacher, was kidnapped in Canada and returned to Algeria by her brother Massoud, a wealthy businessman who disapproved of their marriage. Zeggar was forced into another marriage but eventually escaped and was reunited with Maschino.

86. The term *intégrisme* refers to a conservative Roman Catholic movement of the early twentieth century, which supported all of the popes and their teachings. In French discussions of Islam, it is often used where in English one would use the term *fundamentalism*. The term *fondamentalisme* also exists in French, but is used far less frequently.

87. "Whatever the religion of the prince, such is that of his region," from the Peace of Augsburg (1555), a settlement between Lutherans and Catholics in Germany.

88. Max Weber used this phrase in *The Protestant Ethic and the Spirit of Capitalism* and elsewhere.

89. Zoroastrianism was the state religion of the pre-Islamic Persian Empire.

90. The Lebanese civil war began in 1975, when Christian Phalangists attacked Palestinians.

91. The terms refer to traditional Bedouin head covering and robes.

92. Orkan was the fourteenth-century founder of the Ottoman Empire; Cyrus the Great was a Persian king of the sixth century BCE; Khosroe Anushirvan was a Persian king of the sixth century CE who scored victories against the Byzantine Empire.

93. This is a reference to Foucault.

94. This is another reference to Foucault.

95. Dateline apparently added by the newspaper's editors. Foucault had not been in Iran for two months.

96. Shapour Bakhtiar was the last prime minister appointed by the shah. He had been a member of the moderate wing of the National Front, which now expelled him.

97. While this article was ostensibly a response to Julliard's December 1978 discussion of religion and politics in *Le Nouvel Observateur*, as Rodinson acknowledged later (see "Critique of Foucault on Iran," app., 267–77), his real target had been Foucault.

98. Eugène Pottier, a participant in the Paris Commune of 1871 and the author of the "Internationale."

99. The Roman Emperor Julian (r. 360–63), later termed "the Apostate," attempted to revive paganism and persecuted Christians, this after Constantine (r. 307–37) had begun the process of actively encouraging the Christianization of the Empire. Many Church officials renounced Christianity during Julian's persecution.

100. Manichaeism, a third-century offshoot of Zoroastrianism with an ascetic bent, viewed the world as torn by a dualistic struggle between the forces of good and evil. It

penetrated the Roman world, including Christianity, as well as the Near East and China. The Mazdakites were a late fifth-century Persian religious sect that opposed the three "demons" of envy, wrath, and greed. Charged with communistic beliefs concerning property and gender relations, Mazdak and tens of thousands of his followers were eventually massacred by the state.

101. See the essays later collected in Rodinson 1993b.

102. The reference to premodern Christianity's tendency to spread by winning over the rulers of existing states, such as Rome, as against early Islam's inclination toward founding new states in the areas it conquered.

103. [Rodinson's note] See the sketch by one of the best French specialists on contemporary Iran, Paul Vieille, in the interesting roundtable on the Iranian revolt published in *Peuples méditerranéens*, no. 5 (October–December 1978): 123ff. [Bani-Sadr et al. 1978]. See also Vieille 1975.

104. Félix Dupanloup (1802–78) was a liberal French Catholic bishop. Tomás de Torquemada (1420–98) was the notorious Spanish Grand Inquisitor who burned some two thousand people at the stake.

105. In her 1973 book on China, later translated into English, Claudie Broyelle (1977) had glorified the position of women in Maoist China, but in a subsequent one, first published in French in 1977, she and her husband Jacques Broyelle had harshly criticized the Maoist regime as totalitarian (Broyelle, Broyelle, and Tschirhart 1980).

106. Here and below, the references were to Foucault's article, "What Are the Iranians Dreaming About?" published in October in *Le Nouvel Observateur*, the only one of his Iran articles then available in French (app., 203–9, here specifically 208).

107. Broyelle and Broyelle were here referring to a lengthy conversation between Foucault and two young Maoist intellectuals (Foucault 1972b). Foucault's interlocutors were André Glucksmann, by 1979 a participant in Foucault's journalism project and today a well-known "New Philosopher" and writer on totalitarianism, and Benny Lévy (1945–2003), who became Jean-Paul Sartre's secretary from 1974 to 1980 (under the name Pierre Victor) and later wrote on Judaism and philosophy.

108. "Firmans" are decrees from a king or sultan.

109. Probably an allusion to *Le petit Larousse illustré*, an abridged and illustrated version of the famous dictionary; a marabout is a North or West African Muslim holy man or hermit, sometimes also a trickster figure.

110. Léon Daudet (1867–1942) was a well-known writer with monarchist and virulently anti-Semitic political views. Daudet served for many years as editor of the notoriously reactionary newspaper *Action française*.

111. René Andrieu (1920–98) was at that time the quite Stalinist editor of *L'Humanité*, the Communist Party newspaper.

112. These are not exact quotations, but an apparent attempt to evoke Foucault's position during the 1972 debate with the Maoists.

113. Pierre Debray-Ritzen was a conservative child psychiatrist, critical of Foucault ever since the publication of *Madness and Civilization* (1961).

114. Maurice Blanchot (1907–2003) was a prominent writer and literary critic.

115. Foucault refers to the Portuguese Revolution of 1974–76, which overthrew a fascist regime in power since the 1920s.

116. This refers to the Ligue Communiste Révolutionnaire (LCR), a Trotskyist party with links to the Belgian economist Ernest Mandel.

117. Ellipsis points in original.

118. The noted liberal historian François Furet (1927–97) had recently published a widely read interpretation of the French Revolution (1981).

119. Foucault refers to Marx's comment on religion, just after the one about the "opium of the people," but less widely known: "Religion is the sigh of the oppressed creature, the heart of a heartless world, just as it is the spirit of spiritless conditions. It is the *opium* of the people" (1843, 175).

120. God Is Great.

121. Ellipsis points in original.

122. Ellipsis points in original.

123. The shah had made a state visit to Washington in January 1978. President Jimmy Carter termed him a defender of human rights, while Iranian students demonstrated in the streets outside.

124. This is very likely a reference to Rodinson.

125. This refers to the 1943 Warsaw Ghetto Uprising against the Nazis.

126. The word is used in the sense that a roof hangs over a building. This notion of "overhang" also has some affinities with the Marxian term *superstructure*. Since the French word *plomb* means "lead," *surplombé* also could be translated as "weighed down."

127. Max Horkheimer (1895–1973) was a Frankfurt School philosopher and sociologist.

128. Sadeq Khalkhali (1926–2003) headed the revolutionary courts. He gloated publicly over the more than five hundred executions he ordered, later complaining that he had executed too few people. He also advocated the destruction of non-Islamic historical monuments. Reza Afshari (2001) has suggested that in the decade 1979–88, the Khomeini regime carried out about twenty thousand political executions.

129. [Rodinson's note] On Ali Shariati (1933–1977), see the brief remarks in Richard 1980, 110ff. and Richard 1995. There is a selection of his writings in French (Shariati 1982). The choices of the editors and translators could be questioned; they artificially privilege certain aspects of Shariati's thought, the appeal of which was perhaps due to his use of ultramodern language (the influence of Sartre, Fanon, etc.) to call for a shake-up of Islamic values in order to turn them into "national" ones. The preface by Jacques Berque partially corrects the way in which the translators have understood the ideas of the author.

130. Here and elsewhere in this article, Rodinson ignored Foucault's philosophical repudiation of humanism, of which he was surely aware.

131. [Rodinson's note] Max Weber carried out the most far-reaching analysis of charisma. He stressed that it was a "specifically creative revolutionary force in history," showing as well its singular instability, while also studying its forms (Weber 1978, 1117). Because, under its varied forms, charisma puts forward "'natural' leaders in moments of distress—whether psychic, physical, economic, ethical, religious or political—[who] were

neither appointed officeholders nor 'professionals' in the present-day sense (i.e., persons performing for compensation a 'profession' based on training and special expertise), but rather the bearers of specific gifts of body and mind that were considered 'supernatural' (in the sense that not everybody could have access to them)," it is clear that charisma of a religious character has the best chance of guaranteeing the perpetuation of these "supernatural" gifts (Weber 1978, 1112–13).

132. As noted earlier, after the 1963 protests a handful of Grand Ayatollahs recognized Khomeini as an ayatollah in order to save his life.

133. According to the shariat (Muslim religious law).

134. From the "Internationale." In the Roman Republic, the Tribunes were upper-class citizens elected by the plebeians to represent them, since the latter were not permitted to speak publicly on their own behalf.

135. [Rodinson's note] The Iranian Revolution has already been the focus of a great deal of literature from many points of view. I will limit myself here to mentioning several French translations that give some idea (no more than that) of Khomeini's writings: Khomeini 1980, 1979a, 1979b. The most competent and profound analysis can be found in Keddie 1981, with a chapter by Yann Richard. Recall above all Richard 1980, cited earlier.

References

Abedi, Mehdi, and Gary Legenhausen, eds. 1986. *Jihad and Shahadat: Struggle and Martyrdom in Islam*. Houston: Institute for Research and Islamic Studies.

Abrahamian, Ervand. 1982. *Iran between Two Revolutions*. Princeton, NJ: Princeton University Press.

———. 1993. *Khomeinism*. Berkeley and Los Angeles: University of California Press.

———. 1999. *Tortured Confessions: Prisons and Public Recantations in Modern Iran*. Berkeley and Los Angeles: University of California Press.

Afary, Frieda. 1983. "Women, Islam, and the Iranian Revolution." Unpublished paper.

Afary, Janet. 1996. *The Iranian Constitutional Revolution of 1906–11: Grassroots Democracy, Social Democracy, and the Origins of Feminism*. New York: Columbia University Press.

———. 1997. "The War against Feminism in the Name of the Almighty." *New Left Review* no. 224 (July–August): 89–110.

———. 2001. "Portrait of Two Islamist Women: Escape from Freedom or from Tradition?" *Critique* 19 (Fall): 47–77.

———. 2004a. "The Human Rights of Middle Eastern and Muslim Women: A Project for the Twenty-first Century." *Human Rights Quarterly* 26, no. 1: 106–25.

———. 2004b. "Seeking a Feminist Politics for the Middle East after September 11." *Frontiers: A Journal of Womens Studies* 25, no. 1: 128–37.

Afary, Janet, and Reza Afshari, eds. 2001. *Non-Muslim Communities in Iran*. Special issue, *Iran Nameh* 19, nos. 1–2.

Afkhami, Mahnaz. 2002. "At the Crossroads of Tradition and Modernity: Personal Reflections." *SAIS Review* 20, no. 2: 85–92.

Afshari, Reza. 2001. *Human Rights in Iran: The Abuse of Cultural Relativism*. Philadelphia: University of Pennsylvania Press.

Akhavi, Shahrough. 1980. *Religion and Politics in Contemporary Iran*. Albany: State University of New York Press.

Al-Ahmad [Al-e Ahmad], Jalal. 1982. *Plagued by the West (Gharbzadegi)*. Trans. Paul Sprachman. Delmar, NY: Caravan Books. First published 1963.

Alaoui, Hassan. 2004. "Maxime Rodinson n'est plus: un parangon de la coexistence." *Le Matin* (Morocco), May 25.

Albala, Nuri. 1978. "Un phénomène de rejet." *Le Monde*, November 9.

Alcoff, Linda Martin. 1996. "Dangerous Pleasures: Foucault and the Politics of Pedophilia." In *Feminist Interpretations of Michel Foucault*, ed. Susan J. Hekman, 99–135. University Park: Pennsylvania State University Press.

Aldrich, Robert. 2003. *Colonialism and Homosexuality*. New York: Routledge.

Almond, Ian. 2004. "'The Madness of Islam': Foucault's Occident and the Revolution in Iran." *Radical Philosophy* 128 (November): 12–22.

Amin, Camron Michael. 2002. *The Making of the Modern Iranian Woman*. Gainesville: University Press of Florida.

Anderson, Benedict. 1983. *Imagined Communities: Reflections on the Origins and Spread of Nationalism*. London and New York: Verso.

Anderson, Kevin B. 1995. *Lenin, Hegel, and Western Marxism: A Critical Study*. Urbana: University of Illinois Press.

"Appel des artistes et intellectuels iraniens en faveur de Salman Rushdie." 1992. *Les Temps Modernes* 549 (April).

'Aqeli, Baqir. 1993. *Ruz Shomar-i Tarikhi-yi Iran*. 2 vols. Tehran: Nashr-i Goftar.

Aquinas, Thomas. 1953. *The Political Ideas of Thomas Aquinas*. Ed. Dino Bigongiari. New York: Hafner Press.

Aristotle. 1995. *Politics*. Trans. Ernest Barker; revised by R. F. Stalley. New York: Oxford University Press.

Arjomand, Said Amir. 1984a. *The Shadow of God and the Hidden Imam: Religion, Political Order, and Societal Change in Shi'ite Iran from the Beginning to 1890*. Chicago: University of Chicago Press.

———. 1984b. *From Nationalism to Revolutionary Islam*. Albany: State University of New York Press.

———. 1988. *The Turban for the Crown: The Islamic Revolution in Iran*. Oxford: Oxford University Press.

Arthur, Marylin. 1987. "From Medusa to Cleopatra: Women in the Ancient World." In Bridenthal, Koonz, and Stuard 1987, 79–106.

Ashraf, Ahmad, and Ali Banuazizi. 1985. "The State, Classes, and Modes of Mobilization in the Iranian Revolution." *State, Culture and Society* 1, no. 3: 3–40.

———. 1996. "From the White Revolution to the Islamic Revolution." In *Iran after the Revolution: Crisis of an Islamic State*, ed. Saeed Rahnema and Sohrab Behdad, 22–44. London and New York: I. B. Tauris.

Atabaki, Touraj. 1993. *Azerbaijan: Ethnicity and Autonomy in Twentieth-Century Iran*. London: British Academy Press.

Ayoub, Mahmud. 1988. "Diverse Religious Practices." In *Shi'ism: Doctrines, Thought, and Spirituality*, ed. Seyyed Hossein Nasr, H. Dabashi, and V. R. Nasr, 258–62. Albany: State University of New York Press.

Azari, Farah, ed. 1983. *Women of Iran: The Conflict with Fundamentalist Islam*. London: Ithaca Press.

Babayan, Kathryn. 1996. "Sufis, Dervishes, and Mullas: The Controversy over Spiritual and Temporal Dominion in Seventeenth-Century Iran." In Melville 1996, 117–38.

Bakhash, Shaul. 1990. *The Reign of the Ayatollahs*. New York: Basic Books.

Balta, Paul. 1979a. "Le gouvernement tente d'enrayer la montée des exigences de l'extrême gauche." *Le Monde*, February 17.

———. 1979b. "Matine-Daftary, petit-fils de Mossadegh, annonce la création d'un 'Front national démocratique.'" *Le Monde*, March 7.

Banani, Amin. 1961. *The Modernization of Iran, 1921–1941*. Palo Alto, CA: Stanford University Press.

Banisadr [Bani-Sadr], A. H., C. Brière, A. Chenal, A. P. Lentin, and P. Vieille, interrogées par E. Bolo. 1978. "La Révolte de l'Iran, table ronde." *Peuples méditerranéens* 5:107–28.

Baraheni, Reza. 1977. *The Crowned Cannibals: Writings on Repression in Iran*. Introduction by E. L. Doctorow. New York: Vintage.

Bartky, Sandra. 1990. *Femininity and Domination*. New York: Routledge.

Baudrillard, Jean. 2001. "L'Esprit du terrorisme." *Le Monde*, November 3.

Bayat, Mangol. 1991. *Iran's First Revolution: Shi'ism and the Constitutional Revolution of 1905–1909*. New York: Oxford University Press.

Beeman, William O. 1979. "Cultural Dimensions of Performance Conventions in Iranian Ta'ziyeh." In Chelkowski 1979, 24–32.

———. 2002. "Ta'ziyeh as Performance." Lecture at the Asia Society and Lincoln Center Festival. New York, July 13.

Behrooz, Maziar. 2000. *Rebels with a Cause: The Failure of the Left in Iran*. London: I. B. Tauris.

Berman, Paul. 2003. *Terror and Liberalism*. New York: W. W. Norton.

Bernauer, James, and Michael Mahon. 1994. "The Ethics of Michel Foucault." In *The Cambridge Companion to Foucault*, ed. Gary Gutting, 141–58. New York: Cambridge University Press.

Bérubé, Michael. 2002. "Nation and Narration." *Context: A Forum for Literary Arts and Culture*, 10.

Best, Steven, and Douglas Kellner. 1991. *Postmodern Theory*. New York: Guilford.

Bill, James A., and William Roger Louis, eds. 1988. *Musaddiq, Iranian Nationalism, and Oil*. Austin: University of Texas Press.

Birnbaum, Pierre. 1996. "Catholic Identity, Universal Suffrage, and 'Doctrines of Hatred.'" In Sternhell 1996, 233–51.

Bonakdarian, Mansour. 1991. "The Left Opposition to Sir Edward Grey's Iranian Policy, 1906–1912." PhD diss., University of Iowa.

Boone, Joseph A. 1995. "Vacation Cruises: or, The Homoerotics of Orientalism." *PMLA* 110 (January): 89–107.

Bordo, Susan. 1988. "Anorexia Nervosa: Psychopathology as the Crystallization of Culture." In Diamond and Quinby 1988, 87–118.

Boroujerdi, Mehrzad. 1996. *Iranian Intellectuals and the West*. Syracuse, NY: Syracuse University Press.

Bridenthal, Renate, Claudia Koonz, and Susan Stuard, eds. 1987. *Becoming Visible: Women in European History*. 2nd ed. Boston: Houghton-Mifflin.

Brière, Claire, and Pierre Blanchet. 1979a. *Iran: la révolution au nom de Dieu*. Paris: Éditions du Seuil.

———. 1979b. "Corruption de la terre." *Le Monde*, May 11.

Brière, Claire, and Maria-Antonietta Macciocchi. 1979. "Premier bilan de la délégation des femmes en Iran." *Libération*, March 24.

Brinton, Crane. 1967. "Romanticism." In *Encyclopedia of Philosophy*, 7:206–9. New York: Collier-Macmillan.

Bromberger, Christian, and Jean-Pierre Digard. 1978. "Les causes de la révolte." *Le Monde*, September 30.

Browne, Edward G. 1956. *A Literary History of Persia*. 4 vols. Cambridge: Cambridge University Press.

Broyelle, Claudie. 1977. *Women's Liberation in China*. Preface by Han Suyin. Atlantic Highlands, NJ: Humanities Press. First published 1973.

Broyelle, Claudie, Jacques Broyelle, and Evelyne Tschirhart. 1980. *China: A Second Look*. Atlantic Highlands, NJ: Humanities Press. First published 1977.

Butler, Judith. 1990. *Gender Trouble: Feminism and the Subversion of Identity*. New York and London: Routledge.

Cahen, Claude. 1977. "La changeante portée sociale de quelques doctrines religieuses." In *Les Peuples musulmans dans l'histoire médiévale*, 189–207. Paris: Institut français de Damas.

Calmard, Jean. 1996. "Shi'i Rituals and Power." Pt. 2. "The Consolidation of Safavid Shi'ism: Folklore and Popular Religion." In Melville 1996, 139–90.

Carmody, Denise, and John Carmody. 1993. "Homosexuality and Roman Catholicism." In Swidler 1993, 135–93.

Carrette, Jeremy R., ed. 1999. *Religion and Culture: Michel Foucault*. New York: Routledge.

———. 2000. *Foucault and Religion: Spiritual Corporality and Political Spirituality*. New York: Routledge.

Chazi, Hassan. 1978. "Mettre fin à la dépendence." *Le Monde*, November 8.

Chehabi, Houchang E. 1993. "Staging the Emperor's New Clothes: Dress Codes and Nation-Building under Reza Shah." *Iranian Studies* 26, nos. 3–4: 209–29.

Chelkowski, Peter J., ed. 1979. *Ta'ziyeh: Ritual and Drama in Iran*. New York: New York University Press; Tehran: Soroush Press.

———. 1991. "Hengami Ke Na Zaman Zaman Ast va Na Makan Makan: Ta'ziyeh-yi Imam Hussein." *Iran Nameh* 9, no. 2: 212–21.

Chelkowski, Peter J., and Hamid Dabashi. 1999. *Staging a Revolution: The Art of Persuasion in the Islamic Republic of Iran*. New York: New York University Press.

Chomsky, Noam. 2001. *9–11*. New York: Seven Stories Press.

Clément, Catherine. 1979a. "Une délégation de femmes françaises à Téhéran." *Le Matin de Paris*, March 20.

———. 1979b. "Les femmes iraniennes." *Le Matin de Paris*, March 24.

———. 1979c. "L'Iran, une révolution au nom de Dieu." *Le Matin de Paris*, April 7.

Cohen, Mitchell. 2002. "An Empire of Cant: Hardt, Negri, and Postmodern Political Theory." *Dissent* 49, no. 3: 17–28.

Colombel, Jeannette. 1994. *Michel Foucault: La clarté de la mort*. Paris: Éditions Odile Jacob.

Cooper, Roger. 1978. "Riot and 'Quake—Iran's Week of Agony." *Sunday Times Magazine* (London), November 18.

Coroller, Catherine. 2004. "Maxime Rodinson, éclaireur de l'Orient." *Libération*, May 26.

Cottam, Richard. 1988. *Iran and the United States: A Cold War Case Study*. Pittsburgh, PA: University of Pittsburgh Press.

Cronin, Stephanie. 1997. *The Army and the Creation of the Pahlavi State in Iran, 1910–1926*. London: Tauris Academic Studies.

Curtis, Vesta Sarkhosh. 1993. *Persian Myths*. Austin: University of Texas Press.

Dabashi, Hamid. 1993. *Theology of Discontent: The Ideological Foundations of the Islamic Revolution in Iran*. New York: New York University Press.

Daniel, Jean. 2002. *Oeuvres autobiographiques*. Paris: Bibliothèque Grasset.

Davidson, James N. 1997. *Courtesans and Fishcakes: The Consuming Passions of Classical Athens*. London: HarperCollins.

———. 2001. "Dover, Foucault, and Greek Homosexuality: Penetration and the Truth of Sex." *Past and Present* 170 (February): 3–51.

Delacour, Marie-Odile. 1979a. "Paris: un millier de manifestantes pour les femmes iraniennes." *Libération*, March 17.

———. 1979b. "Kate Millett à Orly retour d'Iran." *Libération*, March 20.

Desmet-Grégoire, H., and S. Nadjmabadi. 1979. "Le voile n'est pas seulement une marque d'oppression." *Le Monde*, March 1.

Deveaux, Monique. 1994. "Feminism and Empowerment: A Critical Reading of Foucault." *Feminist Studies* 20, no. 2: 223–47.

Diamond, Irene, and Lee Quinby, eds. 1988. *Feminism and Foucault: Reflections on Resistance*. Boston: Northeastern University Press.

Dosse, François. 1991–92. *Histoire du structuralisme*. 2 vols. Paris: Éditions la découverte.

Dover, Kenneth J. 1989. *Greek Homosexuality*. Cambridge, MA: Harvard University Press. First published 1978.

Dunayevskaya, Raya. 1979. "Iran, Unfoldment of, and Contradictions in, Revolution." In *The Political Philosophic Letters of Raya Dunayevskaya*. Vol. 2. Detroit: News and Letters (March 25).

———. 1996. *Women's Liberation and the Dialectics of Revolution*. Detroit, MI: Wayne State University Press. First published 1985.

Duran, Khalid. 1993. "Homosexuality and Islam." In Swidler 1993, 181–97.

Editors' Note. 1979. "Michel Foucault et l'Iran." *Le Monde*, March 31.

Ehrenreich, Barbara. 2001. "Veiled Threat." *Los Angeles Times*, November 4.

Elwell-Sutton, L. P. 1979. "The Literary Sources of the Ta'ziyeh." In Chelkowski 1979, 167–81.

Enayat, Mahmoud. 1979. "Man az Tekrar-i Tarikh Mitarsam." *Ettela'at* (3 Bahman, 1357/January 23): 4.

Eribon, Didier. 1991. *Michel Foucault*. Trans. Betsy Wing. Cambridge, MA: Harvard University Press.

Eron, Lewis. 1993. "Homosexuality and Judaism." In Swidler 1993, 103–47.

Esma'ili, Husain. 1991. "Daramadi be Nomun Shenasi-yi Ta'ziyeh." *Iran Nameh* 9, no. 2: 223–53.

Esposito, John. 2002. *Unholy War: Terror in the Name of Islam*. New York: Oxford University Press.

Fanon, Frantz. 1967. *Black Skin, White Masks: The Experiences of a Black Man in a White World*. Trans. Charles Lam Markmann. New York: Grove Press. First published 1952.

———. 1968. *The Wretched of the Earth*. Trans. Constance Farrington. New York: Grove Press. First published 1963.

Fischer, Michael M. J. 1980. *Iran: From Religious Dispute to Revolution*. Cambridge, MA: Harvard University Press.

Floor, Willem M. 1983. "The Revolutionary Character of the Ulama: Wishful Thinking or Reality?" In Keddie 1983, 73–100.

Foucault, Michel. 1961. "Préface." In *Histoire de la folie à l'age classique*, i–xii. Paris: Plon.

———. 1963. "A Preface to Transgression." In Carrette 1999, 57–71.

———. 1965. *Madness and Civilization: A History of Insanity in the Age of Reason*. Trans. Richard Howard. New York: Vintage. First published 1961.

———. 1969. "What Is an Author?" In Rabinow 1984, 101–20.

———. 1971. "Nietzsche, Genealogy, History." In Rabinow 1984, 76–100.

———. 1972a. *The Archaeology of Knowledge*. Trans. A. M. Sheridan Smith. New York: Pantheon. First published 1969.

———. 1972b. "On Popular Justice: A Conversation with Maoists." In *Power/Knowledge: Selected Interviews and Other Writings, 1972–1977, by Michel Foucault*, ed. Colin Gordon, 1–36. New York: Pantheon, 1980.

———. 1973. *The Order of Things: An Archaeology of the Human Sciences*. New York: Vintage. First published 1966.

———. 1977a. *Discipline and Punish: The Birth of the Prison*. Trans. Alan Sheridan. New York: Vintage. First published 1975.

———. 1977b. "Truth and Power." In Rabinow 1984, 51–75.

———. 1978a. *The History of Sexuality*. Vol. 1. *An Introduction*. Trans. Robert Hurley. New York: Vintage. First published 1976.

———. 1978b. "Sexuality and Power." In Carrette 1999, 115–30.

———. 1978c. "Table ronde du 20 mai 1978." In Foucault 1994b, 20–37.

———. 1980. "About the Beginning of the Hermeneutics of the Self." In Carrette 1999, 158–81.

———. 1981. "Is It Useless to Revolt?" Trans. with an introduction by James Bernauer. *Philosophy and Social Criticism* 8, no. 1: 3–9.

———. 1983. "On the Genealogy of Ethics: An Overview of Work in Progress." In Rabinow 1984, 340–72.

———. 1984. "What Is Enlightenment?" In Rabinow 1984, 32–50.

———. 1985. *The History of Sexuality*. Vol. 2. *The Uses of Pleasure*. Trans. Robert Hurley. New York: Vintage. First published 1984.

———. 1986. *The History of Sexuality*. Vol. 3. *The Care of the Self*. Trans. Robert Hurley. New York: Vintage. First published 1984.

———. 1991. *Remarks on Marx: Conversations with Duccio Trombadori*. Trans. R. James Goldstein and James Cascaito. New York: Semiotext(e).

———. 1994a. *The Birth of the Clinic: An Archaeology of Medical Perception*. Trans. A. M. Sheridan Smith. New York: Vintage. First published 1963.

———. 1994b. *Dits et écrits, 1954–1988*. Vol. 3. *1976–1979*. Ed. Daniel Defert and François Ewald, with Jacques Lagrange. Paris: Gallimard.

———. 1998. *Iraniha Che Roya'i dar Sar Darand?* [Persian edition of the fall 1978 articles on Iran]. Trans. Hussein Ma'sumi Hamadani. Tehran: Hermes Press.

———. 1999. "Michel Foucault and Zen: A Stay in a Zen Temple." In Carrette 1999, 110–14.

———. 2000a. *Power*. Vol. 3 of *The Essential Works of Michel Foucault, 1954–1984*. Ed. James Faubion. Trans. Robert Hurley et al. New York: New Press.

———. 2000b. "Governmentality." In Foucault 2000a, 201–22.

Foxhall, Lin. 1998. "Pandora Unbound: A Feminist Critique of Foucault's *History of Sexuality*." In Larmour et al. 1998, 122–37.

Franceschini, Paul-Jean. 1979. "*Iran: la révolution au nom de Dieu* de Claire Brière et Pierre Blanchet." *Le Monde*, March 29.

Fraser, Nancy. 1989. *Unruly Practices: Power, Discourse, and Gender in Contemporary Social Theory*. Minneapolis: University of Minnesota Press.

Freeland, Cynthia A., ed. 1998. *Feminist Interpretations of Aristotle*. University Park: Pennsylvania State University Press.

Freud, Sigmund. 1989. *Civilization and Its Discontents*. New York: W. W. Norton. First published 1930.

Friedl, Erika. 1991. *Women of Deh Koh: Lives in an Iranian Village*. London: Penguin.

Furet, François. 1981. *Interpreting the French Revolution*. Trans. Elborg Forster. New York: Cambridge University Press. First published 1978.

Ganji, Akbar. 2002. *Majma' al-Jazayer-i Zendanguneh*. Tehran: Tarhe-Now.

Gasiorowski, Mark J. 1987. "The 1953 Coup d'État in Iran." *International Journal of Middle East Studies* 19, no. 3: 261–86.

Ghafary, Farrokh. 1991. "Daramadi bar Namayeshha-yi Irani." *Iran Nameh* 9, no. 2: 177–85.

Gheissari, Ali. 1998. *Iranian Intellectuals in the Twentieth Century*. Austin: University of Texas Press.

Gillespie, Michael Allen. 1984. *Hegel, Heidegger, and the Ground of History*. Chicago: University of Chicago Press.

Groenhout, Ruth. 1998. "The Virtue of Care: Aristotelian Ethics and Contemporary Ethics of Care." In Freeland 1998, 171–200.

Gueyras, Jean. 1978. "L'Iran après le vendredi noir. Pt. 3. 'Vive Khomeiny!'" *Le Monde*, October 5.

———. 1979a. "Les manifestations des femmes amènent l'ayatollah Khomeiny a nuancer sa position sur le 'voile islamique.'" *Le Monde*, March 13.

———. 1979b. "Les formations de gauche déconseillent aux femmes la poursuite des manifestations de rue." *Le Monde*, March 14.

Habermas, Jürgen. 1995. *The Philosophical Discourse of Modernity: Twelve Lectures*. Trans. Frederick G. Lawrence. Cambridge, MA: MIT Press. First published 1985.

Hadot, Pierre. 1992. "Reflections on the Notion of 'The Cultivation of the Self.'" In *Michel Foucault, Philosopher*, ed. Timothy J. Armstrong, 225–32. New York: Routledge.

Haeri, Shahla. 1989. *The Law of Desire*. Syracuse, NY: Syracuse University Press.

Hafsia, Jalila. 1981. *Visages et Rencontres*. Tunis: Privately printed.

Halimi, Gisèle. 1979. "De l'Islam, des femmes et la révolution en général." *Le Monde*, March 21.

Halliday, Fred. 2002. *Islam and the Myth of Confrontation: Religion and Politics in the Middle East*. London and New York: I. B. Tauris.

Halm, Heinz. 1997. *Shi'a Islam: From Religion to Revolution*. Trans. Allison Brown. Princeton, NJ: Markus Weiner.

Halperin, David, M. 1990. *One Hundred Years of Homosexuality and Other Essays on Greek Love*. New York: Routledge.

Harbi, Mohammed. 2004. "Maxime Rodinson, un marxiste face à l'Islam." *Le Monde*, May 26.

Hardt, Michael, and Antonio Negri. 2000. *Empire*. Cambridge, MA: Harvard University Press.

Hashemi, Gita. 2000. "Between Parallel Mirrors: Foucault, Atoussa, and Me, on Sexuality of History." Master's thesis, University of Toronto.

Hashemi, Manuchehr. 1994. *Davari: Sokhani dar Karnameh-yi Savak*. London: Aras Press.

Hayes, Jarrod. 2000. *Queer Nations: Marginal Sexualities in the Maghreb*. Chicago: University of Chicago Press.

Hegland, Mary Elaine. 1983. "Two Images of Husain: Accommodation and Revolution in an Iranian Village." In Keddie 1983, 218–63.

———. 1998. "Flagellation and Fundamentalism: (Trans)forming Meaning, Identity, and Gender through Pakistani Women's Rituals of Mourning." *American Ethnologist* 25, no. 2: 240–66.

Heidegger, Martin. 1962. *Being and Time*. Trans. John Macquarrie and Edward Robinson. New York: HarperCollins. First published 1927.

Hekman, Susan. 1990. *Gender and Knowledge: Elements of a Postmodern Feminism*. Boston: Northeastern University Press.

Hirshman, Linda Redlick 1998. "The Book of 'A.'" In Freeland 1998, 201–47.

Hitler, Adolf. 1953. *Hitler's Secret Conversations, 1941–1944*. Trans. Norman Cameron and R. H. Stevens. New York: Farrar, Straus, and Young.

Hooglund, Eric J. 1982. *Land and Revolution in Iran, 1960–1980*. Austin: University of Texas Press.

Humayuni, Sadeq. 1979. "An Analysis of a Ta'ziyeh of Qasem." In Chelkowski 1979, 12–23.

Hussain, Asaf. 1985. *Islamic Iran: Revolution and Counter-Revolution*. New York: St. Martin's Press.

Hyam, Ronald. 1990. *Empire and Sexuality*. Manchester, UK: Manchester University Press.

Ingram, David. 1994. "Foucault and Habermas on the Subject of Reason." In *The Cambridge Companion to Foucault*, ed. G. Gutting. Cambridge: Cambridge University Press.

Iraj Mirza, Jalal al-Malek. 1972. *Divan-i Iraj Mirza*. Tehran: Mozaffari Press.

Iran: Foreign Area Handbook. 2002. Washington, DC: Library of Congress, Gulf 2000 Project.

Jahangard, Nasrin. 2004/1382. "Mishel Fuko va Ostureh-yi Qodrat." *Yas* (October/Day 15).

Javadi, Hasan, Manijeh Marashi, and Simin Shekarloo, eds. 1992. *Ta'dib al-Nisvan va Ma'ayib al-Rijal*. Chicago: The Historical Society of Iranian Women and Jahan Books.

Johnson, Douglas. 2004. "Maxime Rodinson: Marxist Historian of Islam." *Guardian*, June 3.

Jospin, Lionel. 1978. "Contre le shah ou contre le P.S." *Le Monde*, September 21.

Julliard, Jacques. 1978. "Marcher sur les deux jambes." *Le Nouvel Observateur*, December 30.

Kandiyoti, Deniz. 1991. "Islam and Patriarchy: A Comparative Perspective." In Keddie and Baron 1991, 23–44.

Kanun-i Nevisandegan-i Iran. 1979/1357. "Kanun-i Nevisandegan-i Iran be Dowlat Hoshdar Midahad." *Ettela'at*, March 1/Esfand 10.

Kar, Mehrangiz. 1987. *Hoquq-i Siyasi-yi Zanan-i Iran*. Tehran: Rowshangaran va Mutale'at-i Zanan.

Katouzian, Homayoun Muhammad Ali. 1993. *Mossadeq va Mobarezeh bara-yi Qodrat dar Iran*. Tehran: Markaz Press.

Kaup, Katia D. 1979. "Les visiteuses de l'ayatollah." *Le Nouvel Observateur*, March 26.

Kazemi, Farhad. 1999. "Feda 'ian-e Eslam." In *Encyclopaedia Iranica*, ed. Ehsan Yarshater, 9:470–74. New York: Bibliotheca Press.

Keating, Craig. 1997. "Reflections on the Revolution in Iran: Foucault on Resistance." *Journal of European Studies* 27, no. 106: 181–97.

Keddie, Nikki R. 1962. "Religion and Irreligion in Early Iranian Nationalism." *Comparative Studies in Society and History* 4, no. 3: 265–95.

———. 1966. "The Origins of the Religious-Radical Alliance in Iran." *Past and Present* 34 (July): 70–80.

———. 1969. "The Roots of the Ulama's Power in Modern Iran." *Studia Islamica* 29:31–53.

———. 1981. *Roots of Revolution: An Interpretive History of Modern Iran*. With a section by Yann Richard. New Haven, CT: Yale University Press.

———, ed. 1983. *Religion and Politics in Iran: Shi'ism From Quietism to Revolution*. New Haven, CT: Yale University Press.

———. 2003. *Modern Iran*. New Haven, CT: Yale University Press. [Expanded version of Keddie 1981.]

Keddie, Nikki R., and Beth Baron, eds. 1991. *Women in Middle Eastern History*. New Haven, CT: Yale University Press.

Kempton, Murray. 1979. "Iran's Revolution: Feminist View." *New York Post*, March 27.

Kepel, Gilles. 2002. *Jihad: The Trail of Political Islam*. Trans. Anthony F. Roberts. Cambridge, MA: Harvard University Press.

Khaki, Reza. 1991. "Ta'ziyehha va Ta'ziyehnamehha." *Iran Nameh* 9, no. 2: 254–67.

Khatami, Mahmoud. 2003. "Foucault and the Islamic Revolution of Iran." *Journal of Muslim Minority Affairs* 23, no. 1: 121–25.

Khomeini, Ruhollah. 1947. *Risaleh-yi Towzih al-Masa'il* [Explanation of problems]. Qom: Ruh Press. [This edition includes material written after 1947 as well.]

———. 1963. "The Afternoon of Ashura." In Khomeini 1981, 177–80.

———. 1970. "Islamic Government." In Khomeini 1981, 27–168.

———. 1979a. *Principes politiques, philosophiques, sociaux et religieux*. Ed. J.-M. Xavière. Paris: Éditions Libres-Hallier.

———. 1979b. *Pour un gouvernement islamique*. Trans. M. Kotobi and M. Simon. Paris: Fayolle.

———. 1980. *Pensées politiques de l'ayatollah Khomeyni*. Trans. Y. A. Henry. Paris: Association pour la diffusion de la pensée française.

———. 1981. *Islam and Revolution: Writings and Declarations of Imam Khomeini*. Trans. and ed. Hamid Algar. Berkeley and Los Angeles: Mizan Press.

———. 1999. *Sahifeh-yi Imam* [Collected lectures, interviews, and fatwas]. 22 vol. Tehran: Mo'aseseh-yi Tanzim va Chap-i Asar-i Imam Khomeini.

Kinzer, Stephen. 2003. *All the Shah's Men: An American Coup and the Roots of Middle East Terror*. Hoboken, NJ: John Wiley and Sons.

Kraft, Joseph. 1978. "View from the Mosque." *Washington Post*, October 29.

Kravetz, Marc. 1979. "Une mission d'information féministe en Iran aujourd'hui." *Libération*, March 19.

Kristeva, Julia. 1997. "Revolution in Poetic Language." In *The Portable Kristeva*, ed. Kelly Oliver, 27–92. New York: Columbia University Press.

Kunstreich, Tjark. 2004. "Lust an der unfreiheit." *Konkret* 8 (August): 35–41.

Kurasawa, Fuyuki. 1999. "The Exotic Effect: Foucault and the Question of Cultural Alterity." *European Journal of Social Theory* 2, no. 2: 147–65.

Lacouture, Jean. 1979. "Iran. Dieu et la Révolution." *Le Nouvel Observateur*, April 14.

Ladjevardi, Habib. 1985. *Labor Unions and Autocracy in Iran*. Syracuse, NY: Syracuse University Press.

———. 1988. "Constitutional Government under Musaddiq." In Bill and Louis 1988, 69–90.

Lambton, Ann K. S. 1965. "Dustur, IV, Iran." In *Encyclopédie de l'Islam*. 2nd ed. Leiden, Netherlands: Brill.

Larmour, David H. J., et al., eds. 1998. *Rethinking Sexuality: Foucault and Classical Antiquity*. Princeton, NJ: Princeton University Press.

Leezenberg, Michiel. 1998. "Power and Political Spirituality: Michel Foucault and the Islamic Revolution in Iran." *Arcadia* Band 33, Heft 1: 72–89.

Le Roy Ladurie, Emmanuel. 1979. "L'Iran de 1979 et la France de 1589." *Le Nouvel Observateur*, January 22.

"Le tout ou rien de l'ayatollah Khomeiny." 1979. *Le Monde*, February 3.

Licht, Fred. 1979. *Goya, the Origins of the Modern Temper in Art*. New York: Universe Books.

Lilla, Mark. 2001. *The Reckless Mind: Intellectuals in Politics*. New York: New York Review Books.

Lindholm, Charles. 1982. *Generosity and Jealousy: The Swat Pukhtun of Northern Pakistan*. New York: Columbia University Press.

Lockman, Zachary. 2004. *Contending Visions of the Middle East: The History and Politics of Orientalism*. Cambridge: Cambridge University Press.

MacCannell, Dean, and Juliet Flower MacCannell. 1993. "Violence, Power, and Pleasure: A Revisionist Reading of Foucault from the Victim Perspective." In Ramazanoglu 1993, 203–38.

Macciocchi, Maria-Antonietta. 1979. "Femmes iraniennes ou marins de Cronstadt?" *Le Monde*, March 30.

Macey, David. 1993. *The Lives of Michel Foucault*. New York: Vintage.

Madaule, Jacques. 1978. "La voix du peuple." *Le Monde*, November 8.

———. 1979. "Une clameur venue du fond des temps." *Le Monde*, January 13.

Mahjub, Muhammad Ja'far. 1979. "The Effect of European Theatre and the Influence of Its Theatrical Methods Upon Ta'ziyeh." In Chelkowski 1979, 137–54.

Manafzadeh, Ali Reza. 1991. "Ta'ziyeh va Binesh-i Trajik." *Iran Nameh* 9, no. 2: 319–27.

Manent, Pierre. 1979. "Lire Michel Foucault." *Commentaire* 7 (Autumn): 369–75.

Marcuse, Herbert. 1962. *Eros and Civilization*. New York: Vintage. First published 1955.

Martin, L. H., H. Gutman, and P. H. Hutton, eds. 1988. *Technologies of the Self: A Seminar with Michel Foucault*. Amherst: University of Massachusetts Press.

Martin, Paul. 1979. "Foucault, l'Iran et la responsabilité." *Le Matin de Paris*, March 31.

Martin, Vanessa. 1989. *Islam and Modernism: The Iranian Revolution of 1906*. London: I. B. Tauris.

———. 2000. *Creating an Islamic State: Khomeini and the Making of a New Iran*. London: I. B. Tauris.

Marx, Karl. 1843. "Contribution to the Critique of Hegel's Philosophy of Law. Introduction." In *Collected Works*, by Karl Marx and Frederick Engels, 3:175–87. New York: International Publishers, 1975.

"Marxist Demonstration in Tehran." 1979. *MERIP Reports* nos. 75/76, 32.

Matin-Asgari, Afshin. 2001. *Iranian Student Opposition to the Shah*. Washington, DC: Mazda Publications.

Matin-Daftari, Maryam. 1990. "Ruz-i Jahani-yi Zan." *Azadi* 2, nos. 7–8: 36–39.

———. 2001. "Cheshm Andaz-i Vaz'iyat-i Zanan-i Irani ba Negahi be Tajrobiyyat-i Gozashteh." In *Barrasi-yi Motale'at va Mobarezat-i Feministi-yi Zanan-i Iran dar Do Daheh-yi Akhir va Cheshmandaz-i Ayandeh*, ed. Golnaz Amin. Berkeley: Proceedings of the Fifteenth Conference of Bonyad-i Pazuheshha-yi Zanan-i Iran.

Matthee, Rudi. 1993. "Transforming Dangerous Nomads into Useful Artisans, Technicians, Agriculturalists: Education in the Reza Shah Period." *Iranian Studies* 26, nos. 3–4: 313–36.

Matzneff, Gabriel. 1978. "L'avenir est intégriste." *Le Monde*, September 30.

———. 1979. "L'autel contre le trône." *Le Monde*, January 13.

Mauriac, Claude. 1986. *Le Temps Immobile 9. Mauriac et Fils*. Paris: Bernard Grasset.

Mayer, Ann Elizabeth. 1995. *Islam and Human Rights: Tradition and Politics*. 2nd ed. Boulder, CO: Westview Press.

Mazzaoui, Michel M. 1979. "Shi'ism and Ashura in South Lebanon." In Chelkowski 1979, 228–37.

McNay, Lois. 1992. *Foucault and Feminism: Power, Gender, and the Self*. Cambridge, UK: Polity Press.

Melville, Charles, ed. 1996. *Safavid Persia*. London: I. B. Tauris.

Memmi, Albert. 1965. *The Colonizer and the Colonized*. Trans. Howard Greenfield. New York: Orion.

Menashri, David. 1980. "Iran." *Middle East Contemporary Survey, 1978*, 3:488–547. New York: Holmes and Meier.

———. 1992. *Education and the Making of Modern Iran*. Ithaca, NY: Cornell University Press.

Merrick, Jeffrey, and Bryant T. Ragan, eds. 1996. *Homosexuality in Modern France*. Oxford: Oxford University Press.

Milani, Mohsen M. 1994. *The Making of Iran's Islamic Revolution*. 2nd ed. Boulder, CO: Westview Press.

———. 1998. "Iranian Revolution (1979)." In *Encyclopedia of Political Revolutions*, ed. Jack A. Goldstone, 248–53. Washington, DC: Congressional Quarterly.

Miller, James. 1993. *The Passion of Michel Foucault*. New York: Doubleday.

Miller, Jean Baker. 2001. "Domination and Subordination." In Rothenberg 2001, 86–93.

Millett, Kate. 1970. *Sexual Politics*. New York: Doubleday.

———. 1982. *Going to Iran*. With photographs by Sophie Keir. New York: Coward, McCann & Geoghegan.

Minc, Alain. 2001. "Le terrorisme de l'esprit." *Le Monde*, November 7.

Mirsepassi, Ali. 2000. *Intellectual Discourse and the Politics of Modernization*. Cambridge: Cambridge University Press.

Moghadam, Valentine M. 1991. "Islamist Movements and Women's Responses in the Middle East." *Gender and History* 3, no. 3: 268–84.

Moghissi, Haideh. 1996. *Populism and Feminism in Iran*. New York: St. Martin's Press.

Momen, Moojan. 1985. *An Introduction to Shi'i Islam*. New Haven, CT: Yale University Press.

Mork, Gordon R. 1996. "'Wicked Jews' and 'Suffering Christians' in the Oberammergau Passion Play." In *Representations of Jews Through the Ages*, ed. Leonard Jay Greenspoon and Bryan F. Le Beau, 153–69. Omaha: Creighton University Press.

Motahhari, Morteza. 1997. *Majmu'eh-yi Asar (Collected Works)*. 11 volumes. Tehran: Sadra Press. First published 1989.

Mottahedeh, Negar. 1999. "Resurrection, Return, Reform: Ta'ziyeh as Model for Early Babi Historiography." *Iranian Studies* 32, no. 3: 387–400.

———. 2002. "Karbala Drag Kings and Queens." Paper presented at the Society for Iranian Studies Biannual Meeting. Bethesda, MD (May).

Murray, Stephen O. 1997. "The Will Not to Know: Islamic Accommodations of Homosexuality." In Murray and Roscoe 1997, 14–54.

Murray, Stephen O., and Will Roscoe, eds. 1997. *Islamic Homosexualities: Culture, History, and Literature*. New York: New York University Press.

Nabavi, Ibrahim. 1999. *Goft va Gu ba Ehsan Naraghi: Dar Khesht-i Kham* [Interviews with Ehsan Naraghi]. Tehran: Jami'h-yi Iraniyan.

Nabavi, Negin. 2001. "Roshanfekran va Bahs-i Farhang-i Bumi dar Iran." *Iran Nameh* 19, no. 3: 263–77.

Najafabadi, Salehi A. 1982. *Shahid-i Javid*. Tehran: Mo'aseseh-yi Khadamat-i Farhangi-yi Rasa. First published 1971.

Najmabadi, Afsaneh. 1993. "Veiled Discourse of Unveiled Bodies." *Feminist Studies* 19, no. 3: 487–518.

———. 2000. "Reading 'Wiles of Women' Stories as Fictions of Masculinity." In *Imagined Masculinities: Male Identity and Culture in the Modern Middle East*, ed. Mai Ghoussoub and Emma Sinclair-Webb, 147–68. London: Saqi Books.

Naraghi, Ehsan. 1978. "Une seule issue: la Constitution." *Le Monde*, November 3.

Nietzsche, Friedrich. 1967. *On the Genealogy of Morals and Ecce Homo*. Ed. and trans. Walter Kaufmann. New York: Vintage.

———. 1976. *The Portable Nietzsche*. Ed. and trans. Walter Kaufmann. New York: Penguin. First published 1954.

Niyazmand, Reza. 1996. *Reza Shah az Tavallod ta Saltanat*. Bethesda: Foundation for Iranian Studies.

Nussbaum, Martha C. 1998. "Aristotle, Feminism, and Needs for Functioning." In Freeland 1998, 248–59.

Nye, Robert A. 1996. "Michel Foucault's Sexuality and the History of Homosexuality in France." In Merrick and Ragan 1996, 225–41.

Olivier, Lawrence, and Sylvain Labbé. 1991. "Foucault et l'Iran. À propos du désir de révolution." *Canadian Journal of Political Science* 24, no. 2: 219–35.

Olson, Robert. 1967. "Death." In *Encyclopedia of Philosophy*, ed. Paul Edward, 2:306–9. New York: Collier-Macmillan.

Paidar, Parvin. 1995. *Women and the Political Process in the Twentieth-Century Iran*. Cambridge: Cambridge University Press.

Paolucci, Paul. 2003. "Foucault's Encounter with Marxism." *Current Perspectives in Social Theory* 22:3–58.

Parsa, Misagh. 1989. *Social Origins of the Iranian Revolution*. New Brunswick, NJ: Rutgers University Press.

Pelly, Sir Lewis, comp., and Arthur N. Wollaston, ed. 1970. *Ta'ziyeh: The Miracle Play of Hasan and Husain*. Farnborough, UK: Gregg International. First published 1879.

"People's Fedayi Open Letter to Khomeini." 1979. *MERIP Reports* nos. 75/76, 31–32.

Petrushevsky, I. P. 1985. *Islam in Iran*. London: Athlone Press. First published 1966.

Pharr, Suzanne. 2001. "Homophobia as a Weapon of Sexism." In Rothenberg 2001, 143–63.

Pinault, David. 1992. *The Shiites: Ritual and Popular Piety in a Muslim Community*. New York: St. Martin's Press.

———. 1998. "Zaynab Bint 'Ali and the Place of the Women of the Households of the First Imams in Shi'ite Devotional Literature." In *Women in the Medieval Islamic World: Power, Patronage, and Piety*, ed. Gavin R. G. Hambly, 69–98. New York: St. Martin's Press.

Plato. 1961. *Collected Dialogues*. Ed. Edith Hamilton and Huntington Cairns. Princeton, NJ: Princeton University Press.

Plutarch. 1957. *On Love, the Family, and the Good Life*. New York: Mentor Books.

Porter, Roy. 1991. "Is Foucault Useful for Understanding Eighteenth- and Nineteenth-Century Sexuality?" *Contention* 1:61–82.

Poster, Mark. 1986. "Foucault and the Tyranny of Greece." Pp. 205–220 in *Foucault: A Critical Reader*, ed. David Couzens Hoy, 205–20. Oxford: Blackwell.

"Quinze mille manifestants ont défilé à Paris." 1978. *Le Monde*, September 14.

Rabinow, Paul, ed. 1984. *Foucault Reader*. New York: Pantheon.

Ramazanoglu, Caroline, ed. 1993. *Up against Foucault: Explorations of Some Tensions between Foucault and Feminism*. New York: Routledge.

Ravandi, Morteza. 1989. *Tarikh-i Ejtema'i-yi Iran*. Vol. 7. Tehran: Fajr Islam.

Reed, Betsy, ed. 2002. *Nothing Sacred: Women Respond to Religious Fundamentalism*. With an introduction by Katha Pollitt. New York: Thunder's Mouth Press/Nation Books.

Rezvani. 1978. "Pour la République de Perse." *Le Monde*, September 17–18.

Richard, Yann. 1980. *Le Chiisme en Iran*. Paris: Adrien-Maisonneuve.

———. 1995. *Shi'ite Islam*. Oxford: Basil Blackwell. First published 1991.

Richlin, Amy. 1998. "Foucault's *History of Sexuality*: A Useful Theory for Women?" In Larmour et. al 1998, 138–70.

Rodinson, Maxime. 1973. *Islam and Capitalism*. Trans. Brian Pearce. Austin: University of Texas Press. First published 1966.

———. 1979. "Les Bahâ'i-s menacés." *Le Monde*, March 20.

———. 1980. *Muhammad*. Trans. Anne Carter. New York: Pantheon. First published 1961.

———. 1981. *Marxism and the Muslim World*. Trans. Jean Matthews. New York: Monthly

Review Press. [The French originals of most of these writings are found in Rodinson 1993a.]

———. 1993a. *L'Islam: politique et croyance.* Paris: Éditions Fayard.

———. 1993b. *De Pythagore à Lénine: Des activismes idéologiques.* Paris: Éditions Fayard.

Roscoe, Will. 1997. "Precursors of Islamic Male Homosexualities." In Murray and Roscoe 1997, 55–86.

Rothenberg, Paula S., ed. 2001. *Race, Class, and Gender in the U.S.* New York: Worth.

Rousseau, G. S. 1972–73. "Whose Enlightenment? Not Man's: The Case of Michel Foucault." *Eighteenth Century Studies* 6, no. 2: 238–56.

Sade, Marquis de. 1992. *The Misfortunes of Virtue and Other Early Tales.* New York: Oxford University Press.

Said, Edward. 1978. *Orientalism.* New York: Vintage Books.

———. 2000a. "My Encounter with Sartre." *London Review of Books* 22 (June 1): 11.

———. 2000b. "Deconstructing the System." *New York Times Book Review,* December 17, 16–17.

Sanasarian, Eliz. 1982. *The Women's Rights Movement in Iran: Mutiny, Appeasement, and Repression from 1900 to Khomeini.* New York: Praeger.

———. 2000. *Religious Minorities in Iran.* Cambridge: Cambridge University Press.

Sarshar, Houman, ed. 2002. *Esther's Children: A Portrait of Iranian Jews.* Los Angeles and Philadelphia: Center for Iranian Jewish Oral History and the Jewish Publication Society.

Sartre, Jean-Paul. 1963. *Search for a Method.* Trans. by Hazel E. Barnes. New York: Vintage. First published 1957.

Sawicki, Jana. 1988. "Identity Politics and Sexual Freedom." In Diamond and Quinby 1988, 177–92.

Schaub, Ua Liebmann. 1989. "Foucault's Oriental Subtext." *PMLA* 104, no. 3: 306–16.

Schimmel, Annemarie. 1975. *Mystical Dimensions of Islam.* Chapel Hill: University of North Carolina Press.

Sebbar, Leila. 1979. "En Iran, le tchador glisse, A Paris, il brûle." *Histoires d'elles* no. 11 (April).

Sedgwick, Eve Kosofsky. 1985. *Between Men: English Literature and Male Homosocial Desire.* New York: Columbia University Press.

Shahidian, Hammed. 1994. "The Iranian Left and the 'Woman Question' in the Revolution of 1978–79." *International Journal of Middle East Studies* 26, no. 2: 223–47.

Shamisa, Cyrus. 2002. *Shahidbazi dar Adabiyyat-i Farsi.* Tehran: Ferdows Press.

Shariati, Ali. 1970. "Jihad and Shahadat." In Abedi and Legenhausen 1986, 153–229.

———. 1980. *Marxism and Other Western Fallacies.* Trans. R. Campbell. Berkeley and Los Angeles: Mizan Press. First published 1977.

———. 1982. *Histoire et Destinée.* Ed. and trans. F. Hamed and N. Yavari d'Hellencourt. Preface by Jacques Berque. Paris: Sinbad.

———. 1986. *What Is to Be Done? The Enlightened Thinkers and an Islamic Renaissance.* Ed. Farhang Rajaee. Houston: Institute for Research and Islamic Studies.

———. 1990. *Collected Works of Ali Shariati*. Vol. 21. *Zan* [Women]. Tehran: Bonyad-i Farhangi-yi Doctor Ali Shariati.

Shaygan, Ali. 1979/1357. "Iran nemitavanad be sadr-i Islam bazgardad." *Ettela'at*, February 25/Esfand 6, p. 8.

Sibalis, Michael David. 1996. "The Regulation of Male Homosexuality in Revolutionary and Napoleonic France, 1789–1815." In Merrick and Ragan 1996, 80–101.

Sick, Gary. 1985. *All Fall Down: America's Tragic Encounter with Iran*. New York: Random House.

Smith, Craig S. 2002. "Shh, It's an Open Secret: Warlords and Pedophilia." *New York Times*, February 21.

Soper, Kate. 1986. *Humanism and Anti-Humanism*. La Salle, IL: Open Court Press.

———. 1993. "Productive Contradictions." In Ramazanoglu 1993, 29–50.

Stauth, Georg. 1991. "Revolution in Spiritless Times: An Essay on Michel Foucault's Enquiries into the Iranian Revolution." *International Sociology* 6, no. 3: 259–80.

Steel, Lola. 1979. "En Iran autant d'ailleurs." *Libération*, March 28.

Steiner, George. 1987. *Martin Heidegger*. Chicago: University of Chicago Press.

Sternhell, Zeev, ed. 1996. *The Intellectual Revolt against Liberal Democracy, 1870–1945*. Jerusalem: Israel Academy of Sciences and Humanities.

Stoler, Ann Laura. 1995. *Race and the Education of Desire: Foucault's History of Sexuality and the Colonial Order of Things*. Durham, NC: Duke University Press.

Swidler, Arlene, ed. 1993. *Homosexuality and World Religions*. Valley Forge, PA: Trinity Press International.

Tabari, Azar, and Nahid Yeganeh, eds. 1982. *In the Shadow of Islam: The Women's Movement in Iran*. London: Zed Press.

Tajik, Mohammad Reza. 1999. *Michel Foucault va Enqelab-i Islami*. Tehran: Mo'aseseh-yi Tose'eh-yi Danesh va Pazuhesh-i Iran.

Taremi, Hasan. 1996. *'Alameh Majlisi*. Tehran: Tarh-i Naw.

Tavakoli-Targhi, Mohamad. 2001. "Tajaddodi Ekhtera'i, tamaddon-i 'Ariyati, va Enqelabi Rowhani." *Iran Nameh* 20, nos. 2–3: 195–236.

Thaiss, Gustav. 1972. "Religious Symbolism and Social Change: The Drama of Husain." In Keddie 1972, 349–66.

———. 1994. "Contested Meanings and the Politics of Authenticity: The 'Hosay' in Trinidad." In *Islam, Globalization, and Postmodernity*, ed. Akbar S. Ahmed and Hastings Donnan, 38–62. London: Routledge.

Tohidi, Nayareh. 1991. "Gender and Islamic Fundamentalism: Feminist Perspectives in Iran." In *Third World Women and the Politics of Feminism*, ed. Chandra Talpade Mohanty, Ann Russo, and Lourdes Torres, 251–60. Bloomington: Indiana University Press.

Triki, Rachida. Forthcoming. "Foucault en Tunisie." *Revue de la société française d'esthétique*.

Tuana, Nancy, ed. 1994. *Feminist Interpretations of Plato*. University Park: Pennsylvania State University Press.

Ullmann, Bernard. 1979. "La Vengeance du Prophète." *L'Express*, April 21.

Vahdat, Farzin. 2002. *God and Juggernaut: Iran's Intellectual Encounter with Modernity.* Syracuse, NY: Syracuse University Press.

Vatandoust, Reza. 1985. "The Status of Iranian Women During the Pahlavi Regime." In *Women and the Family in Iran,* ed. Asghar Fathi, 107–30. Leiden, Netherlands: E. J. Brill.

Vidal-Naquet, Pierre. 1993. "Rodinson et les dogmes." *Le Monde,* July 30.

———. 1998. "Entre Marx et Mahomet." *Le Monde,* April 3.

Vieille, Paul. 1975. *La Féodalité de l'État en Iran.* Paris: Éditions Anthropos.

Wafer, Jim. 1997a. "Muhammad and Male Homosexuality." In Murray and Roscoe 1997, 87–96.

———. 1997b. "Vision and Passion: the Symbolism of Male Love in Islamic Mystical Literature." In Murray and Roscoe 1997, 107–31.

Waldman, Amy. 2001. "Iran Shi'ites Celebrate and Mourn a Martyr." *New York Times,* December 15.

Weber, Marianne. 1998. "Excerpt from 'Authority and Autonomy in Marriage.'" In *The Women Founders of Sociology and Social Theory, 1830–1930,* ed. Patricia Lengerman and Jill Niebrugge-Brantley, 215–20. New York: McGraw-Hill.

Weber, Max. 1978. *Economy and Society: An Outline of Interpretive Sociology.* Ed. Guenther Roth and Claus Wittich. Berkeley and Los Angeles: University of California Press.

Willis, Ellen. 2001. "Bringing the Holy War Home." In Reed 2002, 373–77.

Yarshater, Eshan. 1979. "Ta'ziyeh and Pre-Islamic Mourning Rites in Iran." In Chelkowski 1979, 88–94.

Yeganeh, Nahid. 1993. "Women, Nationalism, and Islam in Contemporary Political Discourse in Iran." *Feminist Review* 44 (Summer): 3–18.

Young, Robert C., ed. 2001. *Postcolonialism: An Historical Introduction.* Oxford: Blackwell Publishers.

Zamanzadeh, Javad. 1994. *Ravankavi-yi Sovar-i Eshq dar Adabiyat-i Farsi.* Bethesda, MD: Iranbooks.

Zinn, Howard. 2002. *Terrorism and War.* New York: Seven Stories Press.

Index